Anonymus

Statistics of the Foreign and Domestic Commerce of the United States

Anonymus

Statistics of the Foreign and Domestic Commerce of the United States

ISBN/EAN: 9783741144905

Manufactured in Europe, USA, Canada, Australia, Japa

Cover: Foto ©Suzi / pixelio.de

Manufactured and distributed by brebook publishing software (www.brebook.com)

Anonymus

Statistics of the Foreign and Domestic Commerce of the United States

STATISTICS

OF THE

FOREIGN AND DOMESTIC COMMERCE

OF

THE UNITED STATES;

EMBRACING

A HISTORICAL REVIEW AND ANALYSIS OF FOREIGN COMMERCE FROM THE BEGINNING OF THE GOVERNMENT; THE PRESENT INTERNAL COMMERCE BETWEEN THE MISSISSIPPI AND ATLANTIC STATES; THE OVERLAND TRADE AND COMMUNICATIONS WITH THE PACIFIC STATES; THE PRODUCTIONS AND EXCHANGES OF THE GOLD AND SILVER DISTRICTS; THE COMMERCE OF THE PACIFIC COAST, AND THE INTERNATIONAL RELATIONS OF THE NORTHERN FRONTIER OF THE UNITED STATES.

COMMUNICATED BY

THE SECRETARY OF THE TREASURY,

IN ANSWER TO

A RESOLUTION OF THE SENATE OF THE UNITED STATES,

MARCH 12, 1863.

WASHINGTON:
GOVERNMENT PRINTING OFFICE.
1864.

IN THE HOUSE OF REPRESENTATIVES, *June* 29, 1864.

Resolved, That there be printed for the use of the House eight thousand extra copies of the report of the Secretary of the Treasury, made in compliance with the resolution of the Senate of the 19th of March, 1863, relating to our foreign and domestic commerce, including as well that on the Pacific coast.

CONTENTS.

Page.

Letter of the Secretary, transmitting the report, with description and classification of contents......1 to 3

FOREIGN COMMERCE OF THE UNITED STATES—TONNAGE AND TRADE.............5 to 117

- Introduction.......... 5
- American and foreign tonnage entered from foreign countries, 1789 to 1821, with the percentage of foreign.......... 6
- American and foreign tonnage entered from foreign countries, 1821 to 1863, with the percentage of foreign.......... 7
- Tonnage in Canadian trade distinguished.......... 7
- Countries, the tonnage from which are less in 1861 than in 1821.......... 8
- Countries, the imports from which, from 1828 to 1860, positively declined.......... 8
- Countries, the imports from which, from [illegible] to 1860, relatively declined.......... 9
- Countries, the imports from which, from [illegible] to 1860, positively and relatively declined.......... 9
- Values of imports into the United States in American and foreign vessels, 1821 to 1863.......... 10
- Values of exports, the produce of the United States, in American and foreign vessels, 1821 to 1863.......... 10
- Values of exports, the produce of the United States, in American and foreign vessels, for the quarter ending September 30, 1863.......... 11
- Values of exports, the produce of the United States, in American and foreign vessels, for the quarter ending December 31, 1863.......... 11
- Imports from foreign countries, in American and foreign vessels, 1862-'63, countries, and values.......... 12
- Tonnage, American and foreign, entering the ports of the United States, third and fourth quarters 1863.......... 13
- Comparison of results.......... 14
- History of the [illegible] navigation laws of Europe, reciprocities and countervailing acts of the United States.......... 14
- National character of tonnage entering the ports of the United States, 1789 to 1863.......... 16
- Comparison of American and British tonnage employed in the foreign trade of the United States, 1840 to 1863.......... 16

TONNAGE AND TRADE, IN FIVE-YEAR PERIODS, 1821 TO 1863.......... 19 to 30

- Tonnage entries of American and foreign vessels from all foreign countries, severally, every fifth year, 1821 to 1863, with the percentage of foreign.......... 21
- Tonnage entries from foreign ports, distinguishing the Canadian, every fifth year, 1821 to 1863, with the percentage of foreign.......... 24
- Tonnage entries for corresponding years, from European countries distinctively, with the percentage of foreign.......... 25
- Tonnage entries for corresponding years, from the West Indies, with the percentage of foreign.......... 27
- Tonnage entries for corresponding years, from Mexico and South America, with the percentage of foreign.......... 27
- Tonnage entries for corresponding years, from Asia, Africa, and miscellaneous places, with the percentage of foreign.......... 27
- Values of the imports and exports of the United States, with the percentage to and from each of the designated geographical divisions, every fifth year, from 1821 to 1863.......... [illegible]
- European trade, distinguishing gold and silver, every fifth year, 1821 to 1863.......... [illegible]
- West India trade, distinguishing gold and silver, every fifth year, 1821 to 1863.......... [illegible]
- Detail of trade with the West Indies, for the years [illegible] and [illegible].......... [illegible]
- Canadian and British provincial trade, distinguishing gold and silver, every fifth year, 1821 to 1863.......... [illegible]
- Mexican and South American trade, distinguishing gold and silver, every fifth year, 1821 to 1863.......... 30
- Asiatic, African and miscellaneous trade, distinguishing gold and silver, every fifth year, 1821 to 1863.......... 30
- Statement of vessels built in the United States, [illegible] to 1863.......... 30
- American tonnage employed in foreign trade, coasting trade, fisheries, and steam navigation, respectively, from 1815 to 1863.......... 31

STATISTICS OF GENERAL TRADE WITH GREAT BRITAIN.......... 32 to 35

- British statement of exports to the United States, 1857 to 1863.......... 32
- Flax and hemp imported into Great Britain, 1857 to 1863 — tons and value.......... 33
- Exports from England of certain articles of foreign production, 1858 to 1863.......... 34
- Exports from England to the United States of certain articles of foreign production, 1862 and 1863.......... 35

CARRIAGE OF FOREIGN PRODUCE IN UNITED STATES VESSELS.......... 35

- Articles of tropical or semi-tropical origin exported from the United States, 1854 to 1863.......... 36
- Articles of tropical or semi-tropical origin, exported from the United States, 1838 to 1863.......... 37

DIRECT TRADE WITH GREAT BRITAIN.......... 37 to 55

- Imports and exports from and to the United States, 1858 to 1863, (British reports).......... 37
- Imports and exports to and from the United Kingdom, 1855-'56 to 1862-'63, (United States official reports).......... 37
- Imports and exports of the precious metals to and from the United States and Great Britain, respectively, 1858 to 1863, (British and American reports).......... 38

Page.

Comparison of cotton receipts in England, for 1861, with the statistics of export from the United States for the same year ... 39
Monthly receipts of cotton in England, from the United States, 1859 to 1861 ... 40
Exports from Great Britain to the United States compared with the official returns of imports into the United States from Great Britain ... 41
Explanation of the deficiency in the British account ... 41
Statement of exchanges between Great Britain and the United States for the seven years, 1856 to 1862, (British records) ... 42
Quantities and values of leading articles imported into England from the United States, 1861, 1862, 1863 ... 43
Imports from the United States into Great Britain for the seven years 1856 to 1862 — quantities and values ... 44
Exports to the United States, the produce and manufactures of the United Kingdom, for the seven years 1856 to 1862 — quantities and values ... 46
Exports to the United States of foreign and colonial produce and manufactures, for the seven years, 1856 to 1862 — quantities and values ... 47
Exports to Great Britain, the produce of the United States, for the four fiscal years 1858-59 to 1861-62 — quantities and values, (from U. S. official records) ... 49
Values of articles the export of which increased from 1860 to 1863 ... 51
The provision trade ... 51

BRITISH TRADE WITH CALIFORNIA ... 52

Imports into England, the produce of California, 1856 to 1862 — quantities and values, (from British official returns) ... 53
Exports to California, the produce and manufacture of the United Kingdom, 1856 to 1862 — quantities and values, (from British official returns) ... 54
Value of foreign and colonial produce exported from Great Britain to California, 1856 to 1862 ... 55

STEAM TONNAGE IN THE FOREIGN TRADE OF THE UNITED STATES ... 55 to [illegible]

Steam tonnage from foreign countries entered at Portland, Maine, 1855 to 1863 ... 56
Steam tonnage from foreign countries entered at Philadelphia, 1851 to 1858 ... 56
Steam tonnage from foreign countries entered at Boston, 1845 to 1863 ... 57
American steam tonnage from foreign countries entered at the port of New York, 1846 to 1863 ... 57
Foreign steam tonnage from foreign countries entered at the port of New York, 1846 to 1863 ... 58
General aggregate of steam tonnage entering the Atlantic ports of the United States, 1846 to 1863 ... 59
Actual steam tonnage arriving from foreign ports, 1846 to 1863 ... 59
Steam tonnage entered at the port of San Francisco from foreign countries, 1853-54 to 1862-63 ... 60
Steam tonnage entered the port of Charleston from foreign countries, 1851 to 1860 ... 61
Steam tonnage entered at New Orleans from foreign countries, 1853 to 1860 ... 61
Steam tonnage entered at Castine, Maine, from foreign countries, 1851-52 to 1862-63 ... 61
Actual steam tonnage employed in the foreign trans-oceanic trade, 1859-63 ... 62

THE ISTHMUS TRADE ... 62

Values of cargoes entering Panama, 1860-62 ... 62
Values of cargoes leaving Panama, 1860-62 ... 62
Number and tonnage of vessels entered at Panama for the year ending September 30, 1862 ... 63
Travel and transportation over the Isthmus of Panama for the year ending September 30, 1862 ... 63

REVIEW OF STEAMSHIP LINES ENGAGED IN THE FOREIGN TRADE OF THE UNITED STATES, JANUARY, 1864 ... 64 to 70

STEAM SHIPPING AND TONNAGE OF GREAT BRITAIN ... 71 to 78

Summary of tonnage entering the ports of Great Britain from foreign countries, 1860 and 1863 ... 72
Number, tonnage, and nationality of vessels entering the ports of the United Kingdom for five calendar years, 1859 to 1863 ... 73
Number and tonnage of registered steam vessels under and over fifty tons, respectively, owned in England, 1860, 1861, 1862 ... 74
Number and tonnage of registered steam vessels owned in England, employed in the home and foreign trade, respectively, in 1860, 1861, 1862 ... 75
Number and tonnage of steam vessels built in the United Kingdom, 1853 to 1862 ... 75
Number, tonnage, and nationality of steam vessels entered and cleared at ports of the United Kingdom, 1860, 1861, 1862 ... 76
Number, tonnage, and nationality of steam vessels entered and cleared at ports of the United Kingdom in 1863 ... 76
Entries of steam vessels at ports of the United Kingdom from the United States, 1853, 1860, 1861, 1863 ... 77
Steam vessels entered and cleared at British ports from and to American countries, 1853, 1860, 1861, 1862 ... 78

TRADE OF THE UNITED STATES WITH CANADA AND THE OTHER BRITISH NORTH AMERICAN PROVINCES ... 78 to 117

Exports of Canadian produce through the United States to the other British North American provinces ... 79
Exports and imports of wheat and wheat flour to and from Canada, 1861, 1862 ... 80
Exports to Canada of wheat, flour, Indian corn, and meal, during the fiscal years 1849 to 1863 ... 81
Exports and imports of wheat and wheat flour to and from Canada, 1863 ... 81
Exports to Canada, 1849 to 1863, (fiscal years) ... 82
Exports to the other British North American provinces, 1849 to 1863, (fiscal years) ... 82
Total exports and imports to and from Canada and the other British North American provinces, 1849 to 1863 ... 83
Imports from Canada, 1850 to 1863 ... 84
Imports from British North American provinces, 1850 to 1863 ... 85
Total imports from Canada and the other British North American provinces, 1850 to 1863 ... 86

Page.

General table of values of imports from Canada into the United States free of duty under the reciprocity treaty, for the half year to June 30, 1855, and the fiscal years 1855-'56 to 1862-'63 ..... [illegible]
General table of imports from the British North American provinces, other than Canada, free of duty under the reciprocity treaty, 1855-'56 to 1862-'63 ..... [illegible]
General table of imports from Canada into the United States paying duty, 1855-'56 to 1862-'63 ..... [illegible]
Analysis of the general tables, averages of domestic exports to Canada ..... [illegible]
Averages of foreign exports to Canada ..... [illegible]
Table of aggregates paying duty in Canada, nine years ..... [illegible]
Table of aggregates paying duty in the United States, nine years ..... [illegible]
Table of values made free to Canada, by the reciprocity treaty, 1850 to 1863 ..... [illegible]
Table of values made free to the United States, 1854 to 1863 ..... [illegible]
Canadian official tables, three years' exports to Canada ..... [illegible]
Statement of the value of the imports into Canada from the United States, 1850 to 1863, with the amount of duties paid ..... [illegible]
Statement of the value of the exports from Canada to the United States, and the total trade, 1851 to 1863 ..... [illegible]
Imports into Canada from the United States, free of duty under the reciprocity treaty, 1855 to 1863 ..... [illegible]
Exports to Canada, the produce and manufactures of the United States, 1850-'51 to 1862-'63 ..... [illegible]
Imports from Canada into United States, free by ordinary laws, 1855-'56 to 1862-'63 ..... [illegible]
Clearances and entrances from and into the lake ports of the United States and European ports, respectively 100
Movement of American produce in and through Canada ..... [illegible]
Value of transit trade through Canada via the St. Lawrence to and from the United States 103
Value of imports from Canada passing through the United States under bond 103
Values of imports into Canada via the United States and the St. Lawrence, respectively, 1850 to 1863 104
Export of United States manufactures to Canada 104
Values of articles, the manufacture of the United States, exported to Canada, paying duty, 1858-'59 to 1862-'63 105
Exports of wheat, flour, corn, and meal, from the United States to the British North American provinces, other than Canada, 1841 to 1863—quantities and values 105
Produce of the United States passing through Canadian canals, the points of origin and destination distinguished, 1861, 1862, and 1863 107
Transportation from American ports to Canada, up and down the St. Lawrence canals 109
Trade of the principal ports of the northern frontier with Canada, 1858 to 1863 110
Summaries of trade at the ports of the northern frontier, eastward and westward of Buffalo, respectively, 1858 to 1863 113
Canadian free ports 113
Imports at the port of Gaspé from countries other than Canada, 1861, 1862, and 1863 114
Exports from the port of Gaspé to British and foreign ports 114
Imports at Sault St. Marie from British and foreign ports, 1861, 1862, and 1863 115
Exports from Sault St. Marie to British and foreign ports, 1861, 1862, and 1863 ..... [illegible]

INTERNAL OR DOMESTIC COMMERCE BETWEEN THE MISSISSIPPI VALLEY AND THE ATLANTIC STATES ..... 117 to 181

DATA—TREATMENT—GENERAL RESULTS ..... 117 to [illegible]
Definition of internal commerce 117
Total values exchanged 117
Internal commerce of Russia and United States, colonial trade of other nations ..... [illegible]
Statistics of domestic commerce, sources ..... [illegible]
Basis of calculation ..... [illegible]
East and west transportation, Mississippi river, and the coasting trade compared ..... [illegible]
Commerce by the grand thoroughfares traversing the meridian of the Alleghenies ..... [illegible]
Exchanges of Atlantic coasting trade ..... [illegible]
Market exchanges at the seaboard, Cincinnati, St. Louis, Chicago, Lake Superior, northwest of St. Paul, of the plains west of the Missouri river, and at New Orleans ..... [illegible]

SPECIFIC CALCULATION OF THE EXCHANGES BETWEEN THE EAST AND THE WEST ..... [illegible] to [illegible]

WESTWARD FREIGHTS ..... [illegible] to [illegible]
Pennsylvania Central railroad, classification of tonnage ..... [illegible]
Westward freight through to Pittsburg ..... [illegible]
Way freight from Philadelphia ..... [illegible]
New York Central railroad, through tonnage ..... [illegible]
Way tonnage, total way and through ..... [illegible]
Erie railroad, through and way tonnage ..... [illegible]
Erie canal, to Buffalo and Oswego, tonnage and values ..... [illegible]
Erie canal, leading articles carried ..... [illegible]
Summary statement, tonnage and values transported westward by the five main lines ..... [illegible]
Population and consumption per capita, west of the Alleghenies ..... [illegible]
Erie canal, leading articles of freight to the western States to 1863 ..... [illegible]
Erie and Champlain canals, westward freight, 1836 to 1862 ..... [illegible]
Transportation tonnage westward from tide-water, on the New York canals, 1857 to 1863 ..... [illegible]
Canadian canals, transportation westward through Welland canal, articles, tonnage, and destination, 1861-'63 134
EASTWARD FREIGHTS ..... [illegible] to [illegible]
Valuations assumed and summary of the four railroads and the Erie canal ..... [illegible]
Pennsylvania Central railroad, articles carried eastward, 1859 to 1863 ..... [illegible]
Through from Pittsburg to Baltimore and Philadelphia ..... [illegible]
Way stations to Philadelphia ..... [illegible]
From Pittsburg to way stations ..... [illegible]
New York Central railroad, tonnage eastward, 1858 to 1863 ..... [illegible]
Erie canal, tonnage to tide-water, produce of the western States and Canada, 1836 to 1863 ..... [illegible]
Erie canal, way freights, produce of New York ..... [illegible]
Lake transportation eastward ..... [illegible]
Freight charge on wheat from Milwaukie and Chicago to Buffalo, from 1858 to 1863 ..... [illegible]

Page.

Lake trade, tonnage of United States vessels employed in, 1830 to 1862 143
Table showing the number, class, tonnage, and valuation of vessels, American and Canadian, engaged in the commerce of the lakes, 1856 to 1862 144
Tonnage of the lakes and the river St. Lawrence January 1, 1860 and 1863 145
Vessels owned at Buffalo, 1850 to 1862 145
Increase of the lake tonnage in 1862 145
Shipping of the port of Milwaukie, 1860 and 1862 146
List of transportation lines on the lakes, 1863 146

TABLES OF PRODUCE SENT EASTWARD FROM THE LAKE CITIES AND PORTS ..... 147 to 15[illegible]

Flour and grain sent from Chicago in 1862, with destination 148
Aggregates of flour and grain sent from Chicago for four years 148
Summary of quantities to Canadian ports in 1862 148
Cattle, animals, provisions, wool, &c., sent from Chicago in 1862 149
Estimated values of produce sent from Chicago in 1862 150
Produce sent eastward from Milwaukie, flour and grain, for ten years, 1853 to 1862 150
Summary of flour and grain from all ports of Lake Michigan in 1862 150
Provisions, wool, whiskey, &c., sent from Milwaukie in 1862, with valuation of all classes of produce 151
Total valuation of Lake Michigan exports, 1862 151
Eastward freights on Wisconsin railroads, 1862 151
Westward freights on Wisconsin railroads, 1862 152

THE LAKE SUPERIOR TRADE:

Transit of vessels through the Sault Ste. Marie canal, monthly, for 1862 ..... 152 to 155
Value of outward shipments for 1862 153
Table of copper shipments, 1855 to 1862 154
Production and export of iron and iron ore, eight years 154

THE LAKE FISHERIES 154, 155
Table of receipts of lake fish at Buffalo, 1854 to 1862 155

TRADE OF LAKE ERIE, EASTWARD ..... 155 to 159

Tables of receipts of produce at Toledo, by various railroads 155
Lines of transportation eastward from Toledo, and quantities shipped in 1862 156
Valuation of produce shipped from Toledo in 1862 157
Trade of Detroit, eastward—quantities for 1860 to 1862 157
Valuation of Detroit exports for 1862 158
Detail of receipts and exports of flour and grain, 1858 to 1862 158

LAKE COMMERCE AT BUFFALO ..... 158 to 168

Receipts of flour and grain at Buffalo and all terminal lake ports for three years, 1850 to 1862 159
Summary of receipts at terminal lake ports for 1862 160
Summary of receipts at New York city, 1860 to 1862 161
Receipts of flour and grain at Buffalo from 1836 to 1862 161
Receipts and exports of provisions at Buffalo, 1847 to 1862 162
Receipts and exports of whiskey at Buffalo, 1850 to 1862 163
Lumber trade of the lakes—receipts and exports at Buffalo, 1848 to 1862 163
Receipts of live stock by lake at Buffalo, 1851 to 1862 164
Receipts and exports of hides and leather, 1858 to 1862 165
Receipts and exports of wool at Buffalo, 1858 to 1862 165
Receipts of lake and other freights via Fort Erie, on the Buffalo and Lake Huron railway, 1862 166
Detail of receipts at Buffalo by lake and railway, 1862 167

GENERAL EXCHANGES, EASTWARD AND WESTWARD, AT BUFFALO ..... 168 to 172

Eastward freights by canal from Buffalo, 1854 to 1862 168
Receipts of westward freights at Buffalo, by canal, 1854 to 1862 169
Detail of exports eastward, by canal, 1860 to 1862 170
Detail of receipts at Buffalo, by canal, 1860 to 1862 172
Comparison of grain and flour receipts of 1862 with 1861 172

LAKE TRADE AT TORONTO, CANADA: Exports of flour and grain, 1856 to 1862, with destination 173

PRODUCE AND GRAIN TRADE OF MONTREAL, CANADA 174
Receipts and shipments at Montreal, 1851 to 1862 175

PRODUCE AND GRAIN TRADE OF OSWEGO, 1861 and 1862 175

SUMMARY OF THE GENERAL MOVEMENT EASTWARD IN FLOUR AND GRAIN 176, 177

Per cent. of receipts at the principal receiving points, 1857 to 1862, including the foregoing eastward movement 176
Variations in the eastward movement, 1858 to 1862 176

GENERAL TABLES OF THE TONNAGE AND TRANSPORTATION OF THE ERIE CANAL ..... 179 to 181
Capacity, tonnage, and aggregate carriage of Erie canal boats eastward 179
Quantities of flour, distinguishing western and New York, reaching tide-water through the Erie canal 179
Tonnage of wheat and flour eastward to the Hudson river on the Erie canal, places of shipment, and total value 180
Tonnage and value of merchandise going to other States by way of Buffalo and Oswego, in each year, 1838 to 1862 180
Estimated value of property coming from, and merchandise going to, other States than New York by way of Buffalo, Black Rock, Tonawanda, and Oswego, 1836 to 1862 180

Page.

COMMERCE OF THE PACIFIC COAST .... 182 to 200

1. The Australian colonies of England 183
2. The Pacific States and Territories of the United States 185
3. The English colonies of Vancouver's island and British Columbia 193
4. Russia in America and Asia 195
5. The Sandwich islands 196
6. The gold product of the Pacific coast 197
7. Movement of treasure to India and China 199

OVERLAND TRADE AND COMMUNICATIONS BETWEEN THE PACIFIC COAST AND THE MISSISSIPPI VALLEY .... 201 to 220

1. The silver production of Nevada 201
2. Agriculture and stock-raising in Utah 202
3. Colorado quartz mining; prospects of agriculture; iron and coal 204
4. Traffic and transportation west of the Missouri river 210
5. Union Pacific railroad; elements of population and business for its support 212
6. Probable extensions of the railroad system of the United States to the Pacific coast:
   a. A southern Pacific railroad route 213
   b. The northern or lake route 216
   c. [illegible] 218

THE MINERAL WEALTH OF LAKE SUPERIOR 221

☞ A statistical map prepared in the Treasury Department to illustrate the text of the report, showing the boundaries of the new Territories at the date of the latest congressional legislation; the railroad communications in operation, in progress, intended, and in prospect between the Atlantic, Mississippi, interior, and Pacific States; the boundaries of the arable districts of British North America upon the northwestern frontier of the United States; the population of all the States and Territories according to the census of 1860, with estimates for the new Territories at later dates; the areas of all the States and Territories furnished by the government Land Office; and the several sites of the gold and silver mines known and worked in the Rocky mountains.

REPORT

OF

THE SECRETARY OF THE TREASURY,

COMMUNICATING,

In compliance with a resolution of the Senate of the 12th of March, 1863, a statistical and general report upon the value and present condition of our foreign and domestic commerce.

TREASURY DEPARTMENT, *June 25*, 1864.

SIR: The following resolution was adopted by the Senate of the United States on the 12th March, 1863:

"*Resolved*, That the Secretary of the Treasury be directed to have prepared and presented to the Senate a statistical and general report upon the value and present condition of our foreign and domestic commerce, including as well that of the Pacific coast; and, further, to suggest what legislation, if any, is necessary to protect the important interests involved."

In response to this resolution, the Secretary has caused to be prepared, and has the honor herewith to transmit, a series of statements covering the wide range of inquiry contemplated by the call of the Senate, as completely as the accessible sources of information have enabled him to do.

The contents of this report may be generally described and classified as follows:

First. A historical and analytic review of the foreign commerce of the United States from the beginning of the government.

Second. An exhibit of the existing internal commerce between the Atlantic and Mississippi States.

Third. The overland trade and communications with the Pacific States.

Fourth. The foreign commerce of the Pacific coast.

Fifth. The international relations of the northern frontier of the United States with British and Russian America.

The first of these general divisions embraces a statement of the tonnage employed and the values exchanged in our foreign commerce generally, with the varying proportions of foreign and American tonnage. It exhibits a general view, historical and statistical, of the carrying trade of our international exchanges, distinguishing the trans-oceanic tonnage from that employed in trade with the British possessions in North America; the course of the carrying trade in the great geographical divisions of our foreign commerce; its increase and decrease with the principal foreign countries; the total value of the exchanges; the international movement of the precious metals; and the periodic changes in the relative value of the imports from and the exports to the several customer countries; to which is added the number, class, and tonnage of vessels built in each year from 1822 to 1863, with the tonnage employed in the coasting trade, the whale, cod, and mackerel fisheries, respectively.

The trade and navigation of the United States with Great Britain, compiled from the official reports of both countries, are given in general, and in sufficient detail to exhibit the extent and fluctuations of this branch of our commerce, the leading articles exchanged in direct and indirect trade, and the direct exchange of commodities, other than the precious metals, between Great Britain and California.

The trade of the United States with Canada and the other British North American provinces is also specially presented, on the authority of both our own and Canadian official reports, showing the extent and character of the exchanges, the kind and value of the transit trade of the eastern and western States through Canada and the St. Lawrence to the ocean.

A general exhibit is made of the steam tonnage engaged in our foreign commerce, and of the Panama Isthmus trade, vessels and cargoes, with a comparative view of the steam shipping and tonnage of Great Britian, and a statement of the steam vessels engaged in American trade entered and cleared in British ports.

The second division of the report, occupied with domestic commerce between the Atlantic and Mississippi States, embraces the quantities and values transported east and west by the great railways of the United States, by the lakes, and by the Welland, Erie, and Champlain canals, and the kind and extent of the shipping of the lakes. The tonnage was obtained from the reports of State commissioners of statistics, boards of trade of the principal cities, transportation companies, and other authoritative sources, and the values estimated by accepted commercial rules.

The interruption of trade between the loyal and disloyal States of the Union, the suspension of the Mississippi river trade, and the non-intercourse of the northern with southern States since the commencement of the rebellion, have rendered the statistics of this large branch of domestic commerce unattainable. The existing records of previous years are known to be both incomplete and unreliable, and no exhibit of it has therefore been attempted in this report.

It will be observed that the data used in exhibiting the east and west trade of the States and Territories relate mainly to the calendar year 1862, which is chosen because in that year its limits were well defined and its character well settled and ascertained.

The third, fourth, and fifth general divisions exhibit the trade of the Pacific coast; its commercial relations with Asia; the movement of the precious metals to India and China; statistics of the population, of mining, of agricultural productions, and of transportation in Nevada, Utah, Colorado, and Kansas, in reference to the construction and support of the Union Pacific railroad; the like statistics of Arizona, New Mexico, western Texas, and Neosho, bearing prospectively upon a railroad from the States of the lower Mississippi to the Gulf of California; similar statisticts of Idaho, Montana, and Dakota, with reference to overland communication between the great lakes and the Columbia river; the situation and prospects of an international route, passing through the northwestern States to the Pacific coast, in British Columbia; the progress of population, mineral wealth, and other material interests anticipated within the present century, in the several belts of interior States traversed by these overland routes to the Pacific ocean; and the condition and prospects of the mining interests of the basin of Lake Superior.

In reference to the existing necessity for the exhibit of our foreign commerce contemplated by the resolution of the Senate, the Secretary begs leave to say that hereafter the requirement, he believes, will be fully met by certain reforms in the annual report of commerce and navigation adopted by the department in the report for 1862-'63, as will be seen by the volume now in type and about to be issued.

The statistics of the internal commerce of the country in the present condition of our national statistics must be gathered from sources that hold no official relations with the Treasury Department; but a knowledge of them has always been required for public and private uses, and in the new condition of our domestic affairs has become more than ever important and necessary to the government and the people. A contribution to the fund of information demanded—believed to be valuable—was prepared in the Treasury Department and published with the finance report of 1863, giving the range of prices of staple articles in the New York market at the beginning of each month of every year from 1825 to 1863. The labor and research bestowed upon the inquiry, the results of which are embodied in the papers now transmitted, will, at least, manifest an earnest endeavor to supply the required information, and the report is submitted as a step towards the more perfect execution of such a work.

The Secretary is not prepared at present to express an opinion in regard to the legislation necessary to protect the important interests to which the Senate's resolution relates. The facts exhibited in the report will doubtless indicate to the wisdom of Congress what measures will best accomplish that end. It is proper to add that the papers now submitted have been prepared under the direction of the Secretary by Messrs. William Elder, James W. Taylor, and Lorin Blodget, gentlemen whose known capacity for intelligent and accurate research and correct appreciation of results supplies a just ground for confidence in their statements and inferences.

With great respect,

S. P. CHASE,
Secretary of the Treasury.

Hon. HANNIBAL HAMLIN,
President of the Senate of the United States.

FOREIGN COMMERCE

OF

THE UNITED STATES.

TONNAGE AND TRADE.

The foreign commerce of the United States has undergone changes within the last forty years, in value, geographic distribution, and agencies employed, which are not indicated by the ordinary official publications with the clearness and force required for the direction of legislation concerning it. The resolution of the Senate recognizes these deficiencies, and is understood to authorize whatever range of inquiry may be demanded for a better exhibition and explication of the history and present condition of our international trade.

The United States began an extraordinarily extended and unusually successful commercial career very soon after the establishment of the government. The condition of Europe for a long period was such that American shipping became of necessity the preferred channel for conducting far the larger share of the commerce of the world. We were not limited to the carriage of merchandise of American production abroad and the return of foreign articles required in our own consumption, but for a series of years entered at, and again exported from our ports, a larger aggregate of values on account of foreign nations than for the entire use of the United States.

It could not, of course, be expected that with the most rapid and successful development of the United States this ascendency in general commerce would be maintained, but the facilities obtained by a preoccupation of extensive and profitable lines of trade between countries possessing no commercial marine directly, and also between these and the commercial and manufacturing states which are their permanent natural markets, should have secured to the shipping of the United States an equal division of all trade between non-commercial states and a share of the carrying trade wherever exclusion by positive legislation does not exist. Still more decidedly should the control of all carrying trade to our own markets have been retained, and the increased consumption of the products of tropical countries necessarily attending on the growth and increasing wealth of the United States, might reasonably be supposed to give employment almost exclusively to American shipping. Crude products of the United States exported, and crude products of tropical latitudes imported for consumption here, constitute a permanent trade which need not pass from American hands.

The statistics of shipping and tonnage, distinguishing the proportions of American and foreign, employed in the commerce of the United States, are the readiest and most directly available guide to the general course of trade from the beginning. Previous to 1821 the statements are designated the "tonnage engaged in the foreign trade," and subsequent to 1821 "the tonnage entered and cleared at all the ports" are the specific statements given. It is probable that the first designation is so nearly identical with the second that no modification of either is necessary in making a continuous comparison, but as a division is required for convenience simply, the first of the following tables bring the series of years down to 1821, of "tonnage engaged in the foreign trade;" and the second gives the tonnage of vessels entered the several ports of the United States for each year of the period following, to 1863.

The large values of foreign merchandise exported from the United States, which are given in detail in another place, necessarily imply the employment of a great amount of American tonnage, since very little of the carrying trade between neutral nations could be in the hands of any belligerent power, and nearly all Europe was long involved in war. Even after the peace of 1815 there were intervals of disturbance, and frequent occasions in which the carrying trade was largely resumed by our shipping. The magnitude of the interest we had in certain years is striking. Beginning at 605,513 tons, in 1790, the tonnage in foreign trade rose to 1,106,512 tons in 1801, and to 1,203,021 tons in 1807, of which but seven per cent. was foreign in the last-named year. The proportions of foreign tonnage to the total engaged in foreign trade for the average of periods of five years, from 1789 to 1821, is as follows: 1789 to 1793, 37.1 per cent.; 1794 to 1798, 10.6 per cent.; 1799 to 1803, 15.6 per cent.; 1804 to 1808, 8.9 per cent.; 1809 to 1813, 9.9 per cent.; 1814 to 1818, 22.1 per cent.; 1819 to 1821, 9.5 per cent.

As a rule, the proportion of American tonnage increased directly with the absolute amount employed. In the two years of least trade, 1789 and 1814, nearly half the tonnage was foreign. In 1811, with nearly 1,000,000 tons engaged, but 3.3 per cent. was foreign; an exceptional state of affairs due to the violence of the European wars then waged. The following is the detail of each description of tonnage employed in the foreign commerce of the United States for each year, from 1789 to 1821, with the calculated proportion of foreign:

American and foreign tonnage engaged in the foreign trade of the United States, 1789 to 1821.

Years.	American, tons.	Foreign, tons.	Total, tons.	Percentage of foreign.	Years.	American, tons.	Foreign, tons.	Total, tons.	Percentage of foreign.
1789	127,329	106,654	233,983	45.5	1806	1,044,005	91,084	1,135,089	8.0
1790	354,767	250,746	605,513	41.4	1807	1,116,241	86,780	1,203,021	7.2
1791	363,810	240,598	604,410	39.8	1808	538,768	47,674	584,442	8.1
1792	414,679	244,278	658,957	37.0	1809	635,479	89,305	724,784	12.6
1793	447,754	163,556	611,310	26.7	1810	906,713	80,316	987,029	8.1
1794	525,649	83,974	609,623	13.8	1811	948,247	33,203	981,449	3.3
1795	580,277	56,832	637,109	8.9	1812	667,817	47,098	715,415	6.5
1796	675,046	46,846	721,892	6.4	1813	237,301	113,827	351,128	32.3
1797	608,078	75,757	683,835	10.6	1814	59,746	48,301	108,047	44.6
1798	522,245	87,760	610,005	14.3	1815	700,500	217,413	917,913	23.6
1799	624,839	107,583	732,422	14.6	1816	877,462	259,724	1,136,186	22.7
1800	682,871	121,403	804,274	15.0	1817	780,136	212,166	992,302	21.3
1801	849,303	157,270	1,006,573	15.6	1818	755,101	161,414	916,515	17.6
1802	798,805	145,519	944,324	15.4	1819	783,579	85,098	868,677	9.8
1803	787,424	163,714	951,138	17.2	1820	801,253	78,859	880,112	8.9
1804	821,962	122,141	944,100	12.9	1821	765,098	82,015	851,098	9.7
1805	922,298	87,842	1,010,140	8.6					

Averages of five-year periods.

Years.	American, tons.	Foreign, tons.	Total, tons.	Percentage of foreign.	Years.	American, tons.	Foreign, tons.	Total, tons.	Percentage of foreign.
1789 to 1793	341,678	201,150	542,798	37.08	1809 to 1813	672,058	74,729	746,891	9.9
1794 to 1798	582,850	69,430	652,099	10.6	1814 to 1818	634,387	179,923	814,310	22.1
1799 to 1803	768,640	139,040	907,706	15.6	1819 to 1821	784,638	82,558	867,196	9.5
1804 to 1808	892,531	87,304	979,735	8.9					

In the next series of years, or from 1821 to 1837, the rapid increase of foreign tonnage is apparent, commencing most decidedly in 1831 and 1832. After this date, notwithstanding the aggregate increase is four-fold in 1849 and seven-fold in 1863, as compared with the average of 1820 to 1830, the proportion of foreign maintains its position at 30 to 40 per cent of the whole. In the tables as they stand a large aggregate of tonnage entering from Canada is included in the American, which is, to a considerable extent, mere ferry tonnage, and should be excluded from the comparison. The average to be so excluded would be 250,000 tons annually for five years previous to 1859, and 500,000 to 600,000 tons for each year from 1859 to 1863, inclusive.

During this period of forty-two years there was no marked event in the history of the United States to affect the progressive advance in general trade. It is evident, however, that, not only was the foreign carrying trade steadily passing from our shipping to other hands, but also the direct commerce of the United States with all other countries was steadily encroached upon, each year adding a greater number of foreign than of American vessels to the general commercial marine. At the date of the introduction of steam in transatlantic commerce the accession of foreign tonnage was more marked than at any other time subsequent to 1832; and correcting the account to transatlantic commerce distinctively, by throwing out the trade with the Canadian border, the proportion of foreign becomes greater.

Aggregate of tonnage entering the ports of the United States from foreign countries, 1821 to 1863, with the proportion of foreign.*

Years.	American, tons.	Foreign, tons.	Total, tons.	Per centage of foreign.	Years.	American, tons.	Foreign, tons.	Total, tons.	Per centage of foreign.
1821	765,098	81,526	846,624	9.6	1843, 9 mo's	1,143,523	534,752	1,678,275	31.8
1822	787,961	100,541	888,501	11.3	1844	1,977,438	916,992	2,894,430	31.6
1823	775,271	119,468	894,739	13.4	1845	2,035,486	910,563	2,946,049	30.9
1824	850,033	102,367	952,410	10.7	1846	2,151,114	959,739	3,110,853	30.8
1825	880,754	92,927	973,681	9.5	1847	2,101,359	1,220,346	3,321,705	36.7
1826	942,206	105,654	1,047,860	10.09	1848	2,393,482	1,405,191	3,798,673	37.0
1827	918,361	137,589	1,055,950	13.03	1849	2,658,321	1,710,515	4,368,836	39.1
1828	868,381	150,223	1,018,604	14.7	1850	2,573,016	1,775,623	4,348,639	40.8
1829	872,949	130,743	1,003,692	13.02	1851	3,054,349	1,939,091	4,993,440	38.8
1830	967,227	131,900	1,099,127	12.0	1852	3,235,522	2,057,358	5,292,880	38.8
1831	922,952	281,948	1,204,900	23.4	1853	4,004,013	2,277,930	6,281,943	36.1
1832	949,622	393,038	1,342,660	29.2	1854	3,752,115	2,132,294	5,884,379	36.2
1833	1,111,441	496,705	1,608,146	30.8	1855	3,861,391	2,083,948	5,945,339	35.05
1834	1,074,670	568,052	1,642,722	34.5	1856	4,385,484	2,286,769	6,672,253	33.3
1835	1,352,653	641,310	1,993,963	32.1	1857	4,721,370	2,464,946	7,186,316	34.3
1836	1,255,384	680,213	1,935,597	35.1	1858	4,385,641	2,279,403	6,665,045	33.4
1837	1,299,720	765,703	2,065,423	37.07	1859*	5,265,648	2,540,387	7,806,035	32.5
1838	1,302,974	592,110	1,895,084	31.2	1860	5,921,285	2,353,911	8,275,196	28.4
1839	1,491,279	624,814	2,116,093	29.5	1861	5,023,917	2,217,554	7,241,471	30.6
1840	1,576,946	712,363	2,289,309	31.1	1862	5,117,685	2,245,278	7,362,963	30.5
1841	1,631,909	736,444	2,368,353	31.1	1863	4,614,808	2,640,378	7,255,078	36.4
1842	1,510,111	732,775	2,242,886	32.6					

In 1862 and 1863 the tonnage entered from Canada amounted to totals quite disproportionate to the commerce, it being:

		American.	Foreign.
1862	tons..	2,487,373	683,411
1863	tons..	2,307,233	743,136

Excluding this, much of which was steam ferry tonnage, the proportion of foreign shipping in the foreign trade of the United States in the fiscal year 1862–'63 was 45.1 per cent. of the whole:—Tonnage in foreign trade, 1862–'63, American, 2,307,465 tons; foreign, 1,897,242 tons.

* A deduction of at least 400,000 tons from American tonnage should be made on this and each following year for the duplicated tonnage of steam ferry-boats at Buffalo chiefly, and in less degree at Ogdensburg and Cape Vincent.

During the fiscal year current, 1863–'64, the reduction of American tonnage has been greatly accelerated from extraordinary and unusual causes, until the direct foreign trade conducted in American bottoms has been almost annihilated.

In the preceding statements it has been the purpose to show the normal course of trade in periods of peace, and to prepare matter for a fair judgment of the state of affairs and the tendencies of trade abroad anterior to the war. It cannot be doubted that there was a serious decline of the foreign trade properly belonging to the United States dating back at least to 1832, and a change in progress, which is more fully disclosed by the statistics giving the values of imports and exports.

The following named countries sent us absolutely less tonnage, both American and foreign, in the year 1861 than in 1821, forty years previous:

		1821.	1861.
Russia	tons..	13,827	12,157
Prussia	tons..	726	400
Swedish West Indies	tons..	13,946	1,684
Sweden and Norway	tons..	13,381	13,330
Danish West Indies	tons..	41,096	14,919
Gibraltar and Malta	tons..	11,666	2,770
French West Indies	tons..	41,729	2,618
Canary islands	tons..	2,329	2,012
Portugal	tons..	20,693	7,417
Honduras and Campeachy	tons..	5,357	3,849
Hayti	tons..	60,119	39,640
Madeira islands	tons..	4,288	1,135
Cape Verde islands	tons..	5,038	2,360

These are comparatively unimportant countries, however, and the diversion of trade from direct channels is not so clearly shown by details of tonnage as by actual imports of merchandise. For the purpose of this comparison of values, two years better representing the periods may perhaps be selected—1828 and 1860—in both of which trade was healthy and importations full, but not excessive. No disturbance of the usual condition of any considerable foreign country existed in either year which could of itself divert trade from its accustomed channels. The total imports in 1828 were $88,509,824, and in 1860 $362,163,941. The re-exports were $21,595,000 in the first-named year, and $26,933,000 in the last named. The following table classifies the details from each country, showing which have increased and which have declined, both positively and relatively:

Countries from which the imports to the United States have positively declined from 1828 to 1860.

Imports from—	In 1828.	In 1860.	Imports from—	In 1828.	In 1860.
Russia	$2,7[illegible]	$1,857,6[illegible]	Gibraltar	$[illegible]95,570	$[illegible]53,9[illegible]
Prussia	1[illegible],0[illegible]	3[illegible],464	French West Indies	[illegible],651	[illegible]
Sweden and Norway	1,570,7[illegible]	614,191	Hayti	2,167,385	2,092,7[illegible]
Swedish West Indies	373,9[illegible]	18,793	Canary islands	2[illegible],740	18,[illegible]
Denmark	117,948	16,509	Madeira	168,010	[illegible]3,773
Danish West Indies	2,2[illegible],1[illegible]	204,616	Cape Verde islands	70,3[illegible]	51,6[illegible]
Dutch West Indies	478,397	395,644	Peru	8[illegible]	3[illegible],432

Countries from which the imports have declined relatively to the total imports.

Imports from—	In 1828.	In 1860.	Imports from—	In 1828.	In 1860.
Holland	$1,[illegible],672	$2,[illegible]	Turkey, the Levant, and Egypt	$505,913	$1,176,620
Scotland	1,[illegible]	4,[illegible]	China	6,[illegible],108	13,556,597
Ireland	711,041	[illegible]	Central America	204,[illegible]	331,[illegible]
Spain on Atlantic	210,[illegible]	651,394	Chili	761,[illegible]	2,[illegible]
Portugal	112,249	146,812	Sicily and Italy	1,[illegible],417	4,[illegible],316
Austria	237,378	722,645			

Countries from which the imports have positively and relatively increased from 1828 to 1860.

Imports from—	In 1828.	In 1860.	Imports from—	In 1828.	In 1860.
Hamburg and Bremen	$1,644,392	$18,[illegible]	Philippine Islands	$[illegible]	$[illegible],168
Dutch East Indies	113,462	[illegible]	Cuba	6,[illegible],135	34,[illegible],976
England	30,476,139	133,[illegible],571	Porto Rico	1,[illegible],130	4,512,[illegible]
British East Indies	1,[illegible]	10,[illegible],312	Azores	78,[illegible]	353,[illegible]
British West Indies	[illegible]	1,[illegible],549	New Granada and Venezuela	1,[illegible]	6,727,[illegible]
Canada and the provinces	447,[illegible]	23,[illegible],381	Brazil	3,[illegible],738	21,214,[illegible]
France on Atlantic	8,[illegible],427	39,130,[illegible]	Buenos Ayres	217,[illegible]	4,[illegible]
France on Mediterranean	804,[illegible]	3,[illegible]			
Spain on Mediterranean	[illegible],476	2,[illegible],437			

The proportions of general increase were a little more than four in 1860 to one in 1828, both being above the average of the general series, and representing two conspicuous points of full and legitimate trade.

The countries from which importations have either positively or relatively declined, are generally those which produce and export crude articles, the exceptions being the countries producing sugar, coffee, and tea. The produce of these last has been immensely stimulated by the growth of population in the United States and the ease of living, and consequent changed habits of the people. This maintains a demand so large that the carriage of supplies is not so easily diverted as in case of crude articles which are the elements of manufacture. It is these last which we are losing chiefly, and of which the loss is important for other reasons than the mere profit of the carrying trade.

It must be observed that these statements refer only to the direct trade from the countries named, and include none of the importations of their products which reach us through other channels. A large and steadily increasing volume of such indirect trade has long existed. The products of Russia reach the United States by way of England and the German states, as do those of Sweden and Norway. Indeed, the tropical products and special exports of the entire list of countries with which our direct connexion appears to have declined, are now brought through the channels named in large proportions, as will be shown by the statements of imports which follow.

As the proportion of foreign shipping engaged in the foreign trade of the United States, is believed to be directly associated with the limitation of our commerce, both direct and indirect, with the greater number of foreign countries, the statements bearing on both points have been introduced indiscriminately. The following summary of the values imported annually by each class of vessels is the natural successor of the detailed comparison of values from each country for 1828 and 1860. The imports have so far been taken as the best illustration of the relations held by the United States to foreign countries, because they were made the basis of a large carrying trade, supplying other countries with merchandise not of our own production, and therefore not permanently within our control. In continuation, the condition of our export trade will be stated, showing to what extent that has undergone modifications similar to those apparent in the import trade.

Value of imports of the United States in American and foreign vessels, 1821 to 1863.

Years.	In American vessels.	In foreign vessels.	Total imports.	Years.	In American vessels.	In foreign vessels.	Total imports.
1821..........	$[illegible]	$4,[illegible]	$62,[illegible]	1844	$94,174,673	$14,260,39[illegible]	$108,435,035
1822..........	76,[illegible]	6,[illegible]	83,241,541	1845	101,[illegible]	16,[illegible]	117,254,564
1823..........	71,511,341	6,067,7[illegible]	77,579,267	1846	106,[illegible],173	15,[illegible]	121,691,797
1824..........	75,[illegible]	5,[illegible]	80,549,007	1847	113,[illegible],337	[illegible]	146,545,638
1825..........	91,[illegible]	4,437,[illegible]	96,340,075	1848	1[illegible]	[illegible]	154,998,928
1826..........	80,779,[illegible]	4,1[illegible]	84,974,477	1849	1[illegible]	[illegible]	147,857,439
1827..........	74,[illegible]	4,51[illegible]	79,484,068	1850	1[illegible]	[illegible]	178,138,318
1828..........	81,851,319	6,[illegible]	88,509,824	1851	163,[illegible]	[illegible]	216,224,932
1829..........	6[illegible]	5,166,[illegible]	74,492,527	1852	15[illegible] 467	54,[illegible]	212,945,442
1830..........	65,[illegible]	4,941,181	70,876,920	1853	191,[illegible]	76,[illegible]	267,978,647
1831..........	[illegible]	9,259,014	103,191,124	1854	217,[illegible]	[illegible]	304,562,381
1832..........	9[illegible]	10,731,007	101,029,266	1855	20[illegible] 149,340	[illegible]	261,468,520
1833..........	98,[illegible]	10,037,5[illegible]	108,118,311	1856	2[illegible]	44,[illegible]	314,639,942
1834..........	113,[illegible],174	12,[illegible],158	126,521,332	1857	2[illegible]	101,773,[illegible]	360,890,141
1835..........	135,[illegible]	14,[illegible]	149,895,742	1858	2[illegible]	[illegible]	282,613,150
1836..........	171,[illegible]	1[illegible]	189,980,035	1859	[illegible]	12[illegible]	338,768,130
1837..........	122,177,[illegible]	1[illegible]	140,989,217	1860	2[illegible]	1[illegible]	362,166,254
1838..........	100,0[illegible]	16,[illegible]	113,717,404	1861	201,544,055	134,106,[illegible]	335,650,153
1839..........	14[illegible]	16,[illegible]	162,092,132	1862	92,274,100	11[illegible]	205,771,729
1840..........	8[illegible]	14,[illegible]	107,141,519	1863	109,744,580	14[illegible]	252,919,920
1841..........	11[illegible]	14,[illegible]	127,946,177	1863, 3d qr....	19,[illegible]	46,114,[illegible]	65,[illegible]
1842..........	[illegible]	11,[illegible]	100,162,087	1863, 4th qr...	18,[illegible]	56,5[illegible]	75,[illegible]
1843, 9 months	49,[illegible]	14,7[illegible]	64,753,799				

Value of exports, the produce of the United States, in American and foreign vessels, 1821 to 1863.

Years.	In American vessels.	In foreign vessels.	Total exports.	Years.	In American vessels.	In foreign vessels.	Total exports.
1821..........	$34,[illegible]	$[illegible]	$43,671,894	1844	$8[illegible]	$[illegible]	$99,715,179
1822..........	[illegible]	[illegible]	49,874,079	1845	7[illegible]	[illegible]	98,455,330
1823..........	[illegible]	6,[illegible]	47,155,408	1846	7[illegible]	[illegible]	101,718,042
1824..........	4[illegible]	7,[illegible]	50,649,500	1847	[illegible],314,47[illegible]	[illegible]	150,574,844
1825..........	[illegible]	8,[illegible]	66,944,745	1848	[illegible]	37,[illegible]	130,203,709
1826..........	[illegible]	6,[illegible]	53,055,710	1849	91,[illegible]	41,[illegible]	131,710,081
1827..........	[illegible]	[illegible]	58,921,691	1850	[illegible]	4[illegible]	134,900,233
1828..........	41,[illegible]	9,[illegible]	50,669,669	1851	137,[illegible]	[illegible]	178,620,138
1829..........	46,[illegible]	8,[illegible]	55,700,193	1852	1[illegible]	[illegible]	154,931,147
1830..........	51,[illegible]	[illegible]	59,462,029	1853	14[illegible]	70,[illegible]	189,869,162
1831..........	49,671,2[illegible]	11,[illegible]	61,277,057	1854	17[illegible]	73,[illegible]	253,390,870
1832..........	[illegible]	16,211,[illegible]	63,137,470	1855	[illegible]	[illegible]	246,708,553
1833..........	52,[illegible]	17,[illegible]	70,317,698	1856	[illegible]	[illegible]	310,586,330
1834..........	61,[illegible]	19,7[illegible]	81,024,162	1857	[illegible]	10[illegible]	338,985,065
1835..........	79,[illegible]	[illegible]	101,189,082	1858	[illegible]	71,[illegible]	293,758,279
1836..........	[illegible]	[illegible]	106,916,680	1859	[illegible]	101,371,[illegible]	335,894,385
1837..........	73,[illegible]	[illegible]	95,564,414	1860	[illegible]	110,[illegible]	373,189,274
1838..........	79,[illegible]	16,17[illegible]	96,033,821	1861	166,[illegible]	[illegible]	228,699,486
1839..........	[illegible]	[illegible]	103,533,891	1862	11[illegible]	[illegible]	213,069,519
1840..........	92,[illegible]	21,[illegible]	113,895,634	1863	1[illegible]	1[illegible]	305,884,998
1841..........	82,[illegible]	23,[illegible]	106,382,722	1863, 3d qr....	13,[illegible]	31,[illegible]	44,[illegible]
1842..........	71,[illegible]	21,[illegible]	92,969,996	1863, 4th qr...	13,[illegible]	[illegible]	71,[illegible]
1843, 9 months	[illegible]	17,[illegible]	77,793,783				

Exports, the produce of the United States, in American and foreign vessels for the quarter ending September 30, 1863.

Ports.	American.	Foreign.	Total.
Passamaquoddy	$273,996	$19,068	$293,064
Other ports of Maine	194,000	18,490	212,490
Portland	133,898	65,870	199,768
Portsmouth, N. H.	....	2,446	2,446
Salem	42,370	2,854	45,224
Boston and Charlestown	774,665	2,597,416	3,372,081
Other ports of Massachusetts	45,914	9,013	54,927
Ports of Rhode Island	22,265	1,507	23,772
New Haven and ports of Connecticut	146,758	4,564	151,322
New York	7,166,068	42,317,700	49,483,768
Champlain	630,705	....	630,705
Lake ports of New York	239,049	799,449	1,038,498
Erie, Pennsylvania	3,552	100,338	103,890
Philadelphia	568,341	1,217,791	1,786,132
Perth Amboy, N. J.	2,238	....	2,238
Wilmington, Delaware	18,095	14,719	32,814
Baltimore	775,482	1,123,328	1,898,810
Key West	....	508	508
New Orleans	48,234	149,407	197,641
Lake ports of Ohio	98,431	362,615	461,046
Detroit	64,271	39,676	103,947
Chicago	315,768	620,976	936,744
Milwaukie	121,110	844,907	966,017
San Francisco	1,937,441	750,956	2,688,397
Oregon	18,556	....	18,556
Puget's Sound	94,656	38,904	133,560
Total	13,604,468	51,030,868	64,635,336

Exports, the produce of the United States, in American and foreign vessels for the quarter ending December 31, 1863.

Ports.	American.	Foreign.	Total.
Passamaquoddy	$341,399	$9,968	$351,367
Other ports of Maine	169,967	40,596	210,563
Portland	457,368	301,717	759,085
Portsmouth, N. H.	....	976	976
Salem, Massachusetts	19,075	1,589	20,664
Boston and Charlestown	1,177,810	2,955,863	4,133,673
Other ports of Massachusetts	66,740	68,850	135,590
Ports of Rhode Island	32,018	360	32,378
New Haven and ports of Connecticut	135,925	26,579	162,504
New York	5,656,859	47,000,400	52,657,259
Champlain	1,080,456	....	1,080,456
Lake ports of New York	168,299	890,640	1,058,939
Erie, Pennsylvania	12,564	75,143	87,707
Philadelphia	804,921	1,578,747	2,383,668
Ports of New Jersey	8,242	10	8,252
Wilmington, Delaware	2,093	11,377	13,470
Baltimore	491,250	1,703,994	2,195,244
Key West	4,986	1,668	6,654
New Orleans	100,839	748,451	849,290
Lake ports of Ohio	17,297	52,655	69,952
Detroit	69,562	356,357	425,919
Chicago	156,638	578,318	734,956

Exports, the produce of the United States, &c.—Continued.

Ports.	American.	Foreign.	Total.
Milwaukie	$6,955	$284,916	$291,871
San Francisco	2,211,883	1,339,666	3,551,549
Oregon	16,594	....	16,594
Puget's Sound	100,588	68,906	169,494
Total	13,284,898	58,144,033	71,428,931

Imports in American and foreign vessels from foreign countries, 1862–'63, *(fiscal year.)*

Countries.	American.	Foreign.	Total.
Russia on the Baltic	$625,838	$97,459	$723,297
Russia on the Black	109,680	116,251	225,931
Russian possessions in North America	27,836	11,912	39,748
Prussia	920	....	920
Sweden and Norway	23,730	309,443	333,173
Swedish West Indies	17,313	14,990	32,303
Denmark	107	....	107
Danish West Indies	132,732	148,999	281,731
Hamburg	205,970	7,507,850	7,713,820
Bremen	104,240	5,664,323	5,768,563
Holland	253,501	1,293,013	1,546,514
Dutch West Indies	49,948	453,504	503,452
Dutch Guiana	162,736	167,303	330,039
Dutch East Indies	230,676	178,076	408,752
Belgium	601,156	1,800,816	2,401,972
England	24,785,786	85,679,841	110,465,627
Scotland	606,856	1,850,920	2,457,776
Ireland	65,104	148,083	213,187
Gibraltar	31,174	60,689	91,863
Malta	22,518	59	22,577
Canada	14,064,716	4,749,124	18,813,840
Other British North American possessions	2,407,869	2,799,565	5,207,434
British West Indies	777,994	1,300,481	2,078,475
British Honduras	110,624	262,800	373,424
British Guiana	110,828	200,721	311,549
British possessions in Africa	1,272,716	430,432	1,703,148
British Australia	3,744	12,353	16,097
British East Indies	4,903,400	513,299	5,416,699
France on Atlantic	3,182,524	4,012,492	7,195,016
France on Mediterranean	1,327,663	2,068,946	3,396,609
French North American possessions	....	44,254	44,254
French West Indies	4,392	17,923	22,315
French Guiana	17,018	....	17,018
Spain on Atlantic	150,340	342,164	492,504
Spain on Mediterranean	892,021	618,044	1,510,065
Canary islands	7,152	3,309	10,461
Philippine islands	1,806,979	76,980	1,883,959
Cuba	16,048,052	5,486,013	21,534,065
Porto Rico	1,787,898	944,578	2,732,476
Portugal	24,092	152,175	176,267
Madeira	9,524	....	9,524
Cape de Verde Islands	13,050	....	13,050
Azores	19,209	27,490	46,699
Sardinia	106,407	199,689	306,096
Tuscany	637,268	345,182	982,450
Papal States	....	21,196	21,196

Imports in American and foreign vessels, &c.—Continued.

Ports.	American.	Foreign.	Total.
Two Sicilies	$1,122,622	$714,415	$1,837,037
Austria	21,837	187,440	209,277
Greece	....	28,012	28,012
Turkey in Europe	27,929	....	27,929
Turkey in Asia	631,147	325,215	956,362
Other ports in Africa	1,193,460	316,620	1,510,080
Hayti	834,398	743,658	1,578,056
San Domingo	98,993	201,988	300,981
Mexico	2,052,415	2,477,169	4,529,584
Central Republic	142,707	41,838	184,545
New Granada	1,710,846	248,022	1,958,868
Venezuela	654,221	874,870	1,529,091
Brazil	5,912,927	5,032,549	10,945,476
Uruguay, or Cisplatine Republic	516,298	124,712	641,010
Buenos Ayres, or Argentine Republic	3,733,010	767,912	4,501,922
Chili	1,601,467	275,446	1,896,913
Peru	51,365	105,236	156,081
Sandwich Islands	629,572	....	629,572
Other islands in Pacific	20,480	88,135	108,615
Japan	61,902	11,949	73,851
China	9,023,327	1,337,737	10,361,064
Whale fisheries	268,356	....	268,356
Uncertain places	103	....	103
Total	109,744,580	143,175,340	252,919,920

American and foreign tonnage entering the ports of the United States, third and fourth quarters of 1863.

Ports.	THIRD QUARTER.		FOURTH QUARTER.	
	American.	Foreign.	American.	Foreign.
Eastport, Passamaquoddy, Maine	25,007	2,641	21,151	2,981
Portland, Maine	11,270	11,730	7,012	24,410
Other ports of Maine	5,658	3,852	2,942	3,268
Portsmouth, New Hampshire	....	2,030	165	1,471
Boston	49,581	168,206	....	....
Other ports of Massachusetts	15,944	15,808	15,144	10,822
Providence and ports of Rhode Island	4,810	8,009	2,537	4,851
New Haven and ports of Connecticut	6,060	2,023	2,987	1,688
New York	218,001	407,505	178,407	371,809
Lake ports of New York	....	....	265,108	192,923
Ports of New Jersey	173	714	....	704
Philadelphia	32,016	14,809	19,575	19,014
Erie, Pennsylvania	603	8,004	2,622	5,258
Wilmington, Delaware	101	....	107	....
Baltimore	13,455	11,001	9,903	18,920
Key West	1,530	601	1,774	2,190
Lake ports of Ohio	9,730	15,530	11,414	6,040
Detroit	45,911	6,983	150,200	60,700
Chicago	40,075	31,237	28,010	17,012
Milwaukie	24,045	16,139	9,106	5,003
San Francisco and Oregon	57,474	15,418	58,175	15,459
	560,688	733,078	780,598	762,044

In regard to the carriage of these exports, the above tables disclose some remarkable facts. Beginning with a proportion averaging less than one-fifth in foreign vessels for the first ten or twelve years, the proportion in 1862–'63 is three-fifths, and for the two remaining quarters, closing the calendar year 1863, the proportion is four-fifths of the whole carried in foreign vessels, and but one-fifth in American; thus precisely reversing the relations of the two classes existing in 1821, and, indeed, continuing to exist to 1831.

But it is important to separate the unusual state of affairs resulting from the war, from the course of events preceding it, and to distinguish the changes then attained, in order to decide upon all the questions involved. Taking the year 1860 as a fair representative of this previous period, the proportion of the total exports which was carried in foreign vessels was 29.6 per cent., and of the five years closing with 1860, 29.5 per cent. For the first five years of the table, 1821 to 1825, the proportion was but 16.6 per cent. carried in foreign vessels.

The change, therefore, is only in part due to the dangers at present incurred by American shipping. Not only are the absolute values large which fell to the hands of foreign carriers previous to 1861, but the proportions are doubled over those existing in the period first stated in the above tables. Taking the comparison further back the disproportion is greater, large encroachments having been established even in 1821 upon the business of American shipping in the carriage of domestic produce to foreign markets.

The imports exhibit a similar course of change from American to foreign hands. The average of the first five years was $5,300,000 in foreign vessels, out of a total of $80,000,000, only 6.6 per cent. In 1832 they had risen to 10 per cent. of the total; in 1848 and 1849 to an average of 20 per cent.; in 1853 to 30 per cent.; and in 1859 and 1860 to 40 per cent. In the fiscal year 1861–'62 they exceeded the total in American vessels by twenty millions of dollars, and in 1862–'63 by thirty-four millions of dollars. In the last six months of the calendar year 1863 they were nearly three times the imports in American vessels, being as follows:

	In American vessels.	In foreign vessels
Quarter ending September 30, 1863........	$19,033,949	$46,114,529
Quarter ending December 31, 1863........	18,935,399	56,551,754
Six months.................... .	37,969,349	102,666,283

The proportions at New York, the chief port of entry, for these two quarters were—

	In American vessels.	In foreign vessels.
Quarter ending September 30.............	7,829,110	38,210,503
Quarter ending December 31	5,994,765	43,321,712

It may be stated that the loss of the great carrying trade conducted by American shipping during the European wars has more than once received earnest public attention. Two or three European States, and particularly France, almost immediately on the establishment of peace, built up a severe system of discriminations against all other shipping than their own. These discriminations were carried to a most injurious length, and were the subject of earnest remonstrance. The effect of the action of France is still seen in the remarkably limited amount of our present direct trade with that country, and for other states the results are quite as striking. In a forcible memorial addressed to Congress by the Chamber of Commerce of New York in 1821, the first decisively adverse effects of the new policy of European states is thus stated:

"It is a lamentable fact that more than half the number of vessels lately arrived at this from foreign ports are dismantled, from the absolute absence of any advantageous object of commercial pursuit; and this state of commerce seems the natural and necessary result of the new order of things which has prevailed since the pacification of Europe. Every restraint that lately shackled the navigation of the principal maritime nations of Europe has been removed, whilst the general trade and navigation of those states are, at the same time, regulated with a studious regard to the interests of their own subjects, so that the United States have not only ceased to be the carriers for Europe, but are deprived of the means of entering into a fair competition in the transportation to foreign countries of the principal products of their own soil."

This is a just statement of the adverse action of France, more particularly, by which the United States shipping was first seriously curtailed of its due share of foreign trade. The discriminations then made by France were not in the form of tonnage dues and port charges so much as in specific charges imposed upon American produce imported in American ships, which charges are stated in this memorial to be as follows:

"The foreign or discriminating duties paid by American vessels importing the following articles into France are: 1⅛ cent per pound (French) on cotton; 1⅛ cent per pound on tobacco; 55 cents per 100 pounds on potashes; which extra duties exceed the whole freight now paid for the transportation of those articles from the United States, whether in French or in American bottoms. To form an estimate of the practical result of these regulations it will be assumed that a vessel of 300 tons register will carry 560,000 pounds weight of tobacco, the difference of duty on which, at 1⅛ cent per pound, would be $6,300, equivalent to *twenty-one* dollars per registered ton; or, in a vessel of the same description carrying 280,000 pounds of cotton and 220,000 of potashes, the difference of duty at 1⅛ cent for the cotton is $4,200, and at 55 cents per 100 pounds on the ashes, is $1,200—together, $5,400—which is equivalent to *eighteen* dollars per registered ton.

"The aggregate tonnage employed in the direct trade to France is estimated at 50,000 tons, in addition to which an indirect trade of considerable extent has been carried on by the circuitous channel of England, the saving in the duties by reshipping our cotton and tobacco thence to France in French vessels, instead of shipping them direct from the United States in American vessels, being more than equivalent to the extra freight and charges attending the additional voyage."

This apparently remote action is here cited because it was one of the events marking the beginning of a system of diversion of our own commerce from direct lines, which has continued to increase to the present time. The export of American produce passes through foreign distributing markets to a great extent, as will be subsequently shown, and the importation of the produce of tropical and non-commercial countries also comes to us at the hands of foreign carriers, and through foreign distributing markets.

The action of the British government in the same direction was even more frequent and persistent, and though interrupted or in other ways rendered nugatory previous to the peace of 1815, the purpose was frequently and distinctly declared. In January, 1791, the British Board of Trade, in a formal report on commercial relations with the United States, announced the policy of giving signal privileges in British home ports to American ships, but refusing all such equality in the ports of the colonies.

"If Congress should propose that this principle of equality should be extended to the ports of our colonies and islands, and that the ships of the United States should be there treated as British ships, it should be answered that this demand cannot be admitted even as a subject of negotiation."

"Many vessels now go from the ports of Great Britain carrying British manufactures to the United States; there load with lumber and provisions for the British islands, and return with the produce of those islands to Great Britain. This whole branch of the trade may be regarded as a new acquisition, and was attained by your Majesty's orders in council before mentioned; which has operated to the increase of British navigation compared with the United States in a double ratio, but (since) it has taken from the United States more than it has added to Great Britain."

Various countervailing acts of the United States aided to neutralize this policy, as has been said, until after the general peace of Europe in 1815. In a commercial convention with England, concluded July 3, 1815, the United States conceded the chief point in controversy, trusting to the great development of our trade with the British colonies, and the energy with which it had been conducted, to maintain it under any circumstances. The United States agreed to the equalization of all the conditions of their commerce with the British European ports, but left the regulations controlling trade with the British West Indies and American colonies without stipulation. The consequences were soon felt. The British authorities re-established their old colonial policy and shut American shipping from the West Indian ports. Vigorous remonstrances were made, and in 1818 Congress enacted that the United States should thereafter be closed against British vessels coming from any British colony or territory that was closed against American vessels by any trade regulation. Again, in May, 1820, Congress further prohibited a circuitous trade that had grown up in evasion of the first act, bringing West India produce through Nova Scotia and Canada. The distress caused in the West Indies by these acts compelled the British Parliament to relax the policy which originated them, and for several years following an imperfect and variable succession of attempts to equalize the trade followed, the general policy of which was to preserve a fair share of it to the United States.

In 1830 the British gained an important advantage, however, by the construction placed on an act of Congress of May 20 of that year. It was claimed by the British and colonial organs that they could take, under this new order, the larger share of the carrying trade in American products away from us, and it is evident from the table of exports of domestic produce previously given that they did so. From 1830 to 1833 the exports in American vessels did not increase at all, while those in foreign vessels doubled.

Year.	In American vessels.	In foreign vessels.	Year.	In American vessels.	In foreign vessels.
1830..........	$51,106,190	$8,355,879	1832..........	$46,025,890	$16,211,580
1831..........	49,671,239	11,006,818	1833..........	52,965,440	17,392,252

The increase of British tonnage in the American trade, resulting from this action, is shown in the tonnage entering the United States from the British West Indies and the provinces for the same years:

Tonnage from West Indies and British Provinces.

Year.	Tonnage from West Indies.		Tonnage from British provinces.	
	American.	British.	American.	British.
1830	22,469	169	130,827	4,002
1831	38,046	23,700	92,672	84,567
1832	61,468	27,209	74,001	108,671
1833	53,[illegible]	31,638	219,[illegible]	208,064
1834	37,081	18,006	173,876	259,884

Total British tonnage entering United States ports:

1829	88,377
1830	80,823
1831	211,270
1832	288,811
1833	383,487
1834	453,495
1835	529,922

Of the result of this change, Pitkin states that it gave to foreign carriers the first decided possession of the carrying trade in American staples. "This great increase in British shipping has been occasioned principally by the circuitous trade, so long the favorite object of British statesmen, and which the American government at last voluntarily yielded. This has thrown into the hands of the British a much greater proportion of the carrying trade of the United States, both in domestic and foreign articles, than they have ever before enjoyed, except at the commencement of the general government. * * * * The circuitous trade thus yielded to the British has given them the carriage of no small proportion of the bulky articles of the south, particularly cotton."

This was written in 1835, and it is evident that the point then made of the introduction of a large proportion of foreign shipping into the trade of the United States deserved all the attention it received. From that time forward no decided acts of either government appear to have modified the course of events. Great Britain relaxed the navigation laws at home in 1854, and by so much favored the employment of American shipping in the trade of the British islands. The great extent to which the entire foreign trade passed to British shipping, and the steady growth of their tonnage entering United States ports, is shown in the following table, which continues the comparison previously begun, from 1830 to 1863:

National character of tonnage entering the ports of the United States—1829 to 1863.

Year.	American.	British.	French.	German or Hanseatic.	Total all countries.
1829	872,949	86,377	14,408	7,815	1,003,892
1830	967,227	87,231	11,236	9,140	1,099,122
1831	922,952	215,887	11,701	11,487	1,204,900
1832	949,622	288,841	22,638	22,351	1,342,860
1833	1,111,441	383,487	20,917	27,859	1,608,146
1834	1,074,670	453,495	23,649	20,122	1,619,720
1835	1,352,653	529,922	15,457	29,400	1,993,993
1836	1,255,384	544,774	19,519	43,254	1,903,697
1837	1,299,720	643,020	26,296	37,523	2,165,423
1838	1,302,974	484,702	20,670	40,021	1,895,124
1839	1,491,979	495,353	22,690	43,343	2,116,053
1840	1,576,946	582,424	30,701	42,424	2,289,330
1841	1,631,909	616,023	17,030	44,918	2,364,353
1842	1,510,111	699,502	15,876	50,286	2,248,828
1843	1,143,523	453,834	[illegible]	40,118	1,678,275
1844	2,010,924	766,747	17,237	60,222	2,917,739
1845	2,035,486	760,093	11,630	64,902	2,940,040
1846	2,151,114	813,987	13,666	69,790	3,110,853
1847	2,101,359	993,210	30,704	92,291	3,321,706
1848	2,393,482	1,177,104	23,970	92,178	3,798,073
1849	2,658,321	1,482,707	31,460	78,596	4,368,898
1850	2,573,016	1,450,539	30,702	80,111	4,348,639
1851	3,054,349	1,659,869	25,252	110,893	4,980,440
1852	3,235,522	1,680,712	25,992	143,900	5,292,880
1853	4,004,013	1,871,210	29,813	183,901	5,281,043
1854	3,752,117	1,748,380	21,857	210,947	5,884,309
1855	3,861,391	1,738,123	14,230	195,370	6,045,339
1856	4,385,484	2,132,822	23,935	152,167	6,872,253
1857	4,721,370	2,070,986	29,307	201,478	7,186,316
1858	4,396,042	1,841,919	16,416	200,741	6,605,843
1859	5,205,648	2,055,110	22,487	257,528	7,806,023
1860	5,921,285	1,918,494	21,557	230,889	8,275,198
1861	4,880,313	1,832,971	15,901	255,336	7,151,355
1862	5,117,685	1,836,006	17,968	270,090	7,372,063
1863	4,487,261	2,096,612	22,312	333,354	7,511,254

To render the above comparison accurate as regards transoceanic commerce, a large reduction of the American tonnage should be made for the entries from Canada. For the ten years, 1854 to 1863, the American tonnage from Canada rose from 1,867,489 tons to 2,307,233 tons—averaging 1,250,000 tons for the first five years, and over 2,000,000 tons for the last five years. The average of British tonnage was about 850,000 tons for the ten years, increasing less from year to year. The transatlantic trade would therefore compare, between American and British, as follows, taking out the actual entries of each class from Canada:

	American, tons entered.	British, tons entered.
1858	3,050,925	928,990
1859	3,283,062	991,644
1860	3,304,000	1,240,458
1861	2,898,427	1,148,058
1862	2,630,312	1,194,580
1863	2,140,128	1,331,478

In the foreign trade of the United States proper, therefore, British shipping approaches much nearer to equality with our own than would appear without the separation of this Canadian trade, a large share of which is really ferry transit, as has before been explained.

TONNAGE AND TRADE IN FIVE-YEAR PERIODS, FROM 1821 TO 1863.

The next following thirteen tables exhibit, respectively, the tonnage arrivals from all foreign ports severally, every fifth year from 1821 to 1863, with the per-centage of foreign to the total; the total tonnage entered from all foreign ports, exclusive of Canada and the other British North American possessions; the like exhibit of the shipping engaged in the United States trade with the several countries of Europe, the West Indies, Mexico and South America, Asia, Africa, and miscellaneous countries, and Canada, respectively; and the total value of the imports and exports, with the percentage of each of the great geographical divisions of our foreign commerce, distinguishing the exchanges of the precious metals from those of ordinary merchandise. These tables are intended to exhibit the progress of our commerce during the last forty-two years, the relative value of our trade with the several customer nations, and the changed proportion of distribution; in effect, a tabled history of our commerce and navigation during the period embraced in the statements.

Two other tables are added: one showing the number, class, and tonnage of vessels built in the United States since 1822, and the other giving their distribution among the various branches of our foreign and home commerce.

General statement exhibiting the tonnage of American and foreign vessels arriv from 1861 to 1863, with the proportion of the for

	Countries.	1851.			1852.			
		American.	Foreign.	Per cent. of foreign.	American.	Foreign.	Per cent. of foreign.	American.
1	Russia	13, 877			17, 349			8, 873
2	Prussia		726	100.0	584	807	61.3	700
3	Sweden, Norway, and Denmark	12, 193	1,169	8.9	14, 761	1, 974	11.8	11, 346
4	Hamburg, Bremen, and other German ports	14, 824	4, 197	22.3	14, 537	4, 858	25.05	13, 824
5	Holland and Belgium	23, 631	1, 401	3.1	28, 892			24, 076
6	England	112, 453	39, 484	25.6	176, 596	39, 373	18.5	122, 348
7	Scotland	4, 737	7, 282	61.3	5, 857	8, 261	51.6	8, 874
8	Ireland	9, 479	3, 018	24.1	13, 927	4, 370	23.8	4, 349
9	France on the Atlantic	11, 431	11, 273	49.6	51, 451	7, 314	12.7	49, 789
10	Spain on the Atlantic	6, 545			8, 483			6, 760
11	Portugal	19, 678	1,013	4.9	21, 045	349	1.6	5, 062
12	Gibraltar	11, 221	425	3.7	9, 348			3, 589
13	Spain on the Mediterranean	4, 747	503	10.6	8, 095			9, 493
14	France on the Mediterranean	3, 700	636	18.3	9, 436			13, 774
15	Italy, Sicily, and Malta	6, 373			9, 095			12, 763
16	Austria	2, 018			8, 315			11, 880
17	Turkey, Greece, Egypt, and the Levant	1, 661	192	10.3	3, 090			3, 916
18	Europe generally	261			474			4, 169
19	French African Possessions							
20	British African Possessions	375			465			829
21	Other ports in Africa	1, 831			9, 625	842	7.8	9, 511
22	Azores	2, 247			1, 721			680
23	Canary islands	2, 329			1, 001			1, 983
24	Madeira	4, 140	148	3.4	2, 548			2, 314
25	Cape de Verd islands	5, 098	94	1.7	2, 098	209	9.4	775
26	British East Indies	4, 546			6, 141			8, 349
27	Dutch East Indies	1, 307			4, 394			2, 883
28	China	6, 029			10, 479			4, 316
29	Other Asiatic ports	1, 632			4, 439			1, 771
30	Philippine islands	763			1, 614			2, 939
31	Australia							
32	Other British colonies, including Australia, until 1841	788			151	63	29.0	948
33	Islands of the Pacific and the northwest coast							375
34	Canada							
35	Other British North American provinces, including Canada, until 1836	111, 989	405	0.3	74, 894	8, 798	10.4	93, 847
36	Cuba	105, 955	4, 478	4.08	122, 910	8, 808	6.2	138, 930
37	Porto Rico	14, 534	43	0.3	12, 899			29, 163
38	Hayti and San Domingo	40, 135	793	1.9	28, 192	1, 137	4.1	26, 448
39	Swedish West Indies	13, 093	863	6.3	6, 294			4, 790
40	Danish West Indies	39, 407	1, 669	4.1	37, 341	1, 433	3.7	27, 301
41	British West Indies and South American colonies	32, 631			97, 231	7, 927	7.5	38, 048
42	Dutch West Indies and American colonies	10, 408	422	2.5	13, 201	1, 977	6.6	11, 899
43	French West Indies and American colonies	41, 729			37, 734	5, 449	12.6	28, 704
44	Spanish American colonies until 1854	24, 870	1, 033	4.4				
45	Mexico				23, 804	6, 063	18.1	22, 377
46	British Honduras	5, 111	246	4.6				1, 458
47	Central America				2, 040			2, 821
48	New Granada and Venezuela				17, 014	3, 844	18.3	9, 174
49	Brazil	10, 399			24, 560	1, 406	5.7	19, 635
50	Uruguay							874
51	Buenos Ayres				3, 054			9, 628
52	Chili				4, 416			3, 729
53	Peru				6, 192			2, 877
54	Other South American ports				1, 290	163	11.8	700
55	Whale fisheries	10, 643			9, 846			19, 391
56	Uncertain places							80
	Total	763, 028	81, 225	9.6	942, 938	105, 654	10.08	985, 939

ing from each foreign country every fifth year from 1821 to 1860, and annually eign to the total tonnage entered at each period.

1831.		1836.			1841.			1846.			
Foreign.	Per cent. of foreign.	American.	Foreign.	Per cent. of foreign.	American.	Foreign.	Per cent. of foreign.	American.	Foreign.	Per cent. of foreign.	
377	6.07	13,944	1,607	10.3	18,370	674	3.5	11,165	319	2.7	1
......	......	311	674	68.5	357	......	......	410	1,375	76.6	2
8,989	50.9	8,645	10,667	55.9	7,407	11,849	61.6	3,348	10,019	74.4	3
12,175	61.3	9,808	38,847	78.3	15,380	85,491	88.4	84,878	63,658	71.3	4
349	1.8	14,771	8,065	36.7	37,012	4,030	9.8	34,617	11,524	25.09	5
84,324	27.4	233,149	107,972	31.4	237,848	194,880	88.8	374,137	107,373	24.6	6
11,046	65.9	4,594	80,065	81.4	8,049	63,118	74.1	30,715	89,874	78.9	7
7,030	61.5	1,945	13,749	87.7	781	17,898	95.8	4,840	85,270	88.8	8
8,866	17.5	73,217	12,889	11.8	107,509	14,656	11.7	103,884	10,728	9.4	9
......	......	7,563	1,713	18.4	12,907	716	5.4	8,119	363	4.3	10
1,451	22.3	7,435	8,919	47.5	13,100	2,465	15.9	6,184	8,657	88.4	11
......	......	3,630	234	6.6	9,377	......	......	8,759	......	......	12
......	......	13,841	2,778	16.7	14,390	2,765	16.4	8,849	4,849	34.6	13
453	3.6	12,108	9,861	44.9	12,730	4,302	25.09	10,670	2,848	21.9	14
150	1.9	21,223	4,418	17.3	26,543	5,854	18.06	85,974	6,629	80.3	15
......	......	6,430	3,806	37.9	6,220	1,461	27.1	5,019	646	10.6	16
......	......	4,788	2,449	33.8	4,168	704	14.4	7,388	1,477	16.6	17
2,030	32.6	......	......	......	......	......	......	......	......	......	18
......	......	......	......	......	......	800	100.0	......	......	......	19
......	......	1,374	......	......	343	......	......	794	......	......	20
......	......	6,623	1,499	18.6	8,131	1,036	14.4	9,418	2,431	20.5	21
397	38.6	1,397	......	......	1,614	......	......	1,612	203	11.1	22
......	......	2,377	193	6.9	2,161	1,088	33.6	1,463	791	35.0	23
......	......	1,848	342	15.3	2,304	140	5.6	1,040	384	27.9	24
......	......	137	......	......	825	......	......	307	......	......	25
......	......	8,658	......	......	6,408	......	......	18,654	......	......	26
......	......	10,383	......	......	307	......	......	3,885	......	......	27
......	......	16,443	......	......	11,898	......	......	18,837	306	1.5	28
......	......	624	......	......	2,979	......	......	1,035	......	......	29
......	......	4,977	......	......	4,308	......	......	6,897	......	......	30
......	......	......	......	......	1,650	......	......	......	......	......	31
......	......	......	......	......	......	......	......	......	......	......	32
......	......	194	......	......	800	......	......	1,859	330	15.3	33
......	......	228,768	233,560	51.1	328,483	280,110	44.9	......	......	......	34
83,893	47.3	55,898	143,883	72.03	87,070	128,301	62.3	850,714	315,879	27.7	35
19,639	12.8	153,373	10,894	6.7	189,645	11,930	5.8	134,905	3,484	2.1	36
3,117	10.3	41,846	1,158	2.7	51,124	463	0.9	51,286	487	.9	37
893	2.5	37,972	639	2.9	35,849	748	2.04	30,844	800	2.5	38
182	5.1	246	......	......	1,092	......	......	650	......	......	39
2,827	9.3	22,040	1,351	5.7	23,487	2,857	11.1	33,046	888	2.8	40
23,780	38.4	41,308	25,738	38.4	71,187	52,543	42.4	87,783	29,638	28.9	41
312	2.6	13,010	78	0.5	17,384	939	5.1	19,048	......	......	42
8,750	9.4	13,685	6,573	32.5	14,445	3,394	19.08	38,400	6,975	15.9	43
......	......	......	......	......	......	......	......	......	......	......	44
11,499	37.9	97,600	3,745	17.3	62,778	3,489	10.09	64,318	7,896	14.6	45
600	27.1	6,804	8,187	24.3	4,335	1,020	19.1	5,329	64	1.1	46
......	......	1,309	357	10.8	8,223	165	6.1	8,430	107	4.2	47
50	0.6	18,484	1,816	2.8	15,151	2,340	13.3	15,089	1,389	8.5	48
1,360	4.3	39,239	4,341	10.0	41,894	4,503	9.7	61,011	4,924	7.8	49
......	......	8,175	......	......	4,437	540	10.8	1,814	......	......	50
......	......	3,201	810	2.9	13,738	2,319	14.4	5,998	987	14.1	51
......	......	8,447	......	......	2,072	300	8.1	4,560	2,281	35.8	52
84	3.5	605	......	......	129	......	......	446	......	......	53
......	......	......	......	......	736	......	......	814	685	72.6	54
......	......	51,349	......	......	38,828	......	......	47,327	......	......	55
......	......	174	511	74.8	......	......	......	167	......	......	56
281,948	23.6	1,255,384	680,213	35.1	1,631,909	736,444	31.1	2,151,114	959,739	30.8	

General statement exhibiting the tonnage of American and foreign vessels

	Countries.	1821.			1826.			
		American.	Foreign.	Per cent. of foreign.	American.	Foreign.	Per cent. of foreign.	American.
1	Russia	9,817	3,268	25.0	7,874	780	8.8	13,683
2	Prussia	283	704	71.8	1,091	349	26.2	....
3	Sweden, Norway, and Denmark	2,680	25,769	90.6	9,477	4,276	31.2	6,318
4	Hamburg, Bremen, and other German ports	21,734	90,379	80.6	37,993	121,701	76.3	4,033
5	Holland and Belgium	27,993	25,720	47.9	54,538	21,983	28.7	40,904
6	England	619,393	411,611	39.9	1,006,413	350,137	25.8	844,988
7	Scotland	18,219	46,215	71.7	26,370	54,170	67.2	19,879
8	Ireland	5,486	74,021	93.1	3,630	11,163	69.7	1,680
9	France on the Atlantic	153,848	29,489	16.3	811,353	94,713	10.4	838,478
10	Spain on the Atlantic	9,940	5,347	35.8	17,088	3,530	17.1	16,538
11	Portugal	981	5,175	84.3	10,879	7,434	40.3	895
12	Gibraltar	509	1,114	68.6	3,203	4,929	60.6	3,713
13	Spain on the Mediterranean	13,101	19,350	66.4	80,710	26,139	25.8	16,777
14	France on the Mediterranean	7,148	14,658	67.8	63,857	7,072	10.1	53,468
15	Italy, Sicily, and Malta	32,258	24,391	46.3	109,033	34,807	24.2	82,088
16	Austria	814	6,391	88.5	4,087	8,788	40.3	2,489
17	Turkey, Greece, Egypt, and the Levant	7,737	2,109	21.3	17,768	4,800	21.3	8,777
18	Europe generally	....	....	....	....	....	....	....
19	French African Possessions	....	....	....	....	....	....	8,172
20	British African Possessions	1,823	370	16.3	8,389	473	8.4	13,080
21	Other ports in Africa	12,675	1,003	7.3	14,137	529	3.6	20,835
22	Azores	1,464	678	28.8	4,538	541	10.6	3,081
23	Canary islands	319	748	70.7	1,149	378	32.8	2,349
24	Madeira	1,068	137	11.3	....	294	100.0	889
25	Cape de Verd islands	111	....	....	2,688	1,307	32.4	2,895
26	British East Indies	19,907	2,813	8.8	65,619	1,338	19.8	109,789
27	Dutch East Indies	3,329	150	4.3	9,169	373	3.9	6,681
28	China	27,367	11,387	29.1	62,194	8,981	12.6	77,854
29	Other Asiatic ports	....	....	....	343	....	....	1,884
30	Philippine islands	9,933	2,549	20.4	24,283	2,118	8.0	29,142
31	Australia	6,381	27,148	80.9	3,085	1,100	26.7	8,370
32	Other British colonies, including Australia, until 1841	....	....	....	....	....	....	....
33	Islands of the Pacific and the north-west coast	21,676	4,253	16.4	17,774	1,073	3.8	33,387
34	Canada	1,013,675	516,363	33.6	1,191,716	1,217,719	50.5	2,417,878
35	Other British North American provinces, including Canada, until 1826	62,458	272,216	85.8	187,754	402,441	68.2	164,082
36	Cuba	333,515	53,162	13.0	816,650	56,082	9.7	670,916
37	Porto Rico	49,336	7,874	14.0	40,301	12,040	23.0	33,709
38	Hayti and San Domingo	39,940	7,830	16.3	46,778	6,630	12.4	40,685
39	Swedish West Indies	874	....	....	981	....	....	1,418
40	Danish West Indies	10,369	5,080	32.7	13,451	2,160	13.8	14,908
41	British West Indies and South American colonies	61,134	44,882	42.3	64,819	38,770	37.4	107,809
42	Dutch West Indies and American colonies	20,145	6,425	23.4	10,272	1,897	14.0	20,064
43	French West Indies and American colonies	4,681	2,353	33.3	8,700	4,643	32.3	6,300
44	Spanish American colonies until 1826	....	....	....	....	....	....	....
45	Mexico	29,407	12,701	30.1	40,408	8,387	17.8	49,879
46	British Honduras	3,016	2,324	43.2	5,173	2,718	34.4	10,167
47	Central America	8,329	209	2.3	61,344	786	11.9	2,431
48	New Granada and Venezuela	183,478	12,668	6.4	152,750	3,720	37.4	103,879
49	Brazil	63,683	22,458	26.05	100,014	12,988	11.8	113,019
50	Uruguay	154	1,628	91.8	1,801	233	12.4	7,898
51	Buenos Ayres	13,328	11,005	45.1	12,544	336	8.5	12,955
52	Chili	30,178	22,398	42.7	13,598	3,336	18.8	17,438
53	Peru	20,168	5,751	22.2	30,948	4,020	11.3	77,330
54	Other South American ports	1,814	1,849	60.3	1,082	....	....	....
55	Whale fisheries	68,624	....	....	63,331	693	1.1	38,077
56	Uncertain places	108	....	....	67	....	....	385
	Total	2,054,348	1,939,091	38.6	4,383,484	2,694,780	38.2	5,021,889

arriving from each foreign country every fifth year, &c.—Continued.

1860.		1861.			1862.			1863.			
Foreign.	Per cent. of foreign.	American.	Foreign.	Per cent. of foreign.	American.	Foreign.	Per cent. of foreign.	American.	Foreign.	Per cent. of foreign.	
3,111	16.6	6,220	3,577	32.4	6,640	2,701	28.3	6,504	4,778	42.3	1
310	100.0	....	400	100.0	....			....	....	....	2
3,679	36.0	8,480	6,273	42.0	1,918	3,294	44.2	470	7,528	94.3	3
170,229	75.9	6,298	161,003	95.1	7,361	190,604	96.2	9,018	179,694	95.2	4
17,303	29.7	41,639	20,843	33.4	34,349	26,729	40.3	39,416	41,254	51.3	5
507,000	37.5	822,683	470,064	36.8	821,447	415,029	36.6	726,800	624,435	46.3	6
62,465	73.9	21,134	34,734	61.7	41,399	27,353	39.7	30,139	40,344	55.6	7
90,314	91.6	1,138	64,734	97.9	23,147	34,344	63.9	23,349	79,647	73.6	8
16,763	7.3	178,167	16,875	8.6	127,703	30,610	11.8	81,442	28,091	26.1	9
3,015	15.4	[illegible]	1,156	10.4	13,026	5,308	19.3	14,410	10,020	41.0	10
8,980	74.4	2,954	5,169	63.4	3,000	8,735	74.1	6,971	13,171	65.4	11
2,430	43.8	971	1,291	65.4	3,821	1,640	30.0	3,285	3,804	54.9	12
20,431	54.9	21,537	11,394	34.6	18,434	8,209	30.8	21,310	11,536	35.1	13
19,757	43.6	14,276	5,349	27.[illegible]	23,579	1,027	4.1	15,361	17,734	53.6	14
47,429	33.8	72,511	20,612	22.1	62,460	17,087	21.5	64,017	24,936	33.2	15
3,730	60.2	3,974	1,251	97.6	361	....	......	....	3,120	100.0	16
5,832	35.4	10,291	2,158	17.3	4,713	....	......	8,069	3,089	34.1	17
....	....	....	....	....	....	....	......	....	....	....	18
1,474	82.1	....	....	....	800	....	......	553	563	50.4	19
4,[illegible]	23.9	10,923	1,137	9.3	10,048	836	7.6	10,831	3,030	21.7	20
1,[illegible]	8.8	19,126	2,256	10.5	13,761	1,735	11.06	18,391	4,846	23.9	21
1,415	61.8	3,800	514	11.7	3,318	379	14.3	1,854	1,520	44.5	22
1,089	30.7	1,027	893	44.9	696	460	40.9	879	973	24.6	23
677	87.4	150	876	86.0	....	....	......	3,843	445	12.07	24
1,980	36.3	1,229	1,121	47.7	1,687	....	......	1,177	1,435	56.0	25
6,280	7.4	68,259	10,329	13.1	27,015	2,874	9.4	43,834	3,564	7.2	26
190	12.8	3,447	2,370	23.00	1,216	430	25.1	2,089	1,194	36.3	27
4,213	5.1	70,293	5,635	7.4	41,200	19,027	31.6	56,392	12,137	17.7	28
3,774	70.0	8,423	....	....	1,751	383	23.0	1,619	....	....	29
1,296	4.2	23,458	1,070	3.4	13,256	730	5.1	23,796	1,520	5.7	30
12,692	36.6	4,078	6,983	62.8	8,118	6,338	44.0	9,000	5,554	38.1	31
....	....	....	....	....	....	....	......	....	....	....	32
1,738	4.0	30,071	1,874	5.4	11,809	570	4.8	9,328	1,050	10.1	33
632,630	28.1	1,856,892	624,679	25.5	2,487,373	681,411	21.5	2,307,850	742,126	24.3	34
473,031	72.7	196,709	463,141	70.3	848,971	377,709	81.7	812,251	430,290	66.3	35
81,798	18.00	418,763	33,110	7.8	379,517	68,533	15.3	389,213	67,426	14.4	36
13,173	31.4	44,508	8,089	15.8	42,377	21,190	33.5	37,244	17,253	31.7	37
7,736	16.02	40,727	5,010	11.0	32,315	23,029	42.1	20,415	31,524	50.6	38
122	8.0	1,541	140	8.3	1,824	1,328	42.3	576	527	47.7	39
8,113	37.9	14,411	3,345	22.9	12,030	3,713	19.8	12,641	11,838	48.5	40
39,544	33.5	82,694	53,825	38.5	69,871	73,724	51.2	78,278	77,048	49.7	41
7,483	27.1	21,297	12,132	36.3	7,923	7,619	49.7	6,622	11,640	63.3	42
3,415	46.9	2,958	4,024	57.5	2,020	8,638	81.4	1,793	7,638	81.1	43
....	....	....	....	....	....	....	......	....	....	....	44
12,744	80.5	27,311	5,509	16.8	30,294	8,074	20.7	42,992	19,646	31.4	45
2,165	17.4	3,165	684	17.7	1,502	2,871	64.7	1,308	4,432	77.3	46
679	18.4	3,023	414	11.9	3,725	1,700	48.3	12,074	2,190	15.3	47
5,010	2.3	169,329	2,441	1.6	164,857	8,396	5.7	165,742	13,857	7.6	48
23,644	22.5	82,829	22,173	20.9	70,913	31,425	30.7	46,323	30,229	39.5	49
417	5.0	6,319	....	....	13,090	677	4.9	4,530	1,009	18.[illegible]	50
3,407	12.6	22,877	1,056	4.4	16,177	4,358	21.2	18,843	3,772	16.6	51
1,316	7.02	24,248	6,301	17.7	15,153	1,339	2.7	15,734	3,078	16.3	52
2,416	2.3	153,678	3,197	2.8	6,053	2,857	32.0	5,031	1,534	64.7	53
....	....	318	....	....	....	....	......	....	....	....	54
....	....	34,738	....	....	34,095	....	......	88,380	....	....	55
....	....	857	....	....	191	....	......	....	....	....	56
2,353,911	28.4	5,023,917	2,217,554	30.6	5,117,085	2,245,278	30.5	4,614,022	2,640,378	36.4	

Statement exhibiting severally the tonnage of vessels from all foreign countries, exclusive of Canada and the other British North American possessions, from Canada and the other British North American possessions, and from all foreign countries, every fifth year, from 1821 to 1860, and annually from 1861 to 1863, with the per-centage of the total foreign tonnage entered at each period.

Years.	Tonnage entered, exclusive of Canada and other British North American provinces.	Percentage of foreign.	Tonnage entered from Canada and other British North American provinces.	Percentage of foreign.	Tonnage entered, inclusive of Canada and other British North American provinces.	Percentage of foreign.
1821	734,950	11.3	111,674	9.3	846,624	9.6
1826	964,270	10.06	83,590	10.4	1,047,860	10.06
1831	1,028,660	19.2	176,240	47.2	1,204,900	23.4
1836	1,279,424	23.6	656,173	67.5	1,935,597	35.1
1841	1,526,987	21.9	801,366	49.0	2,328,353	31.1
1846	1,744,270	25.4	1,366,583	37.7	3,110,853	30.8
1851	3,041,106	31.6	1,052,334	44.9	4,093,440	38.8
1856	3,672,030	22.3	2,900,223	54.0	6,572,253	36.2
1860	4,340,771	28.1	3,934,425	28.8	8,275,196	28.4
1861	3,897,850	27.4	3,343,621	34.3	7,241,471	30.6
1862	3,547,046	32.6	3,815,307	28.3	7,362,353	30.5
1863	3,570,495	41.3	3,684,581	31.6	7,255,076	36.4

Statement exhibiting the total tonnage of vessels arriving from each country in Europe every fifth year from 1821 to 1860, and annually from 1861 to 1864, with the foreign percentage of the total tonnage entered at each period; and showing, also, the total tonnage entered from the whole of Europe in American and foreign vessels, and the percentage of foreign at the several periods.

Years.	Russia.		Prussia.		Sweden, Norway, and Denmark.		Hamburg, Bremen, and other German ports.		Holland and Belgium.		England.		Scotland.		Ireland.		France on the Atlantic.	
	Total tonnage.	Percentage of foreign.	Total tonnage.	Percentage of foreign.	Total tonnage.	Percentage of foreign.	Total tonnage.	Percentage of foreign.	Total tonnage.	Percentage of foreign.	Total tonnage.	Percentage of foreign.	Total tonnage.	Percentage of foreign.	Total tonnage.	Percentage of foreign.	Total tonnage.	Percentage of foreign.
1821	13,427	......	738	100.0	13,391	6.8	18,704	22.3	97,254	5.1	151,077	85.8	11,989	61.3	72,497	34.1	62,704	49.6
1826	17,342	......	501	41.3	18,723	11.8	18,398	25.05	68,902	......	211,863	18.5	13,118	52.6	18,307	33.8	54,863	12.7
1831	9,508	4.07	700	......	14,343	50.9	88,109	43.3	24,465	1.4	307,680	27.4	16,692	63.9	11,408	60.5	69,513	17.5
1836	13,331	10.2	615	44.5	18,319	55.8	44,473	78.3	82,308	30.7	343,721	31.4	24,847	61.4	15,734	87.7	87,298	13.9
1841	19,044	3.5	357	......	19,293	61.6	81,074	68.4	41,045	9.6	432,887	39.0	31,167	71.1	10,683	93.8	124,060	11.7
1846	11,404	2.7	1,794	76.6	13,721	74.4	85,229	71.3	46,189	25.07	572,510	34.6	33,809	72.9	33,278	80.2	114,306	9.4
1851	13,085	25.0	988	72.6	28,430	90.6	112,873	88.6	83,281	47.9	1,001,809	39.9	64,434	71.7	79,508	83.1	162,194	18.3
1856	8,643	8.8	1,480	52.7	13,753	31.2	158,904	78.5	80,309	23.7	1,324,632	43.8	80,340	67.8	14,780	48.7	230,006	10.4
1860	16,624	10.6	310	100.0	8,280	30.6	174,255	85.9	38,380	29.7	1,351,985	37.5	72,804	73.9	30,307	83.4	233,911	7.3
1861	12,157	32.4	400	100.0	14,733	42.6	169,300	95.1	61,522	33.4	1,301,753	35.8	63,882	63.7	53,364	87.9	153,022	8.6
1862	8,549	58.3	....	......	8,810	62.9	108,983	80.5	91,064	40.3	1,298,476	38.6	68,944	39.7	84,693	68.2	228,313	11.8
1863	11,580	42.3	....	......	7,898	94.3	188,613	93.8	71,044	58.3	1,349,305	48.5	68,343	55.6	103,043	73.8	80,493	38.1

Statement exhibiting the total tonnage of vessels arriving from each country in Europe every fifth year from 1821 to 1860, &c.—Continued.

Years.	Spain on the Atlantic.		Portugal.		Gibraltar and Spain on the Mediterranean.		France on the Mediterranean.		Italy, Sicily, and Malta.		Austria.		Turkey, Greece, Egypt, and the Levant.		Total tonnage.		
	Total tonnage.	Percentage of foreign.	Total tonnage.	Percentage of foreign.	Total tonnage.	Percentage of foreign.	Total tonnage.	Percentage of foreign.	Total tonnage.	Percentage of foreign.	Total tonnage.	Percentage of foreign.	Total tonnage.	Percentage of foreign.	American.	Foreign.	Percentage of foreign.
1821	6,283	......	30,683	4.9	16,976	5.3	4,339	18.3	6,373	......	2,019	......	2,114	9.08	280,349	72,087	21.4
1826	5,463	......	31,277	1.6	15,464	......	8,420	......	9,085	......	8,515	......	3,579	......	383,276	64,902	14.4
1831	6,780	......	6,494	22.3	13,182	......	14,267	3.4	12,822	1.9	11,920	......	10,107	20.0	408,772	131,341	24.4
1836	9,376	18.4	10,854	27.5	20,378	15.2	31,927	44.2	25,630	17.3	10,394	37.0	7,245	32.8	441,487	240,142	35.2
1841	17,183	5.4	15,563	15.9	19,599	14.4	16,532	26.02	32,206	18.06	7,220	87.1	4,872	14.6	803,504	251,379	23.8
1846	8,485	4.3	7,163	22.4	17,887	29.3	13,082	22.9	22,206	23.3	3,611	10.5	8,875	16.6	644,171	370,740	36.5
1851	15,487	32.8	6,139	84.3	38,214	57.0	21,802	67.9	61,347	48.3	7,085	88.5	8,868	21.3	916,536	787,879	46.2
1856	20,336	77.1	18,312	40.8	56,985	54.8	37,019	18.1	142,802	24.3	6,949	40.5	22,577	31.3	1,573,736	682,807	30.2
1860	19,571	13.4	3,654	74.4	43,383	52.6	43,925	45.6	139,467	23.6	6,190	60.2	14,879	33.4	1,333,477	914,300	40.7
1861	11,848	18.4	7,417	69.4	34,445	36.6	10,565	37.00	80,128	22.1	4,527	27.6	12,479	17.3	1,230,616	846,697	40.7
1862	29,534	19.3	11,785	74.1	32,137	30.7	85,190	6.4	97,207	17.5	381	......	6,713	......	1,346,022	888,630	32.1
1863	94,420	41.0	30,149	65.4	40,033	38.4	33,085	52.6	98,943	23.2	3,120	100.0	8,944	34.1	1,616,078	1,114,915	38.3

Statement exhibiting the tonnage of American and foreign vessels arriving from the West Indies every fifth year from 1821 to 1860, and annually from 1861 to 1863, with the proportion of the foreign to the total tonnage entered at each period.

Years.	American.	Foreign.	Percentage of foreign.
1821	313,819	8,405	2.6
1826	351,998	20,039	5.3
1831	294,379	53,400	15.3
1836	329,790	46,050	12.3
1841	414,401	72,914	14.9
1846	497,179	60,770	11.0
1851	540,394	129,569	19.3
1856	704,900	122,317	14.8
1860	917,838	195,402	17.6
1861	841,623	141,705	14.4
1862	582,676	201,371	25.5
1863	557,546	244,863	30.5

Statement exhibiting the tonnage of American and foreign vessels arriving from Mexico and South America every fifth year from 1821 to 1860, and annually from 1861 to 1863, with the proportion of the foreign to the total tonnage entered at each period.

Years.	American.	Foreign.	Percentage of foreign.
1821	39,879	1,595	3.8
1826	84,043	11,516	12.0
1831	92,616	17,608	14.1
1836	97,839	14,054	13.4
1841	134,369	16,686	11.0
1846	142,486	17,959	11.2
1851	353,073	94,553	20.7
1856	468,333	41,281	8.1
1860	518,917	61,924	10.6
1861	478,863	43,657	8.3
1862	310,478	62,624	16.8
1863	283,607	71,696	20.3

Statement exhibiting the tonnage of American and foreign vessels arriving from Asia, Africa, and miscellaneous countries every fifth year from 1821 to 1860, and annually from 1861 to 1863, with the proportion of the foreign to the total tonnage entered at each period.

Years.	American.	Foreign.	Percentage of foreign.
1821	39,592	240	0.6
1826	48,135	514	1.0
1831	46,076	337	0.8
1836	107,377	2,444	2.2
1841	79,790	2,813	3.4
1846	105,915	4,337	3.9
1851	104,549	31,098	22.9
1856	260,963	21,211	7.5
1860	340,825	44,298	11.5
1861	276,019	35,315	11.3
1862	167,310	31,596	15.8
1863	187,483	33,608	15.0

Statement exhibiting the total imports and exports of the United States in the respective years given, and the proportions of the total trade with the several designated geographical divisions of the world.

Years.	Imports.	Exports.	Percentage.									
			Europe.		West Indies.		Canada, &c.		Mexico and So. America.		Asia, Africa, and miscellaneous.	
			Imports.	Exports.	Imports.	Exports.	Imports.	Exports.	Imports.	Exports.	Imports.	Exports.
1821	$62,585,724	$64,974,382	64	53	23	18	0.6	3	3	6	8.8	[illegible]
1826	84,974,477	77,595,322	55	55	18	18	0.8	3	13	18	12.9	6
1831	103,191,124	81,310,583	66	62	15	19	1.0	5	10	14	4.0	7
1836	189,980,035	128,663,040	71	73	11	11	1.3	2	9	9	7.7	3
1841	127,946,177	121,851,803	63	72	14	11	1.5	6	13	8	6.5	3
1846	121,691,797	113,488,516	66	69	18	14	1.6	7	11	9	9.6	3
1851	216,224,932	218,388,011	69	78	11	7	5	6	11	6	6.0	3
1856	314,639,942	326,964,908	63	75	10	8	7	9	10	7	8	4
1860	362,163,941	400,122,296	60	78	12	6	6	6	12	6	10	6
1861	334,350,453	249,344,913	60	68	12	10	7	9	10	7	9	6
1862	205,819,823	229,790,280	56	69	14	10	8	9	12	7	8	6
1863	252,919,920	331,809,459	59	68	14	9	9	9	11	9	9	6

European trade.

Years.	Gold and silver.		Trade, exclusive of gold and silver.		Total.	
	Imports.	Exports.	Imports.	Exports.	Imports.	Exports.
1821	$4,390,396	$1,678,190	$36,[illegible]	$32,679,6[illegible]	$40,367,380	$34,357,598
1826	743,036	912,748	46,023,725	41,258,043	46,766,761	42,[illegible],151
1831	321,324	8,974,731	68,[illegible],087	49,438,413	68,983,311	58,413,148
1836	7,179,414	867,773	127,094,[illegible]	88,382,578	134,274,388	94,370,353
1841	634,771	6,674,584	82,358,[illegible]	60,088,439	83,[illegible],260	67,641,023
1846	811,856	2,[illegible],407	83,[illegible],318	76,174,566	80,746,584	78,425,970
1851	1,637,070	25,971,[illegible]	147,[illegible],150	145,615,180	149,544,196	170,[illegible]
1856	636,393	61,[illegible],627	209,316,152	204,[illegible],941	168,954,714	247,[illegible]
1860	172,172	60,[illegible],153	217,639,463	249,[illegible],763	217,[illegible],635	310,670,916
1861	37,403,713	23,[illegible],343	167,031,140	147,271,941	204,434,855	170,[illegible]
1862	12,343,044	30,644,463	105,074,646	137,331,891	117,330,730	136,[illegible],474
1863	254,603	34,301,231	148,[illegible],705	173,[illegible],807	149,311,636	208,001,[illegible]

West India trade.

Years.	Gold and silver.		Trade, exclusive of gold and silver.		Total.	
	Imports.	Exports.	Imports.	Exports.	Imports.	Exports.
1821	$3,257,081	$318,[illegible]	$11,[illegible],701	$11,818,367	$14,[illegible],784	$12,[illegible]
1826	1,611,519	476,975	14,299,712	13,781,777	15,912,230	14,157,710
1831	1,968,394	410,371	14,464,330	11,[illegible]	15,782,723	11,[illegible]
1836	338,457	1,030,497	21,344,251	12,240,[illegible]	21,[illegible],708	13,[illegible]
1841	700,598	417,173	17,842,221	12,300,[illegible]	18,543,536	12,[illegible]
1846	1,304,223	386,473	12,814,030	11,058,[illegible]	14,317,[illegible]	10,[illegible]
1851	606,085	2,312,385	22,701,039	13,163,351	23,307,124	15,[illegible]
1856	167,577	673,107	33,170,914	16,737,615	33,344,391	17,[illegible]
1860	1,794,367	1,024,321	41,811,134	23,5[illegible],053	43,[illegible],497	24,[illegible]
1861	3,276,741	2,411,899	38,218,589	22,041,701	41,504,330	24,[illegible]
1862	166,573	2,058,319	27,395,091	21,925,074	27,561,664	23,[illegible]
1863	418,427	2,081,741	20,474,992	29,[illegible]	20,063,323	31,[illegible]

Trade of the several West India islands in the years 1860 and 1863, showing the change of the balance of trade in the respective years.

1860.

	Imports.	Exports.		Imports.	Exports.
Swedish West Indies	$18,783	$77,916	Cuba	$34,072,970	$12,392,979
Danish West Indies	200,116	1,261,424	Porto Rico	4,512,935	1,721,750
British West Indies	1,804,450	5,398,479	Dutch West Indies	396,614	303,431
French West Indies	18,353	544,211	San Domingo	283,448	169,300
Hayti	2,082,722	2,672,092			
Total	4,174,744	9,947,034	Total	39,294,053	14,637,350

Excess of exports, $5,772,290. Percentage of imports to total, 29 per cent.
Excess of imports, $24,587,673. Percentage of imports to total, 73 per cent.
Percentage of total imports to total trade, 64 per cent.

1863.

	Imports.	Exports.		Imports.	Exports.
Danish West Indies	$391,722	$1,814,619	Swedish West Indies	$72,300	$7,525
British West Indies	2,074,475	7,555,321	Dutch West Indies	510,540	372,316
French West Indies	92,385	901,214	Cuba	21,514,065	14,811,599
Hayti	1,678,337	3,0 ,771	Porto Rico	2,732,476	2,217,723
San Domingo	300,251	481,340			
Total	4,563,130	14,140,258	Total	24,802,398	17,389,185

Excess of exports, $9,579,128. Percentage of imports to total, 24 per cent.
Excess of imports, $7,413,901. Percentage of imports to total, 58 per cent.
Percentage of total imports to total trade, 60 per cent.

Canadian and other British provincial trade.

Year.	Gold and silver.		Trade, exclusive of gold and silver.		Trade, inclusive of gold and silver.	
	Imports.	Exports.	Imports.	Exports.	Imports.	Exports.
1821	$89,413		$408,077	$2,010,004	$495,478	$2,010,004
1830	221,891	$462,230	429,936	2,138,545	651,950	2,5 ,715
1840	377,197	982,010	587,712	3,079,808	964,909	4,061,818
1845	546,474	64,420	1,891,097	2,386,959	2,437,571	2,451,382
1847	475,891	198,100	1,492,248	6,438,463	1,968,187	6,636,563
1849	653,043	251,900	1,314,674	7,154,533	1,967,717	7,406,433
1851	44,677	30	6,648,445	12,014,921	6,693,122	12,014,951
1856	33,807	4,000	21,276,614	29,025,349	21,310,421	29,029,349
1860	278,363	10,400	23,572,798	22,695,928	23,851,161	22,706,328
1861	318,444	69,100	22,724,489	22,676,513	23,042,933	22,745,613
1862	798,970	599,045	18,511,025	20,573,070	19,299,995	21,072,115
1863	6,538,478	3,661,216	17,464,786	27,619,814	24,003,264	31,281,030

NOTE.—The reciprocity treaty between the United States and Great Britain, concluded 5th of June, 1854, went into operation in the trade with Canada, October 18, 1854; with New Brunswick, November 11, 1854; with Prince Edward's island, November 17, 1854; with Newfoundland, November 16, 1855; and with regard to fish from all the provinces, on the 11th of September, 1854.

The aggregate exports (inclusive of specie and foreign merchandise) to Canada and the other British North American possessions for the three years 1852-'53-'54, amounting to $46,816,318, exceeded the aggregate imports 113.4 per cent. The aggregate exports of the five years, from the 30th of June, 1854, (which period covered the first four and a half years of the operation of the reciprocity treaty,) amounted to $132,983,772, exceeding the imports of the same period 61.3 per cent. The aggregate imports of the two years, 1860 and 1861, immediately preceding the rebellion, amounted to $46,814,314, exceeding the exports 2.2 per cent. In the year 1862, the first full fiscal year of the rebellion, the exports, amounting to $21,079,185, exceeded the imports 9.2 per cent.; and in the year ending June 30, 1863, the exports ($30,281,030) exceeded the imports 31.2 per cent.

In the trade with the British North American possessions other than Canada, in the year 1851, the exports amounted to $4,083,783, the imports to $1,736,631. This commerce had gradually grown to double these amounts in 1860; the exports and imports holding about the same ratio, say the former about double the value of the latter. In the year 1863 the exports were $10,928,348, the imports $5,307,424. The Canada trade of 1851 amounted to $12,893,611, of which the exports were 61.5 per cent. In 1860 the total trade was $32,944,787, of which the exports were 43 per cent.; in 1861 the total trade rose to $38,029,383, of which the exports were 52 per cent. In 1856, the year of the greatest trade with Canada previous to 1863, the total amount was $32,371,438, of which the exports were 54 per cent.

Mexican and South American trade.

Years.	Gold and silver.		Trade, exclusive of gold and silver.		Trade, inclusive of gold and silver.	
	Imports.	Exports.	Imports.	Exports.	Imports.	Exports.
1821	$772,532	$211,[illegible]	$1,705,760	$2,434,328	$1,[illegible],318	$2,[illegible],250
1826	542,716	377,333	9,[illegible],438	12,[illegible],737	10,435,109	12,935,310
1831	3,247,664	322,983	8,949,664	10,[illegible],404	11,[illegible],[illegible]	11,338,[illegible]
1836	5,019,922	1,104,223	12,[illegible],217	10,696,015	17,[illegible],139	11,[illegible],[illegible]
1841	8,7[illegible],[illegible]	4[illegible],[illegible]44	13,[illegible],[illegible]	8,[illegible],123	16,4[illegible]7,721	10,042,[illegible]
1846	[illegible],3[illegible]	443,339	12,[illegible],712	8,[illegible],083	13,[illegible],[illegible]	9,[illegible],44[illegible]
1851	1,692,[illegible]	1,468,370	21,431,320	12,429,811	23,123,[illegible]	13,964,1[illegible]1
1856	3,160,343	1,234,390	32,662,793	18,974,339	35,[illegible],112	20,[illegible],139
1860	6,134,434	1,077,000	37,452,323	21,513,294	43,[illegible],[illegible]	22,590,294
1861	4,714,[illegible]	550,857	32,764,[illegible]	16,380,7[illegible]	37,[illegible],[illegible]	16,[illegible],[illegible]
1862	2,641,[illegible]	[illegible],153	22,271,[illegible]	15,[illegible],443	24,916,[illegible]	15,410,[illegible]
1863	1,997,[illegible]	3[illegible],663	25,448,363	25,[illegible],883	27,445,[illegible]	26,197,730

Asiatic, African, and miscellaneous trade.

Years.	Gold and silver.		Trade, exclusive of gold and silver.		Trade, inclusive of gold and silver.	
	Imports.	Exports.	Imports.	Exports.	Imports.	Exports.
1821	$178,444	$7,[illegible],[illegible]	$5,740,378	$5,[illegible],811	$5,[illegible],[illegible]	$13,[illegible],[illegible]
1826	2,795,7[illegible]	2,[illegible],049	7,469,663	2,125,307	11,[illegible],[illegible]	4,[illegible],[illegible]
1831	131,336	1,[illegible],[illegible]	5,919,337	2,334,160	3,[illegible],[illegible]	4,[illegible],[illegible]
1836	110,614	1,[illegible]7,415	14,193,[illegible]	2,452,[illegible]	14,312,[illegible]01	4,[illegible],401
1841	[illegible],[illegible]73	1,[illegible],231	7,324,5[illegible]0	2,407,[illegible]	7,[illegible],4[illegible]	4,[illegible],[illegible]
1846	[illegible],[illegible]	[illegible],132	10,[illegible],271	3,1[illegible],411	10,[illegible],[illegible]	3,5[illegible],573
1851	1,4[illegible],[illegible]	422,363	12,[illegible],328	6,[illegible],7[illegible]	13,[illegible],[illegible]	6,046,[illegible]
1856	307,[illegible]	1,108,171	23,[illegible],[illegible]	11,627,[illegible]	24,[illegible],[illegible]	12,734,130
1860	1[illegible],[illegible]	3,551,305	33,357,[illegible]	16,019,[illegible]	33,[illegible],[illegible]	19,570,344
1861	470,412	2,[illegible],[illegible]	37,27[illegible],641	12,412,910	37,731,[illegible]	14,644,[illegible]
1862	312,[illegible]	3,[illegible],[illegible]	15,169,013	7,[illegible],744	15,[illegible],[illegible]	11,[illegible],[illegible]
1863	125,406	3,873,544	22,317,[illegible]	10,[illegible],093	22,443,471	14,721,[illegible]

SHIPPING OF THE UNITED STATES.

*The number, class, and tonnage of vessels built in the United States, 1822 to 1863.**

Years.	Class of vessels.					Total number of vessels.	Total tonnage.
	Ships.	Brigs.	Schooners.	Sloops and canal boats.	Steamers.		
1822	64	131	260	168	....	623	75,347
1823	55	127	260	165	15	622	75,030
1824	56	156	377	168	26	781	90,939
1825	56	197	538	168	35	994	114,997
1826	71	187	482	227	45	1,012	126,438
1827	58	133	464	241	38	934	104,342
1828	73	108	474	197	33	885	98,375
1829	44	68	485	142	43	673	77,098
1830	25	56	403	116	37	637	58,094
1831	72	95	416	94	34	711	85,962
1832	132	143	568	122	100	1,065	144,539
1833	144	169	625	185	65	1,188	161,626
1834	98	94	497	180	68	937	118,330
1835	25	50	301	100	30	507	46,238
1836	93	65	444	164	124	890	113,627
1837	67	72	507	168	135	949	122,987
1838	66	79	510	153	90	898	113,135
1839	83	89	439	122	125	858	120,988
1840	97	109	378	224	63	871	118,309
1841	114	101	311	157	78	761	118,893
1842	116	91	273	404	137	1,021	129,083

The number, class, and tonnage of vessels, &c.—Continued.

Years.	Class of vessels.					Total number of vessels.	Total tonnage.
	Ships.	Brigs.	Schooners.	Sloops and canal boats.	Steamers.		
1843	58	34	138	173	79	482	63,618
1844	73	47	204	279	163	766	103,537
1845	124	87	322	342	163	1,038	146,018
1846	100	164	576	355	225	1,420	188,204
1847	151	168	689	392	198	1,598	243,732
1848	254	131	701	547	175	1,851	318,075
1849	198	148	623	370	208	1,547	256,577
1850	247	117	547	290	159	1,360	272,218
1851	211	65	522	326	233	1,357	298,203
1852	255	79	584	267	259	1,444	351,493
1853	269	95	681	394	271	1,710	425,571
1854	334	112	661	386	281	1,774	535,616
1855	381	126	605	669	253	2,034	583,450
1856	306	103	594	479	221	1,703	469,393
1857	251	58	504	258	263	1,334	378,805
1858	122	46	431	400	226	1,225	242,287
1859	89	28	297	284	173	870	156,601
1860	110	36	372	289	264	1,071	212,892
1861	110	38	369	371	264	1,143	233,193
1862	60	17	207	397	183	864	175,076
1863	67	34	212	1,113	367	1,823	310,884

* For calendar years 1820 to 1833, fiscal years ending September 30, from 1834 to 1842, and ending June 30 subsequently.

SHIPPING OF THE UNITED STATES.

A comparative view of the registered and enrolled tonnage of the United States, showing the registered tonnage employed in the whale fishery, the proportion of the enrolled and licensed tonnage employed in the coasting trade and fisheries, and the tonnage employed in steam navigation, from 1815 *to* 1863 *inclusive.*

Years.	Registered tonnage.	Enrolled tonnage.	Total tonnage.	Registered tonnage in the whale fishery.	Tonnage employed in steam navigation.	Enrolled tonnage in coasting trade and fisheries.
	Tons.					
1815	854,294	513,833	1,368,127	....	....	462,807
1816	800,760	571,459	1,372,219	....	....	519,059
1817	800,725	590,186	1,399,911	4,871	....	535,798
1818	606,089	619,095	1,225,184	16,134	....	582,309
1819	612,930	647,821	1,260,751	31,700	....	589,247
1820	619,047	661,119	1,280,166	35,391	....	610,976
1821	619,896	679,062	1,298,958	28,070	....	614,711
1822	628,150	696,549	1,324,699	45,449	....	624,618
1823	639,921	696,645	1,336,566	39,918	24,879	631,615
1824	669,973	719,190	1,389,163	33,165	21,610	657,879
1825	700,787	722,323	1,423,110	35,379	23,061	657,899
1826	737,978	796,212	1,534,190	41,757	34,059	770,418
1827	747,170	873,437	1,620,607	45,653	40,197	877,316
1828	812,619	928,772	1,741,391	54,621	39,418	889,050
1829	650,142	610,655	1,260,797	57,284	54,036	610,654
1830	576,675	615,311	1,191,776	39,911	64,471	615,309
1831	620,452	647,394	1,267,846	82,315	34,035	649,360
1832	686,990	752,461	1,439,450	72,868	90,813	751,454
1833	750,026	856,123	1,606,149	101,158	101,049	856,123
1834	857,438	901,469	1,758,907	108,060	122,815	901,469
1835	885,822	939,118	1,824,940	97,640	122,815	939,118
1836	897,774	984,321	1,882,101	144,680	145,536	1,001,322
1837	810,447	1,096,238	1,896,685	127,242	154,761	1,096,238
1838	822,592	1,173,047	1,995,639	119,629	190,410	1,173,047
1839	834,244	1,262,234	2,096,479	131,845	194,908	1,262,234
1840	899,765	1,280,999	2,180,764	136,926	202,339	1,280,999
1841	945,803	1,184,941	2,130,744	157,405	175,168	1,184,940
1842	975,359	1,117,032	2,092,391	151,691	229,461	1,117,032

A comparative view of the registered and enrolled tonnage, &c.—Continued

Years.	Registered tonnage.	Enrolled tonnage.	Total tonnage.	Registered tonnage in the whale fishery.	Tonnage employed in steam navigation.	Enrolled tonnage in coasting trade and fisheries.
	Tons.					
1843	1,009,315	1,149,297	2,158,[illegible]	152,374	[illegible]	1,149,[illegible]
1844	1,068,765	1,211,330	2,280,095	168,293	[illegible],179	1,211,[illegible]
1845	1,095,173	1,321,829	2,417,002	190,695	[illegible],018	1,[illegible],344
1846	1,130,286	1,431,798	2,562,084	182,[illegible]	347,[illegible]	1,319,[illegible]
1847	1,241,313	1,597,733	2,839,045	193,858	[illegible],841	1,[illegible]
1848	1,360,887	1,793,155	3,154,042	192,[illegible]	427,891	1,747,[illegible]
1849	1,438,942	1,895,073	3,334,015	180,186	462,374	1,[illegible]
1850	1,585,711	1,949,743	3,535,454	146,016	525,946	1,[illegible]
1851	1,726,[illegible]	2,046,[illegible]	3,772,439	181,644	[illegible]	1,[illegible]
1852	1,899,448	2,238,992	4,138,440	193,798	643,240	2,1[illegible]
1853	2,103,674	2,303,336	4,407,010	193,[illegible]	514,097	2,3[illegible]
1854	2,333,819	2,469,[illegible]	4,802,902	181,901	676,607	2,411,[illegible]
1855	2,535,136	2,676,804	5,212,001	186,773	770,285	2,513,[illegible]
1856	2,491,408	2,[illegible],149	4,871,652	189,213	673,077	2,[illegible]
1857	2,463,167	2,476,[illegible]	4,940,841	195,771	716,734	2,[illegible]
1858	2,499,742	2,550,068	5,049,808	198,593	729,390	2,[illegible]
1859	2,507,401	2,657,615	5,145,037	185,728	[illegible],436	2,[illegible]
1860	2,546,237	2,807,631	5,353,868	166,841	867,937	2,[illegible],631
1861	2,642,628	2,897,185	5,539,813	145,734	877,203	2,[illegible]
1862	2,[illegible],951	2,820,913	5,112,164	117,713	710,468	2,77[illegible]
1863	2,026,114	3,125,941	5,155,055	99,228	575,516	3,1[illegible]

STATISTICS OF GENERAL TRADE WITH GREAT BRITAIN.

The great extent to which the course of foreign commerce has been diverted in recent years from direct lines to and from the countries of production and consumption gives a constantly increasing degree of importance to the statistics of trade with the countries in whose hands the carrying trade is being absorbed. The first and chief of these intervening countries is England. The statements annually published by that government are very full and comprehensive, and may be taken as the best available illustration of the commerce of the world. There are few articles the produce of any country which are not now largely carried through British ports, and whose quantities, values, and destination do not appear in the British statistics.

In the year 1862 the total value of British exports to the United States was £19,173,907=$92,801,710, of which more than one-fourth was articles wholly of "foreign and colonial produce," their value being £4,846,037, or $23,454,819. The manufactures designated as the produce of the United Kingdom were also made up in great degree of foreign staples, imported crude from the countries of their origin. The comparison of British exports to the United States for several years, distinguishing those of foreign origin, strikingly illustrates the progress of this carrying trade.

Exports from Great Britain to the United States.

	1857.	1858.	1859.	1860.	1861.	1862.
Of the produce and manufacture of the United Kingdom	£18,985,[illegible]	£14,491,448	£22,333,403	£21,667,063	£9,064,504	£14,327,870
Of foreign and colonial produce	1,840,[illegible]	1,[illegible],057	1,864,487	1,240,616	1,951,479	4,846,037

In values of the United States.

	1857.	1858.	1859.	1860.	1861.	1862.
Of the produce and manufacture of the United Kingdom	$91,891,945	$70,138,615	$109,158,490	$104,658,595	$43,872,199	$79,346,691
Of foreign and colonial produce	5,280,227	8,302,804	9,024,117	6,014,581	9,492,106	13,454,019
Totals	97,172,172	78,441,419	118,182,607	110,673,176	53,364,305	92,801,710

The increasing proportion of foreign articles to the total export in the last two years corresponds with the changed direction of commerce noted in the shipping accounts. For 1863 the value of foreign and colonial produce exported cannot be obtained, but the value of the produce of the United Kingdom sent to the United States is nearly the same as in 1862—£15,351,626, or $74,301,869.

The crude staples of British manufactures are now in great proportion of foreign origin. Wool from South America, South Africa, Australia, and other colonies, and also from various continental states of Europe, is imported in immense quantities. Flax, undressed, from Russia, enters equally with the flax of Ireland into linen manufacture. The quantities of flax and hemp imported into England from Russia for six years amount to the following:

Years.	Flax.		Hemp.	
	Tons.	Value.	Tons.	Value.
1857	63,745	$10,625,494	20,035	$4,633,574
1858	40,544	10,070,644	30,281	4,964,263
1859	63,723	12,870,054	35,460	5,075,311
1860	62,442	12,485,601	29,478	4,353,016
1861	47,023	10,913,709	23,043	3,444,245
1862	61,723	10,367,147	30,450	5,304,419

These are but single examples among many, showing the vast quantities of raw materials imported into England for manufacture, the final products of which constitute the exports designated as the "Produce and Manufactures of the United Kingdom." It is, therefore, but reasonable to estimate that a large share of those values are in a certain sense a portion of the indirect commerce between the real countries of production and those of consumption.

The carriage of foreign produce not manufactured in this manner is tending towards concentration in a few hands with great rapidity, and England far exceeds the German states and all others combined in the volume of this business. Taking tropical articles, or staples of almost universal consumption, and particularly those produced by distant countries, such as were for twenty or thirty years from the commencement of the great European wars the especial commerce of vessels of the United States, the results become very decided and conspicuous. The following table compares the quantities of such articles re-exported by England for five years to 1863:

Exports from England of certain articles of foreign production.

Articles.		1859.	1860.	1861.	1862.	1863.
Cocoa	lbs	2,819,248	2,421,370	4,509,277	1,430,814	4,138,[illegible]
Coffee	do	97,246,054	43,081,920	46,[illegible],765	58,[illegible],850	71,[illegible]
Cotton	do	173,157,898	250,428,640	298,287,937	214,714,640	241,770,[illegible]
Cochineal	do	1,048,240	1,878,800	1,021,044	2,107,616	2,[illegible],360
Indigo	do	6,142,464	6,148,992	7,553,730	5,014,[illegible]	6,182,[illegible]
Lac dye	do	404,768	453,304	372,[illegible]	Not given.	Not given.
Logwood	tons	3,750	2,169	3,847	do	do
Terra japonica	do	324	679	1,578	do	do
Cutch	do	765	1,048	[illegible]	do	do
Currants	cwts	117,848	87,375	63,981	102,910	97,[illegible]
Raisins	do	78,377	91,926	41,848	38,431	28,[illegible]
Guano	tons	29,397	10,439	12,410	16,224	7,[illegible]
Hemp	cwts	Not given.	67,441	48,918	73,041	108,[illegible]
Jute, and the like	do	do	42,511	99,479	116,638	183,[illegible]
Hides, dry	do	144,453	141,109	198,298	250,714	[illegible]
wet	do	102,814	110,408	98,966	63,471	78,[illegible]
Oil, palm	do	156,475	184,211	175,050	231,946	[illegible]
cocoa-nut	do	174,748	141,478	218,674	165,778	197,[illegible]
olive	do	30,089	28,110	86,890	90,360	18,[illegible]
petroleum	do			20	63,880	163,[illegible]
Metals: copper	do	47,098	73,516	78,450	172,371	125,[illegible]
tin	do	7,918	10,163	19,173	91,678	[illegible]
Quicksilver	lbs	2,333,996	2,364,378	1,217,039	1,037,380	1,040,[illegible]
Rice	cwts	1,133,075	1,173,050	1,722,148	1,272,049	1,[illegible]
Saltpetre	do	104,347	89,625	18,644	78,499	[illegible]
Seeds: flax and linseed	bush	853,610	981,898	778,078	735,224	732,[illegible]
rape seed	do	1,364,273	855,544	614,548	946,056	476,[illegible]
Silk, raw	lbs	2,132,327	3,153,943	4,086,[illegible]	5,[illegible]	3,[illegible]
waste	cwts	1,563	1,376	823	4,238	1,[illegible]
thrown	lbs	254,297	436,[illegible]	91,[illegible]	177,[illegible]	[illegible]
manufactures of India	pieces	249,[illegible]	112,970	134,849	138,834	73,[illegible]
Spices: cinnamon	lbs	703,[illegible]	691,816	741,977	613,591	912,[illegible]
pepper	do	6,651,824	9,131,827	6,053,034	17,[illegible]	10,911,[illegible]
cassia	do	867,790	612,857	616,438	Not given.	Not given.
cloves	do	[illegible]	704,854	390,037	do	do
nutmegs	do	231,100	64,227	170,470	do	do
ginger	do	1,131,649	701,474	801,760	do	do
pimento	do	2,221,648	2,078,816	2,848,560	do	do
Sugar, brown	cwts	215,517	295,303	471,994	241,470	[illegible]
refined	do	64,674	30,679	33,918	22,711	[illegible]
Molasses	do	60,150	49,973	105,548	51,709	[illegible]
Tallow	do	8,790	9,197	137,850	172,903	32,[illegible]
Tea	lbs	6,416,734	8,399,530	12,447,[illegible]	27,[illegible]	[illegible]
Tobacco	do	11,171,164	6,371,314	7,534,218	12,026,155	10,417,[illegible]
manufactured	do	1,368,319	1,442,561	1,292,040	946,963	2,108,[illegible]
Wines	galls	2,172,738	2,273,308	1,923,253	2,110,425	2,290,773
Wool*	lbs	29,618,998	20,854,041	44,348,318	37,441,812	49,344,377
other	do	8,813,704	4,862,889	9,376,962	10,633,813	14,380,348

* Of British possessions.

The designations of quantity given here to some extent mask the magnitude of a portion of the entries—sugar, rice, oils, dried fruits, tallow, and many other items, being designated in hundred-weights and tons, instead of pounds and gallons. In coffee, sugar, cocoa, indigo, wool, and others, the increase in 1863 is very great even over 1862, and the quantities are more than twice as great as those carried in 1859. In 1863, 41,842,311 pounds of wool were re-exported to the United States. In 1862 the following items are conspicuous among the foreign exports to the United States, which may also be found in the general table of exports of foreign and colonial produce, which follows in another place. They are here contrasted with 1860:

Articles.	1860.	1862.
Coffee ....lbs.	1,901	902,354
Cotton ....lbs.	73,[illegible]	91,547,360
Currants ....lbs.	166,592	1,435,302
Hemp ....cwts.	304	31,440
Indigo ....lbs.	520,648	1,722,000
Rice ....lbs.	58,912	24,147,200
Silk, raw ....lbs.	66,994	101,128
Silk, knubs ....lbs.	3,608	277,312
Skins, goat ....No.	171,556	395,693
Tea ....lbs.	60,[illegible]	2,539,609
Tobacco manufactured ....lbs.	3,392	20,864
Wool ....lbs.	2,841,200	11,578,426

The corresponding quantities for 1863 cannot be obtained, except for wool and one or two other items. Many other articles increase in greater or less degree, as can be seen by reference to the general table of exports of foreign produce to the United States.

Before proceeding to the general statistics of British trade with the United States, as prepared from the official publications of that government, the relation of the United States to the distant tropical carrying trade, and to the carrying trade generally, may be further illustrated. The India trade was for a long time in American hands, and most cargoes arriving from the east for any port of the Atlantic markets broke bulk first in our own ports, and were re-exported in United States vessels to the west of Europe. This India trade also laid the foundation of many manufactures, among them those of morocco leather, silk spinning and silk finishing of piece goods, dyeing, &c. The Calcutta trade continued longest in the possession of United States vessels, being first for a long period carried to Philadelphia with the China trade, and for the last ten years controlled at Boston. It ceased nearly with the breaking up of sailing lines in the east, in 1862 and 1863, through the piracies conducted in the interest of the rebellion.

CARRIAGE OF FOREIGN PRODUCE BY THE UNITED STATES.

Of the total value of the exports of the United States, a proportion varying from one-half in the earlier years to one-fifteenth in 1860 was of articles of foreign origin. For fifteen years, from 1796 to 1810, the exports of domestic produce and of foreign produce were nearly the same; the aggregate for this period being $517,525,900 of domestic and $514,489,291 of foreign exports. In some single years the value of foreign articles carried became very large: in 1799, $45,500,000; in 1801, $46,642,000; in 1806, $60,283,000, and in 1807, $59,643,000. The average for periods of five years each, from 1796 to 1860, shows a large excess in the early periods over those of recent years:

Annual average,	1796 to 1800	$34,190,775
" "	1801 to 1805	37,084,476
" "	1806 to 1810	35,822,607
" "	1811 to 1815	6,818,860
" "	1816 to 1820	18,619,327
" "	1821 to 1825	25,812,023
" "	1826 to 1830	20,114,944
" "	1831 to 1835	21,542,608
" "	1836 to 1840	18,347,791
" "	1841 to 1845	12,115,013

Annual average, 1846 to 1850........................$13,705,293
" " 1851 to 1855........................ 21,968,924
" " 1856 to 1860........................ 23,813,687
Single year 1861........................ 21,145,427
Single year 1862........................ 16,869,641
Single year 1863........................ 25,959,248

Average of first ten years........................$35,637,626
Average of last ten years........................ 22,891,306

A previous table shows the leading articles of foreign produce exported from Great Britain, and approximately the extent of the present carrying trade of that country. The same articles now make up the chief part of the trade of the United States in articles of foreign origin exported, and they have been the conspicuous elements of that trade from the beginning. A rapid increase in the quantities carried by England is observable, and a decline in those carried by the United States. To illustrate this tendency fully, as regards the United States, a comparison of periods of four or five years each, separated by a considerable interval of time, may be made, the first period being from 1824 to 1828, and the last five years ending with 1860. The first division of articles embraces crude staples of tropical or semi-tropical origin, with a few manufactures peculiar to remote countries, and subsequently a list of leading articles not of tropical origin is given:

Articles of tropical or semi-tropical origin exported from the United States.

Articles.	1824.	1825.	1826.	1827.	1828.
Cocoa	$577,938	$495,092	$419,577	$441,221	$345,674
Coffee	2,921,079	3,254,936	1,419,022	2,324,784	1,497,097
Cotton	30,311	88,360	24,852	8,875	22,810
Cotton manufactures of India*	321,204	443,271	336,295	270,448	294,974
Dye-woods	645,391	644,418	459,000	350,448	419,981
Fruits	36,813	55,713	29,522	54,739	39,204
Indigo	513,271	891,974	712,090	864,951	382,709
Opium†	......	......	......	304,290	139,799
Silk, raw	1,407	21,639	132,295	181,150	47,277
Silk manufactures of India	1,816,325	1,390,237	1,651,492	891,975	713,610
Silk manufactures, all other	not named.	1,235,399	1,583,228	814,076	612,874
Spices	600,171	705,120	578,729	305,129	181,307
Spirits, West India	810,951	253,857	253,626	208,806	241,773
Sugar	990,003	1,614,607	1,742,034	1,191,580	889,480
Tea	582,169	1,442,141	1,398,694	778,413	672,924
Cigars, Havana	41,336	33,175	41,460	49,977	39,945
Sulphur	2,653	3,704	696	1,512	4,311
Wines	328,433	448,856	360,485	342,350	327,806

* "[illegible]" only. † Opium was not named previous to 1827. It was undoubtedly largely carried.

The following table gives the values of the same class of articles exported in eight years, ending with 1863. The contrast between the years of the first series in cocoa, coffee, silk, and indigo, and those of the second series, is great:

Exports of foreign articles.

Articles.	1856.	1857.	1858.	1859.	1860.	1861.	1862.	1863.
Cocoa	$81,788	$32,801	$167,080	$148,432	$271,597	$185,948	$144,089	$351,717
Coffee	1,858,416	2,016,804	1,380,970	1,821,730	2,258,091	777,485	1,382,070	1,081,482
Cotton	....	....	....	18,908	10,499	8,730	16,647	771,027
Dye-woods	688,767	878,143	691,331	330,500	318,616	308,599	380,119	485,336
Fruits	188,828	177,237	187,416	152,763	281,445	183,915	190,576	207,449
Indigo	71,670	62,178	300,050	10,348	48,175	34,437	117,240	185,943
Oil, palm and cocoa-nut	....	....	....	....	45,078	178,238	229,721	428,430
Opium	19,870	30,138	42,549	88,943	13,463	31,438	32,049	38,815
Silk, raw	4,955	4,163	94,092	19,974	176,389	121,108	81,418	14,118
Silk, manufactures of	874,530	157,198	254,958	849,378	299,326	278,704	201,109	276,783
Spices	475,308	388,348	414,763	189,845	489,070	388,146	118,317	232,404
Spirits, West India	56,972	42,053	40,808	69,806	118,907	44,498	38,434	31,335
Sugar	1,217,479	1,180,280	4,040,030	2,270,291	8,150,879	3,735,781	1,317,711	1,504,272
Tea	1,082,611	1,430,313	1,324,426	2,467,383	1,985,243	1,358,630	628,918	1,024,783
Cigars	184,242	227,143	165,002	226,214	271,063	125,990	178,609	146,219
Wines	167,910	129,815	172,764	246,013	163,880	181,318	170,801	174,680

In view of the general advance of trade in these articles, the entire list must be regarded as having declined from the first to the second period.

DIRECT TRADE WITH GREAT BRITAIN.

The British official tables of trade and navigation give the following values of imports from and exports to the United States for seven years, ending with 1862; the values being changed to their equivalent in money of the United States:

Years.	Imports from United States.	Exports to United States.
1856	$174,471,281	$109,465,644
1857	162,863,578	97,172,179
1858	165,804,080	70,441,513
1859	165,975,068	118,192,597
1860	216,010,657	110,873,176
1861	230,048,158	63,301,308
1862	134,141,380	92,801,710

Our own account of this trade is made up for fiscal years ending June 30, and it can therefore be compared definitely only in periods. It is impracticable to divide the fiscal year of the United States, and to reconstruct the summaries for calendar years:

Years.	EXPORTS TO GREAT BRITAIN.			IMPORTS FROM GR'T BRITAIN.
	Domestic.	Foreign.	Total.	
1855–'56	$160,742,372	$1,618,435	$162,360,807	$122,268,068
1856–'57	183,650,472	3,195,319	186,845,791	130,413,093
1857–'58	156,015,200	12,080,648	168,094,848	93,780,658
1858–'59	171,155,766	2,790,087	174,045,853	125,764,421
1859–'60	197,280,730	6,060,165	203,340,921	138,696,484
1860–'61	116,583,955	3,951,968	120,535,923	129,910,377
1861–'62	105,894,554	4,699,602	110,594,156	88,481,430
1862–'63	111,436,229	9,181,577	120,617,806	113,136,700

The British account does not include gold and silver bullion or coin, while the account of the United States does. The total value of specie and bullion sent to Great Britain among our exports in the seven years ending with June, 1862, was $236,751,778, and the total received from Great Britain in the same period was $55,894,096.* The detail of this exchange of specie was as follows, as given in the United States record for fiscal years—the British statistics being for calendar years:

	Exports to England.	Imports from England.
1855–'56	$34,161,062	$421,771
1856–'57	50,890,268	4,069,054
1857–'58	39,636,001	0,754,357
1858–'59	41,760,051	147,383
1859–'60	33,360,575	101,371
1860–'61	12,174,820	32,678,440
1861–'62*	24,729,001	11,721,720
1862–'63	50,339,267	238,498

British account.

	Imports into England from United States.	Exports to United States.
1856	Not given	£96,227
1857	Not given	659,110
1858	£4,811,772	202,667
1859	9,672,981	14,342
1860	4,792,582	1,727,220
1861	66,683	7,381,953
1862	10,064,162	37,528
1863	6,147,524	54,195

NOTE.—The importations of gold and silver coin and bullion were exempted by law from entry inwards at the custom house until the passing of the act of 20 & 21 Vict., cap. 62, in the year 1857.

Changing these to United States values they become:

	Imports into England.	Exports to United States.
1856	....	$465,738
1857	....	4,642,092
1858	$23,288,970	980,424
1859	46,817,229	60,415
1860	23,197,306	8,359,448
1861	322,745	35,728,652
1862	48,710,544	181,635
1863	30,434,016	263,303

The account of exports to the United States made up from British records is but $50,690,707 for eight years, against $56,132,595 recorded in the United States as imported from Great Britain, a difference of near five and a half millions of dollars. As the years 1856 and 1863 embrace very small exports, the correction of the United States account to calendar years would not remove the discrepancy. The account of imports into England is also short in British records as compared with our own. Taking the six years fully reported, the total by the British tables is $181,170,815; and by American, for fiscal years, $202,019,715, a difference of $20,848,910. This difference is also too large to be explained by the differences in the years. It is to be noticed, however, that the British entry was by *ounces* both for gold and silver, with a computed value "at the market price at the time of entry." This is probably the chief cause of the discrepancy.

Another and important point to be observed in the general comparison of the statistics is the incompleteness of the return of United States exports in the fiscal year ending June 30, 1861. For the last three quarters of that year certain ports of the southern States failed to make returns of the commerce transacted, which in most cases continued under the flag of the United States very nearly to the close of the fiscal year. At Savannah, Mobile, and New Orleans, the transactions of three entire quarters were not returned to the Treasury Department, and at all the other ports south of Norfolk two entire quarters were not returned. These ports were the channels through which nearly all the cotton, rice, and other staples of the south were exported, and the shipment of these was unprecedentedly active in the first months of 1861, and quite down to June of that year. In the original publication of the statistics of that year no correction was made for these omitted returns, and the effect is shown in the previous table of the total values exported to England as given by the two authorities. That country credits the United States with $239,046,158 in value of exports, while the return, uncorrected for the omission of southern ports, is but $116,583,955.

To make the best correction practicable in the case, it is assumed, as a minimum, that the exports at these ports for quarters not returned were at least equal to the transactions of the corresponding quarters of the previous year. The total value of the exports of those ports during the like period of the preceding year was $161,011,950 of domestic produce, and about $500,000 in value of foreign produce. This correction of the general aggregates cannot so readily be applied to the detail of countries. The great bulk of values was of cotton, and of this but a small proportion was to other countries than England. The evidence afforded by the British statistics is conclusive that the general sum assumed is too small, since the excess admitted by them is $170,000,000 in the three years 1860, 1861, and 1862.*

The British account of cotton alone received from the United States during the year ending with June, 1861, would show near a hundred millions of dollars' worth beyond the quantity officially returned in the United States as having been exported, the last-named aggregate being 207,342,265 pounds, value $22,651,923. The British report, which can in this case be made to conform in time to our fiscal year, credits the United States with 968,006,928 pounds, value $140,961,448.

	Pounds.	Value.
British	968,006,928	$140,961,448
American	207,342,265	22,651,923
Difference	760,664,663	118,309,525

This statement of differences in one article for the period of one year proves that if all the exports were embraced in the correction, a total not less than twenty millions greater would be required for the entire correction. The following table of monthly receipts of cotton in England from the United States shows the course of this trade for three years, and the enormous proportions it reached in 1861, for which year the United States records fail to show what it was:

* This correction was adopted in the finance report of the Secretary of the Treasury of December, 1863, increasing the total of domestic exports for the fiscal year 1860-'61 to $389,711,391, and the foreign to $21,145,427, the aggregate exports being $410,856,818.

Monthly receipts of cotton in England from the United States.

Month.	1859.		1860.		1861.	
	Quantity.	Value.	Quantity.	Value.	Quantity.	Value.
	Cwts.	*Pounds.*	*Cwts.*	*Pounds.*	*Cwts.*	*Pounds.*
January	177,334	[illegible],010	316,856	[illegible]	172,605	[illegible]
February	994,464	3,191,255	1,204,091	3,[illegible]	939,970	3,129,833
March	711,318	2,414,110	1,[illegible]	4,[illegible]	1,494,391	4,[illegible]
April	[illegible],312	2,161,[illegible]	1,[illegible]	3,[illegible],631	1,254,[illegible]	4,[illegible],135
May	[illegible]	2,212,[illegible]	1,233,749	3,814,761	[illegible]	3,[illegible]
June	1,[illegible],547	4,[illegible]	1,610,704	5,[illegible],978	[illegible],813	3,[illegible]
Half year	4,725,153	13,489,[illegible]	7,194,635	21,[illegible]	5,874,835	[illegible]
July	1,1[illegible],967	4,[illegible]	701,192	1,[illegible],551	840,064	3,[illegible]
August	[illegible],291	1,479,504	[illegible],974	1,[illegible],419	440,451	1,[illegible],837
September	351,626	1,[illegible]	179,344	546,010	148,464	657,[illegible]
October	[illegible]	678,[illegible]	130,732	405,011	3,630	10,458
November	221,840	730,851	82,708	175,634	[illegible]	1,465
December	1,440,797	4,641,[illegible]	1,044,250	3,472,111	4,[illegible]	20,[illegible]
Half year	3,861,319	12,759,707	2,768,424	8,418,082	1,442,334	5,[illegible],199
Year	8,586,672	[illegible]	9,963,319	30,069,719	7,317,169	26,670,[illegible]

Converting these into the quantities and values of the United States, the receipts of cotton in England for the three calendar years became:

	Pounds.	Value.
1859	961,707,264	$136,824,762
1860	1,115,891,728	145,537,340
1861	819,522,928	129,084,731

Even after the first of July, when the ports of the United States were closed to all legal trade, and for which no estimate has been made, the quantity of American cotton received in England was very great, amounting to 161,563,808 pounds, value $28,382,723. Probably the larger share of that received in England in July was cleared from southern ports before the last of June, and therefore it properly belongs with the additions made to correct that account in comparison with our own.

Recurring to the summaries of exports and imports between the two countries, compared on a previous page, we may assume a correction of the export values of United States records given for 1860–'61 and 1861–'62, equal to the two values of cotton shown to be in excess in this last calculation, namely: $118,309,525 in 1860–'61, and $28,382,723 in 1861–'62. More clearly, these are corrections on the first and second half years of 1861; and whatever may be the deduction from them on account of the later months of 1861 is fully made up by the export of other articles of which no account has been taken. The addition to the United States is therefore the sum of $146,692,248, still leaving a small deficit in the difference between this sum and $170,000,000 before shown to be the British excess for three years, exclusive of the foreign exports. These foreign exports amount to $14,731,735, leaving the actual difference about ten millions of dollars.

The other portions of the series agree very well with each other. There is reason to believe, however, that the United States record is generally short of the full values as regards produce actually landed for consumption in England. Many cargoes of provisions, grain, and flour clear for Irish or Channel ports for orders; and this was more frequently the case in 1861, 1862, and 1863, than in previous years. Apparently being cleared for British ports, and so recorded at United States ports, they do not enter at those ports, and do not appear in their imports. During the year 1862 one hundred vessels touched at Cork for orders, of which a considerable share ultimately proceeded to continental ports.

It is, moreover, established beyond doubt that there are large deficiencies in the report of outward cargoes, particularly at the port of New York. There being no outward inspection, and clearance being always given on the oath of the shipper or agent, a degree of inaccuracy has grown up, which is mainly the consequence of haste. Undervaluations and imperfect schedules of cargo occur where no intent to evade the law exists, particularly as no questions of revenue are involved. Clearance only on the verification of cargo by an outward inspector, as in nearly every European state, would be the only practicable measure for correcting these omissions, and for securing an absolutely full report of exports.

COMPARISON OF EXPORTS FROM GREAT BRITAIN TO THE UNITED STATES WITH THE REPORTED IMPORTS OF THE UNITED STATES RECORDS.

The chief fact disclosed by these comparisons is the gigantic character of the trade conducted through British ports for other nations, and for the general markets of the world, from which our direct shipping is being withdrawn. Either in the crude form in which they were imported, or in partial or complete transformation as manufactures, vast quantities of the staple products of the United States pass through England to other markets of final consumption in every year.

Taking the aggregates exchanged for six years preceding the war, or including one year of partial disturbance, each single year of the series gives a similar result, and confirms the general conclusion. The British record is short, comparing calendar with the nearest corresponding fiscal years, as follows:

	British statement deficient.	British statement in excess.
1856	$12,600,398	....
1857	33,630,021	....
1858	19.279,145	....
1859	7,571,624	....
1860	27,723,306	....
1861	65,842,071	....
1862	....	$6,320,260

The exports of British produce and manufactures are reported at the "declared real value," or on the statement of the exporter, while the exports of foreign and colonial produce are at "computed real value"—a value determined upon the reported quantities by the officers of the customs. It can scarcely be believed that the values reported when entering United States ports are in excess, nor does there appear any probable correction of these entered values which will remove the discrepancy. The solution is undoubtedly to be found in the account of remittances in the form of bills of exchange drawn against the exports of United States produce, the extent of which remittances can only be inferred from the debt of the United States held abroad, in connexion with other causes.

According to a report of the Secretary of the Treasury, made to the Senate in 1854, the amount of American stocks and loans reported to be held by foreigners June 30, 1853, was two hundred and twenty-two millions of dollars. Large sums were also known to exist of which no report could be obtained, estimated at a total nearly equal to that reported. The increase accruing in the next seven years we do not stop to estimate. French authorities have estimated the capital held by foreigners in United States national, State, and municipal stocks, including bank and railroad stocks, at a total sum of five hundred millions. Dividends and interest paid on this sum, averaging six per cent. per annum, would require remittances to the extent of thirty millions, for which sum there would of course be no commercial equivalent, either in commodities or in money. To this must be added the expenditures of travellers and the remittances of emigrants, together not less than five millions annually. The sum of thirty-five millions, therefore, is in all probability remitted in bills of exchange to Europe, and the excess of our exports over imports in recent years is to this extent accounted for; and whatever remains of the apparent excess of exports to Great Britain over imports may be balanced by the payment there of excesses of importation over exportation with certain other countries with whom our accounts are to some extent settled in England, amounting in 1861 to fifty one millions of dollars, due from us on our trade with the West Indies, South America, Asia, Africa, &c.

The extent of the annual differences appearing on the face of the commercial statements is large, and it does not appear to have attracted the attention its importance deserves. Taking the aggregates exchanged for six years preceding the war, or including one year of partial interruption or disturbance, 1861, as given in the British account, and exclusive of specie, the nominal balance appears highly favorable to the United States. The two sums, 1856 to the close of 1861, are:

Imports into Great Britain	$1,124,750,600
Exports from Great Britain	683,783,700
Difference	440,966,900

Or an average of $73,494,483 annually. Deducting the excess of specie sent to England, for which we must take the statement of the United States, and which was $167,750,401, or $27,958,400 yearly, the balance still remaining is $45,536,083 yearly in favor of the United States. After all consideration has been given to the account of remittances just referred to, the general state of these gigantic exchanges is less unfavorable to the United States than has generally been supposed.

TABULAR STATEMENTS OF EXCHANGES BETWEEN GREAT BRITAIN AND THE UNITED STATES, FOR SEVEN YEARS, 1856 TO 1862, FROM BRITISH RECORDS.

The following tabular statements of the entire exchanges of the United States with Great Britain in detail is copied from the last annual volume of British Trade and Navigation Reports, for 1862. For 1863 only a few specific articles can be obtained, the monthly publications of the British government distinguishing countries only in a few leading articles. The first table embodies such as are so stated by countries, comparing the three years 1861 to 1863 only, and converting the values and quantities to like terms with those of the United States.

This preliminary table shows the enormous development of the petroleum trade within three years, and that grain, flour, and petroleum, have to some extent supplied the place of cotton as the basis of exchange on England. The sum of values of these leading articles is sustained in a most unexpected degree.

Quantities of leading articles.

Articles.	1861.	1862.	1863.
Cotton.............. ....pounds....	819,500,528	13,524,224	6,304,0[illegible]0
Petroleum...... ....gallons....	1[illegible]9,[illegible]	4,07[illegible]	[illegible],417,22[illegible]
Wheat............. ....bushels....	20,0[illegible]1,9[illegible]	29,[illegible].1[illegible]	16,071,[illegible]
Wheat flour........... ....barrels....	1,[illegible]7,4[illegible]	2,249,707	1,2[illegible],911
Indian corn......................bushels....	24,722,816	21,8[illegible]0,3[illegible]	20,774,976
Entered for consumption.			
Wheat................. ....bushels....	20,279,608	30,155,84[illegible]	16,291,489
Wheat flour.......................barrels....	1,989,231	2,[illegible]7,110	1,[illegible]78,411

Values of leading articles.

Articles.	1861.	1862.	1863.
Cotton..........	$129,600,870	$3,117,163	$2,435,125
Petroleum..	8,3[illegible]	6[illegible]2,9[illegible]	2,72[illegible],[illegible]
Wheat............	29,354,411	41,[illegible],514	20,371,[illegible]
Flour..	13,[illegible]4,635	15,471,44[illegible]	7,5[illegible],224
Indian corn...........	22,172,927	16,75[illegible],0[illegible]5	19,2[illegible]6,774

Indian corn, known to be nearly all from the United States, is not distinguished as to countries; but it is assumed as approximately correct.. Other staple exports, as of cured meats, lard, tallow, butter and cheese, and tobacco, are not separately stated in the British reports. They will be found in detail in the comparative table following those taken from the British records, prepared for fiscal years from the United States returns.

Imports from the United States.—(From British official record.)

Articles.	Quantities. 1856.	1857.	1858.	1859.	1860.	1861.	1862.	Computed real value. 1856.	1857.	1858.	1859.	1860.	1861.	1862.
								£.	£.	£.	£.	£.	£.	£.
Ashes, pearl and pot ……cwts.	11,673	33,498	81,[illegible]	15,599	23,910	90,[illegible]	39,770	25,[illegible]	67,550	37,837	81,799	34,344	34,118	63,539
Bacon ……do..	308,397	380,718	145,672	35,170	156,656	387,314	1,037,596	832,114	791,166	535,691	84,639	434,598	844,677	1,819,788
Bark, tanners' ……do..	57,580	80,463	68,128	49,031	59,831	34,459	55,549	33,965	44,925	68,319	30,970	90,041	15,401	31,295
Peruvian ……do..	5,280	6,339	3,[illegible]	8,732	725	428	32	58,[illegible]	65,915	44,473	37,068	13,941	6,[illegible]	816
Beef, salted ……do..	138,437	92,[illegible]	134,[illegible]	168,716	191,821	195,007	178,111	288,[illegible]	524,[illegible]	681,287	373,814	347,439	703,[illegible]	318,[illegible]
Butter ……do..	8,005	1,387	8,319	2,390	62,015	180,500	374,348	7,[illegible]	6,398	9,348	12,659	367,439	815,861	1,179,010
Caoutchouc ……do..	398	2,917	1,[illegible]	8,541	8,085	9,251	676	8,744	18,377	11,891	87,733	94,738	78,394	6,807
manufactures of. lbs..	388,656	304,183	64,[illegible]	130,500	168,715	94,666	60,000	48,396	34,238	9,083	13,036	14,623	9,[illegible]	4,644
Cheese ……cwts.	68,258	49,498	37,708	60,[illegible]	167,430	323,461	353,500	173,508	116,[illegible]	131,098	155,788	623,463	741,[illegible]	788,863
Clocks ……No..	84,958	90,234	103,397	120,[illegible]	162,355	187,619	128,438	39,979	44,916	43,563	82,444	84,[illegible]	42,[illegible]	60,767
Copper ore ……tons	674	2,028	8,354	1,[illegible]	1,617	3,938	1,252	10,791	30,551	44,530	31,101	87,137	71,049	91,887
Copper ……do..		1,461	549	298	397	807	73		171,[illegible]	64,823	89,894	19,[illegible]	73,315	7,168
Corn: wheat ……qrs..	1,978,150	650,734	594,640	38,906	1,499,393	2,307,744	3,724,710	4,677,088	1,912,120	1,429,831	80,909	4,323,[illegible]	4,944,037	8,378,930
pease ……do..			4,[illegible]	5,739	29,737	42,503	15,558			9,111	10,029	84,347	79,650	37,910
maize ……do..	1,000,871	418,[illegible]	394,[illegible]	3,364	430,334	1,721,334	1,519,428	1,801,383	720,945	680,290	4,782	713,737	2,[illegible],357	2,168,037
wheat meal & flour cwts.	2,492,517	1,464,[illegible]	1,764,795	916,462	2,854,[illegible]	3,734,[illegible]	4,[illegible],514	2,892,517	1,294,738	1,331,[illegible]	181,344	1,[illegible]	2,[illegible]	3,837,[illegible]
Cotton, raw ……do..	8,[illegible],643	5,846,[illegible]	7,439,[illegible]	8,[illegible]	8,[illegible]	7,316,[illegible]	124,[illegible]	[illegible],150,[illegible]	21,554,877	24,[illegible]	28,[illegible]	30,[illegible]	23,[illegible]	1,831,377
Guano ……tons	1,247	2,167	4,[illegible]	2,919	347	1,575	69,547	7,163	8,[illegible]	39,[illegible]	17,[illegible]	1,[illegible]	6,[illegible]	630,112
Hams ……cwts.	13,737	13,[illegible]	6,646	2,654	13,[illegible]	88,[illegible]	198,277	47,[illegible]	47,743	19,617	10,544	65,[illegible]	68,343	348,[illegible]
Hemp, undressed ……do..	9,612	183,966	14,645	9,582	67	163	41,[illegible]	8,101	150,247	18,514	7,663	100	187	56,[illegible]
Hides, not tanned ……do..	1,678	28,500	3,[illegible]	16,550	53,591	51,648	13,334	4,867	131,452	7,318	48,333	183,763	108,916	38,[illegible]
tanned ……lbs..			180,344	783,287	1,252,116	1,338,[illegible]	1,873,[illegible]			7,688	38,[illegible]	65,403	38,516	66,375
Hops ……cwts	78	381			38,548	33,375	58,712	175	844			234,[illegible]	171,[illegible]	384,579
Iron and steel, wro't or unwro't.										2,[illegible]	4,[illegible]	7,[illegible]	74,[illegible]	23,409
Lard ……cwts.	131,[illegible]	169,[illegible]	105,[illegible]	87,[illegible]	130,871	973,558	519,316	379,387	561,694	[illegible],464	162,[illegible]	390,[illegible]	799,731	1,[illegible],749
Logwood ……tons	10,739	10,593	5,923	7,334	5,655	4,[illegible]	8,544	65,377	83,010	38,747	30,508	41,481	33,691	87,[illegible]
Oil, spermaceti ……do..	8,778	3,916	3,501	3,[illegible]	3,581	4,159	3,[illegible]	288,[illegible]	314,093	332,[illegible]	348,[illegible]	368,149	[illegible]	223,544
train or blubber ……do..	887	371	370	231	1,[illegible]	1,613	8,[illegible]	12,[illegible]	16,[illegible]	13,[illegible]	7,438	34,[illegible]	64,157	117,033
lard ……cwts.						1,313	43,317			2,633		5,[illegible]	3,[illegible]	101,891
or spirits of turpentine. do..	69,978	88,540	69,378	116,747	197,084	74,838	9,079	319,087	397,528	177,784	912,348	913,917	158,[illegible]	33,141
Oil-seed cake ……tons	58,781	43,139	39,[illegible]	38,438	37,[illegible]	37,345	89,[illegible]	226,104	374,811	269,188	277,[illegible]	314,319	261,578	594,[illegible]
Petroleum ……cwts						9,953	881,048						8,[illegible]	634,[illegible]
Pork, salted ……do..	69,645	58,445	44,[illegible]	69,195	88,042	45,190	163,947	187,[illegible]	68,779	96,043	140,973	108,584	102,[illegible]	333,794
Quicksilver ……lbs..		379,573	164,538			70,508	303,453		38,257	18,018			8,391	38,347
Rice, not rough ……cwts.	80,954	88,764	48,771	51,[illegible]	69,[illegible]	49,366	38,473	77,801	89,[illegible]	84,[illegible]	84,457	81,[illegible]	83,[illegible]	69,[illegible]
rough ……qrs..	6,807	7,168	8,322	2,226		1,673		18,781	21,505	4,[illegible]	2,[illegible]		6,147	
Rosin ……cwts.	517,[illegible]	648,[illegible]	688,[illegible]	698,[illegible]	668,[illegible]	457,[illegible]	67,[illegible]	838,[illegible]	308,254	328,173	308,[illegible]	178,[illegible]	688,128	44,370
Saltpetre ……do..	5	78,[illegible]	10,334	416	368			3	158,[illegible]	19,[illegible]	[illegible]	3,[illegible]		
Seed, clover ……do..	4,[illegible]	38,[illegible]	48,[illegible]	38,458	86,348	79,[illegible]	64,916	18,[illegible]	103,[illegible]	117,[illegible]	188,[illegible]	194,[illegible]	[illegible]	116,161
Skins and furs, undressed, viz:														
Beaver ……No..	8,[illegible]	7,[illegible]	11,871	13,[illegible]	7,[illegible]	6,[illegible]	19,[illegible]	4,[illegible]	3,[illegible]	8,[illegible]	8,[illegible]	9,[illegible]	[illegible]	6,388

Articles														
Dry? ... do.	30,[illegible]	30,[illegible]	17,[illegible]	[illegible]	30,[illegible]	[illegible]	13,710	11,[illegible]	[illegible]	[illegible]	[illegible]	10,[illegible]	10,[illegible]	[illegible]
[illegible] ... do.	44,[illegible]	[illegible]	[illegible]	72,[illegible]	[illegible]	[illegible]	37,[illegible]	[illegible]	[illegible]	17,[illegible]	[illegible]	[illegible]	[illegible]	[illegible]
[illegible] ... do.	[illegible]	[illegible]	[illegible]	[illegible]	11,[illegible]	[illegible]	13,[illegible]	[illegible]	[illegible]	[illegible]	1,[illegible]	[illegible]	14,[illegible]	[illegible]
[illegible] ... do.	[illegible]	72,[illegible]	[illegible]	[illegible]	[illegible]			[illegible]	[illegible]	[illegible]	[illegible]	[illegible]		
[illegible] ... do.	[illegible]	[illegible]	[illegible]	1,[illegible]	1,[illegible]	1,[illegible]	1,[illegible]	[illegible]	[illegible]	[illegible]	[illegible]	74,[illegible]	[illegible]	[illegible]
Other ... do.	[illegible]	1,[illegible]	[illegible]	7,[illegible]	[illegible]	4,[illegible]	4,[illegible]	[illegible]	[illegible]	[illegible]	[illegible]	[illegible]	[illegible]	[illegible]
[illegible] ... do.	481,713	[illegible]	[illegible]	[illegible]	[illegible]	[illegible]	[illegible]	[illegible]	[illegible]	[illegible]	[illegible]	113,[illegible]	[illegible]	[illegible]
Spermaceti, lbs.?								1,[illegible]	[illegible]	[illegible]	[illegible]	7,[illegible]	[illegible]	[illegible]
Sugar, unrefined? ... cwts.			[illegible]	[illegible]	[illegible]	[illegible]	[illegible]			41,[illegible]	[illegible]	[illegible]	[illegible]	[illegible]
Tallow? ... do.	[illegible]	[illegible]	14,[illegible]	19,[illegible]	[illegible]	[illegible]	[illegible]	[illegible]	[illegible]	[illegible]	[illegible]	347,[illegible]	[illegible]	[illegible]
Tar? ... [illegible]	1,[illegible]	[illegible]	673	1,[illegible]	1,[illegible]	[illegible]	[illegible]	12,[illegible]	[illegible]	4,[illegible]	12,[illegible]	[illegible]	[illegible]	1,[illegible]
Tea? ... lbs.	[illegible]	[illegible]	[illegible]	[illegible]	[illegible]	[illegible]	[illegible]	7,[illegible]	[illegible]	[illegible]	[illegible]	43,[illegible]	3,[illegible]	[illegible]
Tobacco, unmanufactured ... do.	[illegible]	[illegible]	[illegible]	[illegible]	[illegible]	[illegible]	[illegible]	1,[illegible]	1,[illegible]	1,[illegible]	1,[illegible]	1,[illegible]	1,[illegible]	1,[illegible]
manufactured ... do.	1,[illegible]	1,[illegible]	1,[illegible]	1,[illegible]	1,[illegible]	1,[illegible]	1,[illegible]	[illegible]	[illegible]	[illegible]	[illegible]	[illegible]	[illegible]	[illegible]
Turpentine? ... [illegible]	[illegible]	[illegible]	[illegible]	[illegible]	[illegible]	[illegible]	3,[illegible]	[illegible]	[illegible]	[illegible]	[illegible]	[illegible]	[illegible]	3,[illegible]
Whale fins? ... [illegible]	[illegible]	[illegible]	[illegible]	[illegible]	[illegible]	[illegible]	[illegible]	[illegible]	[illegible]	37,[illegible]	[illegible]	[illegible]	[illegible]	[illegible]
Wood and timber:														
Not sawed or split? ... [illegible]	[illegible]	[illegible]	[illegible]	[illegible]	[illegible]	[illegible]	4,[illegible]	[illegible]	[illegible]	[illegible]	[illegible]	[illegible]	[illegible]	[illegible]
Deals, battens, &c.? ... do.	[illegible]	[illegible]	[illegible]	[illegible]	[illegible]	[illegible]	[illegible]	[illegible]	[illegible]	[illegible]	[illegible]	[illegible]	[illegible]	[illegible]
Staves? ... do.	[illegible]	[illegible]	[illegible]	[illegible]	[illegible]	[illegible]	[illegible]	173,[illegible]	[illegible]	[illegible]	[illegible]	117,[illegible]	[illegible]	[illegible]
Wool, sheep and lambs'? ... lbs.	[illegible]	3,[illegible]	[illegible]	[illegible]	1,[illegible]	1,[illegible]	[illegible]	1,[illegible]	[illegible]	[illegible]	[illegible]	[illegible]	[illegible]	14,[illegible]
Woollen rags, torn up to be used as wool? ... lbs.						1,771,[illegible]	[illegible]						[illegible]	[illegible]
All other articles								[illegible]	1,[illegible]	[illegible]	[illegible]	[illegible]	[illegible]	[illegible]
Total value								[illegible],647,[illegible]	[illegible]	[illegible]	34,[illegible]	[illegible]	[illegible]	[illegible],713,[illegible]

Exports to the United States, the produce and manufacture of the United Kingdom.

Articles.	Quantities.							Declared real value.						
	1856.	1857.	1858.	1859.	1860.	1861.	1862.	1856.	1857.	1858.	1859.	1860.	1861.	1862.
								£.	£.	£.	£.	£.	£.	£.
Alkali, soda..........cwts	730,[illegible]	830,041	654,977	1,103,990	1,090,380	431,380	1,043,639	317,393	374,160	439,697	576,459	539,976	913,[illegible]	453,094
Apparel..........	....	....	....	....	....	....	....	1,664,313	1,303,191	1,019,634	1,509,227	1,417,592	629,198	703,164
Fire-arms (small).....no.	....	....	10,598	17,[illegible]	16,778	44,73[illegible]	343,[illegible]	....	....	10,527	83,147	84,780	104,990	971,770
Bags, empty..........doz	303,470	192,[illegible]	199,728	187,434	253,419	163,130	183,181	138,090	102,391	92,301	79,440	104,673	74,105	67,808
Beer and ale..........bbls	31,782	25,974	24,[illegible]	23,914	21,305	7,380	7,780	140,067	114,950	108,117	106,[illegible]	100,373	31,43[illegible]	31,440
Bleaching materials.cwts	....	....	97,[illegible]	132,617	137,[illegible]	75,[illegible]	132,[illegible]	....	....	38,[illegible]	62,927	70,146	34,416	62,388
Books, printed..........do.	11,977	11,000	9,178	11,774	12,513	8,537	2,440	152,111	133,037	110,831	138,[illegible]	140,941	62,348	50,[illegible]
Coals..........tons	247,404	197,507	301,004	304,816	330,[illegible]	371,[illegible]	287,449	146,970	133,091	161,946	185,[illegible]	199,779	246,090	202,019
Copper..........cwts	33,189	27,315	18,495	73,818	12,500	3,170	9,370	219,279	140,670	83,590	130,[illegible]	64,347	14,197	41,[illegible]
Cottons..........yards	227,[illegible],736	177,842,814	154,018,134	[illegible],146,[illegible]	[illegible],776,[illegible]	74,080,537	97,375,780	3,771,508	3,070,[illegible]	2,813,580	3,994,711	3,849,915	1,254,343	1,042,338
Cottons..........value	....	....	....	....	....	....	....	640,084	649,035	376,405	612,[illegible]	644,281	394,751	550,311
Drugs and chemicals..........	....	....	....	....	....	....	....	138,037	80,340	113,789	117,670	125,027	52,714	117,333
Earthenware & porcelain.	....	....	....	....	....	....	....	364,449	347,357	278,610	508,045	624,183	216,916	397,916
Glass manufactures..........	....	....	....	....	....	....	....	70,430	46,571	40,090	58,790	87,070	27,378	52,[illegible]
Hardware & cutlery.cwts	149,604	143,694	88,790	183,490	197,430	79,797	49,634	1,229,419	1,031,867	654,407	1,179,039	1,054,909	431,456	399,080
Iron, wr't and unwr't.tons	330,513	202,526	173,908	289,041	294,589	108,054	130,190	3,339,077	3,170,087	1,440,[illegible]	1,949,547	3,138,340	955,533	1,393,713
Lead and shot..........do	4,091	8,344	2,815	3,005	4,137	767	19,100	111,879	61,[illegible]	71,011	67,439	98,531	16,154	892,748
Leather wro't and unwro't	1,744,169	1,193,915	....	....	....	....	....	147,290	109,346	78,469	172,944	123,777	33,651	35,842
Linens..........yards	72,338,208	46,089,479	44,183,[illegible]	64,732,834	80,988,394	31,169,077	65,318,318	2,154,690	1,425,156	1,344,634	1,944,314	1,993,437	642,870	1,694,046
Linens..........value	....	....	....	....	....	....	....	199,220	158,108	138,605	178,509	191,730	87,670	209,549
Machinery and mill work.	....	....	....	....	....	....	....	123,605	46,742	24,778	33,610	42,230	30,724	30,637
Oil, linseed..........galls	1,[illegible],466	[illegible]	771,090	1,081,813	692,780	14,420	85,[illegible]	133,728	82,465	97,697	130,173	74,774	1,990	7,893
Painters' colors..........	....	....	....	....	....	....	....	94,209	82,131	54,354	99,814	73,351	42,337	38,791
Plate and watches..........	....	....	....	....	....	....	....	164,090	108,738	49,291	67,080	83,[illegible]	11,737	16,448
Salt..........tons	343,430	[illegible]	297,000	319,678	339,077	772,380	151,134	174,145	99,741	108,370	99,770	119,[illegible]	79,780	63,231
Silk manufactures..........	....	....	....	....	....	....	....	570,213	540,990	379,090	690,[illegible]	641,[illegible]	169,118	812,148
Spirits..........galls	[illegible],379	683,897	180,795	416,617	425,020	112,[illegible]	172,000	67,940	78,978	43,590	62,470	68,[illegible]	18,030	32,918
Stationery..........	....	....	....	....	....	....	....	69,177	69,185	43,367	72,035	44,034	13,949	38,670
Tin, unwrought.....cwts	3,334	2,672	6,011	6,100	3,517	1,[illegible]	18,330	21,378	25,949	37,090	30,901	33,165	7,323	105,547
Tin plates..........	....	....	....	....	....	....	....	1,059,303	981,477	844,945	1,093,799	1,018,536	417,300	[illegible]
Wool, sheep and lambs', lbs	....	....	882,491	454,948	191,772	1,370,[illegible]	1,933,457	....	....	8,490	32,567	7,205	71,[illegible]	98,530
Woollens, by piece...pieces	698,537	957,030	390,190	930,120	913,107	440,797	1,087,113	1,610,407	1,649,529	1,090,791	1,902,670	1,730,738	852,278	1,831,300
by the yard..yds.	34,514,588	33,443,356	28,442,180	33,607,620	38,537,607	27,594,083	6,380,947	1,463,047	1,428,387	1,324,010	2,113,179	2,446,415	1,108,178	613,070
of value...value.	....	....	....	....	....	....	....	930,250	311,854	203,479	378,438	317,540	82,271	192,735
Woollen yarn..........lbs.	141,344	183,388	130,648	371,[illegible]	118,167	113,438	197,320	14,013	18,430	13,167	38,390	14,[illegible]	14,770	38,919
All other articles....value.	....	....	....	....	....	....	....	....	....	671,343	1,087,538	1,037,714	492,628	665,337
Total value..........	....	....	....	....	....	....	....	21,[illegible]	[illegible]	14,491,448	22,553,[illegible]	21,692,[illegible]	9,064,504	14,387,179

Exports to the United States of foreign and colonial produce and manufactures.

Articles.	Quantities. 1856.	1857.	1858.	1859.	1860.	1861.	1862.	Computed real value. 1856.	1857.	1858.	1859.	1860.	1861.	1862.
								£.	£.	£.	£.	£.	£.	£.
Argol ....cwts.	3,[illegible]	2,[illegible]	4,181	1,[illegible]	4,[illegible]	1,304	2,[illegible]	12,474	8,[illegible]	12,[illegible]	8,[illegible]	[illegible]	5,317	9,047
Arms and ammunition										[illegible]	1,[illegible]	[illegible]	84,051	61,[illegible]
Bark, Peruvian ....cwts.	[illegible]	[illegible]	2,912	4,[illegible]	3,[illegible]	1,[illegible]	[illegible]	7,130	[illegible]	[illegible]	[illegible]	[illegible]	[illegible]	[illegible]
Bristles ....lbs.	9,[illegible]		4,107	[illegible]	[illegible]	7,[illegible]	10,[illegible]	1,[illegible]		[illegible]	3,[illegible]	16,[illegible]	[illegible]	2,[illegible]
Caoutchouc ....cwts.	4,772	710	5,742	1,[illegible]	[illegible]	[illegible]	7,[illegible]	87,974	4,[illegible]	[illegible]	13,[illegible]	3,[illegible]	8,973	[illegible]
Cochineal ....do.	1,073	1,110	2,126	1,316	1,[illegible]	[illegible]	1,636	40,[illegible]	[illegible]	64,[illegible]	[illegible]	33,[illegible]	6,[illegible]	27,990
Coffee ....lbs.			10,389	1,[illegible]	1,[illegible]	12,010	[illegible]			[illegible]	[illegible]	54	307	[illegible]
Cotton, raw ....cwts.			1,[illegible]	[illegible]	[illegible]	[illegible]	[illegible]			3,[illegible]	4,742	1,[illegible]	[illegible],441	1,[illegible]
Cream of tartar ....do.	1,[illegible]	[illegible]	3,063	1,817	8,718	3,[illegible]	1,644	10,[illegible]	[illegible]	14,[illegible]	9,971	17,417	19,251	10,[illegible]
Currants ....do.	2,181	14,[illegible]	21,[illegible]	[illegible],145	1,[illegible]	10,[illegible]	13,916	4,[illegible]	[illegible]	[illegible],472	43,917	1,[illegible]	11,971	[illegible]
Flax, dressed & undressed do.		1,[illegible]	[illegible]	6,[illegible]	[illegible]		377		[illegible]	704	7,[illegible]	[illegible]		1,[illegible]
Gloves, of leather ....pairs.	30,[illegible]	[illegible]	35,[illegible]	15,[illegible]	10,[illegible]	4,[illegible]	3,[illegible]	2,[illegible]	2,[illegible]	3,[illegible]	1,716	1,[illegible]	[illegible]	[illegible]
Gum, animal and copal ....cwts.	2,[illegible]	[illegible]	[illegible]	2,810	2,[illegible]	31	[illegible]	6,[illegible]	5,[illegible]	1,[illegible]	7,874	11,[illegible]	131	[illegible]
Arabic ....do.	7,614	8,347	10,726	[illegible]	4,[illegible]	11,[illegible]	[illegible]	13,316	10,[illegible]	39,[illegible]	37,[illegible]	7,[illegible]	18,381	42,[illegible]
lac dye ....do.	[illegible]	104	1,[illegible]	[illegible]	1,[illegible]	[illegible]	1,[illegible]	9,074	[illegible]	8,[illegible]	1,381	4,[illegible]	3,[illegible]	6,[illegible]
other kinds ....do.	23,[illegible]	10,[illegible]	24,[illegible]	33,[illegible]	24,[illegible]	2,410	16,[illegible]	34,[illegible]	[illegible]	[illegible]	[illegible]	[illegible]	7,[illegible]	46,[illegible]
Hair, manufactures of, or of goat's wool								11,[illegible]	3,[illegible]	18,[illegible]	[illegible]	10,[illegible]		6,[illegible]
Hats or bonnets of straw ..No.	1,[illegible]	1,[illegible]	8,[illegible]	1,340	[illegible]	[illegible]		[illegible]	1,[illegible]	5,[illegible]	5,101	[illegible]	1,[illegible]	
Hemp, undressed ....cwts.	8,[illegible]	3,[illegible]	17,[illegible]	2,[illegible]	[illegible]	1,[illegible]	31,440	4,[illegible]	8,[illegible]	[illegible],710	3,[illegible]	[illegible]	1,[illegible]	[illegible]
jute ....do.	4,[illegible]	1,[illegible]		1,[illegible]	[illegible]	[illegible]	9,[illegible]	3,[illegible]	1,[illegible]		1,[illegible]	[illegible]	1,774	9,[illegible]
Hides, tanned ....do.	724		[illegible]	[illegible]	[illegible]	[illegible]	12,114	2,[illegible]		101,107	[illegible]	47,[illegible]	1,[illegible]	41,[illegible]
Indigo ....do.	2,715	2,[illegible]	5,[illegible]	[illegible]	4,[illegible]	14,[illegible]	15,325	[illegible]	113,[illegible]	[illegible]	[illegible]	154,[illegible]	[illegible]	[illegible]
Iron in bars ....tons	[illegible]	234	241	2,[illegible]	[illegible]	1,118	2,716	6,[illegible]	6,446	4,[illegible]	[illegible]	34,[illegible]	[illegible],447	[illegible]
Linen manufactures										1,[illegible]	[illegible]	5,[illegible]	9,[illegible]	[illegible]
Nitre, cubic ....cwts.			3,176		3,[illegible]	1,[illegible]	10,[illegible]			9,340		8,[illegible]	[illegible]	7,[illegible]
Nutmegs ....lbs.	70,752	[illegible]	[illegible],197	[illegible]	[illegible]	[illegible]	[illegible],136	6,[illegible]	12,[illegible]	11,[illegible]	10,[illegible]	1,[illegible]	7,131	1,316
Oil, turpentine ....cwts.						7,518	4,651						17,[illegible]	[illegible]
Opium ....lbs.	10,801	13,[illegible]	[illegible]	16,720	[illegible]	[illegible],170	[illegible]	8,151	10,[illegible]	[illegible]	[illegible],081	[illegible]	[illegible],704	[illegible]
Pepper ....do.			6,631	[illegible]	14,748	505	2,142,[illegible]			118	871	[illegible]	[illegible]	[illegible],711
Platting of chip, straw, &c do.	3,718	11,[illegible]	17,[illegible]	[illegible]	1,[illegible]		[illegible]	3,718	8,[illegible]	16,[illegible]	[illegible]	1,[illegible]		8
Quicksilver ....do.	34,[illegible]		[illegible]	[illegible]	140,630	[illegible]	[illegible],710	2,974		[illegible]	[illegible]	12,[illegible]	[illegible]	6,321
Rags for paper ....tons			6	[illegible]	[illegible]	[illegible]	2,[illegible]			[illegible]	19,953	2,[illegible]	743	[illegible],548
Raisins ....cwts.	[illegible]	[illegible]	13,[illegible]	17,[illegible]	3,[illegible]	[illegible]	[illegible]	1,[illegible]	1,[illegible]	[illegible],214	[illegible],210	8,[illegible]	30	1,[illegible]
Rice, not in the husk ....do.		1,[illegible]	9,340	2,[illegible]	[illegible]	[illegible],570	[illegible]		573	4,[illegible]	1,[illegible]	[illegible]	[illegible],987	13[illegible]
Saltpetre ....do.	4,019	1,[illegible]	4,[illegible]	2,[illegible]	6,015	[illegible]	51,[illegible]	7,[illegible]	7,[illegible]	6,[illegible]	2,[illegible]	16,164	975	[illegible]
Seeds, linseed ....qrs.			[illegible]		14,[illegible]		19,504			1,[illegible]		37,[illegible]		57,527
Senna ....lbs.	78,[illegible]	74,[illegible]	[illegible]	[illegible]	[illegible]	74,[illegible]	847,[illegible]	1,644	1,[illegible]	[illegible]	[illegible]	1,[illegible]	1,[illegible]	4,137
Silk, raw ....do.	10,[illegible]	[illegible]	73,[illegible]	112,[illegible]	[illegible]	87,[illegible]	101,[illegible]	16,[illegible]	[illegible],170	[illegible],964	114,[illegible]	72,[illegible]	[illegible]	[illegible],075
knubs and husks ....cwts.			[illegible]	[illegible]	34		2,[illegible]			[illegible]	[illegible]	[illegible]		[illegible],614

Exports to the United States of foreign and colonial produce and manufactures—Continued.

Articles.	Quantities.							Computed real value.						
	1856.	1857.	1858.	1859.	1860.	1861.	1862.	1856.	1857.	1858.	1859.	1860.	1861.	1862.
								£.	£.	£.	£.	£.	£.	£.
Silk manufactures:														
Broad stuffs and ribbons..lbs.	3,77?	3,0??	6??	9,0??	4,604	674	8,3??	9,0??	9,?07	8,???	7,0??	10,49?	1,?54	4,707
Skins, goat.....................no.	1??,7??	53,075	377,8??	147,14?	171,35?	123,4??	???,???	11,0??	8,4??	??,47?	14,179	14,3??	11,331	35,0??
Spelter..........................tons.	510	231	6??	1??	84	....	73?	13,1??	9,???	10,31?	2,204	9,0??	....	13,?55
Spirits, brandy, proof.....galls.	43,97?	37,6??	??,6??	47,21?	??,33?	7,0??	10,87?	??,17?	??,8??	7,8??	??,73?	8?,97?	3,3??	4,727
Sugar, unrefined..............cwts.	....	....	7	42	2,741	??,???	1,70?	....	....	11	6?	4,0??	34,5??	1,77?
Tar.................................lasts.	....	....	....	....	1	8	1,04?	....	....	....	....	17	14?	21,490
Tea.................................lbs.	18,41?	1,957,0??	??,387	7?,??4	??,??0	72?,33?	2,5??,5??	977	14?,???	6,3??	5,917	7,047	31,3??	391,0?4
Teeth, elephants'...........cwts.	67?	110	171	70?	15?	3?	8?	??,6??	4,7??	6,341	??,05?	5,0??	2??	1,3??
Tin, unwrought..................do..	1,3??	3,61?	3,3??	1,74?	2??	1,0??	4,377	9,???	19,0??	21,077	13,017	8,3??	6,53?	??,50?
Tobacco, manufactured, and cigars..........................lbs..	??,45?	11,???	3,61?	10,04?	3,37?	31,5??	??,??4	11,0??	2,0??	47?	1,341	33?	1,63?	1,???
Wine................................galls.	??,04?	??,10?	??,73?	61,34?	??,?51	18,14?	??,91?	94,1??	??,081	15,051	??,7??	3?,3??	4,7??	8,147
Wool, sheep and lambs'....lbs..	???,???	3,054,3??	3,3??,74?	3,9??,47?	2,041,3??	10,0??,047	11,5??,???	37,6??	213,6??	16?,4??	4??,???	???,27?	4??,4??	742,15?
Woollen manufactures........	....	....	....	....	....	....	....	8,27?	8??	4,47?	3??	3,147	9,77?	1,5?7
All other articles..............	....	....	....	....	....	....	....	188,???	???,2??	16?,3??	???,3??	2??,???	18?,07?	37?,?77
Total value........................	....	....	....	....	....	....	....	6??,77?	1,0??,?5?	1,3??,???	1,654,497	1,140,616	1,94?,17?	4,04?,?77
Total British and for'n produce.	....	....	....	....	....	....	....	22,616,677	30,076,0??	13,7??,701	24,417,???	2?,?07,6??	11,0??,???	1?,17?,?07
Total value of imports, exclusive of specie, from the United States, brought from page 43.	....	....	....	....	....	....	....	??,047,7??	33,047,5??	3?,???,??5	34,??4,0??	44,7?7,???	??,3??,???	?7,71?,15?

Exports of domestic produce of the United States to Great Britain, (from United States official records.)

Articles.		1869-'70.		1870-'71.		1871-'72.		1872-'73.	
		Quantities.	Values.	Quantities.	Values.	Quantities.	Values.	Quantities.	Values.
Animals			$1,300		$570		94,370		
Apples	bbls	4,116	99,674	32,027	109,373	83,395	37,168	37,395	$100,510
Ashes	cwt	163,000	307,247			4,681	87,[illegible]	5,397	40,338
Bark, oak			73,[illegible]		54,164		84,739		151,[illegible]
Beef	tierces	61,011	1,732,395	41,530	808,719	63,185	1,479,[illegible]	68,[illegible]	1,[illegible],730
Books and maps			94,941		13,465		16,[illegible]		48,917
Brushes and brooms			763		3,109		3,518		11,670
Butter	lbs	3,363,196	439,460	11,117,474	1,649,137	19,346,767	3,077,068	38,983,957	8,150,671
Candles, sperm, &c	do	100,646	31,453	403,858	108,[illegible]	798,816	47,015	[illegible]	75,257
Carriages			8,304		9,525		2,670		3,[illegible]
Cheese	lbs	11,980,419	1,192,456	87,[illegible]	8,[illegible],678	[illegible],834,[illegible]	8,[illegible],047	38,678,334	3,655,119
Clothing			11,316		17,820		10,770		29,674
Cloverseed	bush	104,[illegible]	535,358	188,994	978,310	88,401	990,343	897,851	1,579,913
Copper and brass manufactures			[illegible],630		663,194		416,415		333,017
Cotton	lbs	1,[illegible],138,789	134,[illegible],780	807,342,553	22,651,[illegible]	3,843,389	804,979	9,480,589	5,[illegible]
Cotton manufactures			116,198		193,505		100,[illegible]		34,[illegible]
Drugs and medicines			69,517		54,[illegible]		64,775		122,[illegible]
Fish	bbls	324	1,655	1,308	8,680	1,549	9,604	1,530	b 10,167
Flaxseed	bush	2,394	3,601	68,503	69,528			38,446	90,085
Furs and fur skins			1,[illegible],397		894,318		496,198		1,471,878
Gold and silver coin			14,[illegible],734		8,541,652		12,325,[illegible]		38,074,788
Gold and silver bullion			15,[illegible],326		4,[illegible],110		10,345,507		9,[illegible],168
Gold and silver manufactures			31,613		5,430		6,182		31,[illegible]
Hams and bacon	lbs	19,565,719	1,[illegible],565	44,775,795	4,304,705	194,831,816	8,894,[illegible]	177,828,139	15,044,391
Hemp manufactures: cordage			760		407		3,[illegible]		83,858
Hides			[illegible],765		164,435		145,386		136,110
Hops	lbs	7,[illegible]	737	5,640,[illegible]	1,[illegible],160	4,149,459	834,[illegible]	7,[illegible]	1,377,690
House furniture			696		10,065		14,[illegible]		88,798
Indian corn	bush	1,041,385	1,462,346	6,172,359	5,[illegible],405	14,473,187	8,[illegible],379	10,783,707	7,867,350
meal	bbls	[illegible]	3,497	8,[illegible]	11,673	1,674	6,180	2,330	9,150
India-rubber manufactures			48,931		42,821		7,425		46,304
Iron, pig	cwt	[illegible]	945	1,460	1,731	2,255	4,580		
manufactures and machinery			[illegible],730		447,256		338,147		689,090
Lard	lbs	17,991,656	1,911,419	53,546,953	8,568,293	53,513,077	4,425,695	60,479,176	4,029,948
Leather	do	1,330,390	297,294	672,667	149,632	301,889	103,374	[illegible],352	247,[illegible]
Lumber and timber: boards	M feet	14,375	190,641	18,779	153,118	14,825	177,126	61,166	194,798
other timber			917,474		110,723		321,148		15,937
hewn timber	cub. feet	[illegible],411	173,798	4,180	74,798	4,916	135,080		
Oil-cake			1,313,696		1,301,353		784,775		1,170,435
Oil: lard	galls	1,701	1,566	14,769	14,391	158,563	82,794	1,075,957	103,280
sperm	do	1,318,151	1,[illegible],651	1,401,085	8,072,337	717,396	[illegible],875	1,003,153	1,520,018

Exports of domestic produce of the United States to Great Britain—Continued.

Articles.		1859-'60.		1860-'61.		1861-'62.		1862-'63.	
		Quantities.	Values.	Quantities.	Values.	Quantities.	Values.	Quantities.	Values.
Oil, whale and fish	galls	137,519	$74,981	180,943	$132,398	550,535	$271,430	1,027,306	$292,437
Paints and varnish			19,873		88,297		84,278		198,819
Paper and stationery			8,807		6,644		16,033		99,979
Pork	bbls	59,431	832,178	38,070	896,927	84,030	730,893	40,389	630,389
Printing presses and type			60,874		80,391		97,416		140,130
Quicksilver							80,010		81,578
Rice	tierces	17,539	344,579	5,047	168,758	85	930	304	9,936
Rosin and turpentine	bbls	359,784	884,498	238,430	833,278	34,873	158,347	5,461	70,134
Rye and small grains			307,047		871,804		218,153		834,945
Spirits, distilled	galls	48,141	17,933	93,399	25,715	645,810	387,071	79,425	41,973
Spirits of turpentine	do	2,270,504	1,038,854	1,346,803	513,328			15,163	43,959
Staves and heading	M	4,139	149,405	3,193	185,848	1,198	73,618	1,798	142,811
Tallow	lbs	6,749,909	801,371	358,965	15,768	59,691,008	2,515,914	88,719,327	3,083,379
Tar and pitch	bbls	93,393	64,397	94,719	70,950			2,279	92,748
Tobacco, leaf	hhds	30,059	4,894,049	35,101	4,918,994	16,169	2,894,538	28,999	6,497,933
manufactured	lbs	2,493,644	424,435	1,995,818	288,579	495,123	403,724	1,880,774	834,874
Wax	do	76,473	98,404	81,780	18,421	69,738	22,034	147,443	37,350
Whalebone	do	157,905	130,178	856,440	182,938	67,939	88,416	158,029	150,409
Wheat	bush	1,874,918	2,404,856	84,510,981	31,357,343	22,925,575	29,539,749	97,355,738	35,738,827
flour	bbls	438,547	2,171,917	2,458,117	13,356,811	2,339,448	18,552,168	1,794,468	11,074,908
Wood manufactures			47,398		131,304		97,240		238,379
Wool	lbs	44,949	13,333	428,412	148,374	809,737	117,153	185,074	81,387
All other articles			707,549		1,120,550		1,663,097		4,880,383
Total exports			186,882,759		116,383,955		105,888,554		168,468,158

This table of exports is uncorrected for the omitted record of cotton exported to England, which has previously been shown to be near $129,084,731 for the fiscal year 1860–'61; and several other items, hides, rice, rosin, spirits of turpentine and tobacco particularly, would add several millions of dollars in value.

The increase in the value of certain exports from 1860 forward has been referred to in connexion with the British statistics, but the records of the United States exhibit the fact in a still more striking manner. Butter, cheese, hops, hams and bacon, lard, petroleum and lard oil, tallow and tobacco, are quite as remarkably increased as is flour or wheat. A comparison of 1860 with 1862 and 1863 shows the fact. The year 1861, having no especial relation to the point under consideration, is not given.

Articles.	1860.	1862.	1863.
Butter	$139,460	$3,077,060	$5,159,871
Cheese	1,102,458	2,228,047	3,655,119
Hops	757	674,867	1,577,670
Hams and bacon	1,629,523	8,694,606	15,044,991
Lard	1,811,418	4,455,695	6,059,958
Lard oil	1,583	82,782	835,290
Tallow	901,371	2,615,914	3,093,509
Pork	592,138	750,895	650,659
Tobacco	4,664,042	2,964,232	6,483,921
	11,102,736	25,571,094	42,561,002

The increase on the articles here named, none of which are distinguished in the British return before quoted, is thus $14,470,000 in 1862 over 1860, and in 1863 the very large excess of $31,460,000.

The important article, petroleum, was unfortunately not distinguished in the quarterly returns until July, 1863, the commencement of the fiscal year 1863–'64. The largest proportion of the sum assigned to unenumerated articles for 1862–'63 was for petroleum, which may be approximately stated at $1,000,000 for 1861–'62, and $4,000,000 in 1862–'63.

In view of the omission of cotton and rice almost altogether from the exports to England in the last two years, the general aggregate at which these exports are maintained is remarkable. In 1860, with very large values for these staples, the total was less than thirty millions in excess of 1863, fiscal years.

	Values of 1860.
Cotton	$134,928,780
Rice	346,576
Rosin and turpentine	964,666
	136,240,022

Comparing this with the difference of 1860 and 1863 in the aggregates, it appears that the increase of northern staples supplied $106,250,000 of this loss in cotton, and this during a period of unprecedented trial to the national resources, and of vastly increased domestic consumption.

Some account of the difference in specie exports is due, however, in the above comparison; the exports of specie and bullion to England being $13,000,000 in 1862–'63, against $31,635,000 in 1859–'60. But the production of gold, and the great import of foreign gold from England in 1861 and 1862, had produced a surplus leading naturally to exportation.

BRITISH TRADE WITH CALIFORNIA.

The British official records distinguish the trade with California from that conducted with other parts of the United States. The tables previously given cover the entire trade, California included, and those that here follow are of California alone.

The annual values of this trade converted into terms of the United States are as follows:

	Imports from California.	Exports to California.
1856	$162,827	$2,226,937
1857	5	2,185,260
1858	70,581	2,823,411
1859	139,760	2,224,570
1860	90,455	3,024,985
1861	3,414,968	2,085,691
1862	1,722,294	1,817,236

It is apparent that the direct trade of England with the Pacific coast of the United States is relatively less than with other sections. That trade is a coasting trade to vessels of the United States, and is protected by the laws relating to the coasting trade generally. Clearance to California direct from European ports is far more difficult than transhipment at the Isthmus of Panama. The direct trade of San Francisco with foreign countries is, therefore, larger with the East Indies and China than with European countries.

The magnitude of the trade with the Pacific States opens an inviting field to foreign occupation, but its peculiar circumstances have so far protected it. They may continue to do so in a great degree, if the quality of coasting trade and the laws which preserve it to vessels of the United States are rigidly maintained; but if these were yielded, a very little time would suffice to displace United States shipping in as great a degree in the Pacific as in the Atlantic.

Imports into England from California: British official table.

Articles.	Quantities.							Values.						
	1856.	1857.	1858.	1859.	1860.	1861.	1862.	1856.	1857.	1858.	1859.	1860.	1861.	1862.
								£.	£.	£.	£.	£.	£.	£.
Corn: wheat .... qrs.						140,[illegible]	81,913						[illegible]	[illegible]
wheat, meal, and flour .. cwt.	18,[illegible]					170,[illegible]	13,739	19,709					161,[illegible]	10,[illegible]
Guano .... tons.	413		1,[illegible]	[illegible]				[illegible]		[illegible]	[illegible]			
Nitre, cubic .... cwt.					19,177							13,[illegible]		
Nicaragua wood .... tons.	1,161							17,411						
Quicksilver .... lbs.						[illegible]	138,[illegible]						[illegible]	14,[illegible]
Silver ore .... tons.				152	[illegible]	1[illegible]	[illegible]				1,[illegible]	3,[illegible]	[illegible]	[illegible]
Wood and timber .... loads.			1,[illegible]	1,[illegible]			[illegible]			[illegible]	[illegible]			3,[illegible]
Wool .... lbs.						118,[illegible]	[illegible]						[illegible]	10,[illegible]
All other articles								617	1	[illegible]	19,[illegible]	1,110	10,[illegible]	67,[illegible]
Totals								[illegible]	1	14,[illegible]	[illegible]	18,[illegible]	[illegible]	[illegible]

Exports to California from England, the produce and manufacture of the United Kingdom.

Articles.		Quantities.							Values.						
		1856.	1857.	1858.	1859.	1860.	1861.	1862.	1856.	1857.	1858.	1859.	1860.	1861.	1862.
									£.	£.	£.	£.	£.	£.	£.
Apparel	value								3,417	7,343	7,704	8,344	12,515	14,1[illegible]	10,[illegible]
Bags, empty	doz.	377	[illegible]	3,918	2,[illegible]	14,4[illegible]	6,9[illegible]	[illegible]	210	[illegible]	1,317	1,0[illegible]	3,0[illegible]	[illegible]	5,[illegible]
Beer and ale	bbls.	13,444	9,[illegible]	10,8[illegible]	4,864	4,1[illegible]	4,[illegible]	3,774	51,085	37,[illegible]	43,250	17,341	15,[illegible]	19,518	12,[illegible]
Coal	tons	18,378	8,[illegible]	14,135	3,0[illegible]	8,[illegible]	2,[illegible]	6,348	8,784	4,427	10,170	8,[illegible]	6,[illegible]	14,[illegible]	4,[illegible]
Copper	cwt.	[illegible]	[illegible]		60	[illegible]	[illegible]	[illegible]	2,045	1,5[illegible]		[illegible]	[illegible]	1,[illegible]	435
Cottons, by yard	yds.	[illegible]	10,831,[illegible]	14,1[illegible]	11,547,391	[illegible]	[illegible]	4,674,[illegible]	185,5[illegible]	195,[illegible]	[illegible]	[illegible],974	330,[illegible]	149,[illegible]	[illegible],136
at value									6,0[illegible]	10,617	10,1[illegible]	12,075	19,1[illegible]	10,1[illegible]	7,717
Drugs and chemicals									540	677	[illegible]	[illegible]	370	[illegible]	3,[illegible]
Earthenware and porcelain									9,817	9,750	[illegible]	9,[illegible]	19,[illegible]	[illegible]	13,[illegible]
Glass manufactures									4,1[illegible]	3,[illegible]	10,740	3,5[illegible]	4,[illegible]	6,144	8,73[illegible]
Hardware and cutlery	cwt.	[illegible]	640	2,319	1,367	1,918	1,877	1,9[illegible]	5,914	3,6[illegible]	8,0[illegible]	7,970	9,2[illegible]	10,[illegible]	[illegible],815
Iron	tons	1,679	1,9[illegible]	1,7[illegible]	3,447	3,53[illegible]	4,471	4,51[illegible]	28,47[illegible]	19,7[illegible]	19,077	[illegible]	30,119	37,[illegible]	[illegible]
Jute manufactures															11,[illegible]
Linens, by the yard	yds.	2,118,930	1,714,8[illegible]	1,745,4[illegible]	1,017,0[illegible]	2,014,041	1,8[illegible],948	2,257,3[illegible]	71,573	[illegible]	[illegible]	30,1[illegible]	[illegible]	40,440	[illegible]
Machinery									843	1,[illegible]	[illegible]	613	1,798	[illegible]	
Painter's colors									911	[illegible]	2,350	1,5[illegible]	1,[illegible]	1,[illegible]	1,0[illegible]
Pickles and sauces									7,133	3,[illegible]	4,296	7,674	4,274	3,0[illegible]	2,673
Silk manufactures									[illegible]	2,0[illegible]	1,5[illegible]	1,725	4,[illegible]	[illegible]	1,0[illegible]
Spirits	galls.	[illegible]	71,8[illegible]	[illegible]	[illegible]	34,314	43,7[illegible]	3,0[illegible]	8,41[illegible]	12,519	8,7[illegible]	10,579	8,73[illegible]	7,44[illegible]	4,1[illegible]
Stationery									1[illegible]	457	157	[illegible]	[illegible]	[illegible]	1,411
Tin plates									2,1[illegible]	2,[illegible]	2,[illegible]	1,347	2,[illegible]	4,[illegible]	2,379
Woollens, by piece	pieces	2,73[illegible]	8,371	1,0[illegible]	11,0[illegible]	5,147	4,477	4,[illegible]	30,6[illegible]	15,9[illegible]	[illegible],64[illegible]	[illegible],57[illegible]	13,700	6,917	10,[illegible]
by yard	yds.	[illegible],574	[illegible]	843,381	[illegible]	716,041	[illegible],874	380,057	18,077	19,[illegible]	[illegible],319	37,0[illegible]	[illegible]	[illegible]	[illegible]
at value									[illegible]	1,974	1,7[illegible]	3,1[illegible]	4,194	1,3[illegible]	1,748
All other articles									36,[illegible]	18,378	18,703	30,9[illegible]	35,5[illegible]	[illegible],150	17,[illegible]
Total values		[illegible]							441,878	[illegible]	[illegible]	477,0[illegible]	[illegible]	618,4[illegible]	328,794

Values of foreign and colonial produce exported from Great Britain to California.

Articles.	Computed real value.						
	1856.	1857.	1858.	1859.	1860.	1861.	1862.
	£.	£.	£.	£.	£.	£.	£.
Cotton manufactures			150		200	1,375	[illegible]
Currants	53	63		914			300
Gloves, of leather					130	500	
Nutmegs	8				17		
Quicksilver			2,4[illegible]	2,387	2,101		
Rice, not in husk			4,227				
Silk manufactures of India		168	1,104	564	3,343	2,9[illegible]	900
Spirits: brandy	1,800	1,665	2,361	3,424	2,6[illegible]	1,253	3,6[illegible]
Tea		3	130				
Tobacco and cigars	133	139		297	92		139
Wine	9,770	8,142	8,563	6,182	10,181	2,[illegible]	5,411
Woollen manufactures					785	1,166	
All other articles	6,265	8,287	5,530	7,814	10,911	2,410	7,795
Totals	18,132	18,418	24,733	22,580	30,591	12,446	18,668
Totals of British and for'n produce.	480,111	451,500	321,326	450,623	621,997	430,938	375,492

STEAM TONNAGE IN THE FOREIGN TRADE OF THE UNITED STATES.

Steamships were introduced into the foreign commerce of the United States in 1840, but they were of little importance for the carriage of merchandise until nearly ten years later, when the establishment of American lines to Europe, competing with the British, developed the capacity of steam transportation, and prepared the way for its general introduction into the transatlantic trade. For two or three years previous to 1850 the aggregates of steam tonnage entering the ports of the United States swelled the volume of foreign shipping very sensibly. At a later period, and with large vessels, the increase of this tonnage has been rapid, until it has reached proportions nearly equal to the sailing tonnage of all classes coming from the two or three leading commercial countries of Europe. The system was, in fact, suddenly and almost completely built up in 1848, 1849, and 1850; American lines to Havre, to Bremen and Southampton, and to Liverpool, across the Atlantic, being established simultaneously with one to Havana from Charleston, and the vast, half-foreign California and Isthmus lines. The tonnage of all those goes to swell the aggregate of tonnage published in official reports as arriving from foreign ports; but the entire Isthmus and California trade, including all that touching at Vera Cruz and Havana, either to and from the Isthmus or to and from New Orleans, should properly be separated from that crossing the Atlantic. It is so separated in the following statements, and the effect is to greatly reduce the proportion of American steamship tonnage appearing to be employed in foreign trade. Technically, clearances from Panama for San Francisco are from foreign countries, but, in fact, little or no commerce with foreign countries is represented. Little or none is represented in arrivals at New York from Chagres or Panama, or in arrivals from Cuba of steamers merely touching at that port on their way from Mexico or the Isthmus.

The statistics of steam tonnage employed in the foreign trade of the United States, therefore, require to be stated with several discriminations, to be properly understood. In the aggregate, the proportions of American and foreign appear nearly equal; but when the distinctions just referred to are made, and the absolute foreign trade only is considered, the amount of American tonnage is greatly reduced. For several years, however, or from 1851 to 1857, the American transatlantic steam lines had great success, and attained an ascendency in that trade that appears favorably in the statistics. The arrivals at New York alone were over 120,000 tons for each of several years, and this against an average of about 60,000 tons of foreign. The Isthmus and Cuban arrivals of United States steamers, entered as foreign, amounted to 160,000 tons more at New York, yet the merchandise traffic by them from any foreign country was very small in amount, and the statements should be kept distinct.

There is also a large local trade conducted by steamers with Canada on the great lakes, the tonnage of which is technically classed with that entering from foreign ports, yet which does not represent any considerable trade strictly to be designated foreign. The annual arrivals of this tonnage are 2,300,000 tons or more,* but its character is more nearly that of ferry and passenger transit than anything else. The amount is so little significant of commerce such as the transatlantic trade always must be, whether conducted by steamers or sailing vessels, that it has not been compiled to illustrate the relation of steam to foreign commerce generally.

With the British provinces of the Atlantic coast there has been for many years a moderately active traffic in small steamers. They sometimes come down to Boston or New York, but generally run only between the ports of Maine and Halifax, or elsewhere in Nova Scotia and New Brunswick. When running regularly, the amount of this tonnage is separately stated in the following tables:

Steam tonnage entered at Portland, Maine, from foreign countries.

Fiscal year ending June 30—	Foreign vessels.		
	From Great Britain.	From British N. American provinces.	Total.
	Tons.	Tons.	Tons.
1855	2,907	....	2,977
1856	....	168	166
1857	12,704	....	12,704
1858	5,538	6,854	12,392
1859	4,924	60	4,984
1860	25,075	9,722	34,797
1861	32,267	....	32,267
1862	37,071	2,803	39,874
1863	16,328	234	16,562

There were no entries of American steamers in the foreign trade.

Steam tonnage of foreign vessels entered at Philadelphia from foreign countries.

		Tons.
Fiscal year ending June 30,	1851	3,351
Do	1852	19,734
Do	1853	22,183
Do	1854	19,421
Do	1855	8,643
Do	1856	4,649
Do	1857	20,856
Do	1858	None.
Do	1859	1,416

There were no entries of American steamers.

* No distinct separation of the steam and sailing tonnage of the lakes having been made for years previous to 1858, it is impracticable to state the exact figures, but it is assumed that more than two-thirds of the arrivals are steam. Probably the proportion is nearly three-fourths. The American arrivals of all sorts at lake ports in 1860 were 2,617,276 tons, and of British tonnage 658,036 tons; together, 3,275,312 tons.

Steam tonnage entered at the port of Boston from foreign countries.

Fiscal year ending June 30—	FOREIGN VESSELS.		AMERICAN VESSELS.	Total tons.
	From Great Britain.	From British Am. provinces.	From British Am. provinces.	
1846	11,941	3,204	....	15,145
1847	11,710	308	....	12,118
1848	14,655	184	....	14,839
1849	16,000	....	....	16,000
1850	20,000	....	....	20,000
1851	22,000	....	....	22,000
1852	25,449	....	....	30,449
1853	28,672	....	11,780	40,352
1854	53,667	....	....	53,667
1855	58,114	1,610	....	59,714
1856	67,833	10,629	....	84,465
1857	54,945	7,980	....	62,925
1858	58,824	6,660	385	65,869
1859	58,979	6,445	....	65,424
1860	66,530	7,249	....	73,779
1861	67,283	6,120	....	73,403
1862	54,141	2,838	....	56,979
1863	57,306	....	....	57,306

The entry of steam tonnage at Boston began with the establishment of the Cunard line in 1840, and the arrivals previous to 1846 were 12,000 to 15,000 tons annually; but the exact quantities cannot be obtained.

American steam tonnage entered at the port of New York from foreign countries.

Fiscal year ending—	From British ports.	From Havre.	From Bremen and Hamburg.	From New Granada and Isthmus.	Total tons.
June 30, 1848	923	1,857	9,934	920	13,634
1849	....	6,571	15,230	7,207	29,008
1850	3,951	....	15,230	54,452	73,633
1851	54,783	9,640	12,629	108,172	185,034
1852	63,379	23,502	13,248	157,196	257,385
1853	73,314	26,183	18,548	170,021	288,066
1854	75,302	18,917	13,494	147,227	254,940
1855	60,062	14,929	11,408	162,317	246,770
1856	71,578	45,052	22,373	162,159	301,324
1857	48,649	30,045	23,400	145,238	247,042
1858	38,431	54,213	10,747	103,010	215,401
1859	9,059	51,484	9,069	111,343	171,885
1860	....	68,544	....	170,611	239,155
1861	....	68,880	....	150,534	219,414
1862	....	18,884	....	91,561	110,445
1863	....	....	....	125,015	125,016
Third quarter, 1863	....	....	....	23,985	23,985
Fourth quarter, 1863	6,923	....	....	43,299	49,222

Foreign steam tonnage entered at the port of New York from foreign countries.

Fiscal year ending—	British, from England.	British, colonial.	French, or from Havre.	Bremen.	Hamburg.	Belgian.	Spanish and Cuban.	Total tons.
June 30, 1844.	3,740	....	....	....	....	....	702	4,672
1845.	3,780	....	....	....	....	....	....	3,780
1846.	13,351	....	....	....	....	....	....	13,351
1847.	9,121	....	....	....	....	....	....	9,121
1848.	19,929	....	6,050	....	....	....	640	26,619
1849.	53,997	....	....	....	....	....	....	53,997
1850.	48,065	....	....	754	....	....	1,639	50,458
1851.	41,889	1,293	....	758	....	....	....	43,940
1852.	59,654	....	....	....	....	....	....	59,654
1853.	81,348	....	....	....	....	....	....	81,348
1854.	78,256	....	....	....	....	....	....	78,256
1855.	33,650	4,042	*4,357	6,158	....	....	....	48,206
1856.	39,185	....	4,915	....	1,876	....	1,289	46,265
1857.	137,678	....	15,125	6,612	17,846	11,551	....	188,812
1858.	141,903	....	....	5,402	22,612	3,764	3,193	176,904
1859.	183,354	....	3,916	34,299	37,654	540	4,072	264,785
1860.	221,724	....	....	23,358	50,951	....	3,276	299,309
1861.	256,857	....	....	30,324	46,615	....	....	333,796
1862.	231,043	....	....	39,617	59,252	3,079	1,428	327,731
1863.	220,490	4,724	1,006	34,388	55,737	....	....	397,247
Half year to Dec., 1863..	237,452	4,540	686	34,122	28,678	1,425	681	307,584
Calendar year, 1863.......	401,210	7,264	686	56,692	53,200	1,425	681	521,168

* In part of British ships for this and the two following years.

General aggregate of steam tonnage entering the ocean ports of the United States from 1844 to 1863.

Fiscal year ending—	American.	Foreign.	Total tons.	Fiscal year ending—	American.	Foreign.	Total tons.
June 30, 1844.......	....	4,578	4,578	June 30, 1854.......	100,442	131,348	231,790
1845.......	....	3,780	3,780	1855.......	346,901	120,108	467,009
1846.......	....	88,456	88,456	1856.......	397,410	120,645	518,055
1847.......	....	91,236	91,236	1857.......	333,943	282,173	616,116
1848.......	13,534	41,357	54,891	1858.......	289,296	254,748	544,044
1849.......	28,068	69,837	97,905	1859.......	311,764	318,016	630,780
1850.......	72,633	71,462	144,095	1860.......	384,899	391,016	775,915
1851.......	193,940	69,221	263,161	1861.......	312,900	139,945	732,848
1852.......	264,091	105,737	369,818	1862.......	612,673	144,564	857,239
1853.......	298,826	124,444	423,250	1863.......	847,008	477,863	794,[illegible]

For the fiscal years 1841, 1842, and 1843, an average of about four thousand tons of foreign arrived at New York.

The actual proportion of the tonnage recorded as in the foreign trade of the United States resulting from the entry of steam vessels is very large, both of American and of foreign vessels, but, as has been said, much of it is in fact not what the record appears to make it. The Isthmus trade is really coastwise rather than foreign, and therefore all, or nearly all, the American steam tonnage entering at San Francisco and New Orleans, with the Isthmus arrivals at New

York, should be struck off. The entries at both New York and New Orleans from Cuba and Mexico are in a great degree of steamers merely touching at Havana and Vera Cruz for passengers and mails, and carrying very little freight. A more legitimate trade was for several years conducted by the steamer Isabel, from Havana to Charleston.

On the North Atlantic coast, again, the steamships touching at Portland and Boston appear in some cases to have been regularly entered there, as well as at New York, in most cases, probably, bringing cargo for both ports. The Cunard line had its original terminus at Boston, however, and steamers have constantly fully discharged at Boston and Portland both, when running as part of the regular lines, or as extra ships on them, from Liverpool. The lake steamer tonnage is, of course, entirely excluded, and the direct transatlantic trade is therefore reduced to the arrivals at Portland, Boston, New York, and Philadelphia. Stating this separately, the following is the result:

Actual steam tonnage arriving in foreign trade.

Fiscal year ending—	American.	Foreign.	Total.
	Tons.	*Tons.*	*Tons.*
June 30, 1844	....	4,572	4,572
1845	....	3,780	3,780
1846	....	24,498	24,498
1847	....	21,238	21,238
1848	12,414	41,357	53,771
1849	20,801	69,897	90,698
1850	19,181	70,462	89,642
1851	80,123	69,201	149,324
1852	100,199	105,739	205,938
1853	118,005	144,224	262,229
1854	107,713	151,346	259,059
1855	94,423	120,108	214,531
1856	138,983	119,236	258,219
1857	102,703	262,587	365,290
1858	112,391	254,845	367,236
1859	63,542	336,558	400,100
1860	68,564	387,885	456,449
1861	68,880	439,460	508,340
1862	15,884	424,579	440,463
1863	....	473,114	473,114

To include Charleston, the American totals would be increased about twenty thousand tons annually from 1851 to 1861; but this could not be considered transatlantic trade in the sense represented above, being wholly from Havana.

Steam tonnage entered at the port of San Francisco from foreign countries.

Fiscal years by quarters.	American vessels.			Foreign vessels.	Aggregate tonnage.
	From Isthmus and Nicaragua.	From British colonial ports.	Total American.	From England, colonial ports.	
1853-'54—3d quarter 1853	17,585	....	....	....	....
4th quarter 1853	19,178	....	....	....	....
1st quarter 1854	19,861	....	....	....	....
2d quarter 1854	21,501	....	78,125	....	78,125
1854-'55—3d quarter 1854	19,500	....	....	....	....
4th quarter 1854	20,290	....	....	....	....
1st quarter 1855	19,500	....	....	....	....
2d quarter 1855	19,804	....	79,644	....	79,644
1855-'56—3d quarter 1855	17,563	....	....	354	....
4th quarter 1855	18,441	....	....	745	....
1st quarter 1856	22,916	....	....	144	....
2d quarter 1856	15,894	....	74,814	....	76,057
1856-'57—3d quarter 1856	17,949	....	....	....	....
4th quarter 1856	17,435	....	....	144	....
1st quarter 1857	16,672	....	....	144	....
2d quarter 1857	12,328	....	63,384	....	63,672
1857-'58—3d quarter 1857	12,158	....	....	....	....
4th quarter 1857	13,031	....	....	144	....
1st quarter 1858	12,609	....	....	144	....
2d quarter 1858	14,702	....	52,500	....	52,788
1858-'59—3d quarter 1858	11,928	20,393	....	....	....
4th quarter 1858	11,844	14,958	....	....	....
1st quarter 1859	12,619	10,297	....	144	....
2d quarter 1859	14,854	12,722	110,096	2,314	110,583
1859-'60—3d quarter 1859	21,311	10,861	....	1,995	....
4th quarter 1859	20,912	11,985	....	1,136	....
1st quarter 1860	21,751	9,840	....	....	....
2d quarter 1860	15,102	13,538	125,400	....	128,531
1860-'61—3d quarter 1860	12,842	10,567	....	....	....
4th quarter 1860	17,880	7,079	....	....	....
1st quarter 1861	13,956	5,441	....	....	....
2d quarter 1861	19,374	8,450	94,489	479	94,968
1861-'62—3d quarter 1861	16,572	3,739	....	....	....
4th quarter 1861	16,444	4,012	....	....	....
1st quarter 1862	18,794	10,416	....	....	....
2d quarter 1862	19,563	12,701	102,230	....	102,230
1862-'63—3d quarter 1862	19,140	7,213	....	1,411	....
4th quarter 1862	21,662	7,750	....	1,411	....
1st quarter 1863	21,698	10,546	....	1,977	....
2d quarter 1863	23,175	10,950	121,904	710	126,903

Steam tonnage entered at the port of Charleston from foreign countries.

American vessels only.		Tons.
Fiscal year ending June 30,	1851	14,926
	1852	16,096
	1853	22,000
	1854	22,317
	1855	20,487
	1856	21,204
	1857	21,917
	1858	21,010
	1859	26,781
	1860	26,990
Half year to December,	1860	11,604

For the first three years the entries are in part estimated, the record for one or more quarters of each being lost. All the entries were from Havana.

The steam tonnage arriving at New Orleans from foreign ports was technically large from the commencement of the Isthmus trade to the close of 1860, and all in American vessels. Estimating for the record of two or three quarters, the following is the tonnage, about one-half of which is from Havana, Cuba, and the other half from the Isthmus, Central America, and Mexico. The years 1855, 1856, 1857, and 1860 are complete:

		Tons.
Fiscal year ending June 30,	1855	60,868
	1856	84,571
	1857	76,514
	1858	75,000
	1859	78,000
	1860	88,530

The New York line touching at Havana was mainly a coasting and passenger trade, and this makes up more than half the total. The arrivals from the Isthmus and Mexico were much the same.

At Mobile there were a few arrivals of American steamers from foreign ports, but their amount in any year was small.

On the northeastern frontier, entering at Castine, Maine, (district of Passamaquoddy,) there is a large aggregate of tonnage accumulated by the frequent trips of small American steamers plying to New Brunswick and Halifax. The average of such arrivals amounts to over 60,000 tons annually since 1853, being in the fiscal years—

	Tons.
1854–'55	64,219
1855–'56	67,401
1856–'57	63,178
1860–'61	55,426
1861–'62	75,324
1862–'63	61,444

The intervening years are not readily distinguished. This was all tonnage of American vessels.

The swelled volume of tonnage arriving from foreign countries during the last ten or fifteen years is more largely due to steam than would at first appear, in consequence of the introduction of the items above described. Taking the fiscal year 1859–'60 as an example, the total tonnage reported as arriving in the foreign trade is of—

American vessels .... tons..	5,921,285
Foreign vessels .... tons..	2,253,911
Total .... tons..	8,175,196

Excluding the tonnage from Canada, the American is reduced to 3,304,009 tons, and the foreign to 1,591,575 tons. Deducting, further, for the California and Isthmus trade in American steam vessels—

For entries at New York .... tons..	170,041
For entries at New Orleans .... tons..	88,530
For entries at San Francisco .... tons..	125,400
For entries at Castine, Maine .... tons..	55,000
Total .... tons..	439,571

The tonnage actually entering in the foreign trans-oceanic trade is reduced to 2,564,438 tons. The peculiar conditions attending the technical statements of tonnage and shipping have thus, to a great extent, concealed the injuries which have been suffered in general ocean commerce, misleading to the impression that large accessions were being made to the shipping so employed, when, in fact, great and most injurious reductions were taking place.

THE ISTHMUS TRADE.

The peculiar character of the trade passing the Isthmus of Panama, the tonnage of which appears as entered and cleared for foreign countries, but which, for reasons before stated, is taken as almost exclusively coastwise, is best explained in the consular reports from Panama, from which the following statements are taken. These statements do not distinguish the values from each country entered for consumption—only the total values from all countries.

Values of cargoes entering Panama.

Year ending—	For consumption.	In transit for the U. States.	In transit for Europe.	Total.
September 30, 1860	$1,378,814	$36,846,930	$14,925,250	$53,148,000
1861	1,145,310	60,146,345	13,066,250	61,347,005
1862	2,443,815	28,282,400	27,000,244	*57,870,620

* Including $144,160 in transit for the South Pacific coast.

Values of cargoes from Panama.

Year ending—	Exports of Panama.	In transit from U. S.	In transit from Europe.	Total.
September 30, 1860	$129,000	$8,325,000	$4,400,000	$12,784,000
1861	250,000	10,169,225	2,206,625	12,625,850
1862	2,939,857	11,047,596	6,113,304	24,796,428

In 1860 there was, also, of merchandise exported, in thirty-one British vessels, to the South Pacific coast $3,500,000, and in vessels of other nations $1,200,000. In 1862 there is included in the outward total the following items:

Value of cargoes from Central America to South Pacific.......... $66,000
Value of cargoes from South Pacific to Central America.......... 76,250
Value of cargoes from Europe and elsewhere (treasure)........... 4,444,268
Value of cargoes from Europe and the United States (jewelry)... 578,062

The total values inward and outward are therefore—

Years.	Inward.	Outward.	Total.
In 1859..................................	$57,079,925	$13,857,000	$71,530,925
In 1860..................................	53,148,004	17,4[illegible]1,000	70,632,004
In 1861..................................	64,347,005	12,024,850	76,072,755
In 1862..................................	57,[illegible],020	24,795,423	[illegible],622,049

The very small proportion of trade for consumption in Panama, and of outward exports, the produce of Panama, is decisive that the tonnage of United States steamships on that line cannot properly be regarded as in the foreign trade.

In 1862 further statements of tonnage arrived and cleared are given as follows:

Vessels arrived at Panama, and their tonnage for the year ending September 30, 1862.

Arrived inward.	No.	Tonnage.	Outward bound.	No.	Tonnage.
American ships	60	80,194	American ships	57	80,578
English ships..............	42	30,611	English ships..............	42	30,611
Spanish ships..............	2	475	Spanish ships..............	2	475
French ships	2	536	French ships	2	536
New Granadian and all other.	70	3,350	N. Granadian and all other..	70	3,350
Total................	176	124,156	Total................	173	121,550

The value of cargoes in American bottoms, inward and outward, in 1862 was $59,671,194.

The following statement of the transit of treasure and freight over the Isthmus of Panama in 1862, towards the Pacific and towards the Atlantic, is also from the consular report for 1862 of Alexander McKee, United States consul at Panama.

Travel and transportation over the Isthmus of Panama for the year ending September 30, 1862.

	Towards the Pacific.	Towards the Atlantic.	Total.
Passengers............................number....	21,456	9,700	31,162
Gold ....value....	$1,441,2[illegible]	$34,605,467	$36,040,736
Silver.......................................do......	....	$14,255,935	$14,256,935
Jewelry.....................................do......	$578,062	....	$578,062
American mails.......................pounds....	232,[illegible]	31,964	264,850
English mails.............................do......	35,565	10,127	45,692
Extra baggage.............................do......	345,547	217,901	563,448
Freight by weight........................do......	54,758,378	20,051,641	74,810,019
Freight by measure......................feet......	737,084	33,879	770,963

Of the treasure carried towards the Atlantic there was:

Gold to the United States	$28,401,693
Silver to the United States	10,513
Gold to England	8,091,032
Silver to England	14,196,008

REVIEW OF STEAMSHIP LINES.

As the tonnage accounts appear in the official records the various ocean steamship lines are but imperfectly disclosed. First, after the experimental trip of the Sirius, in 1838, the Great Western ran for several years—1840 to 1846—almost alone to New York. In 1842 and 1843 there were three or four arrivals of the British Queen from Antwerp; but the principal opening of the steamer trade was made by the Cunard line, established in 1840 and 1841, from Liverpool, *via* Halifax, to Boston. There were several of these vessels, the Columbia, the Acadia, the Caledonia, and Britannia, the first four of the line. The Columbia was lost in 1843, and was succeeded by the Hibernia and the Cambria,* to which were added, on the extension of the line to New York, in 1848, the Niagara, Europa, Canada, America, and the Trent and Severn, of the West India line, occasionally came to New York. The Cunard line was the pioneer as a commericial venture strictly. It always carried a larger share of merchandise than other British lines, and larger also than the American line afterwards established to British ports. A French line from Havre appears in the arrivals at New York in 1847, three or four steamers of about 600 tons each, but they disappear in 1848.†

In 1848, simultaneously with the extension of the Cunard line to New York, and its enlargement to a total of 55,000 tons arriving in the fiscal year 1848-'49, there was an American line to Bremen established. The Washington and Herrmann, and a large steamer, the United States, made several trips to and from Havre. The Isthmus lines were begun nearly at the same time, expanding rapidly in 1850 and 1851, and, as they touched at Vera Cruz and Havana frequently, their tonnage appears as foreign arrivals, entering from Mexico and Cuba, though conducting little actual foreign commerce. In 1850 the first arrivals of the Collins line were reported at New York—the Atlantic, Pacific, Arctic, and Baltic. The tonnage by these ships rose to 75,000 tons annually in 1853 and 1854, but the line was abruptly discontinued in 1857.

An interruption of the Cunard line to New York occurred in 1855, amounting to an absolute discontinuance for the entire year, but it was fully resumed in 1856. The tabular statement preceding being for fiscal years, does not show the fact of discontinuance during the calendar year 1855. The line ran to Boston, however, as usual.

In 1856 a French line from Havre was started to New York, composed of the Barcelone, the Lyonnaise, the Alma, and Cadiz, but they made a few trips only. Several British steamers—the Jason, Etna, Alps, &c.—made a few trips also from Havre to New York in 1856 and 1857, but they were not afterwards continued.

From Bremen the Hansa, a Bremen vessel, in 1856 and 1857, made a few trips to New York, and the Jason and Argo, British, after the withdrawal of the

* In the tonnage of arrivals at Boston the capacity of these vessels is given at a much lower figure than when, in 1849, they were reported at New York: the Cambria being at Boston 760 tons, and at New York 1,334 tons; the Hibernia 791 and 1,344 tons; the Acadia 618 and 1,300 tons; the Britannia 619 and 1,161 tons; the Caledonia 615 and 1,116 tons. No sufficient reason appears for the discrepancy; but as it was admitted in the original calculations of tonnage, the materials for this statement must now be made up in the same manner. This discrepancy in the tonnage of the same steamships recorded at Boston and New York continues to the close of the employment of the first line of ships in 1862.

† Entered as the Union, 704 tons; the Philadelphia, 663 tons; the New York, 688 tons; and the Missouri, 669 tons.

Hermann and Washington, American. A line of Belgian steamers was also started in 1856—the Leopold, the Belgique, and Constitution—but soon withdrew. The Hamburg steamers Borussia and Hammonia, and the Bremen line, before referred to, continued in successful operation, between the North German ports and New York, from their beginning in 1856. In 1859 and subsequent years they received the addition of two or three heavy steamers—the Teutonia, Bavaria, and Saxonia, from Hamburg, and the Bremen and New York, from Bremen. Together the amount of this tonnage from Hamburg and Bremen rose rapidly from 1858 forward, amounting to 109,892 tons in the calendar year 1863. The success of the line has been so decided as to lead to a large diversion of the trade of continental Europe through the ports of Bremen and Hamburg, ranking them next to England in the general amount of trade with the United States.

The trade with France, largely carried by the American line of steamers to Havre from 1857 to the close of 1861, is now received through a British-built line, just making its first passages in June, 1864, and a second line of new foreign steamers is also started between Liverpool and New York.

The effect of the establishment of the Bremen and Hamburg lines of foreign steamers on the trade of the United States with those countries is so striking as to require notice here. The following is a comparison, beginning with 1855, of the proportion of American and foreign vessels engaged in the trade of the United States with those ports:

Vessels and tonnage entered the ports of the United States from Hamburg and Bremen.

Period.	American vessels.		Foreign vessels.	
	No.	Tons.	No.	Tons.
Fiscal year 1854-'55	50	30,925	230	[illegible]
1855-'56	[illegible]	[illegible]	214	[illegible]
1856-'57	36	37,411	201	[illegible]
1857-'58	30	[illegible]	245	[illegible]
1858-'59	9	11,223	218	[illegible]
1859-'60	6	4,031	190	170,223
1860-'61	12	[illegible]	[illegible]	161,046
1861-'62	10	7,361	196	[illegible]
1862-'63	9	9,016	183	[illegible]

The conduct of this trade has, therefore, almost wholly passed to other than United States vessels. The value of the trade has also increased beyond all proportion to the tonnage. In 1859-'60 the imports from the two ports were $18,498,607, and the exports $18,378,703—a total trade of $36,877,310, a very little, indeed, of which was carried by American vessels.

PRESENT CONDITION OF FOREIGN STEAM LINES (JUNE, 1864.)

The present condition of the foreign steam lines to the United States is shown in the following table, first embodied in a memorial to Congress by the Chamber of Commerce of New York:

Foreign steam lines to the United States, January, 1864.

Line.	Route.	Name of steamer.	Tonnage of each steamer.	Total tonnage.	Remarks.
Cunard line	Liverpool to New York, and Liverpool to Boston.	Scotia	4,137		Under subsidy.
		Persia	3,096		
		Australasian	2,663		
		China	2,529		
		Arabia	2,945		
		Africa	2,089		
		Asia	2,051		
		Europa	1,751		
		America	2,000		
		Niagara	1,824		
		Canada	1,831	25,870	
Screw line		Kedar	1,876		
		Hecla	1,694		
		Olympia	1,666		
		Sciota	1,704	6,693	
Dale line	Liverpool to New York.	City of London	2,560		Transferred from Philadelphia to New York in 1857.
		City of New York	2,560		
		City of Baltimore	2,367		
		City of Washington	2,390		
		City of Manchester	2,109		
		City of Cork	1,545		
		City of Limerick	1,540		
		Etna	2,215		
		Edinburgh	2,197		
		Kangaroo	1,874		
		Bosphorus Branch	448		
		Glasgow	1,962	23,737	
London and New York Steamship Company.		Bellona	1,700		
		Cella	1,680	3,388	
Anchor line		Union			Not yet completed.
		Avon			
		Una			
		Britannia	1,274		
		Caledonia	1,253		
		United Kingdom	1,155	3,694	
Montreal ocean steamship line.		St. George	1,438		
		St. Andrew	1,380		
		St. Patrick		2,819	
Galway line		Adriatic	4,000		
		Columbia	2,000	6,000	
National Steam Navigation Company.		Louisiana	2,271		
		Virginia	2,747		
		Carolina	2,410	7,428	
Hamburg Amer'n Packet Company.		Saxonia	2,500		
		Hammonia	2,100		
		Teutonia	2,400		
		Borussia	2,100		
		Germania	2,600	11,700	
North German Lloyds steamship line.		America	2,509		Five vessels.
		New York	2,360		
		Hansa	2,992		
		Bremen	2,394	10,135	
Jamaica, Hayti, Nassau, and Havana.		Saladin	516		Under subsidy.
		Corsica	1,047	1,860	
		Aggregate tonnage		104,031	

The Adriatic, here named as one of the Galway line, and now owned abroad, was originally built for the Collins line, and is the only steamer of American build which crosses the ocean. To the list above given, from January to June, 1864, the following have been added:

The General Transatlantic Company's line between New York and Havre.

Washington, 3,204 tons	900 horse power.
Lafayette, 3,204 tons	900 horse power.
Eugenie, (afloat)	900 horse power.
France, (building)	900 horse power.
Napoleon III, (building,)	1,100 horse power.

The National Steam Navigation Company's line, New York to Liverpool.

Virginia	2,876 tons.
Pennsylvania	2,972 tons.
Louisiana	2,166 tons.
Westminster	
Queen	3,612 tons, (building.)
Erin	3,215 tons, (building.)
Ontario	3,212 tons, (building.)
Helvetia	3,209 tons, (building.)

Various propositions for the establishment of new American steam lines to foreign countries have been made during the last year, and it has been claimed that the aid of the government should be accorded to any lines which should be opened, at least to the extent of the aid regularly accorded by the British government in like cases. The circumstances surrounding any such enterprises at the present time are decidedly adverse, unless aid of some decided character is afforded. The national and semi-official character attached to European steamer lines by the governments supporting them undoubtedly goes far toward securing them precedence in passenger carriage, in important and valuable freights, and in every element of security, with the advantages it brings—the consideration of chief importance now in distant voyages. A system of official recognition similar to that which has so long characterized the royal mail steamer lines of Great Britain is urgently needed for the United States.

At the instance of the promoters of a new steam line to Brazil, among others, Congress has just passed an act extending aid in the form of guaranteed payments for postal service.

The following very valuable statements and tables from the memorial of the Chamber of Commerce of New York, before referred to, prepared by John Austin Stevens, jr., esq., secretary, are by permission reproduced here. They cover the several points to which they relate so completely as to render the preparation of similar tables unnecessary, while it would be scarcely possible to equal them in force and completeness. The principal table of existing steamer lines previously copied is given at the close of a history of American steam lines, from which the statement of passages which here follow are taken.

Average passages of the Cunard steamers in 1859.—(From the report to Parliament of the select committee in 1860.)

LIVERPOOL AND BOSTON.

Names of steamers.	No. of passages from Liverpool to Boston.*	Average time of passages.			No. of passages from Boston to Liverpool.	Average time of passages.		
		Days.	Hours.	Minutes.		Days.	Hours.	Minutes.
Niagara	3	15	4	.....	3	11	11	33
Arabia	6	12	19	17	6	10	7	6
America	5	14	20	6	6	11	11	20
Canada	7	14	4	20	6	11	12	50
Europa	6	13	3	.....	5	10	15	13
	27	13	20	33	26	10	20	22

LIVERPOOL AND NEW YORK.

Names of steamers.	No. of passages from Liverpool to New York.†	Average time of passages.			No. of passages from New York to Liverpool.	Average time of passages.		
		Days.	Hours.	Minutes.		Days.	Hours.	Minutes.
Persia	7	11	11	49	7	9	16	57
Asia	6	13	7	34	8	10	20	57
Africa	7	13	4	38	8	10	22	20
Europa	3	15	13	55	3	11	21	5
Arabia‡	1	15	12	.....	.....	.....	.....	.....
	26	13	3	10	26	10	16	40
Reducing Boston to New York distance, the average of all passages is	53	13	20	.....	53	11	3	.....
Cunard line	.....	Average as above.			.....	12	14	6

Average passages of the Collins steamers at several periods.

NEW YORK AND LIVERPOOL.

Names of steamers.	No. of passages from Liverpool to New York.	Average time of passages.			No. of passages from New York to Liverpool.	Average time of passages.		
		Days.	Hours.	Minutes.		Days.	Hours.	Minutes.
1856.—Baltic§	7	12	12	.....	7	11	8	.....
1857.—Atlantic	4	11	13	.....	4	10	[illegible]	.....

NEW YORK AND SOUTHAMPTON.‖

Name of steamer.	No. of passages from Southampton to N. York.	Average time of passages.			No. of passages from N. York to Southampton.	Average time of passages.		
		Days.	Hours.	Minutes.		Days.	Hours.	Minutes.
1860.—Adriatic	5	10	8	20	5	9	10	33

* 2,[illegible] nautical miles. † 3,013 nautical miles. ‡ One trip.

§ The shortest passage across the Atlantic was by the Baltic in 1854; time, 9 days, 16 hours, and 30 minutes.

‖ Distance to Southampton exceeds that to Liverpool 57 miles.

An estimate of the correspondence conveyed by the British American packets (Cunard line) in one year, 1859; of the total British postage thereon; of certain deductions to be made from the total British postage; of the British sea postage remaining after making those deductions; of the cost of sea conveyance, and of the difference between the cost of sea conveyance and the amount of sea postage.—(From the report of the select committee on postal and telegraph contracts made to the House of Commons in May, 1860.)

		No. of letters.	British postage on letters.	No. of packages of printed matter.	British postage on printed matter.
Between the United Kingdom and the United States		4,810,000	£82,500	1,728,000	£7,500
Between the United Kingdom and Canada		963,600	6,000	*471,600	1,600
Between the United Kingdom and the rest of British North America and Bermuda		135,700	†14,550	‡164,950	670
Between the United Kingdom and Havana, Mexico, and California		46,000	2,750	34,100	140
Between intermediate ports		Cannot be stated.	2,700	Cannot be stated.	
Between the continent of Europe and North America, in open mails		115,300	5,650	104,000	480
French and Prussian closed mails		190,500 ozs.	17,930	321,000 ozs.	530
Total British postage on printed matter					10,920
Total British postage on letters					132,050
Total British postage on letters and printed matter					142,970
Deduct for returned letters	£4,835				
Deduct for British inland rate 1½d. per letter on the whole number of letters in the number column	11,000				
Deduct half the postage on the printed matter, with the exception of the 1 centime on the French and Prussian closed mails	5,135				20,970
Total sea postage					122,000
Cost of sea conveyance.					
For conveyance of mails between Liverpool and to Halifax and Boston, and between Liverpool and New York	173,300				
For conveyance of mails between New York and Nassau	3,000				
For conveyance of mails between Halifax and Bermuda and St. Thomas, and between Halifax and St. John's, Newfoundland	14,700				191,000
Loss on the service, viz., difference between sea postage and cost of sea conveyance					69,000

* Of this number only 304,000 (which were despatched from the United Kingdom) produced any British postage.

† Including £1,500 for postage on official letters.

‡ Of this number the papers received in the United Kingdom produced no British postage.

United States mail service abroad, October 1, 1852.

No. of route.	Points.	Distance.	No. of trips.	Contractors.	Am't of pay.	Contract.
		Miles.				
1...	New York, by Southampton, England, to Bremen-Haven, Germany.	3,760	Once a month.	Ocean Steam Navigation Company.—C. H. Sand.	$200,000	With Postmaster General, act of Congress March 3, 1845.
2...	Charleston, So. Carolina, by Savannah, Georgia, and Key West, Florida, to Havana, Cuba.	680	Twice a month.	M. C. Mordecai	50,000	With Postmaster General, acts of Congress March 3, 1847, and July 10, 1848.
3*...	New York to Aspinwall, New Granada, direct.	2,000	Twice a month.	George Law, M. O. Roberts, and B. R. McIlvaine.	290,000	Under contract with Secretary of Navy, acts of Congress March 3, 1847, and March 3, 1851.
	New Orleans, Louisiana, to Aspinwall, New Granada, direct.	1,400				
	New York, via Havana, to New Orleans, Louisiana.	2,000				
4...	Astoria, Oregon, with sundry stoppages.	4,200	Twice a month.	Pacific Mail Steamship Company.	348,250	Contract with Secretary of Navy and Postmaster General, acts of March 3, 1847, and March 3, 1851.
5...	New York to Liverpool...	3,100	26 p'r year	E. K. Collins & Co. ...	858,000	Contract with Secretary of Navy, March 3, 1847, and July 21, 1852.
6...	New York, by Cowes, to Havre, France.	3,270	Once a month.	Ocean Steam Navigation Company.—M. Livingston.	130,000	Contract with Postmaster General, March 3, 1847.
7...	Aspinwall to Panama	60	Twice a month.	....	60,426	Service of Panama railroad under temporary arrangement, act of Congress Mar. 3, 1851, at 22 cents per pound.
					2,446,626	

Table showing the foreign steam communication of Great Britain and the government subsidies.—(From the report of the Postmaster General, 1862.)

No. of lines.†	Destination.	Number of trips.	Companies.	Date of contract.	Subsidy per annum.
12..	Southampton, Vigo, Oporto, and Lisbon.	Three times a month	Peninsula and Oriental Steam Navigation Co.	Admiralty, January 9, 1852.	[illegible]
13..	Southampton to Gibraltar, Malta, and Alexandria.	Four times a month	..........do..........	....	949,600
	Marseilles, Malta, and Alexandria.				
	Suez and Bombay	Twice a month....	..........do..........	Admiralty, January 1, 1853, July 7, 1854.	
	Suez and Calcutta				
	Bombay and China				
14..	Point de Galle and Sydney.	Once a month......	..........do..........	Post office, April 16, 1861.	134,672
15..	Liverpool, Halifax, and Boston.	Weekly	Sir S. Cunard..........	Admiralty, June 24, 1858.	173,340
	Liverpool and New York..				
16..	Halifax, Bermuda, and St. Thomas.	Once a month......	..........do..........	July 1, 1854	14,700
17..	West Indies	Twice a month.....	Royal Mail Steampacket Co.	July 3, 1850......	270,000
	Brazil and River Plate....	Once a month......	..........do..........	January 1, 1851 ..	
18..	Pacific	......do..........	Pacific Steam Navigation Co.	April 1, 1859	25,000
19..	West Coast of Africa......	Once a month, to touch at Madeira, Teneriffe, Sierra Leone, &c.	African Steamship Co..	Sept. 24, 1858	30,000
20..	Cape of Good Hope	Once a month......	Union Steamship Co....	Sept. 13, 1858	33,000

* Of these lines, Nos. 3, 4, and 7 are now in operation—all the others have being withdrawn.
† The preceding numbers are of domestic lines or lines to the continent.

Table showing comparative subsidies to American and British lines in 1857.

AMERICAN.

Line.	Trips.	Distances.	Subsidy.	Gross postage.	Total miles.	Pay per mile.
Collins	26	3,100	$385,000	$415,987	806,000	$2 10½
Bremen	13	3,700	128,407	120,937	96,200	1 34
Havre	13	3,270	84,494	88,474	85,020	1 00½
Aspinwall	24	3,200	290,000	129,610	153,600	1 88½
Pacific	24	4,200	348,250	163,278	201,600	1 70
Havana	24	670	60,000	6,500	32,119	1 86½
Vera Cruz	24	900	29,025	5,900	43,200	67
Total	......	....	1,327,730	*1,045,740	*723,738	†1 60½

* The slight errors in these footings occur in the original. † Average.

BRITISH.

Line.	Trips.	Distances.	Subsidy.	Gross postage.	Total miles.	Pay per mile.
Cunard	52	3,100	£173,340	£163,687 10	304,600	11s. 4½d. $2 74½
Royal Mail	24	11,402	270,000	116,945 00	547,200	9 10 2 46
Peninsula and Oriental	24	*	244,000	179,186 11	798,677	6 01½ 1 55½
Australian	12	14,000	185,000	33,281 13	336,000	11 00 2 73
Bermuda and St. Thomas	24	2,043	14,700	....	98,000	3 00 0 73
Panama and Valparaiso	24	2,716	25,000	5,715 00	130,368	3 10 0 74
West Coast of Africa	12	6,245	23,250	3,196 02	149,880	3 05 0 82½
				French, Belgian, and Dutch postage.		
Channel Islands	156	132	....	74,430 08	41,184	....
Holyhead and Kingston	730	64	....	36,139 00	93,440	....
Liverpool and Isle of Man	119	70	....	10,000 15	16,660	....
Shetland and Orkneys	52	100	....	....	10,400	....
Total	......	....	1,088,797	801,573 07	3,338,821	0 7 2 39

Total average per mile, $2 10½. Average of four principal lines, $2 39.

These subsidies have been gradually increasing from the year 1850, and additions made as new services were required from the lines, growing out of the increased commerce which followed their establishment; and in times of commercial distress, as well as in prosperity, the same sustaining and unfaltering protection has always been afforded by the sagacious and far-seeing policy of the British government.

STEAM SHIPPING AND TONNAGE OF GREAT BRITAIN.

The steam marine of Great Britain is intimately related to that of the United States so far as foreign trade is concerned. The increase of foreign shipping of all classes conducting the foreign trade of the United States is almost wholly British, and the successful lines of steamers newly established, as well as those which have at any time taken the place of American lines, are also nearly all British. The statistics of British shipping are, therefore, essential to the proper consideration of the changes in progress directly affecting American shipping.

The first table which follows shows the tonnage of all classes entering British ports for five years to the close of 1863, the steam tonnage not being separated. The most conspicuous fact apparent in this table is the increase of the aggregate of British tonnage, the fixed position of foreign tonnage, and the decline in tonnage of the United States.

Summary of tonnage entering ports of Great Britain.

	In 1859.	In 1863.
British	5,386,953	7,290,417
All foreign	3,700,597	3,838,529
United States	1,077,948	692,337

The increase of British is near 2,000,000 tons, while that of the United States declines 385,611 tons in five years. A still greater decline is apparent when the maximum year 1861 is compared with 1863, the first giving a total of 1,647,076 tons, and the decline to 1863 being, therefore, 944,739 tons. This decline is undoubtedly due to the immense number of American vessels sold abroad in 1861, 1862 and 1863, the great majority of which were purchased by the British. Thus the increase of steam vessels, which is wholly foreign, combines with the loss of the magnificent fleet of sailing ships, long the pride of United States commerce, to expel the United States flag from the chief centres of foreign commerce.

It is noticeable that France and the German, as well as other continental states conduct a relatively small trade with British ports. The largest item of tonnage is Norwegian, the next Prussian; yet the largest is but a tenth part of the British tonnage; and the total belonging to all other countries is, in 1863, reduced to about half the aggregate of arrivals. The progress made toward the entire control of the British trade by British shipping during the five years covered by the table is very extraordinary, and it is probably mainly due to the rapid development of steam transportation in every line of commerce, and in the carriage of heavy and crude tropical products as well as in the exchanges between states producing the most valuable classes of goods.

Number, tonnage, and nationality of vessels entering the ports of the United Kingdom for five calendar years.

Countries.	1859.		1860.		1861.		1862.		1863.	
	Vessels.	Tons.	Vessels.	Tons.	Vessels.	Tons.	Vessels.	Tons.	Vessels.	Tons.
British United Kingdom and dependencies.	19,909	5,369,053	20,104	5,763,464	21,060	6,304,090	22,356	6,590,140	23,773	7,299,417
Foreign	16,389	3,700,597	18,270	4,292,823	16,529	4,300,470	17,770	4,149,941	18,140	3,838,529
Total	36,294	9,069,650	38,374	10,055,287	37,589	10,604,560	40,126	10,740,090	41,913	11,137,946
United States	1,115	1,077,948	1,417	1,381,021	1,072	1,647,076	1,327	1,179,290	691	692,337
Russian	346	103,302	435	125,612	407	125,295	438	134,689	423	137,067
Swedish	918	151,351	1,119	181,775	945	155,774	863	161,778	1,043	172,417
Norwegian	2,504	528,078	2,662	637,730	2,917	634,438	3,191	657,479	3,309	754,788
Danish	2,771	276,510	2,067	291,753	2,321	225,677	2,634	250,972	2,871	278,318
Prussian	1,536	375,915	1,706	425,436	1,493	373,509	1,652	410,200	1,077	420,164
Mecklenburg and Oldenburg	798	147,341	722	144,098	630	128,949	702	145,593	705	146,033
Hanoverian	804	74,685	870	81,196	778	67,027	801	78,519	910	80,240
Hanse Towns	537	200,868	640	212,066	561	238,984	642	249,139	649	256,041
Dutch	1,443	182,050	1,601	185,098	1,250	153,624	1,440	181,858	1,349	161,634
Belgian	179	43,238	257	64,160	298	61,218	298	64,807	314	60,244
French	2,334	192,113	2,187	180,524	1,646	135,906	2,338	190,043	2,894	238,046
Spanish	271	72,607	244	67,048	253	79,606	277	80,869	377	97,509
Portuguese	124	30,708	147	33,678	143	30,627	98	37,769	87	12,921
Sardinian	148	44,357	248	61,963	249	63,284	290	79,127	250	81,465
Sicilian	119	26,769	167	38,949	124	34,661	160	35,963	74	17,628
Austrian	240	90,985	407	154,058	357	114,774	359	118,843	340	114,388
Greek	74	18,978	89	10,125	67	17,445	39	11,293	30	6,650
Other European countries	34	10,304	38	12,240	66	17,160	98	21,745	120	33,541
Other countries	24	6,513	20	6,355	19	7,288	15	5,210	13	4,301

The statistics of British steam tonnage in foreign trade are somewhat difficult of access. The distinction between registered and enrolled vessels is not there, as in the United States, a general line of separation between the class of shipping in foreign trade and that in the coasting trade. Very narrow seas separate England from several distinct foreign powers, and the most positive form of papers establishing the nationality of a vessel are necessary as well as convenient, therefore. Of the registered steam vessels belonging in England in 1860 and 1861 a large proportion were under fifty tons, as follows:

Years.	Steam vessels of 50 tons or less.		Steam vessels over 50 tons.	
	No.	Tons.	No.	Tons.
In 1860	802	18,471	1,186	433,891
1861	854	19,643	1,268	485,015
1862	808	20,864	1,319	515,270

The employment of British registered steam vessels, not including colonial, as divided between the home and foreign trade in 1860, 1861 and 1862, was as follows, exclusive of river steamers:

Years.	In home trade.		Part native and part foreign.		In foreign trade.	
	No.	Tons.	No.	Tons.	No.	Tons.
In 1860	402	92,254	80	29,803	447	277,437
1861	448	102,795	72	24,024	477	313,365
1862	454	104,020	69	29,463	510	328,310

Total in all, other than river trade.

Years.	No.	Tons.
In 1860	929	399,494
1861	997	441,184
1862	1,033	461,793

The number of steam vessels built and registered in the United Kingdom from 1853 to 1861 was large, and three-fourths or more were built of iron.

Number and tonnage of steam vessels built in the United Kingdom.

Years.	No. of iron.	Whole No.	Tonnage.
1853	117	153	48,215
1854	152	174	64,255
1855	195	231	81,018
1856	175	229	67,573
1857	165	239	59,918
1858	118	153	53,150
1859	106	150	38,003
1860	149	198	53,798
1861	159	201	70,840
1862	181	221	77,338

The preponderance of iron in steamship building began in 1853, and it is noticeable how completely that material has controlled since that time. In the ten years of this table there were 1,501 steam vessels built of iron, out of a total, of all dimensions, of 1,940 only, leaving but 439 built of timber.

The proportion to which foreign-built steam vessels enter into the home or foreign trade of England is relatively smaller than the sailing tonnage, notwithstanding the opening of the coasting trade to foreign bottoms in 1853. The German states and the French have a moderate share in that trade—small, indeed, rather than moderate—while the United States have now absolutely none. The united tonnage belonging to all foreign nations is not one-sixth of the whole.

Number and tonnage of steam vessels of each nation entered and cleared at ports of the United Kingdom in 1860, 1861, and 1862.

Nationalities.	VESSELS ENTERED.					
	1860.		1861.		1862.	
	No.	Tonnage.	No.	Tonnage.	No.	Tonnage.
British	6,631	2,111,735	7,220	2,375,856	7,754	2,645,126
United States	2	2,818	5	7,778	1	618
Russian	24	11,671	23	14,158	21	13,401
Swedish	30	8,190	20	4,911	34	10,021
Norwegian	19	9,282	17	6,647	18	6,085
Danish	69	15,149	34	8,765	35	10,691
Prussian	64	10,456	46	12,461	51	14,657
Hanoverian	26	4,627	22	3,673	28	3,498
Oldenburg and Mecklenburg	22	4,685	21	4,473	20	4,404
Hamburg	197	99,560	176	95,704	200	110,354
Bremen	144	69,188	131	68,257	152	87,743
Lubec	11	3,816	4	1,522	3	1,242
Dutch	269	60,020	297	64,650	298	67,939
Belgian	137	33,981	225	43,086	215	49,121
French	216	20,494	352	45,081	555	71,497
Spanish	58	19,285	89	34,831	118	55,133
Portuguese	11	14,677	7	2,557		
Austrian	1	300	1	341		
Turkish	2	900				
Italian					1	618
Total entries	7,929	2,548,911	8,626	2,801,743	9,466	3,153,440

Nationalities.	VESSELS CLEARED.					
	1850.		1851.		1852.	
	No.	Tonnage.	No.	Tonnage.	No.	Tonnage.
British	6,146	2,041,891	6,818	2,294,898	7,447	2,604,357
United States	4	5,021	8	10,890	1	449
Russian	28	10,875	29	14,009	26	13,654
Swedish	35	7,975	19	4,879	33	11,771
Norwegian	18	8,853	18	6,707	18	6,630
Danish	61	14,065	39	10,601	30	10,863
Prussian	62	15,960	45	11,809	50	14,380
Hanoverian	22	3,658	22	3,603	23	3,657
Oldenburg and Mecklenburg	25	5,409	20	4,360	23	5,107
Hamburg	167	95,024	184	100,048	201	113,836
Bremen	139	66,014	135	70,729	151	65,388
Lubec	11	4,351	7	2,670	5	1,556
Dutch	284	64,183	305	68,252	278	70,433
Belgian	75	24,865	74	24,877	80	20,889
French	49	14,631	61	17,354	80	27,168
Spanish	66	18,071	67	35,487	118	67,103
Portuguese	11	12,825	3	1,304	1	146
Austrian	......	......	1	341	......	......
Turkish and Greek	6	2,672	......	......	......	......
Other countries	4	1,065	3	1,356	17	6,201
Total entries	7,228	2,418,562	7,678	2,672,441	8,588	3,058,950

The contrast exhibited in these three years with the proportion of American steam tonnage employed in trade reaching British ports in 1853 is very striking:

*Number and tonnage of steam vessels of each nation entered and cleared at ports of the United Kingdom in 1853.**

Nationalities.	ENTERED.		CLEARED.	
	Vessels.	Tons.	Vessels.	Tons.
British	3,984	1,170,850	3,668	1,080,000
Swedish	2	180	......	......
Norwegian	2	145	......	......
Danish	17	4,471	18	4,734
Prussian	12	2,788	10	2,350
Other German states	110	32,457	117	31,385
Dutch	184	38,580	185	39,434
Belgian	125	28,898	121	27,858
French	14	1,528	14	1,685
Spanish	14	3,085	13	2,929
Portuguese	......	......	1	205
American, United States	35	46,670	38	51,347
Totals	4,606	1,335,636	4,186	1,258,789

* From the valuable memorial of the Chamber of Commerce before referred to. The various statements and explanations of that memorial cover almost exactly the ground here embraced, and the statistics are necessarily nearly identical. The entire matter of the memorial is extremely compact and clear in its illustration of the present position of British steam vessels in general foreign commerce.

The total tonnage and the number of vessels is more than double in 1862 over 1853, and the increase is almost wholly British, the American almost wholly disappearing in 1862, although creditably large in 1853. The steam marine of Sweden, Norway, Denmark, and the north of Europe generally, shows a very fair development from 1853 to 1861. The French and Spanish share in the increase; and, on the whole, the development of European states in this respect indicates a purpose in each not to be left behind in the progress of ocean commerce.

The British statements of trade in steam vessels to American countries north and south are worthy of attention:

Entrances of steam vessels at ports of the United Kingdom from the United States for 1853, 1860, 1861, *and* 1862.

Years.	British.		American.		Other countries.		Total.	
	No.	Tons.	No.	Tons.	No.	Tons.	No.	Tons.
1853	86	89,293	23	32,053	......	....	109	122,248
1860	154	197,520	......	....	2	3,020	156	200,540
1861	152	206,075	1	2,100	3	3,586	156	211,661
1862	152	227,468	1	618	4	6,316	157	233,402

While, as this table shows, there are now very few entries of steam vessels from the United States at British ports except the British, there are many entrances and clearances of steamers of other countries to and from other ports of the continent southward. Steamers of Spain, France, and Germany are already in the carrying and passenger trade of the tropical countries of this continent. From Cuba one Spanish steamer entered and cleared at a British port in 1860, and three in 1861. From Brazil, twenty-four steam vessels entered in 1853, twenty-four in 1860, and twelve in 1861—sixteen being British and eight of other countries in the ten years first named: In 1861 all but one were British. From St. Thomas (Danish West Indies) there were twenty-four to twenty-eight each year, nearly all British; from New Granada five to seven, and clearances of one or more to almost every American State. This point is of especial importance, since it invades a trade hitherto belonging in great part to the United States. The following table gives the number of these entrances and clearances, with their tonnage, without distinction of nationality:

Steam vessels entered at British ports from American countries.

Nationalities.	1853.		1860.		1861.		1862.	
	No.	Tons.	No.	Tons.	No.	Tons.	No.	Tons.
United States	109	122,248	156	200,546	156	211,661	157	233,402
Cuba	......	....	1	657	3	2,027	......	....
St. Thomas, (Dan. W. I.)	27	44,037	28	43,029	28	49,138	26	48,938
New Granada	......	....	5	1,922	7	3,589	6	3,258
Brazil	24	22,614	24	32,259	19	17,222	13	7,654
Hayti and Mexico	1	673	......	....	......	....	3	1,775

Steam vessels cleared from British ports for American countries.

Nationalities.	1853.		1860.		1861.		1862.	
	No.	Tons.	No.	Tons.	No.	Tons.	No.	Tons.
United States	111	120,113	200	263,151	190	267,505	179	291,975
Cuba	......	....	1	647	4	2,045	8	4,459
St. Thomas, (Dan. W. I.)	25	40,603	27	46,303	27	46,965	28	48,340
New Granada	1	812	......	....	2	1,068	......	....
Brazil	22	21,473	21	30,275	13	6,824	13	17,025
Hayti	......	....	3	1,024	7	3,588	6	2,512
Montevideo and B. Ayres	......	....	1	104	2	331	2	340
Mexico	......	....	......	....	1	464	10	3,903
Chili	1	224	......	....	1	904	......	....

The nationality of these vessels has been in great part stated. None are United States vessels except those trading from the United States, and but four or five of these in 1860 and 1861. Further statistics of this sort, being obtainable only in the British annual volumes of Trade and Navigation, cannot be given for the year 1863. The statements for 1863 undoubtedly develop and extend the changes which the comparison of 1853 with 1860, 1861, and 1862 shows to be in progress. Great numbers of vessels have been built to add to the British steam marine in the last year, and their various lines have been very active in American trade, north and south. As shown previously, the number of steam vessels built in England in 1862 was 221, with a tonnage of 77,358 tons—a greater number than in any previous year.

TRADE OF THE UNITED STATES WITH CANADA AND THE OTHER BRITISH NORTH AMERICAN PROVINCES.

The trade of the United States on the northern frontier with Canada, and on the North Atlantic coast with the British provinces other than Canada, is very closely connected with the internal trade in many respects. The exchanges between the east and the west, to and from United States markets, in many cases pass through Canada, as the transit tonnage of the Welland canal shows. Great quantities of wheat, flour, and other produce enter Canada at Detroit, to return again to the United States at Buffalo and Oswego, and also for export to foreign countries and European markets through the St. Lawrence, and over the railroad line to Portland, Maine. The technical exports and imports of the United States to and from Canada are, for these reasons, much modified when reduced to the facts of actual exchange between the respective markets; but it is not easy to separate the quantities and values so as clearly to disclose these facts, but some evidence in regard to the magnitude of this indirect trade may be obtained from the statistics subsequently given of American produce exported by way of the St. Lawrence; of that carried in both directions on the Welland canal; of the exports to Canada at Detroit, and the imports from Canada at Buffalo, Niagara, Oswego, Ogdensburg, and Cape Vincent, on the St. Lawrence, Champlain, and Vermont.

The trade with the British Atlantic provinces is less subject to modification, and has little connexion with the internal exchanges of the United States. The exports are principally flour, breadstuffs, and provisions, and the imports are coal, fish, oats, stone, and lumber. In the fiscal year ending June 30, 1855, no less than $1,280,000 in value of flour, grain, and other produce of Canada, was exported through United States ports to these provinces—a trade which was large for several years, but which ceased in 1859.

Exports of Canadian produce through the United States to other British provinces.

Fiscal years ending—	WHEAT.		WHEAT FLOUR.	
	Bushels.	Value.	Barrels.	Value.
June 30, 1849			3,773	$20,433
1850	24,902	$25,762	31,758	186,789
1851	24,259	23,132	69,890	346,895
1852	1,680	1,341	119,816	583,821
1853	17,671	16,618	152,369	835,896
1854	2,408	2,951	151,741	1,229,865
1855	1,545	3,683	135,552	1,270,057
1856			7,387	66,898
1857			1,677	14,419
1858			1,751	10,318
1859			267	1,770

In view of the length of time during which the St. Lawrence river is annually closed by ice, and the great facilities afforded by the railroads leading from Canada to Portland, Maine, this channel of exchanges between the provinces and Canada might reasonably be relied upon as a permanent one. Possibly the discontinuance is due to the relative excess of breadstuffs in the United States, and their export in such quantities as fully to occupy the market the Atlantic provinces afford. The exports of wheat, flour, and breadstuffs average more than half the total of United States produce sent to the provinces annually, rising to more than five millions of dollars in value in the year ending June 30, 1863. This trade is evidently for consumption only, and not in transit to any other market, as is the case with much of the wheat and flour export to Canada. It is also all cleared from ports of the Atlantic coast, and does not pass through Canadian channels.

The important relation held by both Canada and the provinces to the export trade in breadstuffs of the United States, and the connexion the trade in them to Canada has with the general internal exchanges of the United States, as before referred to, requires a statement of their quantities and values at the outset of the statistics of general trade on the northern frontier. The export to the provinces is seen to be in the regular and natural increase belonging to a consuming market, while that to Canada is irregular, apparently bearing no relation to any consumption in Canada. Probably the very large export of Indian corn was, however, for consumption in the form of distillation, and is therefore an exception. As an illustration of the trade appearing to exist to and from Canada in wheat and flour, but which is in fact to a great extent a transit trade, the following citations of the transactions of the fiscal years ending June 30, 1861 and 1862, are made:

Exports to Canada, 1861.

Places.	WHEAT.		WHEAT FLOUR.	
	Bushels.	Value.	Barrels.	Value.
From Detroit	9,777	$9,777	7,660	$38,310
Chicago	3,044,337	2,769,416	22,560	104,650
Milwaukie	673,359	635,141	23,108	99,086
	3,727,473	3,414,334	53,334	242,058

Imports from Canada, 1861.

Places.	FLOUR AND BREADSTUFFS.	
	Barrels.	Value.
At Vermont	142,998	$833,061
Oswego	92,893	480,381
Niagara	93,118	500,746
Buffalo	96,159	521,067
Ogdensburg	61,573	307,842
	485,729	2,603,937

Exports to Canada, 1862.

Places.	WHEAT.		WHEAT FLOUR.	
	Bushels.	Value.	Barrels.	Value.
From lake ports of Ohio	340,372	$333,520	992	$4,303
Detroit	408,428	408,886	19,671	98,021
Chicago	1,997,276	1,589,634	26,525	90,643
Milwaukie	1,567,657	1,265,610	30,359	123,037
	4,312,733	3,597,500	77,547	316,004

Imports from Canada, 1862.

Places.	WHEAT.		WHEAT FLOUR.	
	Bushels.	Value.	Barrels.	Value.
At Genesee	42,426	$48,280	632	$2,772
Oswego	1,257,364	1,280,929	78,063	387,778
Niagara	39,617	39,624	140,800	515,258
Buffalo	761,840	748,701	83,300	468,777
Ogdensburg	83,100	43,357	79,280	430,305
Vermont	670,884	673,375	152,805	921,718
Cape Vincent	256,512	231,334	21,778	109,255
Champlain	41,824	43,357	14,222	75,710
	3,112,206	3,088,157	508,510	2,920,527

Exports to Canada of wheat, flour, Indian corn, and meal, for the fiscal years 1849 to 1863, inclusive.

Years.	Wheat.		Wheat flour.		Indian corn.		Meal, rye, &c., value.	Total value.
	Bushels.	Value.	Barrels.	Value.	Bushels.	Value.		
1849	[illegible]	$112,0[illegible]	10,127	[illegible]	[illegible]	$30,265	$5,255	$215,[illegible]
1850	75,610	[illegible]	[illegible]	132,509	[illegible]	42,113	3,[illegible]	[illegible]
1851	[illegible]	[illegible]	51,716	181,550	[illegible]	30,153	[illegible]	[illegible]
1852	[illegible]	[illegible]	[illegible]	[illegible]	[illegible]	[illegible]	[illegible]	413,241
1853	[illegible]	[illegible]	[illegible]	175,64[illegible]	151,416	78,462	[illegible]	[illegible]
1854	185,225	[illegible]	[illegible]	[illegible]	[illegible]	[illegible]	17,107	1,374,973
1855	210,[illegible]	[illegible]	[illegible]	494,061	[illegible]	[illegible]	20,7[illegible]	1,[illegible],140
1856	921,[illegible]	[illegible]	[illegible]	1,310,713	1,766,131	1,037,[illegible]	[illegible]	[illegible]
1857	1,62[illegible],141	[illegible]	[illegible]	212,345	1,161,[illegible]	671,980	[illegible]	[illegible]
1858	2,670,941	[illegible]	[illegible]	[illegible]	[illegible]	[illegible]	[illegible]	[illegible]
1859	1,324,[illegible]	[illegible]	[illegible]	[illegible]	[illegible]	[illegible]	[illegible]	[illegible]
1860	1,120,975	1,010,[illegible]	[illegible]	[illegible]	[illegible]	[illegible]	105,497	[illegible]
1861	[illegible]	[illegible]	[illegible]	[illegible]	[illegible]	[illegible]	[illegible]	[illegible]
1862	[illegible]	3,[illegible],315	118,043	[illegible]	[illegible]	[illegible]	[illegible]	[illegible]
1863	6,51[illegible]	6,717,063	[illegible]	1,100,171	4,211,[illegible]	[illegible]	145,301	[illegible]

In the Canadian trade reports for 1855 it is stated that the trade in flour of the United States was, previous to the reciprocity treaty of 1854, mainly for exportation. Not being entered for consumption, it was bonded, and paid no actual duty.

The detail of imports for 1861 is not given, because it is imperfect, wheat not being distinguished in returns from other grain, and therefore that item not being available for comparison. That for 1863, following, sustains the course of trade apparent in the two previous years:

Exports to Canada, 1863.

Places.	WHEAT.		WHEAT FLOUR.	
	Bushels.	Value.	Barrels.	Value.
From lake ports of Ohio	1,428,511	$1,505,615	895	$1,769
Detroit	345,075	351,746	39,059	220,940
Chicago	1,510,390	1,562,575	78,719	340,850
Milwaukie	2,890,791	3,023,619	40,099	174,020
	6,173,773	6,400,965	158,772	737,579

Imports from Canada, 1863.

Places.	WHEAT.		WHEAT FLOUR.	
	Bushels.	Value.	Barrels.	Value.
At Vermont	28,739	$27,021	112,557	$520,741
Champlain	17,877	18,120	11,548	53,641
Cape Vincent	135,659	133,955	15,993	96,898
Ogdensburg	75,521	78,651	46,718	219,256
Oswego	360,405	375,359	47,303	218,081
Genesee	54,104	60,541	63	264
Niagara	20,052	21,076	81,482	383,267
Buffalo	267,329	291,496	93,323	557,159
	958,254	1,007,219	330,360	2,173,479

Summary of values exchanged, 1862 *and* 1863.

	Value of wheat and flour to Canada.	Value of wheat and flour from Canada.
1862	$3,914,203	$6,[illegible],6[illegible]
1863	7,134,564	3,180,028

It is known that considerable shipments of wheat from Chicago and Milwaukie, in 1863, though cleared for Canada, were really destined for export through the St. Lawrence to Europe. In the Canadian trade reports the value of "goods in transitu from the United States," exported seaward by the way of the St. Lawrence annually, is given, but this is not necessarily distinctive of the produce of the United States actually taking that route to other foreign markets. Flour made in Canada of American wheat may be exported, and even grain, passing in and out without payment of duty, may first be placed in Canadian markets, and again be withdrawn for export abroad.

In the tables just given, showing the exchange of wheat and flour for three years, it will be seen that the largest values are of wheat exported and of flour imported. All the exports are at ports west of Buffalo, and all the imports at Buffalo and eastward. The railroad lines terminating at Buffalo, Niagara, and Vermont, carry large quantities of flour, much of it made in Canada from wheat of the United States imported from the upper lake ports. In any case, the volume imported at all the ports of the border does not differ much from the volume exported; the trade, therefore, being one of convenience in transit, rather than one between producing and consuming markets, so far as wheat and flour are concerned. The modification of the aggregates exchanged between the United States and Canada is, therefore, for the three years, nearly five and a quarter millions of dollars reduction on both exports and imports, or ten and a half millions in the sum total of exchanges for each year.

There are other elements of the trade to Canada in which the movement is similarly indirect, in comparison with other departments of foreign commerce, but none of them are of much importance. The export trade to Canada has undergone many changes since the enactment of the reciprocity treaty, in 1854, the chief of which is the decline of manufactured articles, and the swelling of the general volume with wheat, flour, corn, pork, and salt. In the following tables the exchange of these articles is distinguished, as far as may be done, by the aid of both the American and Canadian records, and separate statements are made of the imports and exports of articles made free of duty by the reciprocity treaty.

The distinction between Canada and the provinces was not made in the export or import returns of the United States previous to 1849, but as the trade with Canada was conducted solely at ports of the northern frontier inland, and that with the coast provinces wholly at Atlantic ports, the compilation has been completed by assuming this division as correct. All the statistics of the trade under the reciprocity treaty were originally reported without separating Canada from the remaining provinces, and the division of values has necessarily been made on the basis just named. In a very few instances small values may have gone from Canada out at the St. Lawrence to enter at Atlantic ports, and similar instances of articles sent from the provinces of the coast inland may have taken place, but the total of such trade in either case would be very small for any single year, or for the aggregate of the series of years.

Exports to Canada.

Fiscal year ending—	Domestic exports.	Foreign exports.	Total exports.
June 30, 1849	$2,320,323	$1,914,401	$4,234,724
1850	4,641,451	1,289,370	5,930,821
1851	5,835,834	2,003,306	7,929,140
1852	4,004,963	2,712,107	6,717,070
1853	4,005,612	3,824,587	7,829,000
1854	10,510,373	6,790,333	17,300,706
1855	9,954,764	8,769,580	18,720,344
1856	15,194,788	5,668,453	20,863,241
1857	13,021,708	3,550,187	16,571,895
1858	13,663,465	3,365,789	17,029,254
1859	13,439,607	4,601,125	18,040,732
1860	11,161,590	2,918,524	14,080,114
1861	11,749,981	2,611,877	14,361,858
1862	11,282,107	1,560,397	12,842,504
1863	*18,430,605	1,468,113	19,898,718

* Including $3,302,190 of unusual export of gold coin.

NOTE.—Previous to 1849 the trade with Canada is not distinguished from the total to all British North American colonies.

Exports to other Provinces.

Fiscal year ending—	Domestic exports.	Foreign exports.	Total exports.
June 30 1849	$3,611,783	$257,760	$3,869,543
1850	3,116,840	501,374	3,618,214
1851	3,254,533	801,250	4,055,783
1852	2,650,134	1,141,822	3,791,956
1853	3,398,575	1,912,968	5,311,543
1854	4,587,771	2,672,383	7,260,154
1855	5,855,878	3,229,798	9,085,676
1856	7,519,909	620,199	8,140,108
1857	6,911,405	770,182	7,681,587
1858	5,975,494	646,979	6,622,473
1859	8,330,060	883,422	9,213,482
1860	7,502,839	1,120,375	8,623,214
1861	7,131,734	1,250,021	8,381,755
1862	7,360,005	890,706	8,250,711
1863	10,198,505	1,183,807	11,382,312

Exports to both Canada and the Provinces, with the total of imports from both.

Fiscal year ending—	Domestic exports.	Foreign exports.	Total exports.	Imports.
Sept. 30, 1821	$2,009,336	$455	$2,009,791	$400,704
1822	1,861,273	16,286	1,877,559	526,817
1823	1,818,113	3,317	1,821,430	463,374
1824	1,773,107	2,617	1,775,724	706,931
1825	2,538,224	1,740	2,539,964	610,788
1826	2,644,105	24,384	2,668,489	650,316

Exports to both Canadas, &c.—Continued.

Fiscal year ending—	Domestic exports.	Foreign exports.	Total exports.	Imports.
Sept. 30, 1827	$2,797,014	$33,660	$2,830,674	$445,118
1828	1,015,328	56,346	1,071,674	447,669
1829	2,724,104	40,805	2,764,909	577,452
1830	3,656,031	130,342	3,786,373	650,303
1831	4,026,392	35,440	4,061,832	864,869
1832	3,566,302	45,083	3,611,385	1,229,536
1833	4,390,091	81,003	4,471,094	1,783,393
1834	3,477,769	57,507	3,535,276	1,548,733
1835	3,900,545	147,343	4,047,888	1,435,166
1836	2,456,415	194,851	2,651,266	2,427,571
1837	2,992,474	296,512	3,288,986	2,359,953
1838	2,481,987	238,504	2,720,491	1,555,570
1839	3,418,770	144,684	3,563,454	2,155,140
1840	5,895,903	204,098	6,100,001	2,007,767
1841	6,292,290	364,273	6,656,563	1,068,187
1842	5,950,143	240,166	6,190,309	1,762,001
June 30, 1843	2,617,006	107,417	2,724,423	857,698
1844	5,361,186	1,354,717	6,715,903	1,405,715
1845	4,844,966	1,309,860	6,154,826	2,020,065
1846	6,042,666	1,363,767	7,406,433	1,937,717
1847	5,819,667	2,165,876	7,985,543	2,343,937
1848	6,399,659	1,982,996	8,382,655	3,046,467
1849	5,932,106	2,172,101	8,104,207	2,820,880
1850	7,758,261	1,790,774	9,549,035	6,644,462
1851	9,060,387	2,954,536	12,014,923	6,693,122
1852	6,655,097	3,853,919	10,509,016	6,110,299
1853	7,404,077	5,736,555	13,140,632	7,550,718
1854	12,204,144	9,352,716	21,556,860	8,927,560
1855	15,806,642	11,999,378	27,806,020	15,136,734
1856	22,714,697	6,314,652	29,029,349	21,310,421
1857	19,936,113	4,326,369	24,262,482	22,124,296
1858	19,638,959	4,012,768	23,651,727	15,806,519*
1859	21,769,627	6,384,547	28,154,174	19,727,551
1860	18,667,429	4,033,899	22,700,328	23,851,381
1861	18,883,715	3,861,898	22,745,613	23,062,163
1862	18,632,012	2,447,103	21,079,115	19,299,995
1863	28,629,110	2,651,920	31,281,030	24,065,423

Imports from Canada.

Year ending—	Free by ordinary laws.	Free by reciprocity treaty.	Total free.	Paying duty.	Total imports.
June 30, 1850	$636,454	....	$636,454	$3,649,016	$4,285,470
1851	1,529,685	....	1,529,685	3,425,786	4,955,471
1852	761,571	....	761,571	3,828,398	4,589,969
1853	1,179,682	....	1,179,682	4,098,434	5,278,116
1854	380,041	....	380,041	6,341,498	6,721,539
1855	760,359	$6,116,137	6,876,496	5,305,818	12,182,314
1856	847,972	15,939,850	16,787,822	610,375	17,398,197
1857	868,753	16,731,984	17,600,737	601,097	18,201,834
1858	367,450	10,900,168	11,267,618	313,953	11,581,571
1859	1,396,377	12,307,371	13,703,748	601,969	14,305,717
1860	2,208,374	16,218,767	18,427,141	434,532	18,861,673
1861	1,659,393	16,327,824	17,987,217	358,240	18,345,457
1862	790,531	14,235,562	15,026,093	227,059	15,253,152
1863	*5,442,868	12,807,354	18,250,222	567,677	18,817,899

* Of this amount the sum of $4,893,185 in gold and silver coin was entered at Champlain.

Imports from other British North American Provinces.

Year ending—	Free by ordinary laws.	Free by reciprocity treaty.	Total free.	Paying duty.	Total imports.
June 30, 1850	$151,145	....	$151,145	$1,207,847	$1,358,992
1851	160,367	....	160,367	1,576,281	1,736,650
1852	218,718	....	218,718	1,301,612	1,520,330
1853	238,568	....	238,568	2,034,034	2,272,602
1854	259,102	....	259,102	1,946,919	2,206,021
1855	140,427	$1,081,200	1,221,627	1,730,793	2,952,420
1856	193,639	3,447,236	3,640,875	184,346	3,824,221
1857	117,589	3,518,226	3,635,815	196,647	3,832,462
1858	195,082	3,852,097	4,047,169	177,770	4,224,949
1859	1,213,013	4,077,045	5,290,058	228,746	5,518,804
1860	526,011	4,227,819	4,753,830	215,878	4,969,708
1861	545,604	3,710,701	4,255,305	162,171	4,417,476
1862	857,654	2,883,990	3,741,644	302,199	4,046,813
1863	1,820,605	2,958,200	4,797,814	409,610	5,207,424

Total imports from Canada and the Provinces.

Year ending—	Free by ordinary laws.	Free by reciprocity treaty.	Total free.	Paying duty.	Total imports.
June 30, 1850	$787,599	....	$787,599	$4,856,863	$5,644,462
1851	1,690,052	....	1,690,052	5,003,070	6,693,122
1852	940,280	....	940,280	5,130,010	6,110,290
1853	1,418,250	....	1,418,250	6,132,468	7,550,718
1854	639,143	....	639,143	8,288,417	8,927,560
1855	998,786	$7,105,337	8,104,123	7,032,611	15,136,734
1856	1,041,611	19,446,080	20,488,097	821,724	21,310,421
1857	1,016,348	20,290,210	21,290,658	827,744	22,124,296
1858	502,632	14,782,255	15,314,787	491,732	15,806,519
1859	2,600,420	16,391,416	18,991,836	733,715	19,727,551
1860	2,734,305	20,446,568	23,180,071	670,411	23,851,391
1861	2,404,907	20,047,625	22,514,529	520,411	23,062,933
1862	1,618,195	17,139,532	18,770,717	520,258	19,299,995
1863	*7,284,573	15,765,563	23,048,136	977,287	24,045,423

* Including $6,355,485 of gold coin.

Articles imported.		Half year to June 30, '55. Quantity.	Half year to June 30, '55. Value.	1855-'56. Quantity.	1855-'56. Value.	1856-'57. Quantity.	1856-'57. Value.	1857-'58. Quantity.	1857-'58. Value.	1858-'59. Quantity.	1858-'59. Value.
Animals			$262,611		$1,360,863		$1,723,909		$1,310,122		$1,139,981
Ashes			22,769		62,328		266,234		153,053		161,659
Bark	cords	110	185	575	1,410	979	1,255	913	618	5	6
Butter	pounds	164,686	19,537	1,185,495	212,136	1,864,199	307,364	1,770,749	274,372	2,314,550	370,199
Cheese	pounds			15,530	1,089	22,349	2,642	28,583	2,375	20,270	1,556
Coal	tons			6	31	137	623	11	69	3	16
Eggs			10,655		30,638		69,990		57,990		44,973
Firewood	cords	3,739	3,690	12,908	30,964	10,910	31,915	16,899	61,763	14,613	40,547
Fish, pickled and other, in barrels	barrels	1,038	5,563	6,670	41,451	3,653	39,233	7,121	49,696	4,409	24,479
dry and other, by weight	pounds	256,862	6,211	2,091,201	81,910	1,404,141	68,165	1,002,787	63,177	1,250,375	42,576
Fish oil	gallons	1,450	902	13,970	14,683	1,978	8,719	1,448	1,569	13,881	5,210
products of, not specified			5,408	?					180		69
Flax and hemp, not manufactured	cwt.	110	673	4,901	2,468	700	8,302	50,644	9,039		8,643
Fruits, dry and green			179		4,610		4,759		1,290		3,601
Furs			29,971		65,817		122,648		31,736		140,297
Grain and flour; wheat	bushels	*1,456,774	2,453,601	3,792,479	6,289,349	2,504,960	3,051,658	2,087,912	2,113,979	1,982,431	1,363,163
wheat flour	barrels	200,770	2,239,900	475,704	4,403,338	1,522,411	4,134,914	347,078	2,443,216	798,683	2,788,096
oats	bushels			†1,173,367	387,299	2,197,600	1,381,326	1,492,874	540,991	8,504,128	2,088,723
oat meal	cwt.								249		578
barley	bushels					875	890			13,303	11,033
all other grains							1,430				673
Gypsum			1,519		572		474		314		2,149
Hides and skins			8,310		149,464		202,314		79,543		157,071
Horses			461		1,378		8,863		1,634		410
Lard	pounds	490	35	2,395	844	378,431	87,696	89,705	7,516	11,800	1,324
Meats, cured, and all other	pounds	112,100	8,083	599,343	50,379	787,058	78,341	215,249	34,915	2,780,913	226,048
Ores of metals	tons	250	1,743	88,372	19,813	3,221	42,924	4,289	206,460	2,733	12,855
Pelts			24,073		132,210		177,598		71,304		89,048
Poultry			603		17,949		32,177		83,193		34,958
Rags	pounds	213,873	4,924	633,946	16,548	374,499	16,950	482,308	14,773	387,058	10,974
Seeds, trees, and plants			2,200		24,014		58,097		14,125		87,267
Slate and stone			941		1,329		7,446		1,518		7,998
Tallow	pounds	1,960	207	7,127	1,014	43,473	6,492	4,080	326	6,314	308
Tar, pitch, turpentine, and balsam			175		1,924		8,900		4,646		2,747
Timber and lumber			571,727		2,318,177		2,013,663		2,438,785		2,544,054
Tobacco	pounds		1,804	69,767	2,850	49,773	3,398	80,430	980	20,540	1,427
Vegetables; potatoes	bushels		98,618	18,790	12,249	98,914	17,436	3,689	4,149	34,230	67,154
Wool	pounds	194,610	81,963	1,498,097	371,363	1,230,135	305,949	808,813	865,045	2,103,408	819,495
Miscellaneous			29		33		1,636		3,800		3,599
Total			3,860,300		13,987,165		18,456,788		10,475,130		11,444,320

* Entered as grain of all kinds, not distinguishing between wheat, oats, and barley. In reality most of it is wheat.
† In this and subsequent years an estimate is made of oats, or of other grain than wheat, by taking the totals at Vermont, Champlain, and Ogdensburg as oats, and all other as wheat.

General table of imports into the United States from Canada, free of duty under the reciprocity treaty, &c.—Continued.

Articles imported.	1859-'60.		1860-'61.		1861-'62.		1862-'63.	
	Quantity.	Value.	Quantity.	Value.	Quantity.	Value.	Quantity.	Value.
Animals	....	$1,653,079	....	$1,720,[illegible]	....	$1,531,437	....	$1,346,721
Ashes	....	183,535	3,933,709	885,314	....	876,168	....	[illegible]
Bark ......cords..	1,893	3,073	1,424	3,6[illegible]	1,182	2,848	3,634	10,959
Butter ......pounds..	3,044,088	500,139	2,976,068	389,068	3,592,321	423,343	2,167,620	323,197
Cheese ......pounds..	88,073	6,028	....	....	121,177	9,707	65,[illegible]	2,049
Coal ......tons..	10	44	37	613	68	615	7	48
Dye-stuffs	....	10	....	....	....	150	....	....
Eggs	....	107,626	....	130,327	....	67,804	....	48,465
Firewood ......cords..	85,918	87,631	92,765	35,767	39,958	89,158	61,940	82,178
Fish, pickled and other, in barrels ......barrels..	7,726	39,549	3,615	34,296	5,343	71,554	3,297	18,719
dry and other, by weight ......pounds..	758,318	33,344	1,481,370	30,496	1,144,649	28,019	851,815	20,343
Fish oil ......gallons..	1,451	1,053	340	277	658	540	2,650	1,487
Flax and hemp, not manufactured ......cwt..	2,066	17,653	5,101	25,890	1,173	11,049	1,948	18,117
Fruits, dry and green	....	4,995	....	2,659	....	6,096	....	6,[illegible]
Furs	....	110,244	....	74,089	....	105,001	....	149,348
Grain and flour: wheat ......bushels..	1,858,160	1,744,647	4,633,444	4,922,190	3,590,630	3,832,840	949,056	1,070,[illegible]
wheat flour ......barrels..	863,847	3,048,175	1,534,470	3,052,890	573,647	2,840,320	600,153	2,137,394
Indian corn ......bushels..	40	450	....	....	67,692	23,806	56,996	14,147
Indian meal ......barrels..	....	....	....	....	281	349	119	48
oats ......bushels..	6,785,381	4,188,858	3,654,380	1,808,277	1,871,830	463,468	2,363,320	1,050,810
oat meal ......cwt..	70	180	....	....	48,135	74,701	15,308	34,331
rye ......bushels..	....	....	....	....	345,623	180,556	10,954	11,577
barley ......bushels..	....	....	....	....	2,080,879	1,089,549	1,810,550	1,509,678
all other grains	....	....	....	....	....	848,830	....	307,573
Gypsum	....	8,473	....	2,436	....	1,750	....	3,310
Hides and skins	....	197,661	....	65,294	....	63,018	....	77,780
Horns	....	1,004	....	294	....	58	....	8,541
Lard ......pounds..	88,752	8,153	....	....	258,700	18,018	56,193	4,857
Meats, cured, and all other ......pounds..	6,288,598	377,790	8,562,994	399,035	2,663,093	197,035	2,977,139	138,075
Ores of metals ......tons..	6,681	300,714	12,907	298,314	40,739	373,439	4,015	680,[illegible]
Pelts	....	149,053	....	94,636	....	101,435	....	117,491
Poultry	....	[illegible]	....	37,063	....	33,176	....	16,304
Rags ......pounds..	1,383,604	34,179	1,377,288	37,070	1,938,[illegible]	59,842	2,816,[illegible]	87,100
Seeds, trees, and plants	....	33,838	....	85,356	....	108,613	....	131,470
Slate and stone	....	6,894	....	1,634	....	1,901	....	3,[illegible]
Tallow ......pounds..	18,449	2,110	....	....	11,818	1,[illegible]	183,636	13,363
Tar, pitch, turpentine, and balsam ......barrels..	....	6,768	....	330	857	1,474	....	2,210
Timber and lumber	....	2,694,198	....	2,709,[illegible]	....	2,036,854	....	2,346,634
Tobacco ......pounds..	9,477	410	3,743	134	30,022	2,192	5,767	[illegible]
Vegetables: potatoes ......bushels..	190,863	92,626	109,397	30,734	....	7,865	....	29,434
Wool ......pounds..	1,656,369	335,698	1,042,385	657,055	1,685,091	563,801	1,907,748	733,049
Miscellaneous	....	2,630	....	947	....	140	....	140
Total	....	16,910,138	....	16,380,377	....	14,284,922	....	12,467,384

General table of imports from the Provinces, other than Canada, free of duty under the reciprocity treaty.

Articles imported.		1853-'54.		1856-'57.		1857-'58.		1858-'59.	
		Quantity.	Value.	Quantity.	Value.	Quantity.	Value.	Quantity.	Value.
Animals			83,689		84,077		618,506		60,960
Ashes			379						
Bark	cords	1,672	7,890	1,432	4,467	1,707	6,095	1,097	3,640
Butter and cheese	pounds	12,391	9,169	31,029	4,343	18,545	9,574	20,313	3,679
Coal	tons	150,446	361,673	130,816	388,852	136,733	397,710	192,718	379,154
Eggs			7,974		6,159		15,053		9,743
Firewood	cords	61,990	152,566	61,741	192,040	45,378	113,815	44,958	137,243
Fish, pickled	barrels	253,915	1,294,817	282,311	1,123,310	257,973	1,124,250	274,835	1,314,040
dry and other	pounds	17,449,543	646,693	11,891,570	409,231	9,443,349	974,676	13,851,060	340,939
oil	gallons	222,819	164,462	288,910	874,563	257,611	130,409	546,449	309,091
products			99,795		82,365		192,738		156,450
Furs			1,415		3,048		3,484		1,731
Fruits, green and dry			1,640		6,343		4,316		3,985
Grain, (nearly all oats)	bushels	63,077	31,647	389,830	111,780	977,608	86,356	769,840	351,169
Barley	do	75	56						
Meal, (oatmeal)	cwt	977	987	337	1,130	5,531	3,089	263	985
Grindstones			59,638		66,821		34,779		40,320
Gypsum			47,067		8,134		10,387		10,444
Hides and skins			69,148		81,441		41,918		84,898
Horns			1,018		1,439		440		844
Meats, (all kinds)	pounds	50,732	3,347	41,139	3,860	34,639	2,008	18,191	1,311
Ores of metals	tons	86	248	95	787	61	311	800	16,854
Pelts			336		1,037		9,683		1,148
Poultry					8,018		218		134
Rags	pounds	331,011	7,886	220,785	8,700	165,498	5,814	116,637	1,094
Seeds and trees			641		1,315		991		1,841
Stone, unwrought			18,631		53,195		69,450		44,394
Timber and lumber			510,745		371,364		444,661		383,519
Vegetables	bushels	380,911	187,301	358,888	337,088	323,680	543,506	952,011	397,219
Wheat	do								
Wheat flour	cwt								
Wool		11,734	2,999	14,785	3,416	16,940	3,756	81,089	4,968
Not enumerated			680		611		378		851
Total			2,458,870		3,289,473		3,655,438		4,666,674

General table of imports from the provinces other than Canada, &c.—Continued.

Articles imported.		1859-'60.		1860-'61.		1861-'62.		1862-'63.	
		Quantity.	Value.	Quantity.	Value.	Quantity.	Value.	Quantity.	Value.
Animals			$3,[illegible]		60,405		81,350		84,458
Ashes			65				498		
Bark	cords	2,538	10,090	1,610	6,019	898	1,758	891	3,790
Butter and cheese	pounds	32,654	5,711	91,049	7,304	16,555	1,779	18,049	3,440
Coal	tons	169,879	497,329	204,000	702,163	188,544	614,041	824,767	737,048
Eggs			10,[illegible]		29,357		21,128		14,035
Firewood	cords	40,901	110,159	60,080	182,677	65,617	110,748	38,850	98,537
Fish, pickled	barrels	294,198	1,230,343	197,391	913,377	177,589	682,404	127,598	478,919
dry and other	pounds	8,059,081	940,109	11,858,310	364,705	3,504,098	101,310	3,921,318	113,788
oil	gallons	427,209	809,545	946,897	131,329	110,000	61,814	203,363	118,730
products			954,417		315,198		182,178		188,613
Furs			8,738		1,400		1,341		785
Fruits, green and dry			3,740		1,370		85,430		411
Grain, (nearly all oats)	bushels	1,087,634	204,821	448,000	182,174	280,137	150,341	939,011	308,389
Barley	do					9,278	8,654	17,845	14,063
Meal, (oatmeal)	cwt	1,148	2,080	402	84	184	824	531	1,804
Grindstones			12,037		50,630		91,049		48,712
Gypsum			13,030		80,181		34,948		130,578
Hides and skins			57,318		87,560		80,460		89,343
Horses			869		221		231		641
Meats, (all kinds)	pounds	34,280	8,161	33,389	1,751	10,531	840	6,983	849
Ores of metals	tons	130	1,065	94	1,870	35	149	57	855
Pelts			3,713		18,034		80,807		63,471
Poultry			876		239		162		58
Rags	pounds	202,676	4,380	803,084	4,354	888,637	5,643	375,957	11,107
Seeds and trees			843		670		1,250		738
Stone, unwrought			78,047		64,508		94,613		18,788
Timber and lumber			635,000		499,171		457,888		471,598
Vegetables	bushels	850,001	233,717	800,703	800,074		884,227		117,438
Wheat	do							6	19
Wheat flour	cwt			1,380	2,736				
Wool	pounds	82,137	4,930	17,418	3,504	31,194	6,008	72,311	98,785
Not enumerated			130		575		13		158
Totals			4,161,000		3,788,410		2,657,593		2,940,430

Imports from Canada paying duty, from 1855–'56 to 1862–'63.

Articles imported.	1855–'56. Quantity.	Value.	1856–'57. Quantity.	Value.	1857–'58. Quantity.	Value.	1858–'59. Quantity.	Value.
Iron, pig ....tons..	1,350	$23,[illegible]	467	$10,298	661	$12,[illegible]	[illegible]	[illegible]
railroad ....do ..	93,[illegible]	[illegible]	10,597	443,530	1,612	113,168	[illegible]	[illegible]
bar, sheet, chains, &c	....	18,[illegible]	....	2,[illegible]	....	2,[illegible]	....	[illegible]
manufactures, not specified	....	7,653	....	16,146	....	18,[illegible]	....	[illegible]
Steel and steel manufactures, cutlery, and arms	....	1,379	....	357	....	785	....	[illegible]
Old iron ....tons..	2,008	[illegible],473	....	21,[illegible]	2,[illegible]	93,167	4,[illegible]	[illegible]
Woollen manufactures	....	3,677	....	4,600	....	4,336	....	[illegible]
Cotton manufactures	....	2,491	....	3,329	....	1,404	....	[illegible]
Silk manufactures	....	1,271	....	1,763	....	063	....	[illegible]
Linens; flax and hemp manufactures..	....	2,[illegible]	....	915	....	434	....	[illegible]
Laces, buttons, and cloth shoes........	....	138	....	[illegible]	....	787	....	[illegible]
Straw bonnets, hats, &c	....	3,[illegible]	....	7,[illegible]	....	4,331	....	[illegible]
India-rubber, and manufactures of........	....	1,0[illegible]	....	2[illegible],[illegible]	....	877	....	[illegible]
Clothing	....	1,[illegible]	....	2,913	....	1,188	....	[illegible]
Furs	....	631	....	1,715	....	615	....	[illegible]
Boots and shoes, leather	....	425	....	2,030	....	701	....	[illegible]
Leather, and all other manufactures of	....	8,641	....	2,[illegible]	....	3,614	....	[illegible]
Hair manufactures and brushes........	....	613	....	4[illegible]	....	133	....	[illegible]
Books	....	1,661	....	6,4[illegible]	....	4,[illegible]	....	[illegible]
Engravings and photographs	....	123	....	45	....	819	....	[illegible]
Paper and manufactures of paper	....	29	....	[illegible]	....	914	....	[illegible]
Musical instruments........	....	137	....	1,0[illegible]	....	1,0[illegible]	....	[illegible]
Watches, jewelry, gold and silver manufactures	....	829	....	333	....	835	....	[illegible]
China and plated ware........	....	7,10[illegible]	....	2,478	....	[illegible]	....	[illegible]
Glassware	....	[illegible]	....	1,0[illegible]	....	158	....	[illegible]
Tin, lead, and zinc manufactures	....	7[illegible]	....	2,316	....	[illegible]	....	[illegible]
Copper and brass manufactures	....	853	....	3,374	....	137	....	[illegible]
Wood manufactures, and wood not specified	....	41,[illegible]	....	77,373	....	92,[illegible]	....	[illegible]
Drugs, dyes, and spices	....	1,326	....	455	....	311	....	[illegible]
Oils, palm and other foreign .. gallons..	420	5[illegible]	120	[illegible]	678	[illegible]	4,[illegible]	2,[illegible]
fish and petroleum ....do..	....	....	....	....	[illegible]	175	....	[illegible]
Tobacco, and manufactures of	....	823	....	617	....	3[illegible]	....	[illegible]
Salt ....bushels..	2[illegible],[illegible]	2[illegible],[illegible]	191,2[illegible]	26,1[illegible]	138,[illegible]	20,878	[illegible]	[illegible]
Wines ....gallons..	11,1[illegible]	7,5[illegible]	1,083	1,4[illegible]	1,334	2,1[illegible]	2,[illegible]	4,[illegible]
Brandy ....do..	4,[illegible]	[illegible],329	3,040	9,161	3,490	13,973	[illegible]	[illegible]
Spirits ....do..	2,719	1,631	1,[illegible]	[illegible]	4,707	4,011	7,3[illegible]	[illegible]
Beer and ale ....do..	[illegible],317	7,116	[illegible],363	3,[illegible]	[illegible],314	8,476	[illegible],476	7,[illegible]
Tea ....pounds..	18	6	4,726	567	40	[illegible]	[illegible]	[illegible]
Coffee ....do..	113	13	3,5[illegible]	354	....	....	....	....
Sugar ....do..	43,170	1,405	[illegible],279	2,011	14,2[illegible]	[illegible]	[illegible]	4,[illegible]
Coal ....tons..	174	623	401	[illegible]	411	7[illegible]	1,[illegible]	3,[illegible]
Wool ....pounds..	[illegible],190	2,405	30	5	....	....	....	....
All other articles........	....	71,610	....	33,437	....	41,434	....	[illegible]
Total........	....	640,373	....	[illegible],097	....	313,[illegible]	....	[illegible]

Imports from Canada paying duty, &c.—Continued.

Articles imported.	1859–'60. Quantity.	Value.	1860–'61. Quantity.	Value.	1861–'62. Quantity.	Value.	1862–'63. Quantity.	Value.
Iron, pig........tons..	590	$7,996	1,076	$14,791	173	$2,[illegible]	40	[illegible]
railroad ....do ..	4,663	170,663	607	14,944	....	....	[illegible]	14,[illegible]
bar, sheet, chains, &c	....	4,430	....	2,207	....	3,[illegible]	....	[illegible]
manufactures not specified........	....	34,607	....	12,7[illegible]	....	5,1[illegible]	....	[illegible]
Steel and steel manufactures, cutlery, and arms	....	2,[illegible]	....	9,[illegible]	....	2,[illegible]	....	[illegible]
Old iron ....tons..	13,115	29,7[illegible]	1,711	21,1[illegible]	925	[illegible]	2,[illegible]	[illegible]
Woollen manufactures........	....	4,0[illegible]	....	3,3[illegible]	....	10,[illegible]	....	[illegible]
Cotton manufactures	....	[illegible]	....	2,1[illegible]	....	[illegible]	....	[illegible]
Silk manufactures	....	2,3[illegible]	....	1,015	....	3[illegible]	....	[illegible]

Imports from Canada paying duty, &c.—Continued.

Articles imported.	1859-'60.		1860-'61.		1861-'62.		1862-'63.	
	Quantity.	Value.	Quantity.	Value.	Quantity.	Value.	Quantity.	Value.
Linens: flax and hemp manufactures	....	$1,657	....	$2,444	....	$2,318	....	$18,777
Laces, buttons, and cloth shoes	....	460	....	246	....	....	....	19
Straw bonnets, hats, &c	....	3,724	....	6,791	....	2,493	....	4,150
India-rubber, and manufactures of	....	11,113	....	53,278	....	97,912	....	13,301
Clothing	....	923	....	749	....	2,105	....	2,154
Furs	....	1,784	....	647	....	538	....	928
Boots and shoes, leather	....	2,978	....	1,869	....	....	....	....
Leather, and all other manufactures of	....	5,079	....	1,164	....	3,904	....	13,783
Hair manufactures and brushes	....	317	....	248	....	146	....	2,213
Books	....	3,243	....	3,752	....	3,848	....	6,298
Engravings and photographs	....	493	....	647	....	56	....	89
Paper and manufactures of paper	....	478	....	60	....	816	....	233
Musical instruments	....	280	....	790	....	....	....	....
Watches, jewelry, gold and silver manufactures	....	7,253	....	635	....	656	....	894
China and plated wares	....	12,310	....	11,611	....	18,739	....	26,409
Glasswares	....	450	....	374	....	942	....	616
Tin, lead, and zinc manufactures	....	1,730	....	1,092	....	1,113	....	7,918
Copper and brass manufactures	....	174	....	470	....	2,090	....	4,572
Wood manufactures, and wood not specified	....	44,219	....	24,407	....	19,340	....	10,292
Drugs, dyes, and spices	....	89	....	108	....	1,619	....	318
Oils palm and other foreign... gallons	3,549	3,210	187	*2,119	534	1,129	721	854
fish and petroleum......do	4,957	4,370	7,030	5,663	8,999	7,043	9,292	2,059
Tobacco, and manufactures of	....	974	....	530	....	67	....	91
Salt......bushels	68,102	9,058	288,890	32,101	136,811	19,865	198,464	37,415
Wines......gallons	1,848	4,659	1,990	2,017	1,753	1,950	1,279	2,256
Brandy......do	6,425	12,930	3,617	7,217	1,600	3,953	1,728	4,516
Spirits......do	5,680	4,076	8,641	4,398	4,764	3,322	1,840	1,154
Beer and ale......do	10,106	1,115	11,582	8,436	1,867	892	1,680	572
Molasses......do	499	117	....	....	8,300	1,123	....	....
Tea......pounds	431	108	1,256	617	1,742	601	19,241	8,081
Coffee......do	....	....	....	....	....	....	10	2
Sugar......do	88,169	1,315	38,290	1,951	85,700	1,337	77,343	3,719
Coal......tons	448	1,017	[illegible]	3,678	271	639	90	299
Wool......pounds	....	....	308,030	61,732	31	18	37,779	15,103
All other articles	....	33,490	....	32,053	....	89,450	....	71,[illegible]
Total	....	434,532	....	339,240	....	327,039	....	425,133

* Of this value $1,618 is essential oil.

† Of this, 15,089 pounds, $1,053, is wool waste.

ANALYSIS OF THE FOREGOING TABLES.

The first general tables given above show an average export trade to Canada of $16,826,797 for eight fiscal years following the enactment of the reciprocity treaty, of which $13,493,739 was the value of domestic produce, and $3,333,059 was the value of foreign goods. There is no marked increase in the exports at the beginning of this period of eight years, the total for 1854 being above the average of the succeeding years, including an unusual export of $3,500,000 of gold coin in 1863. The average for the last four years is $12,933,000 in value of domestic produce exported, against an average of $14,300,000 for the four previous years, which were the first of the full operation of the treaty. The general volume of domestic export trade to Canada has, therefore, declined under its operation.

The foreign exports show a marked decline during the eight years, falling off from $6,790,333 in 1854, and $8,769,580 in 1855, to $1,560,397 in 1862, and $1,468,113 in 1863. It is obvious that the Canadian supply of foreign goods is no longer purchased in the importing cities of the United States, as before the treaty; and the statistics of goods entering Canada, through the United States, under bond, show that to be the mode of receipt substituted for the former. These bonded goods nearly all enter at Portland, and pass over the railroads through Vermont.

Of the exports to Canada, both domestic produce and foreign merchandise, the United States records give no distinction as to those which pay duty and those received free of duty; but the Canadian official tables show that for eight calendar years to 1862, an average of $9.335,865 of these exports paid duty, while an average of $10,720,000 was admitted free of duty. As the record in this case is for calendar years, the annual values cannot be exactly compared with those made up for our fiscal years. The Canadian values are larger generally—a fact to be accounted for by their more rigid inspection of imports than ours of exports, and by the valuation they make of "settlers' goods," "vehicles in use," and a large class of personal effects not usually cleared at our custom-houses.

The imports from Canada show an average value of $16,643,826 for the last eight fiscal years, of which an average of $467,238 only paid duty on entering the United States. The average sum of $16,170,337 entered free of duty, of which $14,443,000 was under the reciprocity treaty, and $1,732,725 was free under other laws. The following are the values admitted free to each country, respectively, contrasted for each year:

Paying duty in Canada.

Calendar years.	Amount.
1855	$11,449,472
1856	12,770,923
1857	9,966,430
1858	8,473,607
1859	9,032,861
1860	8,526,230
1861	8,338,620
1862	6,128,768
1863	3,974,396
Average of 8 years	8,401,481

Paying duty in the United States.

Fiscal years.	Amount.
1854–'55	$5,305,818
1855–'56	640,375
1856–'57	691,097
1857–'58	313,953
1858–'59	504,969
1859–'60	434,532
1860–'61	358,240
1861–'62	227,059
1862–'63	567,677
Average of 8 years	467,238

Under the reciprocity treaty, therefore, duty is paid on goods of the United States entering Canada of the average annual value of $7,934,241 more than the values of duty-paying goods entering the United States from Canada.

The respective values made free by the reciprocity treaty were, from 1856 to 1861, nearly twice as great from Canada, or of Canadian produce, as from the United States, or of United States produce. In 1862 and 1863, in consequence of the enormous increase in the shipments of wheat, flour, and grain nominally to Canada, but really through Canada to other markets, the values became nearly equal.

Reciprocity imports into Canada from the United States.

Calendar years.	Amount.
1856	$8,082,820
1857	8,642,044
1858	5,564,615
1859	7,106,116
1860	7,069,096
1861	9,980,937
1862	14,430,626
1863	12,339,367
Total, 8 years	73,215,623

Reciprocity imports into the United States from Canada.

Fiscal years.	Amount.
1855–'56	$15,959,850
1856–'57	16,731,984
1857–'58	10,900,168
1858–'59	12,307,071
1859–'60	16,218,767
1860–'61	16,327,824
1861–'62	14,205,562
1862–'63	12,607,054
Total, 8 years	115,548,890

The treaty has, therefore, released from duty a total sum of $12,333,257 in value of goods of Canada more than of goods the produce of the United States. The decline in value of American and foreign goods paying duty on entering Canada from the United States, in 1862 and 1863, is due to the decline of trade in all fabrics and manufactures, not to any change in the proportions of free and dutiable, through which our exports are relieved from taxation.

CANADIAN OFFICIAL STATISTICS, WITH DETAILED TABLES OF EXPORTS TO CANADA.

As the distinction between goods entering Canada free and dutiable cannot be derived from the United States returns, the following table is limited to three years, and the Canadian statistics are taken complete for the illustration of that side of the trade. These tables are very full and valuable, furnishing a clear illustration of the character of that trade as it enters Canadian markets.

The Canadian tables that here follow are general tables corresponding to those before given from United States records, and these, with various tables cited elsewhere, are all taken from the annual volumes on the Trade and Navigation of Canada, published by that government.

Statement of the value of the imports into Canada from the United States for 14 years, from 1850 to 1863 inclusive, with amount of duties paid.

[From Canadian official reports.]

Calendar years.	Value of free goods.	Value of duty-paying goods.	Total imports.	Amount of duties paid.	Rate per cent.
1850	$791,128	$5,903,732	$6,694,860	$1,069,814	18.47
1851	1,384,030	6,981,735	8,365,765	1,274,702	18.26
1852	864,620	7,613,063	8,477,693	1,433,195	18.82
1853	1,125,665	10,656,582	11,782,147	1,806,819	16.94
1854	2,083,757	13,449,341	15,533,098	2,209,173	16.42
1855	9,379,204	11,449,472	20,828,676	1,780,679	15.60
1856	9,933,856	12,770,923	22,704,509	2,059,826	16.13
1857	10,258,231	9,966,430	20,224,651	1,605,164	16.10
1858	7,161,858	8,473,907	15,635,565	1,611,711	19.63
1859	8,600,055	9,002,861	17,592,916	1,825,135	20.20
1860	8,740,719	8,536,230	17,273,029	1,759,928	20.64
1861	12,730,768	8,338,620	21,069,388	1,684,892	19.60
1862	19,044,374	6,128,783	25,173,157	....	......
1863	19,134,966	3,974,396	23,109,362	....	......

Of the value of free goods here stated, there was of coin and bullion the following sums:

In 1861 .... $963,308
1862 2,530,297
1863 4,651,679

The values exported, as reported in the United States records, are elsewhere stated for fiscal years, and therefore not directly comparable with these, which are from Canadian reports.

Statement of the value of the exports from Canada to the United States, and the total trade.

[From Canadian official reports.]

Calendar years.	Exports to United States.	Imports from United States.	Amount of the whole trade.
1851	$4,071,544	$8,365,764	$12,437,308
1852	6,284,520	8,477,693	14,762,213
1853	8,936,380	11,782,144	20,718,524
1854	8,649,000	15,533,098	24,182,098
1855	16,737,276	20,828,676	37,565,952
1856	17,979,752	22,704,508	40,684,260
1857	13,206,436	20,224,648	33,431,084
1858	11,930,094	15,635,565	27,565,659
1859	13,922,314	17,592,916	31,515,230
1860	18,427,968	17,273,029	35,700,997
1861	14,386,427	21,069,388	35,455,815
1862	15,063,730	25,173,157	40,236,887
1863	22,534,074	23,109,362	45,643,436

Imports into Canada from the United States, 1855 to 1863, free of duty under the reciprocity treaty. (Prepared from official documents of Canada.)

Articles imported.	1855.		1856.		1857.	
	Quantity.	Value.	Quantity.	Value.	Quantity.	Value.
Animals ...number.	7,470	$507,[illegible]	16,700	$473,[illegible]	16,[illegible]	$[illegible]
Ashes	....	8,[illegible]	....	7,107	....	16,15[illegible]
Bark ...cords.	....	3,[illegible]	8[illegible]	2,9[illegible]	1,[illegible]	[illegible]
Broom-corn	....	24,101	....	39,[illegible]	....	32,670
Burr and grindstones	....	21,100	....	17,[illegible]	....	16,[illegible]
Butter ...pounds.	147,840	25,7[illegible]	237,[illegible]	44,967	218,810	3[illegible]
Cheese ...do...	1,0[illegible]	103,9[illegible]	1,343,000	153,[illegible]	1,[illegible]	152,[illegible]
Coal ...tons.	60,0[illegible]	[illegible]	81,000	345,361	94,[illegible]	40[illegible]
Cotton, raw	....	13,[illegible]	....	17,531	....	3,[illegible]
Dyestuffs	....	18,9[illegible]	....	25,[illegible]	....	15,[illegible]
Eggs	....	1,[illegible]	....	10,57[illegible]	....	18,57[illegible]
Fish	....	102,47[illegible]	....	122,[illegible]	....	192,415
oil ...gallons	[illegible],155	1[illegible],110	[illegible],159	2[illegible]	198,[illegible]	162,371
products of	....	4,871	....	[illegible]	....	[illegible]
Firewood ...cords	....	30,[illegible]	84,717	[illegible]	31,673	44,218
Fruits, dried	....	14,391	....	[illegible]	....	32,[illegible]
not dried	....	140,9[illegible]	....	137,2[illegible]	....	157,2[illegible]
Flax, hemp, and tow, not manufactured	....	[illegible],170	....	[illegible]	....	75,[illegible]
Flour ...barrels	19[illegible],[illegible]10	1,613,74[illegible]	13[illegible],100	7[illegible]	312,640	1,2[illegible]
Furs, skins and tails, not dressed	....	87,[illegible]	....	64,[illegible]	....	[illegible]
Grain, all kinds ...bushels	9,469,[illegible]	8,711,9[illegible]	3,45[illegible],211	2,7[illegible]	3,7[illegible]	3,[illegible]
Gypsum	....	12,[illegible]	....	6,[illegible]	....	7,[illegible]
Hides and pelts	....	60,0[illegible]	....	80,000	....	10[illegible]
Lard ...pounds.	....	91,[illegible]	....	142,132	....	3[illegible],740
Manures	....	11,9[illegible]	....	11,100	....	1[illegible]
Meal ...barrels.	6,[illegible]	40,0[illegible]	8,[illegible]	3[illegible],715	14,2[illegible]	[illegible]
Meat of all kinds ...cwt.	109,098	1,019,711	15[illegible]	1,417,771	90,[illegible]	[illegible]
Ores of metals	....	43[illegible]	....	5,[illegible]	....	11,[illegible]
Pitch and tar ...barrels.	3,200	[illegible],457	....	7,[illegible]	2,353	[illegible]
Plants and shrubs	....	37,[illegible]	....	63,[illegible]	....	21,1[illegible]
Poultry	....	1,73[illegible]	....	6,941	....	8,[illegible]
Rags	....	1,[illegible]01	....	[illegible]	....	2,[illegible]
Rice ...pounds.	[illegible]	42,673	[illegible]	40,171	[illegible]	[illegible]
Seeds	....	1[illegible]	....	67,71[illegible]	....	1[illegible],415
Skins	....	[illegible],504	....	[illegible]	....	17,1[illegible]
Stone and marble ...unwrought	....	57,113	....	6[illegible],791	....	72,[illegible]
Tallow ...pounds	....	3[illegible]	....	[illegible],301	3,[illegible]	[illegible]
Timber and lumber	....	[illegible],411	....	[illegible]	....	[illegible]
Tobacco, unmanufactured ...lbs	719,[illegible]	[illegible]	[illegible]	10[illegible]	950,[illegible]	1[illegible]
Turpentine	....	2,[illegible]	....	28	....	....
Vegetables	....	11,735	....	34,[illegible]	....	[illegible]
Wool	....	7,[illegible]	....	[illegible]	....	[illegible]
Free by reciprocity treaty	....	7,725,572	....	8,0[illegible]	....	8,[illegible]
Specie and bullion	....	....	....	....	....	*
All other free goods†	....	1,[illegible]	....	1,[illegible],768	....	1,[illegible],177
Total free of duty	....	9,379,[illegible]	....	9,[illegible]	....	10,[illegible],921

Imports into Canada from the United States, &c.—Continued.

Articles imported.	1858.		1859.		1860.	
	Quantity.	Value.	Quantity.	Value.	Quantity.	Value.
Animals ...number.	10,170	$240,1[illegible]	[illegible]	$224,677	14,9[illegible]	$[illegible]
Ashes	....	[illegible]	....	12,[illegible]	....	31,[illegible]
Bark ...cords.	525	9,117	600	2,570	3[illegible]	[illegible]
Broom-corn	....	20,[illegible]	....	20,[illegible]	....	[illegible]
Burr and grindstones	....	13,[illegible]	....	14,3[illegible]	....	15,[illegible]
Butter ...pounds	43,[illegible]	7,[illegible]	2[illegible],719	40,335	1[illegible],398	[illegible]
Cheese ...do...	1,[illegible],675	[illegible]	791,410	[illegible]	[illegible]	[illegible]
Coal ...tons.	[illegible]	[illegible]	[illegible],537	[illegible]	[illegible]	304,[illegible]
Cotton, raw	....	11,[illegible]	....	17,307	....	[illegible]
Dyestuffs	....	[illegible],343	....	[illegible]	....	4[illegible]

* Specie not distinguished until after 1857.

† An average value of [illegible] annually, is of articles of foreign origin.

Imports into Canada from the United States, &c.—Continued.

Articles imported.	1858.		1859.		1860.	
	Quantity.	Value.	Quantity.	Value.	Quantity.	Value.
Eggs		92,497		81,980		[illegible]
Fish		78,030		108,994		[illegible]
oil ... gallons	95,000	78,906	129,963	73,046	172,000	[illegible]
products of		798				[illegible]
Firewood ... cords	94,805	47,657	19,800	40,810	81,307	[illegible]
Fruit, dried		21,929		35,414		[illegible]
not dried		89,071		915,600		[illegible]
Flax, hemp, and tow, not manufactured		44,372		87,301		[illegible]
Flour ... barrels	192,250	739,540	377,082	2,040,643	167,000	[illegible]
Furs, skins and tails, not dressed		37,564		114,530		[illegible]
Grain, all kinds ... bushels	3,001,725	2,078,464	1,760,835	1,739,077	3,430,983	2,[illegible]
Gypsum		5,307		11,767		[illegible]
Hides and pelts		125,001		250,030		[illegible]
Lard ... pounds	347,983	41,310	875,805	53,049	316,300	[illegible]
Manures		12,134		12,791		[illegible]
Meal ... barrels	6,492	81,064	37,984	125,408	7,830	[illegible]
Meat of all kinds ... cwt	93,600	641,966	64,720	801,451	54,150	[illegible]
Ores of metals		8,078		2,349		[illegible]
Pitch and tar ... barrels	2,300	6,204	3,345	8,479	4,370	[illegible]
Plants and shrubs		38,647		24,423		[illegible]
Poultry		1,542		1,034		[illegible]
Rags		943		3,873		[illegible]
Rice ... pounds	402,180	18,162	600,254	18,549	300,480	[illegible]
Seeds		79,356		84,111		148,[illegible]
Slate		15,790		32,767		3,[illegible]
Stone and marble, unwrought		51,480		49,063		62,[illegible]
Tallow ... pounds	3,909,904	401,803	2,976,216	309,038	3,282,918	[illegible]
Timber and lumber		115,271		97,435		64,[illegible]
Tobacco, unmanufactured ... lbs	1,380,074	135,493	1,964,498	148,974	1,987,433	196,[illegible]
Turpentine		31				14
Vegetables		18,614		66,109		12,[illegible]
Wool		11,101		69,173		70,[illegible]
Free by reciprocity treaty		5,564,613		7,106,116		7,[illegible]
Specie and bullion		15				14,[illegible]
All other free goods*		1,597,328		1,453,909		1,[illegible]
Total free of duty		7,161,956		8,560,035		8,[illegible]

Imports into Canada from the United States, &c.—Continued.

Articles imported.	1861.		1862.		1863.	
	Quantity.	Value.	Quantity.	Value.	Quantity.	Value.
Animals ... number	10,[illegible]	$333,519	23,110	$347,809	25,300	$[illegible]
Ashes		30,842		34,477		17,[illegible]
Bark ... cords	930	3,650	1,010	4,115	1,650	6,[illegible]
Broom corn		50,867		32,259		34,[illegible]
Burr and grindstones		16,159		13,[illegible]		13,[illegible]
Butter ... pounds	541,854	68,545	815,500	104,[illegible]	644,547	97,[illegible]
Cheese ... do	2,152,900	177,776	1,907,010	174,456	2,807,040	[illegible]
Coal ... tons	171,861	458,665	108,805	437,391	103,547	[illegible]
Cotton, raw		53,606		56,460		[illegible]
Dyestuffs		53,739		60,976		[illegible]
Eggs		1,136		1,850		4,[illegible]
Fish		145,832		154,415		[illegible]
oil ... gallons	121,015	63,081	[illegible],450	109,630	183,365	[illegible]
products of		197				[illegible]
Firewood ... cords	89,033	57,012	84,049	47,230	79,384	[illegible]
Fruit, dried		64,808		61,113		72,948
not dried		244,994		370,511		378,170
Flax, hemp, and tow, not manufactured		73,476		108,080		[illegible]
Flour ... barrels	148,008	701,713	[illegible],130	1,[illegible],679	133,439	[illegible]
Furs, skins and tails, not dressed		103,285		119,898		[illegible]
Grain, all kinds ... bushels	7,223,738	5,408,163	10,[illegible],750	7,876,919	6,182,083	[illegible]
Gypsum		11,742		13,300		12,[illegible]

* An average value of $500,000 annually, is of articles of foreign origin.

Imports into Canada from the United States, &c.—Continued.

Articles imported.	1861.		1862.		1863.	
	Quantity.	Value.	Quantity.	Value.	Quantity.	Value.
Hides and pelts		[illegible]		$350,000		[illegible]
Lard ...pounds.	156,915	[illegible]	[illegible]	63,341	[illegible]	41,757
Manures		7,319		9,418		7,648
Meal ...barrels	6,954	17,114	91,075	44,363	10,000	[illegible]
Meat of all kinds ...cwt.	52,280	600,101	137,270	1,060,249	193,650	1,270,[illegible]
Ores of metals		5,871		12,316		18,003
Pitch and tar ...barrels.	2,120	8,620	3,008	13,085	2,863	11,138
Plants and shrubs		63,361		85,693		63,639
Poultry		2,214		3,604		4,459
Rags		10,793		6,981		11,323
Rice ...pounds.	128,010	3,629	[illegible]	2,746		84
Seeds		108,135		80,348	2,044	87,345
Slate		3,064		1,419		1,014
Stone and marble ...unwrought.		65,958		43,167		87,076
Tallow ...pounds.	2,043,[illegible]	842,474	1,443,000	129,516	1,[illegible]	102,[illegible]
Timber and lumber		171,[illegible]		94,774		62,941
Tobacco, unmanufactured ...lbs.	1,[illegible]	163,349	6,289,840	841,364	8,[illegible]	1,327,610
Turpentine		58				64
Vegetables		55,607		61,219		47,729
Wool		197,[illegible]		333,070		[illegible]
Free by reciprocity treaty		9,960,237		14,420,026		12,279,397
Specie and bullion		867,308		2,510,197		4,631,979
All other free goods*		1,878,510		2,093,431		2,143,920
Total free of duty		12,722,755		19,044,374		19,124,[illegible]

* An average value of $500,000 annually is of articles of foreign origin.

Exports, the produce and manufactures of the United States, to Canada for three years, 1860–'61 *to* 1862–'63.

Articles exported.	1860-'61.		1861-'62.		1862-'63.	
	Quantity.	Value.	Quantity.	Value.	Quantity.	Value.
Animals: horses and mules ...number.	815	$17,987	553	[illegible]	329	$27,144
cattle ...do.	153	3,981	1,100	22,799	1,108	41,252
hogs ...do.	4	20	1,869	13,302	8,668	80,976
sheep		2,650		1,737		1,453
Apples ...barrels.	19,810	47,011	37,867	84,717	77,839	177,458
Ashes ...cwt	311	1,571	2,041	10,701	1,[illegible]	8,771
Bark, oak		1,364		10,497		10,309
Beef ...barrels.	116	1,719	374	3,725	794	2,310
Beer and ale ...gallons.	25,147	9,770	18,443	1,656	69,352	72,828
Books		106,724		62,804		35,184
Bricks, lime, and cement		6,561		95,205		22,390
Butter ...pounds.	67,794	9,407	663,583	71,472	694,940	78,718
Cables and cordage ...cwt.	2,474	30,179	940	11,214	672	6,653
Candles ...pounds.	15,502	2,123	20,075	3,074	18,110	1,944
Carriages		11,117		25,054		11,801
Cheese ...pounds	372,767	37,045	687,991	76,870	705,614	55,374
Clover seed ...bushels.	2,645	10,012	1,376	5,736	3,416	18,947
Coal ...tons.	73,349	251,031	94,446	371,011	92,606	400,974
Copper and brass manufactures		16,909		32,230		30,874
Cotton, raw ...pounds.	136,630	13,214	82,915	11,712	146,851	64,930
Cotton manufactures		403,381		244,447		64,475
Drugs and medicines		60,350		95,958		110,646
Earthenware		12,347		18,147		8,244
Fish, dry ...cwt.	3,803	86,817	8,076	90,819	7,077	32,712
pickled ...barrels.	840	6,656	972	5,[illegible]	1,109	7,732
Fire-engines		1,865		4,300		3,000
Flaxseed ...bushels.					4,150	8,973
Furs		23,409		35,774		39,372
Glassware		83,860		191,381		47,103
Gold and silver coin				225,300		3,592,140
Gunpowder ...pounds.	2,029	3,097	36,125	2,612	9,779	1,325
Hams and bacon ...do.	50,170	4,508	310,263	19,834	805,580	63,579
Hats, wool and fur		79,010		69,305		14,079
Hemp ...tons	130	8,808	97	5,027	140	14,107

Exports, the produce and manufacture of the United States, &c.—Continued.

Articles exported.	1860-'61.		1861-'62.		[illegible]	
	Quantity.	Value.	Quantity.	Value.	Quantity.	Value.
Hemp manufactures, not specified	....	13,[illegible]	....	84,394	....	[illegible]
Hides	....	179,481	....	187,[illegible]	....	[illegible]
Hops ... pounds	60,350	12,344	157,990	18,763	87,613	[illegible]
House furniture	....	134,250	....	199,[illegible]	....	[illegible]
India-rubber manufactures	....	10,136	....	1,151	....	[illegible]
Indian corn ... bushels	1,891,740	810,346	3,218,439	1,010,942	4,911,[illegible]	1,[illegible]
Indian meal ... barrels	2,385	5,559	3,964	10,971	9,476	[illegible]
Iron, pig ... tons	461	37,[illegible]	1,970	32,532	710	16,[illegible]
bar ... do	166	8,322	400	23,051	140	[illegible]
castings ... do	300	31,651	214	16,191	275	[illegible]
nails ... pounds	193,530	8,624	816,255	8,340	138,490	[illegible]
manufactures, not specified	....	790,751	....	722,[illegible]	....	[illegible]
Jewelry	....	12,954	....	11,046	....	5,[illegible]
Lard ... pounds	40,831	4,449	761,[illegible]	70,799	400,373	[illegible]
oil ... gallons	2,[illegible]	1,973	2,377	1,771	7,406	[illegible]
Lead ... pounds	4,720	435	89,[illegible]	2,732	[illegible]	[illegible]
Leather ... do	87,[illegible]	29,310	143,313	81,[illegible]	182,706	[illegible],457
boots and shoes ... pairs	95,283	106,649	73,[illegible]	69,770	21,962	[illegible]
morocco leather	....	....	....	1,795	....	4,031
Marble and stone manufactures	....	97,377	....	97,[illegible]	....	[illegible]
Musical instruments	....	122,[illegible]	....	100,987	....	67,445
Oil-cake	....	....	....	4,004	....	[illegible]
Oil, linseed ... gallons	14,[illegible]	10,716	2,327	1,676	1,[illegible]	1,[illegible]
whale and fish ... do	109,972	114,749	104,161	99,[illegible]	68,418	[illegible]
Onions	....	943	....	505	....	[illegible]
Paints and varnish	....	39,907	....	39,046	....	[illegible]
Paper and stationery	....	74,773	....	72,376	....	[illegible]
Pork ... barrels	10,341	163,743	51,410	689,[illegible]	84,[illegible]	[illegible]
Potatoes ... bushels	1,500	614	17,382	7,[illegible]	14,041	[illegible]
Printing materials	....	5,534	....	4,250	....	1,[illegible]
Rice ... barrels	217	3,858	170	2,430	1	[illegible]
Rosin, tar, pitch, and turpentine ... do	12,420	37,517	5,754	29,[illegible]	1,[illegible]	17,[illegible]
Rye and small grain	....	40,670	....	57,[illegible]	....	119,[illegible]
Salt ... bushels	471,723	128,952	356,409	214,[illegible]	530,912	257,[illegible]
Soap ... pounds	30,[illegible]	3,424	23,499	1,574	13,[illegible]	1,[illegible]
Spirits, from grain, &c. ... gallons	11,[illegible]	11,167	30,655	7,576	11,167	4,[illegible]
Spirits of turpentine ... do	4,[illegible]	2,908	2,921	3,479	310	545
Sugar ... pounds	2,471,566	241,011	1,182,627	85,[illegible]	190,[illegible]	10,449
Molasses ... gallons	61,537	31,[illegible]	31,910	15,179	13,[illegible]	4,718
Tallow ... pounds	954,612	90,880	1,534,553	144,[illegible]	1,080,787	[illegible]
Tobacco, not manufactured ... hogsheads	1,375	80,469	1,204	75,311	3,401	[illegible]
snuff ... pounds	17,624	7,078	12,356	3,924	12,567	3,[illegible]
manufactured ... do	2,453,531	663,875	577,755	[illegible]	235,[illegible]	[illegible]
Vinegar ... gallons	10,688	1,816	14,741	2,371	11,[illegible]	[illegible]
Wax ... pounds	57	13	3,000	1,317	7,[illegible]	[illegible]
Wheat ... bushels	4,144,029	3,871,230	4,538,474	3,801,315	6,313,801	6,717,[illegible]
Wheat flour ... barrels	81,617	444,840	118,643	538,738	232,190	1,162,171
Wool ... pounds	221,700	66,740	411,048	138,958	165,[illegible]	85,[illegible]
Wood manufactures	....	38,502	....	49,051	....	[illegible]
lumber and timber	....	35,341	....	70,345	....	[illegible]
All other articles	....	1,084,156	....	632,[illegible]	....	[illegible]
Total	....	11,749,941	....	11,843,107	....	14,[illegible]

The detail of imports from Canada which pay duty during the period of the reciprocity treaty shows that very few of such imports are the produce or manufacture of Canada originally. The chief articles are iron, salt, foreign spirits and wines, beer and ale, and foreign dry goods. It is not easy to identify any item of consequence produced in Canada, other than "manufactures of wood," which is an item made up of local products in part, at least.

The detail of imports free by ordinary laws exhibits a very irregular trade of this sort. The chief values are of articles of the United States brought back, personal effects, and unusual movements of coin and bullion.

Imports from Canada free by ordinary laws.

Articles.	1855-'56.	1856-'57.	1857-'58.	1858-'59.	1859-'60.	1860-'61.	1861-'62.	1862-'63.
Produce of the United States returned	$549,734	$460,871	$73,948	$130,159	$726,659	$1,414,756	$430,067	$173,444
Personal effects	352,574	339,979	102,858	253,197	271,863	194,430	220,433	271,095
Animals, living	3,040	1,070	4,673	810,704	1,142,717	305,919	2,612	965
Coin and bullion				9,000			4,126	4,792,196
Seeds and trees	40,068	65,313	38,043	43,990	27,695	60,171	39,675	53
Copper ore	5,864			2,220	8,330	2,644		
Plaster	3,354	557	1,739					
Paintings	2,000	380	40	300	743	400		
Shingle and stave bolts			3,449	10,004	14,481	10,646	6,071	3,620
Produce of American fisheries				6,965	1,970			
Other articles	1,374	894	3,476	23,380	10,148	7,591	*23,017	†143,096
Total	697,972	868,753	357,430	1,346,377	2,348,373	1,939,260	738,831	5,387,773

* Including 9,410 pounds indigo, $[illegible].
† Including 13,766 pounds tea, $10,247; 80,763 pounds indigo, $14,[illegible].

The detail of imports from the Provinces other than Canada, free by other laws than the treaty, is also shown to be mainly of United States produce returned and specie in small amount. The following are the items:

Years.	Specie.	Produce of U. S. returned.	Gypsum.	Animals living.	Other articles.
1854-'55		$14,651	$103,920	$775	$59,175
1855-'56	$33,807	14,248	109,074	431	35,179
1856-'57	14,930	25,968	88,314	839	17,751
1857-'58	21,643	28,539	80,444	3,618	60,858
1858-'59	18,847	673,567	78,600	6,000	23,230
1859-'60	4,018	110,098	97,034	5,449	37,059
1860-'61	61,651	81,610	80,832	4,621	3,711
1861-'62	28,301	63,623	9,425	125	9,707
1862-'63	5,542	94,257	90,003		10,500

The import trade from the British Atlantic provinces is very small in actually free articles other than those affected by the reciprocity treaty. On the Pacific coast there is a receipt of bullion from Victoria at San Francisco, the value of which is given in the published commerce and navigation reports as imports from British North American provinces. It has been separated from the above statement, though in other statements of trade with the provinces the small trade of San Francisco with British Columbia in duty-paying articles has not been separated. The bullion brought to San Francisco from British Columbia began in 1850, and was, in 1861-'62, $756,423, and in 1862-'63, $1,663,642.

The record of imports and exports at United States ports of the lake district almost invariably confines the transactions to Canada, the exceptions being only one outward shipment from Milwaukie to England in 1861, value $46,061, and one similar shipment in 1863, value $3,381. It has therefore been necessary to consider all the trade of the lake district as conducted with Canada, although the registered entries and clearances of vessels show frequent transactions direct with English ports. The following is the detail of actual entrances and clearances at these lake ports for European ports, through the St. Lawrence, from the official returns:

Fiscal years.	No.	Clearances.	Tons.	No.	Entrances.	Tons.
1855–56	......	......	......	....	......	......
1856–57	1	Chicago to England.....	379	....	......	......
1857–58	1	Chicago to England.....	183	1	England to Chicago...	183
	9	Cleveland to England....	3,244	1	England to Cleveland..	372
	3	Detroit to England......	987	1	England to Detroit....	382
1858–59	16	Chicago, Detroit, and Cleveland to England...	5,761	7	England to same ports.	2,401
	2	Same ports to Hamburg..	633	....	......	......
	1	Same ports to Spain.....	347	....	......	......
1859–60	5	To England and Scotl'd..	1,438	10	From England	3,575
1860–61	5	To England and Ireland. .	1,791	8	From England	2,838
1861–62	......	......	......	3	From England	1,168
1862–63	1	To England...........	394	1	From England	394

Undoubtedly the outward shipments by these vessels were considerable, and a few imports are specified in the statistics of soda ash, iron, salt, &c. But the trade is not a permanent one in any sense. In the last fiscal year but a single vessel cleared and entered, and it can therefore scarcely be necessary to make a distinct and precise account of it as of a permanent trade. This practical neglect of the St. Lawrence river as an outlet to western produce of the United States, under the circumstances controlling that route for the last four or five years, is particularly significant, and decisive as to the channels this trade prefers. Not only the treaty of reciprocity, but the careful and inviting legislation of Canada in regard to tolls and tonnage duties, have united to remove all obstacles to the free employment of this route for the export of breadstuffs and provisions from the western States. Great hopes were entertained in Canada of the commerce that would be thus developed, but the united efforts of the two governments have proved of little effect in opening a channel preferable to that made up of the lakes, the canals, and railroads of the United States. The statistics of downward freight through the Welland canal show that most American produce entering that canal returns again to American ports. The tables of this Welland canal tonnage, given here from the official Canadian reports, are particularly instructive on the point of the destination of both upward and downward freight.

The following extracts from the report of the Hon. W. P. Howland, finance minister of Canada in 1862, state very compactly and forcibly the principal facts connected with the expected occupation of the St. Lawrence river as a line of outward transit for produce of the western States. They are from the Canadian Trade and Navigation report for 1862:

Movement of American produce in and through Canada.

The movement of property on the provincial canals shows a steady increase. On the Welland canal the movement was:

	Tons property.	Tonnage of vessels.
In 1859	709,611	856,918
1860	944 084	1.139 509
1861	1,020,483	1.517.672
1862	1,243,774	1,476,842

And on the St. Lawrence canals the movement was:

In 1859	631,769	785,688
1860	733,696	824,465
1861	866,908	1,009,469
1862	964,894	1,019,230

The movement on the Welland canal has, therefore, increased 7½ per cent. in 1861 over 1860, and in 1862 15 per cent. over 1861. Whilst on the St. Lawrence canals the movement of tonnage has increased in 1861 by 22 per cent. over 1860, and in 1862 by 6 per cent. over 1861.

In this connection I propose to consider the effect which the removal of the tolls from the St. Lawrence canals, and the reduction of those on the Welland, has had on the movement of property through those works.

That the movement of property by the St. Lawrence route has been greatly augmented during the past three years is sufficiently apparent from the figures above given, and we may congratulate the country thereon; but that this increase has been due to the remission of the tolls is not to be assumed without taking into account other circumstances which have mainly influenced the direction of trade.

First among these circumstances may be stated the greatly increased production of cereals in the western States, and the figures presently introduced will show that in proportion to that increase, and to the whole volume of agricultural produce moved from Lakes Erie and Michigan to tide-water, we have not obtained so large a traffic since the removal of the tolls as we obtained prior to the adoption of that policy.

The following statement shows the quantity of grain sent eastward from the lake regions, including Canada, during the last seven years:

Years.	Flour.	Wheat.	Corn.	Other grain.	All reduced to bushels.
	Barrels.	*Bushels.*	*Bushels.*	*Bushels.*	
1856	3,[illegible],449	19,[illegible],358	14,[illegible],639	4,[illegible]	67,707,769
1857	3,397,964	16,763,285	[illegible],779,[illegible]	9,256,914	44,7[illegible],[illegible]
1858	4,499,813	21,243,859	10,495,554	5,088,097	[illegible]
1859	3,700,274	16,865,706	4,423,008	4,261,051	41,[illegible]
1860	4,108,037	32,334,391	16,075,778	7,712,[illegible]	[illegible]
1861	6,533,809	40,[illegible]	29,524,622	10,6[illegible],115	119,2[illegible]
1862	8,359,910	50,699,130	32,965,923	10,844,909	136,3[illegible]

The following statement shows the proportion of wheat and flour which has passed from the western States to tide-water by the St. Lawrence and Erie canals, respectively, during the same period, (all being reduced to bushels of wheat:)

Movement of American breadstuffs.

Years.	Down the St. Lawrence.	Through Erie canal.	Total to tide-water.
1856	1,209,612	15,342,833	16,553,445
1857	1,930,280	10,601,532	12,531,812
1858	1,876,933	13,757,283	15,634,216
1859	1,0[illegible],750	10,371,9[illegible]	17,300,725
1860	1,846,468	23,0[illegible]	2[illegible],75[illegible],468
1861	3,103,153	34,447,[illegible]	37,550,983
1862	5,320,054	3[illegible],240,131	41,560,185

NOTE.—The above statement is computed by adding to the importations from United States ports at Kingston the quantities sent down the St. Lawrence canals from the United States to the Canadian ports, and it is assumed that all the imports at Kingston were sent down by St. Lawrence canals. The movement on the Erie canal during the first six years is taken from the canal auditor's reports; that for 1862 is from "Hunt's Merchants' Magazine." The statement [illegible] only to wheat and flour.

Hence it appears that of the whole quantity of western wheat and flour which was transported to tide-water through the New York and Canadian canals during the past seven years, we obtained for the St. Lawrence route, in 1856, 7.3 per cent.; 1857, 15.4 per cent.; 1858, 12.01 per cent.; 1859, 16.08 per cent.; 1860, 7.16 per cent.; 1861, 8.26 per cent.; 1862, 11.4 per cent.

These are the principal commodities which have heretofore passed through the St. Lawrence canal. If we include with them the Indian corn, which figures so largely in the Welland and Erie canal returns, the percentage will become still less favorable to us, and the proportions will be still further reduced by bringing into the comparison the cereal products of the western States which are carried to tide-water by the several railroads converging at the Atlantic ports.

While we have failed to obtain so large a proportion of the western trade, since the removal of the tolls, as we obtained in 1859 and the preceding years, the tolls levied on that (the Erie) canal which is the chief competitor with the St. Lawrence route have been materially increased, as the following comparison of tolls on the three principal articles will show:

Toll per 1,000 pounds per mile.	1860 and previous years.	1862.
On corn	2 mills.	2½ mills.
On flour	2 "	3 "
On wheat	2 "	3 "

This increase is equivalent to an advance of seventy cents per ton on wheat and flour from Buffalo to tide-water, and of forty cents per ton from Oswego to tide-water; whilst the advance on corn is equivalent to thirty-five cents per ton from Buffalo, and to twenty cents per ton from Oswego.

The rates of freight have also increased by the Erie canal, and they have increased in a still greater ratio by the St. Lawrence. During the four years next preceding 1859 the average freight for flour from Lake Ontario ports to Montreal was $1 84½ per ton. In 1860, the year in which the tolls were removed from the St. Lawrence canals, the rate of freight was $2 11½ per ton; in 1861 it was $2 56½; in 1862 it was $2 61; so that the increase over the average of the four years preceding 1859 was seventy-two cents in 1860, seventy-two in 1861, and eighty-one in 1862. If we add to these figures the tolls remitted, we find that the forwarder received over the average rates which they obtained in the four years above alluded to, in 1860, forty-nine cents per ton; in 1861, ninety-four cents, and in 1862, one dollar and three cents per ton, together with the tolls on the tonnage of his shipping.

Comparing in a similar manner the rates of freight obtained for carrying wheat, we have a still more striking example of the advanced rates which the forwarders have been able to exact. The average freight rates for wheat from Lake Ontario ports to Montreal, in 1855, 1856, 1857, and 1858, was $1 81 per ton; in 1860, $1 31; in 1861, $2 72, and in 1862 it was $2 71 per ton. Thus the advance over the average rate during the four years first named was, in 1860, $1 21; in 1861, $1 13; in 1862, $1 13. Adding the tolls relinquished by the province, it will be seen that the advance obtained by the forwarder has been, in 1860, $1 43, and in 1861 and 1862, $1 35 per ton, together with the tolls due to the tonnage of his vessels.

Whatever else may be urged in favor of free canals, it certainly cannot be said that the policy of 1860 has been productive of benefit, either to the producer or consumer of western breadstuffs; and from the advance which has taken place in the freights by the St. Lawrence route, as well as in both tolls and freight by the competing route to tide-water at Albany, it is abundantly manifest that the forwarder can pay a moderate toll without unduly trenching on his profits.

It can be shown from reliable data that, in so far as the actual cost of transportation (including therein the canal tolls recently imposed) is concerned, western produce can be carried to tide-water much cheaper by the St. Lawrence than by any competing route; and we must trace our failure to obtain for our canals a greater proportion of the western trade to other causes than the charges heretofore imposed for the use of those works. I am persuaded that the chief cause of that failure lies in the absence of sufficient competition among forwarders engaged in the St. Lawrence trade; in the financial relations between shippers engaged in the western trade and the capitalists of New York; and, finally and chiefly, in the lower rates of ocean freights from New York to Europe, occasioned by the greater competition at that port than is to be found at Quebec or Montreal. It is gratifying to know that the Canadian forwarder has been able to obtain the advanced rates above quoted, but we cannot find therein a justification of that policy which, in addition to other advantages, would give him the free use of costly works which complete the grandest system of inland navigation in the world, and have not been constructed without imposing heavy burdens on the country. If it could be shown that the tolls remitted had gone in mitigation of the comparatively high rate of ocean freight to which our trade is subject, we might find in that fact some reason for making our canals absolutely free. But it has been shown that this has not been the result. The tolls have gone to enhance the profits of the forwarder whose freight tariff has been regulated, not by the cost of doing his work, but by the competition with which he has had to contend. There is but one course open for securing that quota of the western trade which the advantages of the St. Lawrence route gives us reason to anticipate. If we can give to the owners of the largest vessels now profitably engaged in the trade of Lake Michigan the option of trading to Kingston and the St. Lawrence, or to Buffalo, as may be found most profitable, we shall have thrown down the barrier which now forces the main current of trade into the Erie canal. We shall have more than balanced the greater insurance and freights charged from our sea-ports to Europe over the corresponding charges from New York, and we may thereafter expect Quebec and Montreal to take rank amongst the greatest grain marts of this continent. All of which is respectfully submitted.

W. P. HOWLAND, *Minister of Finance.*

QUEBEC, *May* 13, 1862.

This very full and impartial statement has been copied at length because of its decisive bearing on the question which was, a few years since, considered a great and practical one for the western producing States, namely: whether they were to anticipate relief to the pressure of their export trade when the St. Lawrence should be fully opened to them.

The transit trade through Canada, inward and outward, by way of the St. Lawrence, is incompletely given in the Canadian trade reports, as follows:

Statement of the transit trade through Canada, viâ the St. Lawrence, to and from the United States.

[From Canadian authorities.]

Calendar years.	Values to the U. States.	Values from the U. States.
1854	$195,327	
1855	18,015	
1856	13,493	
1857	183,790	
1858	26,916	
1859	76,318	
1860	21,505	
1861	622,514	$3,505,511
1862	490,298	5,198,920
1863	512,245	8,997,818

The transit trade through the United States to Canada is another important element of the mutual exchanges, one of which the volume is unexpectedly large, larger than the export of United States produce by way of the St. Lawrence. It is conducted almost wholly over the railroads leading from Portland, Maine, to the frontier of Vermont, and makes up the larger half of the business of the sub-port of entry of Island Pond, Vermont.

Value of imports into Canada passing through the United States under bond.

1855	$4,463,774
1856	4,926,522
1857	5,582,643
1858	2,057,024
1859	4,546,491
1860	3,041,877
1861	6,669,952
1862	5,509,427
1863	6,172,483

The rapid increase of this traffic is remarkable. It affords a channel for steamer freight that appears to be preferred to the slower course by way of the St. Lawrence. The comparison of the use by Canada of the two channels of imports is as follows: showing that more than a third of the import trade of Canada enters now at United States ports, and is transported over our railroads under bond.

	Imports via United States	Imports via St. Lawrence.
1855	$4,463,774	$12,738,373
1856	4,926,922	16,989,513
1857	5,582,643	14,378,094
1858	2,057,024	10,768,161
1859	4,546,491	11,472,754
1860	3,041,877	13,327,160
1861	5,688,952	16,726,541
1862	6,508,427	17,601,019
1863	6,172,483	16,439,930

Evidently the advantages of unrestricted transit to and from sea are quite as valuable to the business of Canada as to that of the United States. The preponderance of steamship traffic in the carriage of all classes of merchandise is increasing the transportation of railroad lines such as these from Portland and Boston to Canada.

EXPORT OF UNITED STATES MANUFACTURES TO CANADA.

The reduction in the value of manufactured articles of the United States exported to Canada in recent years as compared with an earlier period has been referred to. In the following table the extent of this reduction and its relation to particular articles is shown, the comparison being for the years 1853 to 1863. Undoubtedly this decline cannot be a natural result between two countries in such proximity maintaining open and equal commercial relations. Especial causes only could produce such a decline in the face of the very great increase of manufactures in the United States during these years, and their development in superior fabrics of every sort. The Canadian tariffs are chiefly levied *ad valorem* on the invoice values of goods at the point of purchase for importation into Canada, whether that be in the United States or in Europe, and the consequence is a practical difference against purchasing in the United States which increases with every accession to prices here, and has now attained to the full nominal measure of the duty levied. The increase in the price of fabrics, caused by the successive tariff acts of the United States and by the internal duties levied, has steadily increased this difference, in connection with the higher rates of *ad valorem* duty levied in Canada, until it now amounts very nearly to a prohibition of purchases in the United States of duty-paying articles. A duty of twenty per cent. on invoices made in England, can scarcely fail now to amount to two such percentages when the same or similar goods are purchased in the United States, simply through the duplication of prices attained here.

Efforts have been made in Canada to obviate the difficulty in some measure by admitting United States invoices at a reduction to gold values, but nothing has been settled on. While these conditions continue, the trade to Canada in articles not covered by the reciprocity treaty, or otherwise free, will remain very small, and that market for manufactures will practically cease to exist.

Values of manufactured articles of the United States exported to Canada, and paying duty.

Articles.	1858-'59.	1859-'60.	1860-'61.	1861-'62.	1862-'63.
Cotton manufactures	$369,016	$314,491	$403,691	$248,442	$94,495
Hemp manufactures, (including cordage.)	32,702	21,971	43,664	16,378	10,565
Iron manufactures, (all other than pig.)	761,619	716,507	839,421	773,381	396,007
Leather boots and shoes	211,147	137,475	106,048	66,770	22,860
Tobacco, manufactured	1,205,084	660,834	681,875	203,681	76,058
Glasswares	85,252	77,061	83,950	121,381	87,032
Earthenware	9,350	11,151	12,347	12,147	8,244
House furniture	130,765	124,251	124,250	158,829	66,716
India-rubber manufactures	13,917	5,908	10,158	1,151	528
Carriages	20,449	109,419	11,117	35,064	11,501
Books	154,034	79,134	106,324	92,858	25,104
Paper and stationery	78,825	61,431	74,272	78,376	66,171
Jewelry	15,069	5,760	12,954	11,046	5,044
Hats	116,150	90,100	70,018	49,565	14,076
Tin manufactures	15,451	20,565	4,302	1,375	....
Marble and stone manufactures	53,883	100,000	97,977	97,002	48,293
Trunks and umbrellas	5,470	1,575	2,577	1,957	1,434
Clothing	9,373	16,055	11,163	8,404	1,328
Wool manufactures	45,146	49,517	36,603	40,051	68,392
Candles and soap	11,450	8,079	9,558	4,583	2,428
Paints and varnish	27,193	32,521	30,000	30,640	30,054
Copper and brass manufactures	60,511	49,658	16,000	32,268	50,871
Musical instruments	104,634	91,732	122,800	100,007	97,415
Printing materials	1,771	3,437	5,634	4,259	1,260
Other enumerated	21,990	5,886	12,776	8,100	4,754
Unenumerated manufactures	624,534	542,028	549,003	394,229	401,297
Total	4,185,618	3,548,114	3,601,643	2,690,930	1,510,608

PREPARED PROVISIONS, ETC., EXPORTED FREE OF DUTY.

Articles.	1858-'59.	1859-'60.	1860-'61.	1861-'62.	1862-'63.
Beef	20,608	78,637	1,718	3,789	9,310
Pork	542,079	477,328	165,745	559,184	670,433
Hams and bacon	64,394	53,470	4,862	19,828	63,670
Butter	15,250	40,154	6,847	71,472	76,718
Cheese	60,198	38,898	37,843	66,870	55,294
Lard	69,642	163,723	4,498	70,789	40,579
Tallow	113,013	130,893	90,800	144,062	105,338
Vinegar	6,646	3,728	1,816	2,321	2,008

SPIRITS AND LIQUORS PAYING DUTY.

Articles.	1858-'59.	1859-'60.	1860-'61.	1861-'62.	1862-'63.
Spirits	33,820	68,341	11,167	7,576	6,720
Beer and ale	2,707	1,924	2,733	1,656	22,832

The exports of prepared provisions, being nearly all free of duty, are fairly maintained. That of liquors has nearly ceased, and an enormous stimulus has been given to distillation in Canada of corn imported free from the United States.

The export of wheat and flour to the coast provinces has been referred to as a large and direct trade to a market for consumption. It constituted the chief part of the export trade previous to the enactment of the reciprocity treaty, breadstuffs having always been admitted free of duty into the colonial ports of the Atlantic coast.

Exports of wheat, flour, corn, and meal from the United States to the Provinces, other than Canada, from 1849 to 1863.

Year ending—	WHEAT.		WHEAT FLOUR.		INDIAN CORN.		MEAL, CORN AND RYE.		Total values breadstuffs.	Total domestic exports.
	Bushels.	Value.	Barrels.	Value.	Bushels.	Value.	Barrels.	Value.		
June 30, 1849	305,383	$332,765	274,891	$1,518,929	221,442	$120,791	211,045	$625,001	$2,004,169	$3,011,783
1850	198,319	214,779	214,034	1,051,548	90,552	57,731	142,832	421,112	1,744,768	3,116,840
1851	216,971	220,310	200,064	943,357	101,109	60,109	92,341	290,610	1,621,365	3,234,553
1852	180,672	165,108	106,117	688,950	141,185	86,221	42,121	137,718	1,076,001	2,650,134
1853	234,717	208,856	171,640	784,498	158,895	105,404	40,284	135,090	1,233,888	3,798,575
1854	148,882	216,280	145,590	955,484	188,134	149,089	95,485	378,295	1,880,733	4,623,771
1855	98,323	188,614	193,122	1,733,395	100,444	154,214	130,795	708,804	2,792,427	5,855,878
1856	147,925	209,960	337,010	3,120,787	183,379	136,774	145,409	611,959	4,158,479	7,510,909
1857	142,588	221,560	436,211	2,881,883	140,616	98,340	101,898	370,774	3,578,777	6,011,405
1858	103,043	132,187	491,802	2,618,913	100,841	85,810	66,255	248,480	3,084,730	5,075,494
1859	74,670	100,717	549,088	3,068,171	110,092	83,320	53,440	210,049	3,365,257	8,320,080
1860	68,421	90,019	578,153	3,044,243	117,284	85,915	52,941	206,881	3,427,098	7,502,839
1861	19,880	28,563	520,358	3,065,219	61,804	48,875	69,789	188,020	3,330,648	7,133,734
1862	13,748	16,582	605,835	3,199,288	113,077	65,358	62,855	254,182	3,535,330	7,389,945
1863	70,804	110,333	732,384	4,420,748	171,964	131,522	74,478	280,238	4,946,871	10,198,505

The fisheries of the coast provinces constitute a large natural market for provisions and breadstuffs which can never be supplied so cheaply from Canada as from the United States. The average imports from them are scarcely half the exports, as will be seen by comparing the annual totals of trade with the provinces, and but a very small proportion of these imports pay duty on entering the United States. The average annual value paying duty is $216,172, for the eight years of the operation of the treaty, while for the five years preceding, the average paying duty was $1,750,000.

Table of trade through the Canadian canals in produce of the United States, distinguishing the points of origin and destination, for the years 1861, 1862, and 1863.

EASTWARD OR DOWNWARD TRADE THROUGH THE WELLAND CANAL.

From United States ports.	1861.		1862.		1863.	
	To Canadian ports.	To United States ports.	To Canadian ports.	To United States ports.	To Canadian ports.	To United States ports.
	Tons.	*Tons.*	*Tons.*	*Tons.*	*Tons.*	*Tons.*
Agricultural implements, castings, &c.	....	26	6	10	2	6
Ashes, pot and pearl	4	121	9	79	219	66
Apples, fruits, and cider	6	165	30	132	368	35
Bark	103	....	164	....	170	....
Barley	....	....	....	728	6	3,329
Beef, pork, hams, and bacon	701	2,132	400½	6,160½	3,509	6,459
Butter and cheese	12	129	23	395½	33	66
Clover seed	6	122	....	194	....	384
Coal	53,603	1,542	47,619	1,231	41,627	1,649
Corn and corn meal	30,830	113,793	65,402	93,648	355	....
Cotton	....	128	....	1	....	....
Fish	7	59	11½	24½	2	13
Flour	1,265	41,612	1,869	48,610	17,900	53,246
Furniture	7	90	3	71	15	09
Hemp and flax	....	17	....	130	69	83
Hides	13	173	....	351	0.1	195
Horns and bones	....	25	....	49	15	18
Horses and cattle	1	13	7	....	1	9
Iron and nails	39	376	1	622½	83	503
Lard and tallow	23	417	14½	1,056½	258	1,323
Leather	....	15	....	35	....	....
Oats	1	573	1,373	2,112½	....	69
Oils, (all)	625	615	757	340	1,523	160
Oil-cake	....	303	....	439	300	38
Ores	....	262	....	1	2,533	....
Potatoes	....	9	64½	40	....	....
Hay and broomcorn	18	118	....	48	10	11
Rags	1	60	....	49	41	24
Rye and rye meal	361	1,960	2,476	1,301	678	1,040
Salt	40	....	47½	....	21	....
Stoneware	119	101	76½	73½	52	107
Stone	8,166	555	2,135	132	6,149	147
Tobacco, (mostly manufactured)	....	602	....	171½	39	....
Wheat	105,923	238,318	161,224½	236,478½	118,982	230,100

Table of trade through the Canadian canals, &c.—Continued.

From United States ports.	1861.		1862.		1863.	
	To Canadian ports.	To United States ports.	To Canadian ports.	To United States ports.	To Canadian ports.	To United States ports.
	Tons.	*Tons.*	*Tons.*	*Tons.*	*Tons.*	*Tons.*
Whiskey	....	1,249	16½	1,837	31	1,529
Wool	....	133	....	253½	....	359
All other articles	54	634	53½	661½	8,191	770
Total	211,910	404,634	283,081½	447,294½	203,653	309,665
Lumber and timber	6,713	22,887	1,910½	24,257	94,783	131,997
Total all classes	217,692	427,521	285,192	471,521½	298,436	441,662

WESTWARD OR UPWARD TRADE THROUGH THE WELLAND CANAL.

Agricultural implements, tools, &c	2	295	5½	199	5	295
Apples, &c	7	255	7	300	130	481
Beef, pork, hams, &c	4	11	28	1	32	5
Bricks, cement, lime, clay, and slate	76	4,029	121½	4,278½	299	5,829
Butter and cheese	2	43	4	42	10	72
Chalk and whiting	....	171	....	565	1	162
Coal	1,568	12,301	1,744½	7,038	2,055	24,552
Coffee	....	611	....	304½	....	302
Copperas	....	24	....	6	....	6
Corn	3,029	....	3,049	....	27,487	72,979
Cotton	17	6	....	....	3	23
Dyes	....	....	3	204	....	193
Earthware and glassware	1	550	....	1,969	78	1,161
Fish	2	1,234	3	9,300	60	5,729
Flour	6	5	24½	....	4,339	129
Furniture	6	714	7½	857½	19	1,501
Gypsum	2	39	4	687	65	229
Hemp	....	271	....	360	1	341
Horses, cattle, and sheep	2	205	....	29	0	223
Iron, nails, and spikes	67	9,358	21½	14,081½	1,274	40,622
Junk and oakum	5	52	3½	165½	10	122
Leather	....	13	2½	139½	....	9
Mahogany	....	8	....	19	....	50
Marble	8	916	5	900	340	3,085
Molasses	....	809	....	1,310	6	2,723
Oats	4	....	114	....	....	3
Oils	1	620	11½	453	64	791
Ores, (iron)	....	2,076	....	6,310	....	21,889
Paints	1	339	½	602	10	630
Pitch, tar, and turpentine	6	75	1	73	20	90
Rye	253	....	618	....	501	....
Salt	1,935	72,672	2,155½	112,952	2,068	102,969
Ship stores	....	47	....	278	3	378
Soda ash	....	308	....	784½	14	615
Sugar	6	2,140	107	3,791½	295	3,891
Tin and steel	....	325	....	571½	14	584

Table of trade through the Canadian canals, &c.—Continued.

From United States ports.	1861.		1862.		1863.	
	To Canadian ports.	To United States ports.	To Canadian ports.	To United States ports.	To Canadian ports.	To United States ports.
	Tons.	*Tons.*	*Tons.*	*Tons.*	*Tons.*	*Tons.*
Tobacco	1	30	....	190½	16	17
Wheat	3,580	9	5,307	....	18,106	....
Whiskey	30	9	....	5	368	14
Window glass	....	122	1	70	38	193
Other articles	45	4,283	75	9,303½	4,269	19,676
Lumber	130	200	1,463½	981	5,083	10,497
Total	10,185	116,240	14,004½	171,673½	67,478	323,244

Transportation by the St. Lawrence Canal from American ports to Canada, (down and up.)

[From Canadian official reports.]

Articles.		1861.	1862.	1863.
Ashes	tons	9	80	100
Apples and vegetables	do	12	3,027½	6,101
Beer, cider, and vinegar	do	....	....	186
Butter and cheese	do	....	120	753
Cement, lime, and bricks	do	233	83	447
Coal	do	3,910	3,479	423
Corn, barley, and grain	do	3,221	3,867	300
Cotton	do	9	....	....
Flour	do	309	3,417	1,107
Gypsum	do	187	....	11
Hemp	do	....	98	80
Hides	do	10	34	20
Iron	do	5	89½	63
Lard and lard oil	do	....	34½	471
Live stock	do	94	123	93
Ores	do	114	2,658	1,976
Pitch, tar, and rosin	do	158	428	241
Pork	do	66	694	849
Salt	do	27	121	98
Sugar	do	457	391	102
Molasses	do	1,160	75	124
Tobacco	do	40	174½	10
Wheat	do	5,143	3,254	7,637
Spirits	do	60	58	16
Stone	do	....	667	395
Lumber and staves	do	166	145	563
Firewood	do	1,540	....	391
Other articles	do	413	409	777
Total		16,637	22,001	23,118

Summaries of the trade of the principal ports of the northern frontier with Canada.

Exports and imports for eight years, 1856 to 1863 inclusive, as reported from the following collection districts:—Vermont: Ports of Burlington and Island Pond, Vt.—Champlain: Rouse's Point and Plattsburg, N. Y.—Oswegatchie: Ogdensburg, N. Y.—Cape Vincent: Including Sackett's Harbor with Cape Vincent, N. Y.—Oswego: Port of Oswego only.—Genesee: Rochester.—Niagara: Niagara and Suspension Bridge, N. Y.—Buffalo Creek: Buffalo.—Presque Isle: Erie, Penn.—Cuyahoga: Cleveland, Ohio.—Sandusky and Miami: Sandusky and Toledo, Ohio.—Detroit.—Mackinaw, Mich.—Milwaukie, Wis.—Chicago.

District and period.	Domestic exports.	Foreign exports.	Total exports.	Imports.
DISTRICT OF VERMONT. (*Burlington and Island Pond.*)				
Year ending June 30, 1856	$350,607	$690,843	$1,031,450	$1,560,118
1857	253,069	365,401	618,470	2,709,193
1858	237,066	727,949	965,665	2,106,089
1859	295,649	840,905	1,136,545	1,802,694
1860	257,089	526,619	783,708	2,731,857
1861	244,657	614,416	859,073	3,477,911
1862	197,803	441,584	639,387	3,163,794
1863	195,303	541,358	736,661	2,527,698
DISTRICT OF CHAMPLAIN. (*Rouse's Point and Plattsburg.*)				
Year ending June 30, 1856	2,354,795	1,164,009	3,518,804	1,718,413
1857	1,076,135	1,240,927	2,317,062	2,334,402
1858	853,028	1,134,531	1,992,459	1,559,806
1859	2,150,431	2,352,209	4,502,640	2,360,084
1860	997,296	912,963	1,910,259	2,538,062
1861	819,671	740,244	1,559,915	2,187,675
1862	752,050	898,076	1,651,032	1,021,944
1863	*4,553,630	600,088	5,159,718	7,648,279
DISTRICT OF OSWEGATCHIE. (*Ogdensburg, N. Y.*)				
Year ending June 30, 1856	774,605	739,676	1,514,281	1,809,805
1857	941,115	45,400	990,515	2,452,840
1858	487,043	107,163	594,206	961,116
1859	356,251	71,455	427,706	1,017,941
1860	223,705	20,810	244,515	974,153
1861	179,343	18,840	198,183	675,017
1862	144,293	15,687	159,979	1,131,810
1863	344,464	....	344,464	703,404
DISTRICT OF CAPE VINCENT. (*Including Sackett's Harbor, N. Y.*)				
Year ending June 30, 1856	600,690	208,609	865,365	1,006,473
1857	506,695	221,622	728,317	1,291,457
1858	465,807	267,605	733,319	1,253,423
1859	351,833	199,169	550,802	890,694
1860	181,220	160,238	341,458	847,007
1861	205,383	117,372	322,755	769,600
1862	399,416	119,515	518,931	709,909
1863	269,836	106,744	375,580	416,786

* Including an unusual export of $3,376,977 of gold and silver coin.

Summaries of the trade of the principal ports, &c.—Continued.

District and period.	Domestic exports.	Foreign exports.	Total exports.	Imports.
DISTRICT OF OSWEGO.				
Year ending June 30, 1856	$4,737,750	$690,357	$5,471,107	$5,391,878
1857	3,069,587	476,531	3,536,068	3,782,899
1858	1,849,780	197,163	2,046,052	1,870,774
1859	1,732,642	358,813	2,091,395	3,617,709
1860	1,448,220	137,450	1,585,670	4,875,889
1861	2,075,895	273,285	2,351,100	6,801,130
1862	1,350,598	69,913	1,420,501	3,557,408
1863	1,203,610	712	1,259,322	2,053,633
DISTRICT OF GENESEE. (*Rochester, N. Y.*)				
Year ending June 30, 1856	737,910	....	737,810	1,117,301
1857	174,611	10,968	185,579	919,734
1858	157,469	14,658	172,021	279,047
1859	166,156	7,884	174,040	358,785
1860	230,710	9,302	239,012	719,451
1861	245,254	....	245,254	337,467
1862	273,844	1,660	275,404	177,303
1863	310,352	....	310,352	158,897
DISTRICT OF NIAGARA. (*Niagara and Suspension Bridge, N. Y.*)				
Year ending June 30, 1856	874,892	184,713	1,059,605	1,055,740
1857	1,540,774	177,558	1,718,332	1,531,357
1858	1,140,587	273,551	1,414,138	916,909
1859	1,734,405	650,123	2,384,528	1,649,844
1860	1,648,755	657,005	2,305,760	2,172,615
1861	2,184,444	510,374	2,694,818	1,890,971
1862	1,288,759	170,174	1,458,933	1,580,793
1863	358,857	9,447	368,304	1,990,544
DISTRICT OF BUFFALO.				
Year ending June 30, 1856	859,664	80,865	940,529	1,837,220
1857	869,371	72,599	941,970	1,601,410
1858	621,603	80,600	702,203	1,390,024
1859	773,312	140,863	914,185	1,689,845
1860	616,100	89,025	705,125	2,677,730
1861	573,877	69,105	643,982	2,573,358
1862	517,948	15,853	533,801	2,684,078
1863	497,626	96,504	594,230	2,220,439
DISTRICT OF PRESQUE ISLE. (*Erie, Pa.*)				
Year ending June 30, 1856	89,094	....	89,094	4,380
1857	49,976	....	49,976	4,019
1858	49,160	....	49,160	1,806
1859	30,121	....	30,121	2,769
1860	30,069	....	30,069	7,478
1861	37,019	....	37,019	2,700
1862	104,067	....	104,067	4,791
1863	190,408	....	190,408	11,449
DISTRICT OF CUYAHOGA. (*Cleveland, Ohio.*)				
Year ending June 30, 1856	764,690	....	764,690	434,719
1857	585,449	....	585,449	231,347
1858	297,615	....	297,615	180,819

Summaries of the trade of the principal ports, &c.—Continued.

District and period.	Domestic exports.	Foreign exports.	Total exports.	Imports.
Year ending June 30, 1859	$310, 906	....	$310, 906	$161, 934
1860	187, 412	....	187, 412	236, 991
1861	369, 200	....	369, 200	181, 273
1862	248, 021	....	248, 021	117, 105
1863	653, 411	....	653, 411	130, 083
DISTRICTS OF SANDUSKY AND MIAMI. (*Sandusky and Toledo, O.*)				
Year ending June 30, 1856	290, 302	....	290, 302	28, 754
1857	348, 540	....	348, 540	36, 919
1858	42, 046	....	42, 046	18, 474
1859	62, 015	....	62, 015	105, 012
1860	97, 308	....	97, 308	92, 693
1861	313, 846	....	313, 846	62, 353
1862	613, 320	....	613, 320	47, 929
1863	*995, 444	....	995, 444	84, 884
DISTRICT OF DETROIT.				
Year ending June 30, 1856	895, 624	....	895, 624	643, 998
1857	1, 487, 253	$15, 353	1, 502, 606	1, 018, 308
1858	6, 168, 031	20, 676	6, 188, 707	663, 001
1860	3, 024, 624	....	3, 024, 624	1, 048, 027
1860	3, 820, 932	....	3, 820, 932	960, 529
1861	330, 752	....	330, 752	542, 853
1862	1, 631, 012	125, 803	1, 757, 815	628, 021
1863	1, 948, 302	60, 298	2, 008, 600	740, 958
DISTRICT OF CHICAGO.				
Year ending June 30, 1856	1, 345, 923	....	1, 345, 923	277, 404
1857	1, 583, 096	308	1, 583, 404	368, 325
1858	1, 713, 077	....	1, 713, 077	222, 830
1859	1, 269, 385	....	1, 269, 385	03, 588
1860	1, 163, 183	....	1, 163, 183	00, 214
1861	3, 622, 343	....	3, 622, 343	77, 348
1862	9, 363, 275	....	9, 363, 275	01, 383
1863	3, 544, 085	....	3, 544, 085	134, 204
DISTRICT OF MILWAUKIE.				
Year ending June 30, 1856	345, 493	....	345, 493	27, 604
1857	622, 044	....	622, 044	5, 817
1858	543, 280	....	543, 280	108, 604
1859	829, 088	....	829, 088	28, 946
1860	187, 111	....	187, 111	3, 425
1861	785, 872	....	785, 872	8, 220
1862	1, 425, 088	....	1, 425, 088	6, 810
1863	3, 323, 637	....	3, 323, 637	24, 479
DISTRICT OF MACKINAW, MICH.				
Year ending June 30, 1856	....	....	....	35, 400
1857	....	....	....	250
1858	....	....	....	0, 853
1859	....	....	....	19, 312
1860	....	....	....	15, 500
1861	....	....	....	13, 863
1862	....	....	....	3, 334
1863	....	....	....	31, 208

* Nearly all this amount was exported in the quarter ending September 30, 1862, at Toledo.

Summary at ports eastward of Buffalo, including Buffalo.

Year.	Domestic exports.	Foreign exports.	Total exports.	Imports.
1856	$11,435,919	$3,845,132	$15,281,051	$10,074,457
1857	8,451,227	2,611,074	11,062,301	16,632,371
1858	6,873,912	2,897,044	9,770,956	10,380,037
1859	7,680,629	4,127,332	12,197,961	12,782,024
1860	6,087,095	2,506,412	8,103,507	17,588,793
1861	6,428,534	2,295,606	8,724,140	17,785,093
1862	4,912,016	1,733,336	6,645,352	14,545,374
1863	*7,705,738	1,299,943	9,005,681	17,610,097

* Including an unusual export of $3,376,977, at the district of Champlain, of gold and silver coin.

Summary at ports westward of Buffalo.

Year.	Domestic exports.	Foreign exports.	Total exports.	Imports.
1856	$3,619,476	....	$3,619,476	$1,653,019
1857	4,577,029	$15,691	4,592,720	1,622,584
1858	7,813,109	20,676	7,833,785	1,283,507
1859	6,890,229	....	6,890,229	1,460,308
1860	6,494,096	....	6,494,096	1,396,880
1861	6,359,141	....	6,359,141	890,600
1862	6,365,532	125,803	6,491,335	767,087
1863	10,565,285	80,298	10,645,583	1,167,302

CANADIAN FREE PORTS.

By an act of the Canadian legislature which went into operation November 20, 1860, the harbor and district of Gaspé Basin, in the Gulf of St. Lawrence, was constituted a free port into which goods of every description might be imported, either for consumption or for re-exportation, without the payment of duties. An extended line of coast was embraced in this district, with Anticosti Island and the Magdalen islands, the whole area of territory being quite large, but the number of inhabitants small. The district itself is incapable of much development, and the consequences as to making it a depot of trade for re-export do not appear to be important. It is mainly used as a point of outward shipment of fish and lumber, and of importation of spirits, groceries, and manufactured goods. These imports are not, however, apparently much beyond the consumption of the islands and fisheries of the vicinity. The countries from which they come are evidently transatlantic mainly, and not in great proportion from the United States. Whatever may be the advantages conferred on the fisheries and local interests of the vicinity, there does not appear to be any general importance attaching to the establishment of this as a free port.

Imports at the port of Gaspé from countries other than Canada.

Articles.	1861.		1862.		1863.	
	Quantity.	Value.	Quantity.	Value.	Quantity.	Value.
Wines and spirits..galls.	30,013	$20,125	38,740	$20,342	61,301	$33,228
Coffee..............lbs.	11,133	1,464	17,766	3,348	39,510	6,316
Sugar...............lbs.	121,449	8,226	244,542	13,625	142,070	9,031
Molasses............galls.	62,697	15,553	111,722	21,988	87,429	19,929
Tea.................lbs.	77,655	24,339	98,868	35,617	103,783	39,109
Tobacco.............lbs.	62,000	11,492	53,067	17,207	50,995	15,964
Clothing..............	....	13,263	....	16,991	....	12,106
Manuf's and dry goods..	....	126,835	....	120,024	....	119,854
Other dutiable articles...	....	48,543	....	57,858	....	61,815
Free goods............	....	104,529	....	107,050	....	118,271
Totals............	....	374,729	....	420,180	....	428,623

Exports of the port of Gaspé to British and foreign ports.

Articles.	1861.		1862.		1863.	
	Quantity.	Value.	Quantity.	Value.	Quantity.	Value.
Fish, dry..........cwt.	142,021	$415,549	184,678	$560,948	180,961	$603,347
pickled.......bbls.	75,037	161,841	27,252	35,067	33,929	59,754
oil..........galls.	42,459	18,876	78,115	43,258	58,360	36,857
Furs and skins.........	....	6,390	....	17,185	....	7,820
Timber and lumber.......	....	10,202	....	19,069	....	31,675
Butter, lard, and pork...	....	1,477	....	3,160	....	6,157
Wheat, flour, and grain..	....	2,015	....	2,664	....	3,238
Other articles..........	....	6,135	....	8,491	....	5,904
Totals............	....	630,477	....	691,075	....	751,852

A second and more important free port, as regards the commerce of the United States, was at the same time established at Sault Ste. Marie, and embracing the whole Canadian coast of Lake Superior and Lake Huron. The district has 400 miles of lake coast, and the adjacent islands are also included. Very little practical importance has resulted from the opening of this port up to the close of 1863; but its proximity to a rapidly developing country on both sides of the boundary indicates that it will interfere materially with the commerce of other districts should it continue a free port. The following were the imports for the three years of its establishment; but it is impossible to say what proportion was from the United States:

Imports into Sault Ste. Marie from British and foreign ports.

Dutiable.	1861.		1862.		1863.	
	Quantity.	Value.	Quantity.	Value.	Quantity.	Value.
Spirits	10,245 gals.	$3,177	8,718 gals.	$3,002	5,078 gals.	$2,560
Coffee	131 lbs.	26	209 lbs.	73	3,554 lbs.	690
Tea	8,748 lbs.	4,648	6,330 lbs.	3,400	14,531 lbs.	8,331
Tobacco	3,601 lbs.	963	1,280 lbs.	571	7,371 lbs.	2,854
Spices	50 lbs.	25	44 lbs.	7	115 lbs.	24
Fruits, dry	639 lbs.	113	5,845 lbs.	385	7,247 lbs.	733
Sugar	33,631 lbs.	2,692	41,374 lbs.	2,022	100,304 lbs.	8,902
Molasses	214 gals.	98	163 gals.	78	....	....
Soap	7,103 lbs.	410	3,035 lbs.	185	7,310 lbs.	516
Malt liquors	1,043 gals.	297	6,458 gals.	1,250	360 gals.	147
Wines	174 gals.	365	413 gals.	628	605 gals.	1,009
Clothing	....	2,227	....	4,037	....	13,415
Woollens	....	25,118	....	22,203	....	16,834
Cottons	....	6,710	....	6,675	....	7,042
Leather manufactures	....	1,101	....	1,482	....	3,190
Hardware	....	2,672	....	6,432	....	4,711
Glass and earthenware	....	255	....	91	....	677
Machinery	....	1,048	....	781	....	394
Iron and steel	....	3,098	....	1,375	....	634
Gunpowder	....	4,865	....	4,992	....	4,308
Candles	....	1,229	....	1,448	....	675
Hay	47 tons.	503	47 tons.	660	28 tons.	465
Other articles	....	5,016	....	5,418	....	13,457
Total dutiable	....	60,615	....	67,587	....	88,506
Free goods	....	20,189	....	22,833	....	27,306
Total imports	....	92,704	....	90,420	....	115,872

Exports of the port of Sault Ste. Marie to British and foreign ports.

Articles.	1861.		1862.		1863.	
	Quantity.	Value.	Quantity.	Value.	Quantity.	Value.
Copper .... tons.	....	....	....	....	1,495	$125,176
Copper ore .... tons.	3,129	$210,471	3,114	$250,408	3,658	245,304
Fish, pickled ...... bbls.	1,210	5,033	50	258	290	1,479
Knees, planks, &c.	....	1,401	....	4,250	....	....
Other wood	....	125	....	3,020	....	1,630
Animals, horses, &c.	....	160	....	450	....	200
Furs	....	17,000	....	40,764	....	56,029
Maple sugar and veg'tab's	....	532	....	421	....	....
Indian bark work	....	761	....	257	....	29
Other articles	....	....	....	....	....	242
Totals	....	235,518	....	305,852	....	430,546

The trade of this port or district is evidently limited altogether to the local consumption and production of the few inhabitants at present occupying it. Its exports of copper and copper ore are the chief productions, and are three times the value of its imports.

The trade of the same port with Canada is very small, the imports and exports being in—

	Imports.	Exports.
1861	$39,179	$95
1862	41,743	74
1863	57,199	253

The chief product, copper and copper ore, comes to the United States.

INTERNAL OR DOMESTIC COMMERCE

BETWEEN THE

MISSISSIPPI VALLEY AND THE ATLANTIC STATES.

DATA—TREATMENT—GENERAL RESULTS.

In the division of this report relating to internal commerce it is assumed that the exchanges conducted within the limits of the United States have attained to a magnitude entitling them to the designation of commerce in the broadest and fullest sense of the term, and to the care and regard of the national authorities as commerce is with foreign countries.

Though these exchanges pass through no official record of valuation it is still assumed that the statistics of the transportation lines afford the basis of a reasonably close approximation to a calculation of their value.

It is assumed that the carriage of produce or manufactures the average distance of three hundred miles from the producing point to the market of consumption, entitles such quantities and values to be ranked with the general mass of exchanges defined as internal commerce. This is limited, however, to transportation east and west, since that, more definitely than in other directions, represents natural movements from producers to consumers.

As a measure of this exchange between the east and the west, all quantities are taken which pass the line of the Alleghanies in either direction, including the extension of their line, or meridian, through Upper Canada. And an addition is made to the quantities reported as carried in through freight across this line, of one-half the way freight of the five great carriers eastward of the Alleghanies to tide-water. These carriers are the Erie canal, the New York Central and Erie railroads, the Pennsylvania railroad, and the Baltimore and Ohio railroad.

Assigning values to the quantities so taken, which are the quantities and market values of 1862, it is found that the aggregate value of westward commerce in that year, including the deliveries of merchandise of all classes at a distance of 300 miles from the Atlantic seaboard, was nearly the sum of $616,000,000; and that the return freight, eastward, of inland produce and merchandise passing the line of the Alleghanies, attained the value of $522,000,000. The total trade is, therefore, $1,138,000,000.

As a general check on the calculation, it is estimated that a population of ten millions west of the Alleghanies is supplied with most of its merchandise by this westward carriage, and that they have taken, under circumstances of unusual activity and ability to supply themselves, fifty dollars in value each of all classes of articles and representatives of value.

To represent this internal movement in such manner that an independent judgment may be formed of it by every one, the statistics of quantities transported in both directions are given in condensed form from the reports of the various transportation authorities, yet with enough detail to show precisely what the exchange is.

The commerce of the lakes is stated in the fullest manner from the trade reports of the cities on its borders. Their immense fleet of vessels, with the recent increase and present tonnage; the lines of propellers of recent establishment, and their railroad connections in transit and at the east with the statistics of shipment at western ports and of receipt at eastern terminal points, are embodied very fully. Calculations of value based on the quantities identified in this way, appear to sustain the calculations applied directly to the tonnage of the great roads and the Erie canal which complete the transportation from the west.

The receipts and shipments of all leading articles of produce are given at the chief ports and cities of the lake district, including Toronto and Montreal, in Canada.

The data used relate mainly to the year 1862. No earlier year is taken to represent our internal or domestic commerce proper; because, before the rebellion the import and export trade of the United States to a considerable extent traversed the southern ports; because it was a full year, but not excessive; and because in that year there was a very complete severance of the domestic commerce of the north from that of the south and from the foreign. The occasional comparisons with other years are made for specific and subordinate purposes.

The "year" intended in this division is the calendar; and the values are at the prices ruling in 1862, before any extraordinary rise had taken place.

INTERNAL OR DOMESTIC COMMERCE.

The extent of the territory of the United States is so great, and the diversity of production in its various parts so much beyond the ordinary diversity belonging to any single or continental government, that the exchanges conducted within its limits rise to the full measure of importance which belongs to commerce in its general sense. The articles exchanged are carried to great distances, and they are of the natural surplus of the districts from which they are taken, supplying a natural want in the districts to which they are carried. Subtropical staples are exchanged for the field crops and forest products of the coolest belt of the temperate latitudes in one direction; and in another the extremes of maritime and of continental interior climates are exchanged. Trade of this comprehensive character must be regarded as permanent, and as entitled to rank next to the highest in national interest and importance. If possible, it should be as regularly stated and as definitely known through authentic statistics, as the external trade of the country in imports and exports is known.

Russia alone, of European states, conducts a trade analogous to that of the United States between its various districts. Great efforts have at all times been made by that government to foster and encourage those inland exchanges, and much of the strength and of the display of accumulated resources which occasions have at various times developed in Russia, may undoubtedly be ascribed to its command of the products of an entire continental zone, and to its constant, though almost silent, interchange of these products from all points within the widely separated coasts that constitute its boundary. The other European states exchange very largely with their colonies, and almost wholly by sea; the statistics of this trade being regularly given as a branch of their foreign commerce. Strike from the commerce of England, France, Spain, and Holland, the trade they conduct with their own colonies, near and remote, and the volume would be greatly reduced. During the last twenty years the development of the interior of this continent, and of the new territorial area of the United States, has drawn a large share of the means, the energy, and activity which in European states finds its proper field of activity in foreign commerce, to the hitherto unnoted trade of the plains, the interior, and the Pacific coast. The district of the great lakes is alone a vast field for this display of commercial energy, and the Mississippi valley has long constituted another, and almost equal field. The railroad system connecting the Atlantic cities with the interior has recently developed the same general character, and has risen to gigantic importance as an agent in actual exchanges of merchandise. The tonnage movement of the great railroads from the interior eastward to the Atlantic cities in 1863 was little, if at all, inferior to the tonnage delivered by transatlantic shipping arriving at the ports of the entire Atlantic coast. The railroad freight tonnage reached a total of nearly 3,500,000 tons, and deducting from the shipping arrivals of the Atlantic ports a small proportion for that which came from American ports north or south of the United States in transit to Europe, the total remaining does not largely exceed the amount just stated.*

The difficulty of assigning definite quantities and values to these internal exchanges is great, since there is no uniform system of record through which they pass. The railroads and canals are, with one exception, private corporations; and though they usually report with great fulness the quantities of the leading articles transported, values are given only in the case of the New York State canals. In many things these reports of the transportation companies are sufficiently full and clear for the purpose of calculating the values exchanged, and it is only necessary to institute a system of estimates, based on the known prices of leading articles. These are readily determined, and there appears no insuperable difficulty in making up calculated total values which will attain a reasonable approximation to accuracy. On the New York canals the precedent of estimating values per pound for freight of all kinds has been set for years in the official reports of the auditor general, and the results of such estimates have been accepted without question.

As a basis for the calculation, it is assumed that goods carried the distance of three hundred miles from the place of production to the place of consumption should be included in the account of domestic or internal commerce. Very large quantities of produce and of manufactured goods are carried much further than this in the United States, as in the very heavy shipments from New York and other Atlantic cities to Chicago, St. Louis, and other points on the Mississippi and Missouri rivers. Probably the assumption of three hundred miles as the minimum of distance would raise the average distance to five hundred miles, in consequence of the preponderance of freights of eight hundred to one thousand miles; so that it would be reasonable to assume two hundred miles as the minimum, and to include all transportation for this last-named distance in the general account. In regard to manufactured goods, domestic and foreign, sent westward, the average distance for those sent to the entire region west of the Alleghanies is little, if at all, short of eight hundred miles. The return trade eastward has a somewhat shorter line.

The calculation of values for this internal exchange must be made from the commercial statements voluntarily put forth by the transporting companies, or compiled by Boards of Trade for commercial information. These sources of information are much more abundant and uniform for the trade between the Atlantic coast and the interior, than for that between the northern and southern States, and along the Mississippi river and valley, north and south. The lines of transportation north and south are neither so regular nor so much pressed with constant business as those leading east and west. Vast as the freights were which were carried on the Mississippi, outward and inward, they were subject to great variations in successive years, and no trustworthy record of them has been preserved. At the east, the coasting trade was always the chief

---

*The total tonnage entered in all the ports of the United States during the fiscal year ending June 30, 1863, was 7,255,076 tons. Deducting an aggregate of 3,050,369 tons arriving from Canada, (the larger share of which is mere ferry tonnage,) and also 273,635 tons arriving at San Francisco and other Pacific ports, there remain 3,931,072 tons as the total arriving from all quarters at all the Atlantic ports.

During the calendar year 1863 the Pennsylvania railroad delivered 704,171 tons at its eastern terminus, while in 1862 the New York Central delivered 1,084,128 tons, and the Erie 971,332 tons. Adding to the last two an advance of 15 per cent. reported in 1863 over 1862, and the three sum up 3,044,960 tons. Adding 500,000 tons for all other roads, the total exceeds 3,500,000 tons.

reliance for carriage, and this was also subject to great and irregular variations. No entrances or clearances of cargo being ever required, the best that can be done is to roughly estimate it by the tonnage capacity of the shipping through which it was conducted.

With the progress of the age in perfecting railroads, the contrast between land and water carriage has been steadily reduced to smaller and smaller proportions, until even the lakes and rivers lying in the direct line of east and west carriage have become merely the equals of the railroad lines. They are but portions of the general lines, and are preferred or rejected at intervals, according to the temporary exigencies of business.

The more important mass of this internal commerce is over the broad northern belt occupied by the great railroad lines, and in which the great lakes, the New York canals, and the Ohio river now only divide the transportation with these roads. All these cross a natural line of geographical division between the east and the west at the Alleghanies, and the continuation of their line from the point where they cease as mountains, due northward, across the Erie canal, the New York Central railroad, and the Canadian lines of transportation, may be taken as of the same geographical significance. There is no line equally well defined in any other part of the United States over which the entire volume of natural exchanges now passes between the two sections. The trade of the Mississippi river has been, and must always remain, much less definite, since an alternative is offered at each extremity for transportation by other modes of conveyance. The outlet for western produce to foreign tropical markets geographically near the mouth of the Mississippi, is now in many respects more convenient by lake and railroad first to the Atlantic coast, than by the most unrestricted use of the Mississippi and the New Orleans markets.

The calculation of transportation east and west may be simplified by taking the entire carriage of the great leading lines, and rejecting that of the subordinate lines. In the entire carriage of the Erie canal the trade passing over Lake Ontario is embraced. A small proportion of the lake trade, which has been estimated by the best Canadian authorities at not more than ten per cent., passes northward of Lake Ontario, or goes out at other ports or outlets than the New York canals, or by railroad to Portland, Maine. This proportion can be taken directly from Canadian statistics, or can be added simply as a percentage on the total values of the lake trade otherwise made up. As there are lateral roads and canals, as well as intermediate lake ports, which represent fragments of the general trade east and west, and which deliver or receive their freight at points on the great roads far along their line from either terminus, it is a necessary and just simplification to take the entire business of the great lines, and reject the smaller ones altogether, as has been said. Thus the New York and Erie road has tributary lines on the north connecting it with Buffalo, with Lake Ontario, and with the Hudson river; on the south it has a great tributary leading from Central Ohio; the business of all being conducted between markets really separated by an average distance not less than three hundred miles.

For the measure of the trade between the east and the west, therefore, it is proposed to take the entire freight carriage of the Baltimore and Ohio railroad, the Pennsylvania railroad, the Erie and Central railroads, in New York, the Erie canal, the Welland canal, and the Grand Trunk railroad of Canada; or to estimate for such transportation on these last named as properly belongs to the trade entering from the United States, and again returning, as has been stated above, viz: ten per cent. of the carriage of the Erie canal.

Before proceeding to give the statement of values so exchanged between the west and the east across the Alleghanies and their line continued northward, it may be proper to state at what other points this domestic commerce should be noted in order to obtain an adequate account of it. The coastwise trade of the Atlantic coast in part belongs to it, as does also the barge transportation through the New Jersey canals, and through the Chesapeake and Delaware canal. But there are no railroad lines in the eastern States whose traffic would be included, beyond the amount which would be reached at the eastern extremities of the great lines before named. That which is local, or may be carried but fifty or one hundred miles on the eastern end of either of the great roads or canals, is again taken up by minor roads and carried to cities along the coast a distance sufficient to make up the distance assumed as the minimum. No eastern roads need, therefore, be taken into the account, if the entire movement on the great lines before named is considered.

The coastwise trade is, in ordinary times, made up of elements that may be estimated with a fair approximation to accuracy. The coal of Pennsylvania is carried coastwise to the extent of near one-fourth the annual production. The products of the fisheries are, to the extent of two-thirds their total in quantity and value, also carried in the coastwise trade, embracing in this calculation the produce of the whale fisheries. The lumber of the southern States is carried northward, that of the Susquehanna eastward, and that of the coast of Maine southward, each in quantities and proportions which may be estimated. Naval stores, rice, and cotton were carried from the planting States in large quantities, as they undoubtedly will be again. Grain and flour from the James river, the Chesapeake, and the coasts of Maryland and Delaware, have been carried to the eastern States in great quantities. Lastly, the manufactures and machinery produced in all the New England States, New York, Pennsylvania, New Jersey, Delaware, and Maryland, have been carried coastwise to the entire south, from the Delaware bay to Texas. The value of these manufactures has always been large; and though the trade is now greatly checked, it constitutes a traffic which will revive promptly, and will attain far greater proportions hereafter than it has at any previous time.

In the west there are at least three central points at which exchanges are conducted rising to the full dignity of commerce. Cincinnati is the first of these, as a point of exchange between the States north of the Ohio, and those producing many things essentially distinct south of the Ohio. The hemp and tobacco of Kentucky are not, however, fully noted in the statistics of trade at Cincinnati. The cotton and iron of Tennessee come to the Ohio river only in small quantities also.

St. Louis is the next general commercial centre the trade of which is not embraced in the account of exchanges between the east and the west. The entire trade of St. Louis, and of such points southward to the mouth of the Ohio river as are now increasing in trade through the Illinois Central railroad or otherwise, should be taken into the exhibit of domestic commerce.

Chicago is a large receiving point, and a larger distributor both of agricultural produce and of manufactured goods than either of the cities first named, but a large share of its exchanges will be noted in the statistics of trade over the great railroad and lake lines. The exchanges here conducted are so extensive, however, that they should be given separately, subsequently estimating what proportion may be taken as included or not included in other statements of internal exchanges.

The Lake Superior trade, now only at the moderate proportions of ten or twelve million dollars in value shipped outward, and twelve millions (including mining machinery) shipped inward, is a distinct and notable item of trade. The copper nd iron produced there are largely smelted and wrought at Detroit, Cleveland, Pittsburg, and Buffalo, but a small share of its products being shipped direct to the Atlantic cities. There is a considerable lumber trade of the upper lakes, and a trade in the salt, fish and local products of the State of Michigan which occupies a class of lake coasting vessels in a profitable and important business, which does not go much beyond the cities of the lake shores.

Beyond all these is the trade of Saint Paul and the northwestern border, and of Leavenworth and the great plains to the gold region; which constitutes a distinct and very important division, not only for what it now is, but in view of its rapid expansion, and the enormous development it is soon to attain.

At the south, New Orleans was always a focal point for extensive domestic exchanges, conducted both coastwise and by the Mississippi river. We can now merely state to what these exchanges attained before the disturbances which have destroyed that trade for the time, and which leave it doubtful to what extent and in what time they will be resumed.

SPECIFIC CALCULATION OF THE EXCHANGES BETWEEN THE EAST AND THE WEST.

I. WESTWARD FREIGHTS.

The reports of the Pennsylvania railroad are more full and complete as regards the details of articles carried than those of any other line of transportation so extensive, and they may therefore be taken as the best to initiate the calculation of values proposed. Prices may be assigned to almost every article in detail, if desired, and the total value may be so deduced, or an average may be taken with less labor which will closely approximate the same result. The general classification into which these articles are thrown is the same as that employed in describing the freight of the New York and Erie and the New York Central roads, and therefore a classified price, calculated to agree with the total derived from the average of all articles in detail, could be used with safety for all similar statements of freight aggregates. Thus the detailed list of articles appears to show that one third of the tonnage carried westward on the Pennsylvania road is properly described as dry goods, another third as drugs and groceries, and the remaining third as iron and heavy goods. If this division is correct, it is not material whether the values assigned per pound to each be absolutely correct, so that their total does not exceed the total deduced by a calculation of values for each article. For the year 1862 the westward freight of this road was as follows:

From Philadelphia to Pittsburg......	256,204,920 pounds, or	128,102 tons.
From Baltimore to Pittsburg........	34,206,488 pounds, or	17,103 tons.
Totals......................	290,411,408 pounds, or	145,205 tons.

The schedule of articles shows a large preponderance of dry goods, drugs, medicines and dyes, groceries, boots, shoes, and hats, and similar articles of high relative value. It is well known that the maximum often assumed by carriers as the limit of value at which they will compensate shippers for goods lost in their care, is usually insisted upon by losers as being below their true value. This maximum is one dollar per pound; but as it is usually applied to other goods than those here distinguished as the third class, or heavy goods, it is but an incidental proof favoring an increase of the general average of prices. It is proposed to assume an average value of forty-three and one-third cents per pound for this westward freight; and in dividing it into three equal portions, to assign one dollar per pound to the dry goods, or highest class, twenty cents per pound to the drugs and groceries, and ten cents per pound to the iron and heavy goods.

1. Dry goods...............	96,803,803	pounds, at $1 per pound.........	$96,803,803
2. Drugs and groceries......	96,803,803	pounds, at 20 cents per pound...	19,360,761
3. Iron and heavy goods.....	96,803,802	pounds, at 10 cents per pound...	9,680,381
Totals................	290,411,408	pounds, at 43⅓ cents per pound..	125,844,945

This is of through freight only, and that which, being carried farthest, may be presumed to average the highest value per pound. During the year 1862 the price of many descriptions of dry goods had largely increased as compared with 1860, and this was particularly true of the classes most largely carried to the interior markets—cotton and cotton-mixed goods, coarse woollens, and leather manufactures. It is, in fact, probable that the values here assumed are too low, and that a total value higher by some millions would be more nearly correct for the year 1862; but as this year is exceptional as compared with former years, it may be better to retain a relatively low rate—one certainly not requiring abatements for over-estimate.

Next, the quantities carried locally on the Pennsylvania road from its eastern terminus to points along its line require to be considered. For reasons elsewhere stated it is assumed that these freights passing through, or departing from, each terminus, belong in the general account, since there is nothing taken for the freights of other roads connected with, and continuing the business of, the great lines. The record of the local freight of the Pennsylvania road is incomplete, in consequence of the employment on it of "cars of individual transporters," who do not make return of their business in the statements of the company, merely paying tonnage rates or mileage rates for their cars in bulk. For 1862 the total reported as carried by cars of the company from the eastern terminus westward, but not through to Pittsburg, is 91,565,194 pounds, to which may be added for the individual transporters at least enough to raise the aggregate to 100,000,000 pounds, or 5,000 tons, of 2,000 pounds each. Of this freight about one-eighth is dry goods, one-fourth groceries, and the remainder, five-eighths, heavy goods. For groceries and heavy goods it is perhaps necessary to reduce the prices taken in the former case, as follows:

1. Dry goods....	12,500,000	pounds, at $1 per pound.........	$12,500,000
2. Groceries, &c.	25,000,000	pounds, at 15 cents per pound ...	3,750,000
3. Heavy goods............	62,500,000	pounds, at 6 cents per pound	3,750,000
Totals...............	100,000,000	pounds, at 20 cents per pound ...	20,000,000

These are minimum quantities and values, which should not be excluded from the account of movements westward. Probably the larger share of the articles have already been brought from points averaging a hundred miles beyond the eastern terminus of the road—New York and the New England States—and they are to be carried at least a hundred miles further, on the average, before being distributed to consumers.

The detailed tables which follow are given for their general value in illustrating the trade of the east with the interior. Were such details accessible for the great roads of New York, a similar diversity and corresponding general divisions would undoubtedly appear. The Central road of New York carries a larger proportion of light and valuable goods, and the Erie road a larger proportion of heavy goods, the two together averaging very nearly the same in classification and in values with the Pennsylvania road.

Articles carried westward on the Pennsylvania railroad.

1.—THROUGH TO PITTSBURG, FROM PHILADELPHIA AND BALTIMORE.

Articles.	1859.	1860.	1861.	1862.	1863.
	Pounds.	*Pounds.*	*Pounds.*	*Pounds.*	*Pounds.*
Agricultural implements	225,378	51,035	28,807	245,380	105,443
Agricultural products, not specified	1,858,997	308,690	867,346	340,621	1,343,198
Bark and sumac	160,771	94,085	98,630	178,157	3,336
Barrels, empty, (oil barrels)		224,160	1,770,157	5,670,270	13,704,187
Books and stationery	2,478,417	1,329,651	715,908	680,073	1,040,185
Boots, shoes, and hats	8,615,406	8,762,194	4,891,418	4,837,429	5,983,451
Brown sheeting and bagging	9,878,049	3,524,048	6,086,102	4,690,925	1,438,934
Carriages and wagons		90,095	85,830	179,377	957,824
Cedar and willow ware	105,073	989,136	119,327	231,390	258,913
Coffee	10,815,235	6,781,574	14,508,948	7,015,700	7,998,753
Confectionery and foreign fruits	3,540,979	2,730,892	2,744,877	645,930	1,876,155
Copper, tin, and lead	2,058,028	5,057,382	3,567,443	2,777,500	7,308,764
Cotton		109,731	323,910	968,310	31,800
Dry goods	87,277,296	64,472,760	43,225,829	73,81[illegible],478	80,328,433
Drugs, medicines, and dyes	8,413,409	12,817,838	12,341,640	31,380,863	11,375,835
Earthenware and queensware	6,170,840	6,620,067	3,306,529	6,299,376	7,922,857
Feathers, furs, and skins		6,770		77,813	94,590
Fresh meats and fish				309,351	75,093
Flour and meal	164,655			90,349	2,085
Furniture and oil-cloth	2,455,304	2,799,683	549,391	2,340,473	2,548,578
Glass and glassware	1,191,763	1,047,644	548,678	848,147	621,785
Grain of all kinds	2,030,335	8,910		217,873	64,756
Grass and other seeds	976,436	58,864	143,378	173,870	73,659
Green and dried fruits	311,463	89,078	86,960	3,819,103	3,718,890
Groceries, except coffee	19,286,903	22,850,187	27,181,460	65,107,985	64,854,645
Guano and phosphate of lime	178,159	17,370		18,231	10,599
Hardware	10,870,368	10,734,309	10,024,098	9,192,943	21,500,597
Hemp and cordage	1,928,499	2,718,629	1,574,400	1,085,513	1,365,853
Hides and hair	808,478	183,119	191,449	388,153	995,348
Iron, pig and blooms	14,250			835,827	138,380
rolled	1,792,109	1,877,525	1,898,199	2,501,217	3,417,832
railroad	4,402,925	987,210	33,129	1,945,408	1,813,180
Leather	3,617,360	880,288	2,694,526	2,434,838	741,738
Lime and plaster		402,887	331,848	425,758	783,436
Machinery and castings	4,783,963	1,211,636	9,074,107	11,878,913	15,928,498
Marble and cement	2,199,250	2,508,389	2,086,345	2,181,337	3,843,634
Malt and malt liquors	174,165	111,087	99,230	383,546	112,985
Nails and spikes	872,073	134,597	292,290	221,887	365,675
Oil, (not coal or petroleum)	2,892,270	2,925,333	1,544,998	1,477,830	733,230
Oysters	309,001	319,710	799,853	1,738,070	2,044,859
Paper	2,840,394	3,973,048	2,019,587	1,853,879	1,387,514
Powder			863,081	8,973,015	7,038,094
Salt	1,344,325	1,908,198	3,581,778	6,833,964	635,374
Salt meats and fish	8,574,180	4,544,560	3,349,094	11,991,327	5,822,388
Soda-ash, (pot and pearl)	17,889,845	19,916,433	5,088,835	13,701,119	13,745,930
Soap and candles	383,645	890,204	191,137	318,114	897,701
Tobacco and cigars	2,839,786	2,806,871	2,785,801	2,434,708	2,682,458
Tar, pitch, and rosin	1,007,648	1,813,079	432,890	1,177,053	417,171
Wines and liquors, foreign	4,881,134	3,842,798	2,010,346	1,049,578	131,388
Whiskey and alcohol	359,003	10,350	30,619	2,821,920	1,837,382
Woollen yarns	378,438	829,030	383,853	378,430	133,738
Miscellaneous	1,179,823	797,880	94,030	64,738	999,846
Government goods					1,118,846
Total pounds	207,677,089	189,491,308	179,633,600	280,441,406	277,878,389
Total tons	103,839	90,747	89,818	143,308	138,[illegible]

Articles carried westward on the Pennsylvania railroad—Continued.

2.—TO WAY STATIONS, FROM PHILADELPHIA.

Articles.	1859.	1860.	1861.	1862.	1863.
	Pounds.	*Pounds.*	*Pounds.*	*Pounds.*	*Pounds.*
Agricultural implements	310,196	224,889	195,475	137,030	150,997
Agricultural products, not specified	2,804,396	1,718,315	864,324	309,419	630,763
Bark and sumac	142,154	10,495	8,450	11,303	1,430
Boots, shoes, and hats	861,470	801,539	733,991	2,036,813	954,048
Books and stationery	808,843	714,419	136,894	437,394	149,449
Carriages		109,555	1,984,085	163,139	101,735

Articles carried westward on the Pennsylvania railroad—Continued.

2.—TO WAY STATIONS, FROM PHILADELPHIA.

Articles.	1859.	1860.	1861.	1862.	1863.
	Pounds.	*Pounds.*	*Pounds.*	*Pounds.*	*Pounds.*
Cedar ware	164,722	192,682	190,068	213,197	184,840
Coffee	4,954,813	3,134,507	2,213,221	1,298,301	410,763
Confectionery and fruits	1,332,815	1,343,511	817,498	323,235	865,953
Coal	50,277,775	23,004,600	84,965,400	....	15,069
Copper, tin and lead	1,170,455	970,479	480,262	423,327	1,866,151
Cotton	3,455,105	4,043,264	353,765	78,602	65,374
Dry goods	8,440,126	9,557,622	7,817,107	8,506,659	7,246,163
Drugs, medicines, and dyes	2,191,973	2,730,514	2,134,144	2,212,430	1,469,191
Earthenware and queensware	1,313,297	1,353,282	972,734	1,066,448	1,171,072
Fish and meats, fresh	98,573	....	8,310	66,070	73,639
Flour	621,853	196,447	601,244	183,410	442,675
Fruits, green and dry	42,924	991,578	853,161	511,549	556,498
Furniture	1,102,129	1,257,535	941,628	1,362,814	765,849
Glass and glassware	678,767	867,195	642,417	254,294	604,547
Grain of all kinds	798,108	469,607	346,957	7,048,311	916,857
Grass and other seeds	31,522	50,937	53,894	65,974	159,000
Groceries, except coffee	20,906,037	20,752,162	15,370,773	14,563,927	23,044,649
Guano and phosphate of lime	456,180	830,866	691,736	261,424	421,740
Hardware	4,029,921	2,870,815	2,675,481	3,716,444	6,229,060
Hides and hair	2,664,818	2,039,840	2,575,501	1,691,100	2,086,815
Hemp and cordage	610,624	654,322	191,169	749,229	198,683
Iron, pig and bloom	4,577,929	1,921,439	2,070,840	7,158,152	2,892,958
rolled	6,313,093	4,812,794	2,344,477	5,340,369	10,414,511
railroad	1,100,324	716,153	417,097	2,509,500	896,718
Leather	511,957	570,979	731,129	494,761	348,988
Lime and plaster	....	1,008,848	816,507	2,294,147	3,114,509
Live stock	733,470	796,700	1,140,015	415,815	997,060
Lard, lard oil, and tallow	598,073	18,540	14,168	50,631	59,153
Lumber and timber	918,439	1,090,091	1,364,840	334,125	613,007
Machinery and castings	4,100,670	3,801,548	3,064,830	3,323,791	7,878,549
Marble and cement	4,541,798	4,659,569	565,330	2,944,678	3,440,611
Malt and malt liquors	1,077,921	1,115,094	3,037,113	491,980	987,959
Nails and spikes	475,555	633,891	457,908	311,612	1,040,718
Oil, petroleum	....	....	34,015	621,837	376,974
other	637,353	1,394,755	939,411	176,616	891,319
Oysters	442,200	853,071	849,659	180,579	399,804
Paper and rags	3,102,844	2,153,132	1,225,125	1,197,467	1,975,973
Powder	....	....	852,635	530,195	898,346
Salt	7,379,699	5,900,581	6,790,116	4,489,853	6,363,335
Salt meats and fish	6,256,867	4,807,915	5,375,496	3,972,390	4,948,640
Soap and candles	6,349,900	57,679	....	177,019	177,773
Soda-ash	309,005	198,907	87,470	221,171	399,669
Tobacco and cigars	1,047,948	863,777	794,975	779,788	764,644
Tar, pitch, and rosin	852,327	613,141	837,854	71,369	13,659
Wines and liquors, foreign	1,195,971	927,060	1,207,519	1,059,126	141,750
Whiskey and alcohol	866,710	948,391	89,710	167,394	1,959,946
Wool and woollen yarn	427,774	495,135	917,723	161,280	928,890
Miscellaneous	7,971,628	2,207,907	20,650,268	222,072	472,117
Government goods	....	....	....	....	2,941,626
Total pounds	173,731,080	134,614,840	128,267,904	91,565,194	160,979,099
Total tons	86,866	67,309	64,134	45,782	80,049

The local freight taken up at all points of the line for carriage beyond the mountains is unnoted in the previous calculation of through freights. This was in 1861 and 1862 as follows:

1861.—Coal, 23,947 tons; other merchandise, 114,126,409 pounds.

1862.—Coal, 5,701 tons; other merchandise, 207,484,614 pounds.

The portion of this taken up at stations east of the mountains may safely be assumed to be one-half, giving a value, at a minimum of five cents per pound, of over $5,000,000.

From the calculation of both branches of the local freight carried, that departing from the east to way stations, and that arriving at Pittsburg from way stations, it is clear that a sum not less than $10,000,000 might be assumed as the value of that carried an average distance of three hundred miles from producer to consumer, and of $5,000,000 for that crossing the line of the Alleghanies in the general east and west exchange.

Next in accessibility and fulness are the statistics of transportation over the New York Central road. Specific articles are named only in a very few instances, but a classification is adopted which distinguishes "Products of the Forest," "Products of Animals," "Vegetable Food," "Other Agricultural Products," "Manufactures," and "Merchandise"—terms too vague, as at present applied, to correspond with any commercial or financial usage. In the traffic westward the terms "Merchandise" and "Manufactures" largely predominate, and in that sent eastward the chief amounts are of vegetable food and products of the forest and of animals. For the freight going westward it is scarcely possible to separate and distinguish articles at all. The following table comprises the tonnage of such trade, as given in the reports of the company, for six years:

Through tonnage westward over the New York Central railroad.

Articles.	1858.	1859.	1860.	1861.	1862.	1863.
	Tons.	*Tons.*	*Tons.*	*Tons.*	*Tons.*	*Tons.*
Products of the forest......	160	88	97	43	92	71
Products of animals	410	673	972	873	395	1,108
Vegetable food............	9	924	5	13	14	1
Other agricultural products	1,071	1,414	1,077	863	1,078	1,335
Manufactures	2,590	2,737	2,216	3,245	3,651	10,574
Merchandise..............	74,206	102,001	108,488	104,750	140,834	183,499
Other articles	4,624	6,001	6,143	6,154	8,069	11,216
Totals...............	83,133	113,839	118,077	116,941	101,013	213,794

Way tonnage westward over the New York Central railroad.

Articles.	1858.	1859.	1860.	1861.	1862.	1863.
	Tons.	*Tons.*	*Tons.*	*Tons.*	*Tons.*	*Tons.*
Products of the forest.....	4,788	7,264	6,892	5,794	6,955	10,744
Products of animals......	6,090	9,297	10,958	10,014	8,585	1,108
Vegetable food...........	4,956	19,368	19,420	11,601	8,594	17,760
Other agricultural products	3,624	5,238	7,789	7,899	5,792	8,717
Manufactures	13,942	15,772	23,543	21,854	24,701	24,852
Merchandise..............	50,292	63,089	71,571	68,327	67,387	76,414
Other articles	20,528	29,640	44,055	44,764	40,278	43,769
Totals...............	103,224	149,654	178,928	170,353	162,292	101,551

Totals way and through.

	1858.	1859.	1860.	1861.	1862.	1863.
Manufactures	10,522	18,509	25,758	25,099	28,712	41,946
Merchandise..............	124,548	165,090	180,059	173,077	214,221	259,904
All other classes.........	45,287	79,793	91,108	89,098	80,372	104,015
Aggregates..........	180,357	263,392	297,925	286,274	323,305	405,345

As this road runs parallel with the Erie canal, and is further relieved of heavy and cheap freight by other canals and by Lake Ontario, no necessity appears to exist for a reduction of values for either division of the freight below the averages assumed for the through and way freight of the Pennsylvania road.

Under the assumption that way freights are properly included, for reasons before stated, the two totals of freights westward may be divided in three equal parts, to which the values before taken for dry goods, groceries, and heavy goods, respectively, may be applied. When put together, the "merchandise" amounts to two-thirds of the whole, or to 214,221 tons, out of 323,305 tons, which is sufficient proof of the generally high grade of the goods carried.

Values of through freight westward.

53,671 tons, at $2,000	....	$117,342,000
53,671 tons, at $400	....	21,468,400
53,671 tons, at $200	....	10,734,200
161,013 tons.	Total value	149,544,600

Values of way freight westward.

20,286½ tons, at $2,000	....	$40,573,000
40,573 tons, at $300	....	12,171,900
101,432½ tons, at $120	....	12,171,900
162,293 tons.	Total value	64,916,800

By the calculation here assumed the total value of the westward freight of this road in 1862 was $214,461,400—a sum which appears excessive. Yet the elements of the calculation are sustained by all the facts that can be obtained bearing on the quality and value of the goods sent westward by such mode of conveyance. The westward tonnage of the Erie canal, the associate of this line of transportation, which must, from the nature of the case, carry the larger share of cheap and heavy freight, has for years been officially estimated at the average value of 18 cents per pound. The total values here given for railroad freight average on all the classes about forty cents per pound—a little more than twice the rate assumed for canal freight. When the advance in values existing in 1862 is considered, this average price cannot be considered excessive.

Westward transportation on the Erie railroad.

The westward freight of the Erie railroad is not classified in the reports of that company, although the eastward freight is, sufficiently for all practical purposes. It is undoubtedly altogether similar to the business of the other roads, so far as the through freight is concerned. The way or local traffic is probably more exclusively or distinctively a local trade, and a greater portion of heavy and low-priced goods is carried. It is proposed, therefore, to take the same divisions applied to the other roads in valuing the through tonnage, and to assume for the local tonnage a classification and prices lower than those applied to the Pennsylvania line.

The tonnage westward for three years is stated as follows in the report:

Year.	Through.	Way.	Total.
	Pounds.	*Pounds.*	*Pounds.*
1861	175,667,350	845,467,060	1,021,134,410
1862	299,793,230	1,106,011,030	1,405,804,260
1863	319,840,110	1,253,210,350	1,573,050,460

Applying the calculation assumed for through freight, we have:

99,931,077 pounds, at $1	$99,931,077
99,931,077 pounds, at 20 cents	19,986,215
99,931,077 pounds, at 10 cents	9,993,107
299,793,230 pounds. Total value	129,910,399

The way tonnage of this road undoubtedly requires a reduction to lower classes and values than those before employed. It reaches a very large aggregate for the year 1862, not less than 553,005 tons of 2,000 pounds. Of what chief articles this immense amount is made up the reports of the company do not state; but it may perhaps embrace some considerable amounts of coal, stone, wood, or other freights of the lowest class, carried between points along its line. Assuming that 300,000 tons of the way freight is of this class, and not properly of goods exchanged between remote points of production and consumption, the remaining 253,005 tons may be taken as similar to the way freights before considered—one eighth being of goods worth one dollar per pound, one-fourth being worth 15 cents per pound, and the remainder six cents per pound, viz:

31,626 tons, at $2,000 per ton	$63,252,000
63,252 tons, at $300 per ton	18,975,600
158,127 tons, at $120 per ton	18,975,240
253,005 tons. Total value	101,202,840

Stone, lumber, and coal, for local consumption, being thus excluded, the proportion of goods of a general character assumed to be carried, both for consumption along the line and for further distribution by the lateral roads connecting with Buffalo on the north and with Pennsylvania and Ohio on the south, does not appear unduly large. The values are large in the aggregate, it is true, but the business is enormous in comparison with any other interior line of land carriage in the world.

There remain to be considered the carriage of merchandise by the Erie canal, and such small portion as the Canadian lines carry westward—this last being really so small in tonnage westward that it hardly need be embraced at all. In eastward tonnage it is important, for many reasons which do not apply to goods going westward.

The Erie canal carried the following aggregates of freight westward for fourteen years to 1862, inclusive:

Year.	To Buffalo.	To Oswego.	Total.	Value at 18 cts. per lb.
	Tons.	*Tons.*	*Tons.*	
1849	68,020	20,297	88,315	$31,793,400
1850	79,405	35,091	114,496	41,218,560
1851	99,918	74,981	174,899	62,963,640
1852	143,787	76,012	219,799	79,127,640
1853	163,192	98,560	261,752	94,230,720
1854	167,550	64,329	231,879	83,476,440
1855	145,530	74,936	220,466	79,367,760
1856	114,596	68,917	183,513	66,064,680
1857	74,733	43,393	118,126	42,525,360
1858	47,350	29,540	76,890	27,680,400
1859	72,767	26,109	98,876	35,595,360
1860	72,030	47,652	119,682	43,085,520
1861	35,278	17,184	52,462	18,886,320
1862	52,945	18,094	71,039	25,574,040

The valuation here made is that of the auditor general in the annual reports of the "Trade, Tolls, and Tonnage of the Canals of New York," the table just given being copied from that report for the year 1862.

It is apparent from this table that the business of the canal rose to higher proportions as a carrier of merchandise westward before the completion of the railroad than since that time. The railroads of that vicinity were first consolidated in a single organization and adapted to the purposes of successful freight business in 1853 and 1854—not completely until the latter year. The quantities and values attain their maximum, therefore, in 1853, and after this date they steadily decline from $94,230,000 to $25,574,000. No change in the price per pound assigned to this freight is made in the series of years of which we here take account. It may be of interest to cite the values taken in earlier years, which were in 1836, '37, and '38, 12½ cents per pound; in 1839, 15 cents; in 1840, 16 cents; in 1841, 18 cents; in 1842, 15 cents; and from 1843 to 1846, inclusive, 17½ cents. All subsequent to 1847, and including that year, was estimated, as in the table copied, at 18 cents per pound. A list of articles constituting the tonnage in 1862 is given, from which it is evident that the valuation per pound should be increased for that year. It appears that the chief articles are sugar, molasses, coffee, crockery, iron, iron manufactures, and general merchandise, the proportions of which are as follows:

Sugar	16,230	tons of	2,000	pounds.
Molasses	4,598	"	"	"
Coffee	1,005	"	"	"
Iron and steel	2,198	"	"	"
Railroad iron	2,553	"	"	"
Nails	994	"	"	"
Crockery	2,535	"	"	"
Merchandise	40,576	"	"	"

It is evident that these articles made up the bulk of the traffic in previous years as well as in 1862, and that the average value per pound was greater in that year than in 1860. No more direct effect of the increased duties on imports and the high internal taxes levied could be produced than upon the staples named above, and undoubtedly the 18 cents average of 1860 should be 22 or 23 cents at least in 1862. Assuming it at 23 cents, there is added to the value of the entire carriage of the canal the sum of $7,103,900, making the total $32,077,940, instead of $25,574,040.

The general summary of quantities and values deduced from these several calculations presents the following aggregates, embracing only the three chief railroads and the Erie canal, and taking no account of various lines which carry a less proportion westward than they do eastward. A small estimate should be added for the business of the Baltimore and Ohio railroad, which is usually one of the large carrying lines, but which, in consequence of the interruption of its business then, caused by the war, had very little through trade westward during the year 1862:

	Tons.	Value.
Pennsylvania railroad—Through	145,205	$125,841,945
Way	60,000	20,000,000
Erie railroad—Through	149,696	129,910,399
Way	253,005*	101,202,840
New York Central railroad—Through	161,013	149,544,600
Way	162,293	64,916,800
Erie canal—Through	71,039	25,674,040
Totals	992,451	616,993,624

* Exclusive of 300,000 tons rejected as being merely local.

Adding a small estimate for the Baltimore and Ohio railroad, we have, approximately, 1,000,000 tons of merchandise carried westward from the seaboard to the interior, exclusive of merely local consumption, and of all deliveries not more than fifty miles from the eastern terminal points of the several great lines, and a value for this commerce of more than $600,000,000.

It must be borne in mind, in considering whether these quantities and values are excessive or not, that several important partial or lateral outlets of this trade have not been noticed at all. The railroad from Portland, Maine, to Canada is one of these, the Champlain canal another, and the railroads of northern New York also add something, together furnishing a moderately large amount which, being shipped through Canada, reaches some port of the lakes to enter the States south or west of the lakes for consumption. The proportions of this trade are, under any aspect of the case, and with any abatements from these quantities and values which the best corrected judgment may make, so vast that they cannot fail of due appreciation after being once brought to attention.

It is apparent that in this calculation quantities and values are embraced which do not pass the meridian of the Alleghanies for the exclusive consumption of the population beyond that line. Even if the limit of distance assumed were 300 miles, there would be from fifty to one hundred miles of the length of each of the New York lines east of this assumed meridian that would be supplied by a carriage far enough to constitute a part of the general trade. By making a deduction for such portion of, say twenty millions of dollars, the preceding estimates may be verified by another and wholly distinct test, namely, by computing the consumption *per capita* of the entire population of the Trans-Alleghany States and parts of States. Portions of New York and of Pennsylvania, portions of Kentucky and Tennessee, and all the remaining northwestern States this side the Rocky mountains, received their supplies of both foreign and domestic merchandise wholly through these lines during the year under consideration. The population of these States in 1860 was as follows:

Ohio	2,339,511
Michigan	749,113
Indiana	1,350,428
Illinois	1,711,951
Wisconsin	775,881
Iowa	674,913
Minnesota	172,123
Kansas	107,206
Missouri	1,182,012
Nebraska	28,841
Estimate for other Territories	200,000
Parts of New York and Pennsylvania	350,000
" " Kentucky and Pennsylvania	250,000
	9,891,979

The natural increase on the reported population of 1860 would add something more, and it may safely be assumed that the population supplied beyond the Alleghanies in that year was in round numbers ten millions. The estimated value of the merchandise of all classes supplied to this population we have reduced to $597,000,000, from which should further be taken an amount o. special war material and public property probably above 15 millions in value, as here computed from its tonnage. The sum remaining to apply to individual consumption would then be near 580 millions of dollars, or fifty-eight dollars *per capita* of the population.

This is, of course, the consumption of both domestic and foreign merchandise, and it places upon the personal consumption of the people all the usual demand of valuable goods for ordinary public uses. The circumstances existing in all parts of the country for that year greatly stimulated the demand for articles required for other than ordinary personal use, for which it would be reasonable to make a deduction in comparing consumption with that of ordinary times.

It has been shown by the comparison of imports and population for a series of years, that the average annual consumption of foreign goods *per capita* in the United States has attained to ten dollars, for a period of ten years preceding the war.

Year.	Imports consumed.	Population.	Consumption per capita.
1852	$195,656,060	24,604,261	7.96
1853	250,420,187	25,348,[illegible]	9.88
1854	279,712,187	26,102,[illegible]	10.71
1855	233,[illegible],227	26,985,739	8.67
1856	298,261,364	27,698,310	10.77
1857	336,914,524	28,593,079	11.81
1858	251,727,[illegible]	29,378,771	8.57
1859	317,873,053	30,200,134	10.60
1860	335,220,919	31,429,891	10.66
1861	315,004,738	32,373,386	9.73
Average of ten years			9.92

This consumption was calculated upon the basis of the entire population of the United States, of course including three and a half to four millions of slaves of the southern States. Excluding the slaves, and taking only the active population, such as are embraced in the northeastern States, the consumption *per capita* would be increased at least one half.

And again, the previous calculation is based upon the entry or invoice value of imports only, not including duties paid, or the cost of handling and shipment.

The values assigned to the freight carried are, of course, in excess, so far as they relate to foreign articles, being those which actually attach to the goods at the line of transit to their western consumers. For both the reasons here named it would be safe to assume that sixteen dollars for each inhabitant would represent the goods of foreign origin transported.

The greater portion of the goods carried, are, however, of the produce and manufacture of the eastern States. As some guide to the proportion of these, the census estimate of $2,000,000,000 of domestic manufactures in 1860 may be taken. Deducting from this aggregate $45,000,000 exported to foreign countries, there remains an amount consumed by 31,000,000 of inhabitants of $1,955,000,000, or $63 for each person. Here, again, the contrast between the slave and the free population requires an addition when applied to the people of the northwestern States, increasing the same to $70 or $75.

Of this sum of $75 worth of movable goods, of the classes usually exchanged from one State to another, it is probable that not more than one-third were made or produced in the section beyond the Alleghanies, and that two-thirds were sent there from the manufacturing east. Nearly all textile fabrics, cordage and leather manufactures, were carried from the east. Drugs, medicines, chemicals, iron, steel, and the finer manufactures of machinery, tools and cutlery, books, paper and paper manufactures, brass and copper manufactures, and manufactured clothing of all classes. Taking these proportions as correct, there are more than $30 worth of all these domestic products consumed, and the division of values will be as follows:

Value of foreign produce consumed........................	$160,000,000
Value of domestic produce and manufactures..........	350,000,000
Value of public property included........................	18,546,000
	528,546,000

This classification of values consumed is only intended to aid the discussion by such light as may in this way be thrown upon it. There are no settled rules applicable to such cases, and the circumstances are in the present case, for many reasons, peculiar. The activity of trade and exchanges increases far more rapidly than the population has done for the past twenty years, a result in part due to the increased power of consumption and command of means by the people, and in part to the greater cheapness and promptness of transportation. The proportion of foreign values transported by these lines to the western States for consumption is largely increased in 1862 by the necessity to obtain sugar and coffee almost wholly from the Atlantic cities, instead of the Mississippi river, as in former years. The loss of New Orleans sugar is an important item, as the heavy tonnage of these articles in the following statement shows:

Tonnage of leading articles on the Erie canal, in 1862, to the several western States.

States, &c.	Sugar.	Molasses.	Coffee.	Iron manufactures.	Crock'ry & glassware.	Other merchandise.
	Tons.	*Tons.*	*Tons.*	*Tons.*	*Tons.*	*Tons.*
To Ohio..................	2,551	750	194	636	457	10,430
Michigan..............	2,397	759	172	602	249	4,173
Illinois................	7,730	1,607	416	1,477	1,029	13,009
Wisconsin	1,940	1,017	174	2,372	440	5,756
Indiana	104	263	8	42	58	634
Minnesota...........	66	29	....	6	6	28
Iowa	101	53	15	371	65	640
Kentucky	28	....	....	60	1	439
Missouri	12	13	....	350	30	1,641
Canada	1,301	210	20	40	78	1,670
Total to other States..	16,230	4,958	1,005	5,735	2,535	40,576
Left in New York	11,407	4,592	630	10,294	1,550	36,258
Total moved from tide-water	27,637	9,550	1,635	16,029	4,085	70,834

For this large way tonnage no estimate has been made to represent the general westward commerce, though by the most rigid rules of classification there would be a share of it coming within the definitions properly applying to these exchanges. Actual deliveries to consumers at points three hundred to five hundred miles from the seaboard would probably cover one-third of the way freight above described as being left in New York.

The Champlain canal is also a channel for large shipments to Canada, and in some cases for western localities through Canada. In the following table the entire movement of merchandise from tide-water by both the Erie and Champlain canals is given, distinguishing that going out of the State from that left within its limits, and giving also the internal movement westward on these lines, from one point to another along them.

Movement of merchandise westward on the New York canals.

Year.	Tonnage going westward from tide-water.					Internal movement westward.
	By Erie canal.		By Champlain canal.		Total from tide-water.	
	To western States.	Left in N. York.	To Vt. and Canada.	Left in N. York.		
1836	39,893	67,677	5,165	6,194	117,849	10,006
1837	25,291	61,799	4,573	4,821	96,484	8,293
1838	34,689	71,257	5,611	6,409	117,049	6,341
1839	34,197	75,910	7,291	7,177	124,575	7,711
1840	22,055	70,979	6,941	6,945	105,960	6,061
1841	31,040	85,860	6,813	9,101	132,814	8,413
1842	24,081	59,755	4,906	5,399	94,213	7,233
1843	37,335	63,199	6,709	6,443	113,686	5,523
1844	42,415	78,557	7,930	6,714	136,810	8,314
1845	49,618	77,883	8,837	8,404	144,742	6,708
1846	58,330	85,542	10,611	8,642	163,125	6,674
1847	76,893	115,787	12,475	11,040	216,195	9,705
1848	91,872	121,895	14,520	14,374	242,661	18,797
1849	87,890	122,414	17,046	9,406	236,815	18,620
1850	115,043	112,446	16,894	13,128	256,499	12,871
1851	177,623	143,410	17,124	11,073	349,230	16,174
1852	219,790	153,182	14,248	8,859	396,067	24,208
1853	281,762	134,932	13,227	16,490	426,401	31,928
1854	231,879	112,366	6,583	21,084	371,913	34,110
1855	220,466	104,257	4,473	13,788	342,902	31,440
1856	183,513	139,104	5,810	19,498	347,925	23,893
1857	108,185	60,915	11,603	7,616	188,160	34,794
1858	76,890	61,176	5,621	5,909	149,696	34,755
1859	94,676	66,649	8,569	7,568	109,664	41,618
1860	119,682	60,247	11,537	8,071	205,537	44,923
1861	58,402	40,818	8,096	10,285	117,601	17,495
1862	71,039	61,503	3,598	10,080	146,220	21,701

Tonnage of "Manufactures," "Merchandise," and "Other articles," (not merchandise,) going westward from tide-water.

Year.	Manufactures.	Merchandise.	Other articles.
1852	34,371	396,067	93,089
1853	39,671	420,401	118,169
1854	40,209	371,913	137,660
1855	40,147	342,902	174,608
1856	54,775	347,925	198,396
1857	31,880	188,160	167,094
1858	25,047	149,696	126,316
1859	22,003	109,664	137,290
1860	32,039	205,537	109,108
1861	19,620	117,601	233,133
1862	65,340	146,220	271,397

Westward transportation on the Canadian canals.

The westward movement on the Canadian canals is at present a part of the general carriage of merchandise from eastern to western markets within the United States. For reasons before stated, it is not proposed to calculate values for this tonnage and add them to the totals previously made up, the way business of the great roads and of the canal being in part taken to cover these values. A large business is done on the Welland canal in articles originally from the United States and destined to markets south of the lakes. The following is the Canadian official account of the—

Westward or upward trade through the Welland canal.

From United States ports.	1861.		1862.	
	To Canadian ports.	To United States ports.	To Canadian ports.	To United States ports.
	Tons.	*Tons.*	*Tons.*	*Tons.*
Agricultural implements and tools	2	296	6½	189
Apples and green fruit	7	256	7	303
Beef, pork, and beans	4	11	29	1
Bricks, cement, lime, clay, and slate	70	4,029	121½	4,278½
Butter and cheese	8	43	4	49
Chalk and whiting	....	171	....	505
Coal	1,668	12,331	1,744½	7,028
Coffee	....	631	....	394½
Copperas	....	84	....	5
Corn	3,029	....	3,049	....
Cotton	17	6	....	....
Dyes	....	....	3	904
Earthenware and glassware	1	556	....	1,808
Fish	2	1,234	3	2,380
Flour	6	5	24½	....
Furniture	5	714	7½	537½
Gypsum	9	39	4	687
Hemp	....	271	....	303
Horses, cattle, and sheep	2	305	....	29
Iron, nails, and spikes	67	9,559	21½	14,081½
Junk and oakum	5	64	3½	165½
Leather	....	13	2½	133½
Mahogany	....	6	....	19
Marble	6	016	5	000
Molasses	....	809	....	1,346
Oats	4	....	114	....
Oils	1	680	11½	439
Ores of iron	....	2,970	....	6,340
Paints	1	338	½	609
Pitch, tar, and turpentine	0	75	1	73
Rye	253	....	018	....
Salt	1,905	72,679	2,155½	112,998
Ship stores	....	47	....	278
Soda ash	....	308	....	784½
Sugar	5	2,140	107	3,791½
Iron and steel	....	325	....	671½
Tobacco	1	39	....	190½
Wheat	3,596	2	5,307	....
Whiskey	39	9	....	5
Window glass	....	122	1	79
Other articles	45	4,293	75	9,393½
Lumber	130	900	1,443½	981
Total	10,816	116,940	14,908½	171,673½

Some portion of this tonnage is of articles of low value per ton, the least valuable being coal, iron ore, lumber, and salt. Iron ore is taken from mines in Canada near Kingston, and the salt is mainly the product of the works of central New York.

As this table gives the entire upward or westward trade of the Welland canal, it affords a striking proof of the preponderance of trade on that canal in articles carried from one market in the United States to another. The return trade eastward exhibits the same excess of freights destined to United States markets, as will appear in the table corresponding to this, illustrating transportation eastward.

II. TRANSPORTATION EASTWARD.

The eastward freight over these great lines of transportation is in some respects better known and more readily determined as to both quantities and values than that carried westward. The chief items that compose it are well known staples of agricultural produce, each of which has been carefully calculated at all the points of shipment at the west, and of receipt at the east. For the last eight or ten years, however, the quantity of miscellaneous freight has been rapidly increasing, including a share of manufactured goods. The tables of the Pennsylvania road are again the best to illustrate the present condition of the trade, and a table of articles carried for five years to 1863 is here given, corresponding to the table of articles carried westward.

By a careful analysis of values of the specified articles of western freight sent eastward over the Pennsylvania railroad in 1862, it appears that the average, exclusive of coal, is very nearly ten cents per pound. The New York canal freight is estimated by the auditor of the canal department, in his annual reports to average two cents per pound in value; an average which is applied there only to the lowest grad e of western freight. Railroad freight is unquestionably far more valuable per ton than that now carried on the Erie canal. The freight carried over the chief New York roads is not stated in detail in their reports. The Erie road in part classifies the freight sent eastward from Dunkirk, but not its entire eastern business. Evidently the proportion of fourth-class freight is larger than on any other road, but as a great share of this is live stock, pork, beef and meats, the value is not so low as if grain was carried. Some of these weights and quantities are as follows, for 1863:

		Pounds.
Live stock	46,989 cattle, 258,089 hogs, 21,454 sheep, 4,306 horses,	111,051,918
Fourth-class freight		343,943,094
Miscellaneous freight		58,116,982
Flour, 1,078,102 bbls		215,620,400
Total pounds		728,732,994

This is all from Dunkirk. The freight received from the Atlantic and Great Western should be included also, but it is placed in the aggregate of "way freight," and it is believed to be a just division to take one-half the way freight eastward as the proper associate of that classed as "through." The totals are therefore as follows:

Through eastward	942,627,210
Way eastward (one-half of 1,002,037,030)	501,018,510
	1,443,645,720

The value of this, at ten cents per pound, is $144,364,672.

The freight carried over the two great railroads of New York is not specified in detail in the reports of those roads. That of the New York central road is in part classified as products of the forest, of animals, vegetable food, and manufactures; but such distinctions are now only general and do not suffice to base estimates of value on. The division made in that report of aggregate tonnage eastward in the year ending September 30, 1862, is as follows:

	Tons.
Products of the forest	32,462
Of animals	350,050
Vegetable food	461,337
Other agricultural products	38,376
Manufactures	63,411
Merchandise	28,884
Other articles	89,609
Total tons	1,064,129

or pounds 212,825,600.

This distribution indicates a generally high grade of value. Products of animals cannot be less than twelve cents per pound on an average, and the remaining classes, other than vegetable food, going much higher. The average cannot be less than ten cents per pound.

Taking from the above aggregate one-half the way freight eastward, there remain—

Through freight	616,177 tons.
One-half way freight	223,975 tons.
Total	840,152 tons.

or 1,680,304,000 pounds; at ten cents, value $168,030,400.

The several great railroad lines, therefore, carried an estimated value of freight eastward, across an assumed line of division between the west and the east, as follows:

The New York Central	$168,030,400
New York and Erie	144,364,572
Pennsylvania	113,000,000
Baltimore and Ohio, (estimated)	25,000,000
Total, four roads	450,394,972

With these total values of eastward freight by the great railroad lines should be connected the value of the eastward freight of the Erie canal, the details of which are given in subsequent tables. That value is officially stated by the auditor general for the year 1862 at $72,131,136 for "property coming from other States" alone. The way freight is not taken into account. The summary of values transported eastward thus becomes:

By the four railroads	$450,394,972
By the Erie Canal	72,131,136
Grand total	522,526,108

The various railroads of Canada carried a portion of the western produce of the United States sent eastward to markets within the United States and for export; but as the account of way tonnage taken on the New York roads is large, it may be considered as merely covering the amount so carried by Canadian lines. Certain branches of the Central railroad of New York probably bring to it portions of the freight going by way of the Welland canal and Lake Ontario, and leaving that lake at Oswego. Some moderate amount is carried to the New York and Erie by its connecting roads to Buffalo. Together, the minor avenues of railroad carriage eastward, north of Pennsylvania, will complete the account, and sustain the aggregates above given under any possible diminution the calculation might require for the leading roads.

The following tables give the detail of eastward freight in very full and satisfactory form over the Pennsylvania road, which has been taken as the basis of the calculation. Values approximating as nearly as could be estimated from current prices were computed in detail on each of the items of this freight, the result being an average on the whole amount a fraction less than ten cents per pound. Possibly the resulting values are too great; but as the freights of these roads have been taken as representative quantities, and as much miscellaneous carriage of produce and merchandise eastward occurs which cannot be noted on either of them, the final sum of values is believed to be too small, rather than too large.

Among the larger unnoted items is the freight of all kinds through Canada which returns to the United States at Oswego, Cape Vincent, Ogdensburg, through the canal to Lake Champlain, and over the railroads leading into Vermont from Canada. Again, there are lateral roads carrying from various points to connect as way freight on some one of the great lines. The Erie road receives immense accessions in this way.

Cattle, sheep, horses, and all descriptions of live stock, also continue to be driven in large numbers from every part of the West, and over all the common roads of the country, from the Maryland line to Lake Erie. The aggregate of their value is less now than formerly, so many take the railroads in preference; yet the total value of animals so moved cannot be less than two or three millions of dollars annually.

The calculation of eastward freights on the great lakes is given at length, and with the fulness which that most important trade demands, in the following separate section. From the statements of the total movement eastward, with which it closes, another estimate of values may be made, covering the business in flour and grain in 1862:

Flour	barrels.. 6,350,910,	value, estimated	$50, 150, 460
Wheat	bushels.. 60,600,130,	value, estimated	63, 373, 912
Corn	bushels.. 32,085,922,	value, estimated	16, 492, 961
Other grain	bushels.. 10,844,039,	value, estimated	5, 422, 470
Total			135, 448, 603

It is difficult to make any further calculation on specific articles—provisions, metals, textile raw materials, or the very large value of animals.

Articles carried eastward on the Pennsylvania railroad.

1.—THROUGH FROM PITTSBURG TO PHILADELPHIA (AND BALTIMORE).

Articles.	1859.	1860.	1861.	1862.	1863.
	Pounds.	*Pounds.*	*Pounds.*	*Pounds.*	*Pounds.*
Agricultural implements	193, 508	113, 305	93, 735	82, 810	89, 310
Agricultural products, not specified	1, 029, 361	1, 400, 260	21, 088, 011	1, 631, 468	858, 897
Bark, oak	3, 555	4, 390	....	29, 637	3, 300
Books and stationery	303, 744	846, 050	120, 079	874, 030	165, 123
Boots, shoes, and hats	4, 675	12, 140	32, 895	180, 918	81, 081
Brown sheetings and bagging	64, 579	8, 945	173, 315	1, 048, 770	141, 200
Butter and eggs	6, 657, 308	9, 135, 438	19, 310, 840	20, 179, 278	7, 358, 538
Carriages	....	8, 345	877, 767	506, 858	81, 410
Cedar-ware	99, 141	5, 965	3, 150	860, 603	8, 020
Coal	937, 006	....	420, 500	....	....
Coffee	....	1, 095	....	281, 488	6, 740
Copper, tin, and lead	1, 672, 104	1, 399, 057	3, 426, 255	1, 334, 161	1, 674, 724
Cotton	17, 817, 569	28, 671, 375	23, 732, 819	14, 921, 367	19, 636, 070
Drugs and medicines	758, 491	1, 315, 775	1, 611, 243	1, 349, 814	321, 541
Dry goods	592, 543	874, 195	3, 801, 007	6, 164, 852	789, 823
Earthenware	349, 779	356, 230	971, 125	387, 874	174, 404
Fresh meats and poultry	454, 443	2, 943, 847	3, 467, 629	4, 654, 130	7, 615, 177
Feathers, furs, and skins	....	356, 447	849, 835	940, 111	812, 827
Flour	64, 882, 273	85, 252, 948	208, 979, 455	185, 626, 081	109, 435, 850
Furniture	449, 005	530, 318	570, 875	416, 409	619, 728
Fruits, green and dry	843, 991	442, 070	1, 796, 900	1, 061, 105	1, 164, 988
Ginseng	182, 134	100, 390	95, 440	79, 340	29, 181
Glass and glassware	2, 353, 718	3, 345, 637	2, 777, 051	4, 511, 971	3, 857, 499
Grain, all kinds, not specified	14, 350, 273	34, 734, 447	65, 983, 853	70, 390, 660	72, 324, 083
Grass and other seeds	1, 958, 273	6, 432, 516	6, 634, 872	8, 143, 310	9, 829, 879
Groceries, not coffee	1, 424, 103	2, 101, 791	1, 279, 583	5, 953, 375	5, 071, 007
Guano and bones	259, 385	578, 319	348, 764	531, 850	4, 235, 164
Hardware	359, 872	800, 948	678, 736	1, 705, 457	950, 347
Hemp and cordage	765, 404	795, 163	1, 373, 736	4, 250, 673	4, 283, 643
Hides and hair	2, 674, 910	1, 838, 370	1, 827, 358	1, 040, 704	2, 773, 082
Iron, blooms and pig	16, 913	....	....	4, 017	....
Iron, rolled	178, 817	410, 941	747, 015	9, 798, 530	13, 088, 173
Lard, lard oil, and tallow	10, 446, 367	17, 390, 731	27, 755, 089	37, 020, 395	34, 294, 299
Leather	1, 703, 631	1, 751, 899	2, 846, 835	8, 90, 567	1, 870, 003
Live stock	65, 103, 736	67, 254, 690	132, 194, 358	228, 892, 011	270, 713, 380
Lumber and timber	579, 949	690, 425	605, 733	970, 290	2, 230, 900
Machinery and castings	848, 185	1, 911, 658	6, 320, 083	8, 253, 670	548, 307
Malt and malt liquors	1, 166, 134	429, 871	1, 253, 349	2, 847, 191	8, 447, 500
Marble and cement	374, 890	316, 547	183, 925	2, 0, 167	408, 335
Nails and spikes	....	95, 849	172, 900	318, 674	348, 534
Oil, coal and petroleum	468, 860	13, 392, 674	193, 513, 501	140, 848, 278	196, 467, 725
Oil, other	....	(with coal oil)	334, 679	1, 307, 048	191, 614
Paper and rags	2, 453, 070	2, 374, 737	1, 029, 455	1, 124, 873	2, 675, 358
Pot and pearl ashes	655, 947	367, 481	408, 973	541, 481	374, 145
Powder	....	....	174, 898	3, 083, 139	3, 839, 812
Salt meats	31, 178, 251	42, 079, 444	64, 892, 007	101, 189, 476	89, 051, 734
Soap and candles	1, 404, 535	989, 818	2, 891, 232	4, 188, 747	3, 107, 535
Straw boards	....	1, 028, 615	....	973, 020	653, 894
Tar, pitch, and rosin	....	25, 255	30, 070	302, 875	1, 466, 170
Tobacco	4, 198, 778	6, 258, 413	48, 465, 815	69, 613, 202	37, 301, 068
Wines and liquors, not specified	....	166, 929	2, 9, 1, 077	3, 419, 867	401, 165
Whiskey and alcohol	11, 981, 236	25, 364, 544	34, 200, 619	37, 714, 244	59, 353, 141
Wool and woollen yarn	355, 765	3, 679, 530	6, 321, 144	5, 342, 711	6, 444, 984
Miscellaneous	877, 780	232, 763	37, 741	873, 601	391, 546
Total pounds	259, 533, 638	352, 014, 718	772, 878, 278	1, 003, 707, 969	873, 818, 881
Total tons	129, 767	176, 007	386, 439	502, 861	436, 810

2.—FROM WAY STATIONS TO PHILADELPHIA.

Articles.	1859.	1860.	1861.	1862.	1863.
	Pounds.	*Pounds.*	*Pounds.*	*Pounds.*	*Pounds.*
Agricultural products, not specified	1, 874, 150	2, 827, 494	2, 210, 179	851, 145	7, 648, 890
Butter and eggs	4, 630, 307	5, 341, 578	6, 135, 324	7, 164, 539	3, 884, 804
Bark	1, 483, 385	5, 732, 857	2, 865, 838	1, 889, 044	1, 532, 897
Carriages and implements	91, 589	189, 403	617, 449	316, 873	335, 895
Coal	818, 853, 843	844, 582, 139	820, 310, 379	305, 102, 841	387, 932, 897
Copper, tin, and lead	92, 474	59, 895	....	41, 953	887, 853
Drugs and dyes	843, 084	184, 925	74, 878	25, 981	880, 973
Dry goods, boots and shoes	2, 131, 001	1, 898, 847	822, 390	885, 079	948, 738
Flour	39, 388, 464	49, 718, 700	81, 607, 947	45, 477, 898	65, 384, 329
Feathers and furs	33, 853	4, 443	6, 250	97, 233	9, 679

Articles carried eastward on the Pennsylvania railroad—Continued.

2.—FROM WAY STATIONS TO PHILADELPHIA.

Articles.	1859.	1860.	1861.	1862.	1863.
	Pounds.	*Pounds.*	*Pounds.*	*Pounds.*	*Pounds.*
Fertilizers	813, 700	886, 658	459, 569	977, 680	628, 507
Fruits, green and dried	857, 077	62, 017	168, 678	142, 985	8, 150, 798
Furniture	569, 771	612, 609	344, 601	438, 919	795, 737
Fresh meats and poultry	1, 944, 163	852, 083	634, 349	1, 492, 144	898, 283
Glass and earthenware	34, 468	13, 169	73, 708	82, 159	15, 674
Grain, all kinds	47, 141, 734	45, 037, 738	38, 425, 918	68, 169, 045	43, 279, 749
Grass and other seeds	1, 959, 331	2, 473, 039	1, 981, 303	2, 971, 139	2, 981, 873
Groceries, all kinds	377, 644	87, 949	816, 376	378, 414	11, 985, 845
Hardware	1, 075, 911	438, 091	280, 298	875, 649	1, 345, 370
Hemp and cordage	87, 638	87, 393	119, 616	87, 410	169, 083
Hides and hair	81, 044	148, 517	15, 427	33, 349	81, 698
Iron, blooms and pig	8, 172, 489	2, 738, 225	3, 614, 739	7, 477, 329	4, 391, 397
rolled	6, 861, 498	14, 483, 531	13, 028, 306	17, 432, 981	21, 899, 830
railroad	159, 524	4, 863, 807	6, 810, 450	....	53, 458
machinery and castings	846, 617	673, 093	422, 661	1, 307, 148	1, 017, 858
Lard and tallow	341, 350	294, 049	491, 394	450, 411	405, 191
Leather	3, 451, 951	3, 574, 549	3, 979, 997	3, 053, 749	4, 077, 533
Live stock	33, 731, 594	28, 998, 143	25, 798, 770	35, 370, 327	38, 871, 940
Lumber and timber	67, 891, 443	80, 078, 974	44, 810, 380	88, 039, 676	97, 027, 134
Marble and cement	1, 882, 239	1, 148, 767	3, 315	58, 585	10, 556, 891
Malt and malt liquors	80, 834	61, 739	91, 535	169, 058	1, 983, 019
Marketing	....	1, 794, 577	1, 373, 789	3, 391, 146	....
Nails and spikes	1, 349, 638	3, 346, 958	856, 715	915, 063	1, 184, 359
Paper and rags	1, 670, 674	2, 179, 217	1, 351, 946	1, 412, 213	2, 190, 177
Powder	....	....	....	323, 300	479, 187
Salt meats	183, 940	348, 349	111, 983	119, 798	1, 329, 898
Straw boards	161, 460	1, 637, 263	135, 450	349, 470	697, 170
Tobacco	813, 679	1, 383, 027	990, 016	2, 073, 944	3, 898, 757
Tar, pitch, and rosin	....	....	....	181, 434	11, 178
Nickel ore	181, 800	173, 900	....	....	....
Wines and liquors	....	44, 600	34, 945	674, 314	1, 178 714
Whiskey and alcohol	8, 137, 567	6, 815, 530	1, 967, 716	3, 838, 594	2, 938, 380
Wool and wool yarn	254, 618	894, 703	994, 676	829, 771	2, 230, 548
Miscellaneous	2, 329, 980	4, 094, 824	822, 607	73, 954	980, 819
Total pounds	446, 790, 507	497, 152, 713	430, 110, 439	582, 222, 160	710, 479, 858
Total tons	223, 397	248, 581	215, 055	291, 118	356, 239

3.—FROM PITTSBURG TO WAY STATIONS.

Articles.	1861.	1862.	1863.
	Pounds.	*Pounds.*	*Pounds.*
Agricultural implements	608, 998	375, 079	811, 464
Agricultural products, not specified	1, 965, 307	427, 530	812, 614
Books, &c	20, 561	21, 649	44, 890
Boots, shoes, and hats	41, 028	65, 976	89, 797
Butter and eggs	81, 474	81, 449	12, 309
Carriages	150, 985	82, 414	67, 510
Cedar ware	199, 498	157, 119	238, 098
Coal oil, petroleum	1, 547, 979	6, 407, 311	4, 146, 809
Coffee	346, 767	124, 300	144, 465
Confectionery and foreign fruit	94, 062	42, 518	92, 043
Copper, tin, and lead	154, 398	156, 277	175, 819
Cotton	88, 100	971, 509	197, 778
Drugs, medicines, and dyes	455, 489	270, 904	119, 987
Dry goods	467, 164	620, 313	316, 980
Earthenware and China	167, 297	211, 994	121, 063
Feathers and furs	8, 367	11, 716	3, 573
Flour	6, 038, 710	8, 163, 377	5, 169, 674
Fresh meats and poultry	39, 970	87, 700	116, 737
Furniture	564, 644	699, 679	785, 518
Fruits, green and dry	379, 079	197, 776	914, 528
Glass and glassware	424, 749	419, 790	738, 070
Grain of all kinds	1, 428, 860	1, 883, 985	5, 701, 659
Grass and other seeds	39, 065	87, 374	941, 197
Groceries, except coffee	3, 097, 078	2, 349, 250	3, 704, 343
Hardware	565, 014	574, 451	2, 064, 541
Hemp and cordage	291, 965	31, 938	44, 770
Hides and hair	1, 079, 816	692, 801	1, 630, 294
Iron, pig and blooms	503, 026	709, 769	151, 498
rolled	2, 143, 004	3, 173, 338	3, 053, 890
railroad	9, 408, 083	4, 215, 300	11, 101, 078

Articles carried eastward on the Pennsylvania railroad—Continued.

2.—FROM PITTSBURG TO WAY STATIONS.

Articles.	1861.	1862.	1863.
	Pounds.	*Pounds.*	*Pounds.*
Iron ore	....	....	[illegible]
Lard, lard oil, and tallow	178,666	322,987	[illegible]
Leather	37,414	98,119	47,780
Live stock	89,940,000	76,545,816	[illegible]
Lime and plaster	50,164	20,100	[illegible]
Lumber and timber	3,017,720	3,[illegible],291	[illegible]
Machinery and castings	1,066,034	1,113,135	[illegible]
Malt and malt liquors	1,054,073	835,727	[illegible]
Marble and cement	341,808	234,327	[illegible]
Nails and spikes	1,007,463	851,972	[illegible]
Oil, not coal	67,327	19,719	[illegible]
Paper and rags	901,438	322,474	797,697
Pot, pearl, and soda ash	76,547	8,140	19,794
Powder	....	....	[illegible]
Salt	734,978	818,248	[illegible]
Salt meats and fish	2,567,907	3,044,513	[illegible]
Soap and candles	440,165	234,972	[illegible]
Tobacco	326,474	444,363	[illegible]
Wines and liquors, foreign	137,330	74,628	[illegible]
Whiskey and alcohol	4,775,373	6,300,546	[illegible]
Wool and woollen yarn	93,971	43,413	81,444
Miscellaneous	106,646	131,328	43,538
Total pounds	139,754,173	128,476,311	[illegible]
Total tons	69,877	64,238	77,194

Through tonnage eastward over the New York Central railroad.

	1858.	1859.	1860.	1861.	1862.	1863.
	Tons.	*Tons.*	*Tons.*	*Tons.*	*Tons.*	*Tons.*
Products of the forest	1,709	2,149	2,478	2,901	2,141	1,[illegible]
Products of animals	104,257	112,910	133,241	168,[illegible]	254,954	[illegible]
Vegetable food	114,072	101,298	133,[illegible]	223,179	297,231	[illegible]
Other agricultural products	1,818	8,171	5,608	13,054	[illegible]	33,541
Manufactures	3,733	3,817	[illegible]	14,[illegible]	17,447	13,910
Merchandise	361	1,439	[illegible]	[illegible]	3,[illegible]	[illegible]
Other articles	3,363	5,133	[illegible]	11,353	[illegible],819	11,[illegible]
Total	[illegible]	[illegible]	[illegible]	435,956	616,177	610,[illegible]

Way tonnage eastward over the New York Central road.

	1858.	1859.	1860.	1861.	1862.	1863.
Products of the forest	17,991	[illegible]	[illegible]	31,979	39,[illegible]	[illegible]
Products of animals	82,319	81,847	78,191	74,389	95,058	[illegible]
Vegetable food	182,517	158,171	[illegible]	[illegible],679	175,108	[illegible]
Other agricultural products	11,838	13,973	[illegible]	[illegible]	17,416	[illegible]
Manufactures	27,124	34,710	44,870	40,813	43,914	[illegible]
Merchandise	8,573	12,234	18,[illegible]	18,[illegible]	23,348	[illegible]
Other articles	34,135	38,[illegible]	46,919	51,[illegible]	[illegible]	[illegible]
Total	349,775	[illegible]	[illegible]	443,078	417,951	[illegible]

Totals way and through.

	1858.	1859.	1860.	1861.	1862.	1863.
Manufactures	31,417	[illegible]	[illegible]	[illegible]	[illegible],411	47,[illegible]
Merchandise	9,934	13,[illegible]	[illegible]	18,[illegible]	[illegible]	50,371
All other classes	537,699	518,[illegible]	[illegible]	[illegible]	971,[illegible]	[illegible]
Aggregates	579,050	[illegible]	[illegible]	[illegible]	1,054,[illegible]	1,044,[illegible]

EASTWARD FREIGHT OVER THE ERIE CANAL.

Tons arriving at tide-water by way of the Erie canal, the produce of the western States or Canada.

Year.	Products of the forest.	Products of Agriculture.	Manufactures.	Other articles.	Total.
1836	5,400	48,000	654	165	54,219
1837	7,637	47,540	471	601	56,255
1838	9,211	72,972	600	630	84,233
1839	28,644	91,329	801	857	121,671
1840	21,241	134,600	1,267	1,040	158,148
1841	45,398	173,437	3,702	1,639	224,176
1842	31,098	185,898	2,639	1,851	221,477
1843	30,775	214,655	2,077	2,869	250,376
1844	64,088	230,155	853	2,029	308,025
1845	91,225	308,422	2,563	4,730	304,651
1846	87,010	410,111	2,920	6,873	506,830
1847	117,323	683,138	5,608	6,871	812,840
1848	142,433	489,478	5,600	12,083	650,164
1849	214,250	535,538	6,146	12,716	768,650
1850	328,022	491,810	7,848	23,519	850,299
1851	368,702	687,124	14,471	15,375	1,088,292
1852	331,892	778,810	21,642	14,026	1,151,076
1853	444,000	727,655	21,355	18,600	1,213,600
1854	320,077	677,085	10,640	25,379	1,091,391
1855	348,215	709,653	10,239	24,763	1,092,870
1856	535,707	658,147	2,851	17,735	1,212,550
1857	430,604	548,374	10,078	24,942	1,019,998
1858	301,139	851,929	19,085	28,946	1,273,099
1859	550,406	420,807	8,608	54,803	1,034,703
1860	647,705	1,177,091	5,808	68,461	1,898,975
1861	385,210	1,761,929	18,248	53,015	2,168,425
1862	683,346	1,968,441	14,170	48,820	2,694,687

WAY FREIGHT EASTWARD OVER THE ERIE CANAL.

Tons arriving at tide-water, the produce of New York, by way of the Erie canal, including the contributions of the lateral canals.

Year.	Products of the forest.	Products of Agriculture.	Manufactures.	Other articles.	Total.
1836	208,760	117,670	10,152	28,105	364,901
1837	174,207	98,172	7,879	51,193	331,251
1838	189,733	101,053	6,729	38,501	336,016
1839	157,075	63,713	5,885	37,014	261,690
1840	110,352	159,623	5,308	24,613	300,167
1841	192,121	92,493	9,676	14,663	308,344
1842	125,623	102,030	7,740	23,273	258,672
1843	202,810	124,313	21,465	30,391	378,902
1844	288,768	135,171	27,579	40,255	491,791
1845	328,055	224,058	40,619	61,433	655,130
1846	320,838	202,474	31,857	45,493	600,662
1847	328,652	192,224	30,037	70,596	618,412
1848	264,649	164,714	19,250	85,668	534,183
1849	227,847	200,471	18,399	51,348	498,069
1850	269,804	200,403	15,217	35,563	521,680
1851	183,681	108,433	15,401	54,858	462,365
1852	250,674	136,649	14,222	51,360	452,728
1853	391,224	168,017	20,045	58,462	637,741

Tons arriving at tide-water, the produce of New York, &c.—Continued.

Year.	Products of the forest.	Products of Agriculture.	Manufactures.	Other articles.	Total.
1854	357,690	148,330	10,440	79,707	603,167
1855	220,865	43,024	22,320	41,030	327,830
1856	173,079	118,164	24,725	58,083	374,540
1857	60,824	64,381	13,747	48,249	197,201
1858	147,511	23,421	17,843	34,813	223,588
1859	228,450	84,107	14,920	65,917	311,394
1860	166,667	120,258	15,135	77,036	379,096
1861	104,004	109,791	7,510	69,783	291,184
1862	143,240	118,006	5,419	64,080	331,357

TRANSPORTATION EASTWARD ON THE GREAT LAKES.

The commerce of the great lakes might of itself be taken as the measure of the internal exchanges of the northern States east and west, adding to its quantities about half the freight of the Erie railroad, and the whole carried on the Pennsylvania Central and the Baltimore and Ohio roads. But as the business of the Erie canal and the New York railroads is somewhat more definitely stated, and as nearly all the produce and merchandise moved on the lakes goes finally over one or the other of these lines, the calculations of lake commerce which here follow are regarded as duplications of the quantities and values previously given. It will be seen that they sustain the aggregates first taken, and furnish evidence that cannot reasonably be doubted that these exchanges between the east and the west constitute the most gigantic system of internal commerce the world has known.

The shipping employed on the great lakes has had various alternations of fortune, being sometimes highly profitable, and therefore stimulated to great development in both sailing and steam vessels. It first began to be conspicuous in 1833, and rose rapidly in the five years succeeding to 50,000 tons. In 1843 an increase again began, which, with but one or two partial reverses, as in 1857, has continued to the present time. An immense and highly profitable business has been done by lake shipping in the carriage of grain and flour during the last four years, beginning with the fall trade of 1860, the consequence of which was a great increase of building in all classes of vessels adapted to the trade. The following table shows the high prices paid for freight on wheat from Milwaukie and Chicago to Buffalo during the months of navigation from 1859 to 1863. It is taken from the report of the Chamber of Commerce of Milwaukie for 1863.

Table showing the monthly range of freights on wheat to Buffalo, in cents per bushel.

Months.	1859.	1860.	1861.	1862.	1863.
April	....	....	8 a 8	10 a 8	9 a 7
May	....	....	6½ a 10	10 a 5	8 a 9
June	....	....	7½ a 6½	5½ a 10	10½ a 8
July	....	....	6½ a 4	8½ a 10	7 a 4
August	....	....	5 a 13	5 a 9	4 a 6
September	4 a 7	17 a 14	11 a 15	14 a 8	6 a 7
October	7½ a 9½	13 a 20	15½ a 24	8 a 17	6½ a 12½
November	10 a 6	12½ a 10	14½ a 20	14 a 15	9½ a 8

These prices are much above the average in previous years, and they have developed the lake shipping to an unprecedented extent. The following table is the official record of tonnage existing at all the ports of the lakes and St. Lawrence river at the close of each year from 1830 forward:

TONNAGE OF VESSELS OF THE UNITED STATES, OF ALL CLASSES, EMPLOYED IN THE LAKE TRADE.

The annual totals of registered and enrolled tonnage at all the lake ports, officially reported to the Treasury Department.

	Tons.		Tons.
1830	7,728	1847	131,659
1831	8,870	1848	160,250
1832	12,736	1849	177,077
1833	15,226	1850	186,790
1834	19,044	1851	200,807
1835	29,709	1852	221,235
1836	32,000	1853	251,492
1837	37,480	1854	280,564
1838	49,159	1855	339,193
1839	46,935	1856	369,950
1840	48,262	1857	398,709
1841	54,569	1858	395,140
1842	59,608	1859	422,381
1843	66,938	1860	450,726
1844	73,124	1861	475,678
1845	86,071	1862	547,165
1846	101,545	1863	611,398

The tonnage here recorded includes all descriptions of enrolled tonnage in river and canal trade, and it therefore exceeds the amount actually employed in east and west transportation. There is also a small abatement to be made on account of the character of the official record, the law requiring the name and tonnage of each vessel to be retained until official notice of its loss or transfer is received. On this account perhaps fifty thousand tons is of vessels lost or transferred to other districts, the exchange of papers in regard to which is incomplete.

Perhaps the best record of the vessels and tonnage actually employed in this trade is that made up by the western Boards of Trade, great care being taken to perfect this record at Chicago, Milwaukie, Detroit, Toledo, Cleveland, Buffalo, and Oswego. The Chicago Board of Trade make the following report of both American and Canadian shipping in the lake trade in their report for 1862:

Table showing the number, class, tonnage, and valuation of vessels, American and Canadian, engaged in the commerce of the lakes, 1858 to 1862.

Class.	American.			Canadian.		
	No.	Tonnage.	Valuation.	No.	Tonnage.	Valuation.
1858—Steamers	79	48,631	....	67	24,781	....
Propellers	113	66,994	....	14	4,197	....
Tugs	69	6,306	....	6	415	....
Barks and brigs	129	42,502	....	37	10,793	....
Schooners	830	177,170	....	212	32,950	....
Total	1,213	337,153	....	335	73,148	....
1859—Steamers	68	40,240	$1,779,000	54	21,403	$949,900
Propellers	118	55,657	2,217,100	16	4,127	140,600
Tugs	72	7,179	450,600	17	2,021	184,800
Barks	32	9,666	482,800	15	5,730	134,000
Brigs	64	30,452	456,000	14	3,295	76,400
Schooners	833	173,382	4,378,000	197	32,198	778,300
Total	1,198	323,150	9,811,800	313	63,663	2,305,900
1860—Steamers	75	47,333	2,439,840	77	25,830	1,499,680
Propellers	190	57,910	3,250,390	97	7,249	407,800
Barks	44	17,829	684,540	23	7,842	246,420
Brigs	76	21,595	484,850	16	3,815	94,340
Schooners	831	172,336	5,233,085	217	38,702	898,560
Total	1,216	316,503	11,092,105	360	76,717	3,140,300
1861—Steamers	65	42,683	1,480,800	63	21,107	1,010,200
Propellers	107	60,018	2,823,000	15	4,602	176,000
Tugs	91	9,155	645,700	22	4,812	202,300
Barks	48	19,616	469,000	19	7,153	189,500
Brigs	75	22,124	475,800	15	4,223	101,000
Schooners	843	180,357	4,555,000	222	33,771	882,300
Total	1,229	333,953	9,608,400	356	75,658	2,549,300
1862—Steamers	66	43,693	1,403,800	64	28,104	1,080,200
Propellers	122	69,039	2,344,800	16	6,154	181,000
Tugs	132	17,890	922,800	22	8,482	208,300
Barks	60	20,555	786,800	22	7,671	224,500
Brigs	75	22,124	460,700	14	4,223	107,000
Schooners	908	190,423	6,439,900	229	35,083	872,500
Total	1,363	361,977	11,364,100	367	88,896	2,607,800

At Buffalo the report of E. P. Dorr, secretary of the Board of Lake Underwriters for 1862, shows the following numbers, tonnage, classes, and value of vessels engaged in the lake trade:

Comparative statement of the tonnage of the northwestern lakes and the river St. Lawrence on the first day of January, 1862 and 1863.

Class of vessels.	1862.			1863.		
	No.	Tonnage.	Value.	No.	Tonnage.	Value.
Steamers	147	64,669	$2,607,900	143	53,692	$2,190,300
Propellers	203	60,951	2,814,900	254	70,253	3,573,300
Barks	62	25,118	621,600	74	33,903	982,900
Brigs	86	25,871	501,100	65	24,631	526,200
Schooners	989	204,900	5,248,900	1,008	227,631	5,955,550
Sloops	15	2,800	11,850	16	667	18,770
Barges	......	....	....	3	3,719	17,000
Totals	1,502	383,309	11,602,450	1,643	413,026	13,257,020

The following are the numbers and tonnage of each class owned and registered in the district of Buffalo:

Class of vessels.	1859.		1860.		1861.		1862.	
	No.	Tonnage.	No.	Tonnage.	No.	Tonnage.	No.	Tonnage.
Steamers	12	10,198	13	10,206	9	7,598	8	5,753
Propellers	49	29,046	57	33,255	48	34,665	57	34,558
Tugs	30	2,810	32	2,774	36	9,613	66	4,700
Barks	8	4,045	10	4,834	9	4,201	18	7,674
Brigs	17	5,611	18	5,555	19	6,603	15	5,090
Schooners	133	34,608	135	33,415	118	29,454	134	34,314
Sloops, &c	....	....	....	....	....	....	9	3,409
Scows	....	....	....	....	....	....	....	350
Barges	....	....	....	....	....	....	....	210
Totals	249	80,378	265	80,159	239	78,065	307	96,150

The following is the increase of the lake marine in 1862, distinguishing American and Canadian vessels, as reported by the same authority:

Class of vessels.	UNITED STATES VESSELS BUILDING.			CANADIAN VESSELS BUILDING.		
	No.	Tonnage.	Value.	No.	Tonnage.	Value.
Steamers	3	1,114	$93,550	2	970	$72,750
Propellers	5	3,815	276,125	6	1,960	147,000
Propeller tugs	8	1,194	80,550	....	....	....
Barks	2	1,037	46,665	6	2,600	121,050
Schooners	38	15,546	654,570	10	3,100	139,500
Barges	....	....	....	19	6,600	198,000
Totals	56	21,706	1,150,455	43	15,230	678,300

SUMMARY.

	Aggregate tonnage.
5 steamboats	2,094
11 propellers	3,775
8 steam tugs	1,184
6 barks	3,737
48 schooners	17,646
19 barges	6,600
99 vessels building—total tonnage	37,026

The Milwaukie Chamber of Commerce reports, as engaged in the trade of that port alone, the following number and tonnage of vessels in 1862 and 1863:

Class of vessels.	1862.		1863.	
	No.	Tonnage.	No.	Tonnage.
Steamers	7	2,546	9	5,753
Propellers	......	....	69	38,541
Barks	8	3,487	70	28,893
Brigs	8	2,481	20	6,925
Schooners	107	19,330	406	81,769

No explanation is given of the sudden and great increase in propellers and schooners in 1863 over 1862, but it is probably due to the connecting of lines regularly at Milwaukie in 1863 which did not previously connect there. The names of several propeller lines of recent establishment are given in the report, however, the eastern connections of which indicate the destination of their freight.

1. The People's Line and Western Transportation Co.: Twelve propellers to Buffalo, Erie railroad and Erie canal.

2. The New York Central Line: Ten propellers to Buffalo, New York Central road and Erie canal.

3. The Grand Trunk Line: Eight propellers to Sarnia, Canada, Grand Trunk railroad.

4. Evans's Line: Seven propellers to Buffalo, New York Central and Erie canal.

5. Northern Transportation Citizens' Line: Eight propellers to Oswego and New York canals.

6. Great Western Railway Line: Seven propellers to Sarnia, Canada, Great Western railroad.

7. Detroit and Milwaukie Railroad Line: Two steamships to Grand Haven, Michigan.

8. Montreal Propeller Line: Five propellers weekly, to Montreal, Canada.

It will be observed that three of these lines are to Canada, and that two, having 15 propellers, connect with railroads of Canada at Port Sarnia, nearly opposite Detroit. This is the point in Canada at which the large quantities of western produce enter in transit to eastern markets of the United States. Though appearing in the statistics as exports to Canada, they are not such in fact, merely taking that as a shorter route at certain seasons to the markets of the Atlantic seaboard.

The Detroit statistics compare 1857 with 1860 and 1862, as follow:

Class of vessels.	1857.			1860.			1862.		
	No.	Tons.	Value.	No.	Tons.	Value.	No.	Tons.	Value.
Sail vessels.....	849	225,419	$7,599,700	581	173,735	$4,422,600	851	355,101	$8,336,470
Steam propellers.	117	59,891	2,959,500	77	43,390	1,620,900	120	65,458	3,228,500
Total......	966	285,310	10,559,200	658	217,125	6,043,500	971	420,559	11,564,970

This statement shows a greater decline in 1858 to 1860 than is apparent from other evidence, but it also shows the decline to have been more than recovered in 1862. While the commerce of the lakes was undoubtedly much depressed in 1858 and 1859, the subsequent high prices of freight, and the vast amount of produce forwarded, restored it to the fullest proportions that could have been anticipated under any circumstances.

The Chicago statement copied above shows that 1,730 vessels, with an aggregate capacity of 450,893 tons, were engaged in lake commerce of a general character, east and west, in 1862, of which one-fifth was Canadian, or foreign. Undoubtedly the business of 1863 was enlarged by 50,000 tons in addition, making 500,000 tons as the capacity for that year. We have now to obtain an approximate estimate of the produce and merchandise actually moved by this large fleet. Unfortunately the tonnage reported as entered and cleared at the several ports is an imperfect guide to the business in consequence of the absence of discrimination between vessels entering with passengers and in ballast from those arriving with cargoes. At Detroit, Buffalo, and several other ports, an immense tonnage arrival is reported which is merely ferry and passenger transit, having very little significance in the carriage of merchandise either between domestic ports, or between the United States and Canada.

GRAIN, FLOUR, AND PRODUCE SENT EASTWARD FROM THE LAKE CITIES AND PORTS.

Chicago is the chief exporting city of the lakes in most agricultural staples, though Milwaukie at present exceeds it in the amount of wheat shipped eastward. The business of Chicago is enormous in a great number of articles, of provisions as well as of grain, and its commercial reports have for many years been clear and accurate as to all the conditions of its trade, the receipts and exports by all lines of transportation. The following is a statement of the flour and grain forwarded in detail for 1862, and the totals for nine years, as given in the Board of Trade report of that city for 1862:

Flour and grain forwarded to all points from Chicago in 1862.

Forwarded—	Flour.	Wheat.	Corn.	Oats.	Rye.	Barley.
	Barrels.	*Bushels.*	*Bushels.*	*Bushels.*	*Bushels.*	*Bushels.*
To Buffalo, by lake	648,345	7,535,386	21,946,987	2,119,950	567,711	295,631
Oswego, by lake	1,928	2,613,784	1,411,747	115,025	58,650	34,550
Ogdensburg, by lake	64,969	73,600	331,614	....	600	325
Ontonagon, by lake	6,658	....	8,310	38,520	....	....
Cleveland, by lake	....	9,800	45,925	....	....	....
Cape Vincent, by lake	....	102,580	199,118	....	....	....
Saginaw, by lake	....	3,500	8,096	9,020	....	....
Other United States ports, by lake	4,994	97,114	185,960	37,949	1,000	3,873
Collingwood, Canada, by lake	199,753	83,900	479,647	36,289	48,180	9,044
Port Colborne, Canada, by lake	953	508,050	1,984,960	35,470	46,900	32,065
Kingston, Canada, by lake	14,634	1,415,650	1,764,010	850	50,030	....
Toronto, Canada, by lake	....	....	211,877	50,311	18,865	....
Montreal, Canada, by lake	6,876	83,425	64,000	....	....	....
Sarnia, Canada, by lake	28,466	351,146	640,679	....	13,778	1,475
Goderich, Canada, by lake	168,938	662,874	663,278	34,387	4,419	1,775
Wellington Square, Canada, by lake	....	9,150	....	....	....	....
St. Catherine's, Canada, by lake	....	85,925	....	....	....	....
Prescott, Canada, by lake	358	16,550	38,250	....	6,501	....
Windsor, Canada, by lake	....	4,630	4,050	....	3,025	....
Belleville, Canada, by lake	368	....	7,150	....	....	....
By Illinois and Michigan canal	640	....	....	228,749	....	347
Chicago and Rock Island railroad	637	....	....	1,750	....	4,163
Illinois Central railroad	3,772	5,892	....	31,272	9,630	15,911
Chicago, Belvidere, and Quincy railroad	198	1,436	....	....	....	5,943
Chicago and northwestern railroad	436	....	47,541	....	....	....
Chicago and Alton railroad	....	....	....	....	....	39,474
Chicago and Milwaukie railroad	3,172	45,082	31,259	9,399	....	13,378
Michigan Southern railroad	595,034	67,838	32,075	113,739	3,040	4,948
Michigan Central railroad	171,334	130,931	31,167	109,977	4,167	38,195
Pittsburg, Ft. Wayne, and Chicago railroad	213,573	42,414	64,940	133,770	3,300	49,689
Total forwarded	1,739,849	13,808,898	29,452,410	3,112,366	871,796	538,165

In this table seven lines leading inland or northward along the lake shore are included, which together took 9,085 barrels of flour, 52,380 bushels wheat, and 465,000 bushels of other grains. These quantities are so small that they will not practically reduce the following aggregates for nine years, in which they cannot be distinguished.

Total quantities of flour and grain forwarded to eastern markets from Chicago for nine years.

Forwarded—	Flour.	Wheat.	Corn.	Oats.	Rye.	Barley.
	Barrels.	*Bushels.*	*Bushels.*	*Bushels.*	*Bushels.*	*Bushels.*
1854	111,677	2,359,925	6,636,054	3,429,647	....	147,611
1855	163,419	6,298,155	7,517,625	1,888,538	....	92,013
1856	216,386	8,334,430	11,129,668	1,014,677	....	19,051
1857	259,648	9,846,052	6,814,615	506,778	....	17,993
1858	470,402	8,850,257	7,726,964	1,319,068	7,369	139,020
1859	698,331	7,168,676	4,349,380	1,183,703	134,404	464,918
1860	698,132	12,402,197	13,700,113	1,091,816	136,649	567,449
1861	1,600,980	15,835,953	24,373,725	1,633,237	300,813	225,534
1862	1,739,849	13,808,898	29,452,410	3,112,366	871,796	538,165

The destination of this movement is very largely to Canada, Collingwood, Goderich, Sarnia, Kingston, Port Colborne, Montreal and Toronto being the points. The quantities so sent in 1862 were: flour, 420,544 barrels; wheat, 3,098,424 bushels; corn, 6,005,061 bushels; oats, 157,252 bushels; rye, 200,059 bushels; barley, 71,910 bushels. These were nearly one-fourth the total quantities sent eastward, except in oats and barley.

The quantity of flour sent eastward by railroad is very great, amounting to

672,961 barrels, or more than one-third of the whole. Of this a portion probably took the lake again at Detroit or Toledo, one-half or more being carried entirely through by railroad.

The shipments or transportation of other articles from Chicago eastward is somewhat difficult of calculation, lake and railroad carriage being to a great extent blended in the statements. The trade in provisions outward is largely increasing, particularly in fresh pork products. The Board of Trade report for 1862 says: "The progress made in pork-packing in Chicago during the past two years is without a parallel in the history of any other city in the United States. During the past two seasons a large proportion of the hogs cut have been made up into English middles, for the Liverpool and London markets. In the early part of this season nearly every packing house in the city was engaged in this branch of the business. The favor with which Chicago brands have been received in the leading markets of England warrants us in the belief that the trade will be one of permanence."

From this statement it may be reasonably inferred that the statement following of hogs, cattle, and cut meats forwarded is mainly to eastern markets, whether by railroad or by lake.

Cattle, hogs, meats, whiskey, wool, lead, &c., sent from Chicago, 1862.

	Cattle.	Hogs, live.	Hogs, dressed.	Beef.	Pork.	Cut meats.	Lard.
				Bbls.	*Bbls.*	*Lbs.*	*Lbs.*
By lake	735	419	....	82,345	108,735	925,000	34,150
Chicago and Milwaukie railroad	1,338	2,190	31	....	....	47,642	[illegible]
Michigan Southern railroad	30,657	141,817	11,481	59,509	49,498	24,546,533	21,682,941
Michigan Central railroad	51,657	97,686	24,446	86,236	89,431	22,522,734	20,112,178
Pittsburg, Fort Wayne, and Chicago railroad	38,757	204,481	8,631	11,637	11,005	21,438,608	17,610,164
Total	109,304	446,423	44,630	149,838	192,549	71,840,797	54,476,[illegible]

Cattle, hogs, meats, whiskey, wool, lead, &c., sent from Chicago, 1862—Continued.

	Tallow.	Hides.	High wines or whiskey.	Wool.	Lead.	Seeds.
	Lbs.	*Lbs.*	*Bbls.*	*Lbs.*	*Lbs.*	*Lbs.*
By lake	365,000	4,651,990	17,551	132,480	1,376,000	1,420,695
Chicago and Milwaukie railroad	32,000	149,550	11,915	....	67,151	49,160
Michigan Southern railroad	2,439,943	2,658,751	12,407	371,603	846,111	974,764
Michigan Central railroad	4,637,733	2,156,153	97,264	680,374	....	2,3[illegible],061
Pittsburg, Fort Wayne, and Chicago railroad	963,853	5,081,853	14,747	916,627	3,080,496	1,133,[illegible]
Total	8,460,531	15,212,[illegible]	65,[illegible]	2,083,084	4,171,7[illegible]	5,9[illegible]

The preponderance of railroad carriage in these articles is very great; barrelled pork, beef, whiskey, hides, wool, and lead being largely carried by lake, and pork only in excess over the carriage by railroads.

A rough estimate of values may be affixed to these quantities deduced from the prices current reported in Chicago in 1862, but the conditions are subject to so much change that it will be but a rough estimate.

Articles.	Quantity.	Price.	Amount.
Flour............bbls..	1,730,800	$5 00	$8,654,000
Wheat............bush..	13,756,000	95	13,068,200
Corn............do..	30,000,000	32	9,600,000
Oats............do..	3,000,000	32	960,000
Rye............do..	870,000	50	435,000
Barley............do..	500,000	75	375,000
Cattle............No.	109,304	30 00	3,279,120
Hogs, live............No.	446,425	7 50	3,348,187
Hogs, dressed............No.	44,609	8 00	356,872
Beef............bbls..	149,888	12 00	1,798,656
Pork............do..	192,549	10 00	1,925,490
Cut meats............lbs..	71,840,707	6	4,310,442
Lard............do..	54,476,423	8	4,358,114
Tallow............do..	8,460,500	9	761,440
Hides............do..	15,212,029	14	2,129,683
Whiskey............bbls..	85,084	12 50	1,063,550
Wool............lbs..	2,083,084	50	1,041,542
Lead............do..	6,171,748	6	370,305
Seeds............do..	5,990,426	8	479,234
Total estimated value............	....	....	57,654,334

PRODUCE SENT EASTWARD FROM MILWAUKIE.

The produce sent from Milwaukie is next to that of Chicago in amount and value. The following are the shipments eastward, nearly all by lake throughout, though a part crossing Michigan by railroad in 1861, 1862, and 1863, for ten years, to 1863 inclusive:

Exports of flour and grain from Milwaukie.

Year.	Flour.	Wheat.	Oats.	Corn.	Barley.	Rye.
	Barrels.	*Bushels.*	*Bushels.*	*Bushels.*	*Bushels.*	*Bushels.*
1854............	145,032	1,800,452	404,999	164,900	331,339	113,443
1855............	181,568	2,641,740	13,833	112,132	63,379	20,030
1856............	188,455	2,761,979	5,443	218	10,398	....
1857............	228,442	2,681,311	9,775	472	890	....
1858............	206,644	3,994,213	562,067	43,958	63,178	5,378
1859............	282,956	4,732,957	209,078	41,364	53,210	11,577
1860............	457,343	7,568,608	94,082	37,294	28,056	9,735
1861............	674,474	13,300,495	1,200	1,485	6,220	29,810
1862............	711,405	14,915,680	79,094	9,480	44,800	128,301
1863............	663,586	12,837,620	831,600	88,969	133,449	84,047

The exports of flour and grain from all the lake ports in 1863 were as follows:

	Flour.	Wheat.	Oats.	Corn.	Barley.	Rye.
	Barrels.	*Bushels.*	*Bushels.*	*Bushels.*	*Bushels.*	*Bushels.*
Racine............	12,457	717,998	2,148	69,065	....	....
Kenosha............	....	198,470	6,210	....	13,790	400
Sheboygan............	19,011	255,436	9,701	....	560	....
Port Washington....	4,164	76,880	3,443	50	4,169	2,560
Green Bay............	140,397	586,805	....	....	....	....
Milwaukie............	663,586	12,837,620	831,600	88,969	133,447	84,047
Chicago............	1,630,691	10,369,391	5,564,650	25,674,062	658,735	835,133
Total in 1863......	2,301,664	24,751,073	6,410,042	25,832,206	810,133	919,712

The shipment of provisions eastward from Milwaukie in 1862 was large:

Beef, 33,174 barrels, 3,217 tierces, equal to	7,599,900 pounds.
Pork, 56,434 barrels, equal to	11,286,800 pounds.
Bacon, 12,665 boxes, equal to	5,382,625 pounds.
Lard, 20,897 barrels and kegs, equal to	5,177,593 pounds.
Tallow, 4,750 barrels, equal to	1,106,750 pounds.

Other produce shipments were:

Butter, 1,068,967 pounds, value	$138,965
Wool, 1,314,210 pounds, value	657,105
Hides, No. 32,941, value	98,823
Seeds, 8,684 pounds, value	26,052
Whiskey, estimated 20,000 barrels, value	180,000

The value of the produce of all classes shipped at Milwaukie is approximately as follows, for 1862:

Flour	$3,557,020
Wheat	14,169,896
Other grains	126,278
Beef	436,692
Pork	564,340
Bacon	322,958
Lard	414,207
Tallow	95,000
Butter, wool, &c	1,000,945
Total	20,787,336

To which may be added, for grain and flour shipped from Racine, Kenosha, Sheboygan, and Green Bay, $2,590,685, giving an aggregate approximately as follows:

Chicago	$57,854,333
Milwaukie	20,787,336
Other ports of Lake Michigan	2,590,685
Total value	81,232,354

Eastward freights on the Milwaukie and Prairie du Chien and the Milwaukie and La Crosse railways in 1863.

Articles.		Milwaukie and Prairie du Chien.	Milwaukie and La Crosse.
Flour	barrels.	106,201	235,623
Wheat	bushels.	4,502,197	5,764,325
Rye	bushels.	85,043	41,041
Barley	bushels.	132,677	118,157
Oats	bushels.	780,216	103,500
Corn	bushels.	100,638	3,138
Beans	bushels.	11,275	9,513
Grass seeds	bushels.	8,344	350
Live hogs	No.	55,027	5,093
Dressed hogs	pounds.	10,780,215	9,407,769
Cattle	No.	22,112	4,325
Eggs	pounds.	277,416	172,171

Eastward freights, &c.—Continued.

Articles.	Milwaukie and Prairie du Chien.	Milwaukie and La Crosse.
Butter .... pounds.	1,300,680	563,084
Lard .... pounds.	1,774,824	12,016
Tallow .... pounds.	210,604	117,948
Wool .... pounds.	440,601	259,940
Hides .... pounds.	1,722,629	2,308,895
Potatoes .... bushels.	....	27,063
Pork and beef .... barrels.	....	1,065
Farm products, not specified .... pounds.	....	300,873
Horses .... No.	....	1,993
Barrels, empty .... No.	....	9,478
Staves .... pieces	....	435,300
Lumber .... feet.	....	2,661,198
Pig iron .... pounds.	....	3,450,165
Ice .... tons.	....	680
Agricultural implements .... pounds.	....	251,914
Shingles .... bunches.	....	6,993
Stave bolts .... cords.	....	150
Merchandise .... pounds.	....	2,770,498
Machinery .... pounds.	....	119,690
Miscellaneous .... pounds.	....	8,064,694

Westward freight over the Milwaukie and Prairie du Chien and the Milwaukie and St. Paul railroads in 1863.

Articles.	Milwaukie and Prairie du Chien.	Milwaukie and St. Paul.
Merchandise .... pounds.	47,101,020	76,508,498
Machinery .... pounds.	327,057	992,691
Agricultural implements .... pounds.	3,504,650	2,191,156
Miscellaneous .... pounds.	9,706,469	9,659,137
Lumber .... feet.	9,060,673	6,679,686
Shingles .... No.	6,951,250	3,332
Laths .... feet.	976,745	182,080
Hoops .... No.	16,371	100,006
Staves .... pieces.	349,942	350,000
Hides .... pounds.	....	216
Coal .... tons.	6,328	2,968
Pig iron .... tons.	60	878
Bark .... pounds.	....	60,000
Bricks .... M.	780	219
Stone .... tons.	....	18
Salt .... barrels.	55,107	43,942
Cement .... barrels.	3,070	4,404
High wines .... barrels.	2,054	8,003
Flour .... barrels.	734	1,425
Wheat .... bushels.	....	1,949
Barrels, empty .... No.	14,448	9,288
Horses, cattle, and sheep .... No.	7,317	10,112
Pork and beef .... barrels.	....	2,043
Corn .... bushels.	....	5,650
Wool .... pounds.	....	15,309
Farm products, not specified .... pounds.	....	1,034,719

There are various minor products of the vicinity of Lake Michigan which constituted items of noticeable value in these exports—in the Milwaukie trade reports cranberries, beans, eggs, staves, shingles, brick, &c.—but their aggregate value is small. At ports of the lake further northward there are furs, fish, lumber and wood in large amount. The fisheries of the straits are extensive and profitable, and though great quantities are now sent west, for consumption in Illinois, Wisconsin, and the vicinity, there is a more considerable portion going eastward to all parts of the lake district. From all miscellaneous sources, however, not more than two or three millions of dollars in value would be added to the outward or eastward trade of the Lake Michigan district.

THE LAKE SUPERIOR TRADE.

The next important accession to the lake trade going eastward is the export trade of Lake Superior, mainly the product of its copper and iron mines. The following statement of the superintendent of the ship canal at the Falls of the Sault Ste. Marie shows the transit of vessels through that canal monthly for 1862:

Months.	Schooners.		Propellers.		Steamers.		Total.
	No.	Tons.	No.	Tons.	No.	Tons.	Tons.
In April	......	....	1	744	1	786	1,530
May	28	6,856	20	10,698	28	19,991	37,345
June	146	49,336	18	9,834	27	18,812	77,982
July	100	29,093	18	9,900	25	17,646	56,739
August	135	42,608	21	11,677	24	17,537	71,820
September	100	32,850	22	10,849	29	20,109	63,808
October	29	8,742	14	7,549	23	16,198	32,489
November	5	1,310	7	3,813	17	12,776	17,899
Total	543	175,395	121	65,124	174	124,853	350,612

The character of this trade is such that this movement would necessarily represent an equal number of vessels and amount of tonnage each way, as all vessels that go up return again the same season unless lost. The eastward movement of the year 1863 would therefore be:

271 schooners	tons..	82,797
60 propellers	tons..	32,561
87 steamers	tons..	62,416
Or 418 vessels of all classes	tons..	177,774

The shipments outward for 1862 were estimated by the same authority to be 150,000 tons of iron and iron ore, and 9,300 tons of pure or native copper, valued together at $12,000,000. Very little else was shipped outward—a few furs, copper ore from the Canadian side, and minor articles. The inward or westward shipments of merchandise, machinery for working mines, supplies to miners, &c., are estimated to have been of the value of $10,000,000 for the same year.

The following statement of the production and shipment of copper from the opening of the mines in 1845 will show the development already attained:

Aggregate shipments of copper from Lake Superior from 1845 to 1862.

				Value.
Shipments in	1845	pounds..	1,300	$290
	1846	tons..	29	2,619
	1847	tons..	239	107,550
	1848	tons..	516	206,400
	1849	tons..	750	301,200
	1850	tons..	640	266,000
	1851	tons..	872	348,800
	1852	tons..	887	300,450
	1853	tons..	1,452	508,200
	1854	tons..	2,300	805,000
	1855	tons..	3,196	1,437,000
	1856	tons..	5,726	2,400,100
	1857	tons..	5,759	2,015,650
	1858	tons..	5,896	1,610,000
	1859	tons..	6,041	1,932,000
	1860	tons..	8,614	2,520,000
	1861	tons..	10,347	3,180,000
	1862	tons..	10,000*	4,000,000

Shipments of the copper districts—four years.

	1859.	1860.	1861.	1862.
Keweenaw district	1,910.3	1,910.8	2,161.9	2,726.8*
Portage lake	1,533.1	3,064.6	4,708.0	4,288.9*
Ontonagon	2,597.6	3,610.7	3,476.7	2,706.1
Carp lake		20.5	......	7.1
Sundry mines		7.6	......	....

The production of iron and the export of iron ore in the Lake Superior region were as follows:

	Tons ore.	Tons pig.	Value.
1855	1,445	.....	$14,470
1856	11,597	.....	92,776
1857	26,184	.....	209,472
1858	31,035	1,627	249,260
1859	65,679	7,258	575,521
1860	116,998	5,660	736,490
1861	45,430	7,970	410,460
1862	115,721	8,590	984,976

The destination of the copper shipped is to Buffalo and eastward, but the iron and iron ore go in part to Cleveland and Pittsburg. Copper is also smelted at Pittsburg to some extent. A very large trade with Lake Superior is conducted at Cleveland, at which point many of these products are first received.

THE LAKE FISHERIES.

The lake fisheries are described in the Buffalo trade report as being located and successful at a great number of points:

"In the Sandusky bay, in the Maumee bay and Maumee river, in the Monroe bay, in the Detroit river, in the St. Clair river and rapids, in Lake Huron from Huron to Point aux Barque, in the Au Sable river, in Thunder bay above Au Sable river, including Sugar island, in Saginaw bay and river, in Tawas bay, between Thunder bay and Mackinac,

* Estimated.

including Hammond's bay, in and about Mackinac at Beaver island and its surroundings, between the De Tour and the Sault, along the eastern shore of Lake Michigan, in Green bay in Wisconsin and Michigan, at Presque Isle, Pennsylvania, in Superior's numerous bays and inlets, are found the principal fishing grounds of the lakes, and the annual catch ranges from sixty to one hundred thousand barrels, valued at four to six hundred thousand dollars. The lake fisheries are only second to the cod fisheries off the Atlantic coast, from Cape Cod bay to Cape Breton, and are a source of very considerable wealth."

The receipts of fish at Buffalo only are fully stated, and the decline apparent in the proceeds of the fisheries received there results from the increased demand for them in the western States generally, and their wider distribution.

Lake imports of fish at Buffalo.

Years.	Barrels.	Years.	Barrels.
1854	11,752	1859	10,391
1855	7,241	1860	26,655
1856	6,250	1861	8,313
1857	5,290	1862	8,647
1858	4,203		

TRADE OF LAKE ERIE EASTWARD

Toledo.

Toledo has within a few years become a point of very extensive shipment of grain and produce eastward. The country adjacent to it, and westward to Lake Michigan, is extremely productive, sending a large annual surplus to distant markets, and the Michigan Southern railroad brings large quantities of flour from Chicago to take water transportation further eastward. In five years, closing with 1862, this road delivered the following extraordinarily large quantities of flour, grain, and other produce, at Toledo:

Articles.	1858.	1859.	1860.	1861.	1862.
Flour..........barrels.	253,156	379,610	394,642	752,309	892,676
Wheat.......bushels.	940,201	1,024,026	1,949,693	2,440,320	2,650,694
Corn...........do...	268,229	100,919	811,372	200,440	258,300
Oats, barley, and rye..	132,630	89,000	179,025	22,025	147,345
Pork..........barrels.	61,212	80,279	62,680	91,738	65,813
Beef...........do...	....	....	47,185	17,829	32,225
Cattle.......number.	1,552	1,253	1,641	2,241	1,603
Hogs, live.......do...	1,552	902	1,307	1,482	3,006
Hogs, dressed.pounds.	3,277,415	4,728,175	3,714,567	5,615,077	6,345,224
Pork, boxes.... do...	....	....	....	....	17,506,593

It will be seen that the new product of cut pork for European markets appears largely in 1862, evidently in greater part from Chicago.

The Dayton and Michigan railroad, leading from the southwest, in western Ohio, also brought a large amount of produce in 1862:

Flour..............barrels.. 156,257	Beef..............barrels.. 4,662
Wheat ....bushels..1,277,006	Pork in boxes....pounds..5,972,536
Corn............ bushels.. 93,422	Dressed hogs.....pounds.. 529,081
Pork.............barrels.. 21,639	

The Toledo and Wabash railroad brought from central Indiana:

Flour............barrels.. 247,389	Pork.............barrels.. 60,978
Wheat...........bushels..2,565,958	Beef.............barrels.. 33,124
Corn.............bushels..2,678,327	Dressed hogs.....pounds..4,302,078
Oats and rye.....bushels.. 66,239	Cut pork........pounds..1,549,267

The Wabash and Erie and Miami and Erie canals delivered at Toledo in 1862:

Flour	barrels..	217,860	Pork	barrels..	28,893
Wheat	bushels..	3,007,204	Beef	barrels..	3,469
Corn	bushels..	738,863	Whiskey	barrels..	21,906
Oats and rye	bushels..	5,621	Bacon	pounds..	2,431,371

Together these lines sum a large aggregate of receipts at Toledo, of which only a small portion has before been noted as leaving Chicago eastward by the Michigan Southern railroad. The total quantities received are:

Flour	barrels..	1,585,325	Whiskey	barrels..	157,115
Wheat	bushels..	9,827,629	Hides	pounds..	6,300,000
Corn	bushels..	3,813,709	Hogs	number..	327,680
Pork	barrels..	167,328	Cattle	number..	74,840
Beef	barrels..	73,480	Sheep	number..	17,400
Lard	pounds..	125,800	Cloverseed	bushels..	60,540
Pork in boxes, and bacon, lbs		27,450,067	Dressed hogs	pounds..	11,176,383

The following is a summary of the receipts of flour and grain at Toledo for three years:

		1860.	1861.	1862.
Flour	barrels..	807,768	1,406,676	1,585,325
Wheat	bushels..	5,341,190	6,277,407	9,827,629
Corn	bushels..	5,386,951	5,312,038	3,813,709
Oats	bushels..	129,689	41,423	234,759
Barley	bushels..	115,992	12,064	63,038
Rye	bushels..	37,787	31,193	44,368
Total grain		11,011,609	11,674,130	13,983,593

The lines of shipment eastward from Toledo are two propeller lines of six to ten vessels each, one connecting with the New York central railroad at Buffalo, and one with the Erie railroad at Dunkirk. There are also vessels running to Oswego, Ogdensburg, Port Colburne, Canada, and other points. The Cleveland and Toledo railroad takes a large amount of flour on the south shore of the lake to Cleveland.

Table showing the shipments of flour, wheat, and corn from Toledo in 1862.

Ports.	Flour.	Wheat.	Corn.
	Barrels.	*Bushels.*	*Bushels.*
To Buffalo	830,702	5,061,216	1,471,218
Dunkirk	498,965	65,050	111,436
Oswego	6,816	3,146,824	741,253
Cape Vincent	....	35,250	69,750
Ogdensburg	38,706	182,335	341,709
Saginaw and Port Huron	550	....	41,000
Cleveland	....	13,500	45,080
Erie	....	....	31,160
Montreal	....	142,500	164,174
Kingston	....	560,814	188,717
Toronto	....	....	73,470
Port Colborne	....	174,270	218,910
Other Canadian ports	2,147	....	60,020
By Cleveland and Toledo railroad	174,307	17,530	157,338
Total	1,547,325	9,492,327	3,697,898

This is all, therefore, the proper eastward trade of the belt embraced in the general calculation, and it is mainly lake commerce strictly. The larger share of the shipments eastward from Chicago by railroad here return to the lake, though they again take the railroads in New York, the Erie at Dunkirk and the Central at Buffalo. The shipments eastward of other produce, pork, beef and provisions, are not given in the trade report* from which the preceding statistics have been taken, but it is assumed that the shipments are at least equal to the receipts. Of pork, beef, lard, tallow, &c., they are undoubtedly much greater than the receipts by railroads and canals, since there is no considerable consumption at Toledo, and a large number of hogs are packed in the city. Live stock, hogs, cattle and sheep, were sent eastward mainly by the Cleveland and Toledo railroad. The numbers by railroads and by lake were:

	Cattle.	Hogs.	Sheep.
By lake	4,093	14,945	1,156
By railroad	85,370	341,640	34,800
Total sent east 1862	89,463	356,585	35,956

The value of this produce leaving Toledo eastward is, approximately—

Flour	$7,736,625
Wheat	9,402,327
Corn	1,479,123
Pork	1,840,608
Beef	891,760
Whiskey	1,571,150
Hides	630,000
Hogs	2,600,440
Cattle	2,245,200
Sheep	35,000
Cloverseed	240,000
Pork in boxes and bacon	1,647,004
Dressed hogs	670,563
Total value	30,969,820

THE TRADE OF DETROIT EASTWARD.

The position of Detroit is one of extensive transit of produce brought by the railroads crossing the State from Lake Michigan, as well as one of importance as a primary market of the produce of the State of Michigan. The Michigan Central railroad carries largely of freight from Chicago, which has once been noted in the statistics of eastward-bound produce. The various branches of this and the other roads in the State make the chief market of their surplus at Detroit. The receipts of flour and grain for three years from all sources were as follows:

Articles.		1860.	1861.	1862.
Flour	barrels	862,175	1,721,140	1,563,878
Wheat	bushels	1,869,623	2,546,111	3,058,232
Corn	do	658,698	1,086,506	583,861
Oats	do	319,588	368,966	402,217
Barley	do	124,882	80,731	165,200
Rye	do	30,843	16,981	18,867

* "The Toledo Blade's annual statement of the trade and commerce of Toledo," published by the Toledo Board of Trade.

The detail of other produce is not at hand for incorporation in this statement. It is known to embrace large quantities of miscellaneous produce—wool, butter, hides, pork, beef and provisions, lard, tallow, seeds, &c. The flour and grain stated above would reach a large valuation, which may be stated at the following approximate sums:

Flour	$9,000,000
Wheat	3,250,000
Corn	500,000
Oats	160,000
Barley and rye	175,000

Estimating five millions of dollars as a minimum value of other produce finding its primary market here, the total value is $18,085,000 furnished at this point to the lake commerce destined for eastern markets.

We find in a late number of the Detroit Tribune a carefully prepared statement of the flour and grain trade of that city for 1863, from which we make up the following table:

FLOUR.

	Receipts—bbls.	Shipments—bbls.
1858	592,387	505,917
1859	605,640	478,918
1860	862,175	809,515
1861	1,321,149	1,261,289
1862	1,543,886	1,445,458
1863	1,143,148	1,033,150

WHEAT.

	Bushels.	Bushels.
1858	886,613	791,870
1859	858,037	739,236
1860	1,814,951	1,607,757
1861	3,005,111	2,705,067
1862	3,593,242	3,419,949
1863	2,174,726	1,862,901

CORN.

1858	236,612	182,587
1859	403,065	132,487
1860	638,698	502,044
1861	1,036,506	980,309
1862	608,861	342,837
1863	352,295	139,616

OATS.

(1858 not given.)

1859	173,364	24,816
1860	399,598	319,205
1861	319,986	253,157
1862	407,247	151,204
1863	662,926	465,057

TOTAL RECEIPTS OF FLOUR AND GRAIN REDUCED TO BUSHELS.

1859	4,177,856
1860	6,441,639
1861	10,514,286
1862	11,827,000
1863	8,527,666

LAKE COMMERCE AT BUFFALO.

From the preceding review of the sources of lake freight and its general shipment eastward, it is apparent that it takes many different routes of actual transit. While the chief one is to Buffalo, connecting them with the Erie canal and the New York Central railroad, there is, first, a large diversion by southern routes; the Pittsburg, Fort Wayne, and Chicago railroad, the Southern Michigan, and the Cleveland and Toledo railroads, all carrying in part to the Pennsylvania Central road, and the two last named to the New York and Erie railroad. Next are other railroads, and several propeller lines terminating at Dunkirk, for shipment over the New York and Erie road; and on the north there are several Canadian lines which draw off large quantities of produce either to Canadian markets, or for transit through Canada to Niagara, Oswego, or other points in the United States eastward. Extensive shipments also take the Welland canal for Lake Ontario without touching at Canadian ports.

The freight passing over the Pennsylvania railroad can only be calculated in the business of that road. Those of the Erie road also have no statistical statement at the point of receipt, and it is only at Buffalo that any definite account of receipts by lake, or from the lake district, can be taken. At this point the statistics are full and satisfactory, and in the very valuable report of the Buffalo Board of Trade for 1862 they are given for a series of years to 1862, inclusive. Here are also definite statements of many items of lake exports—fish, copper, iron, &c., which could not be stated in detail from western sources.

Buffalo is a point of the receipt and shipment equally of quantities coming from other primary or producing markets and destined to other markets of consumption. Oswego, Dunkirk, Ogdensburg, and Cape Vincent are the same for the lake trade. Detroit and Toledo are such in part only. The following statements of receipts may therefore be considered as equivalent to shipments also, and may be grouped as exhibiting the receipts at the eastern extremity of the lakes of the proper trade of the lake district:

BUFFALO.

	1860.	1861.	1862.
Flour....................barrels..	1,122,335	2,159,591	2,846,022
Wheat....................bushels..	18,502,649	27,105,219	30,435,381
Corn....................bushels..	11,386,217	21,024,657	24,288,627
Oats....................bushels..	1,209,594	1,797,905	2,024,932
Barley....................bushels..	262,158	313,757	423,124
Rye....................bushels..	80,822	337,764	791,564
Total grain..............	31,441,440	50,597,302	58,564,078

OSWEGO.

	1860.	1861.	1862.
Flour....................barrels..	121,399	119,056	235,382
Wheat....................bushels..	9,651,564	10,121,440	10,982,132
Corn....................bushels..	5,019,400	4,642,262	4,529,962
Oats....................bushels..	388,416	116,384	187,284
Barley....................bushels..	1,326,915	1,173,551	1,050,364
Rye....................bushels..	244,311	381,687	130,175
Total grain..............	16,630,606	16,435,330	16,878,917

DUNKIRK.

	1860.	1861.	1862.
Flour.................barrels..	542,765	736,529	1,095,364
Wheat...............bushels..	500,688	604,561	112,061
Corn...................bushels..	644,061	230,400	149,654
Oats and rye..........bushels..	8,843	7,175	10,173
Total grain.............	1,153,812	842,136	271,888

OGDENSBURG.

	1860.	1861.	1862.
Flour.................barrels..	248,200	411,888	576,394
Wheat.................bushels..	565,022	677,396	689,930
Corn...................bushels..	867,014	1,119,594	1,120,176
Oats...................bushels..	28,242	2,365	3,336
Barley.................bushels..	7,106	15,151	15,529
Rye.....................bushels..	3,050	3,868	....
Total grain.............	1,470,433	1,818,384	1,828,974

CAPE VINCENT.

	1860.	1861.	1862.
Flour.................barrels..	28,940	65,407	48,576
Wheat.................bushels..	208,678	276,610	316,403
Corn...................bushels..	73,300	124,411	219,309
Oats...................bushels..	27,299	2,994	1.030
Barley.................bushels..	90,614	53,677	31,265
Rye.....................bushels..	20,616	23,305	762
Total grain.............	415.707	481,257	598,829

Summary of receipts at terminal lake ports, 1862.

	Flour, barrels.	Grain, bushels.
Buffalo..........................	2,846,022	56,564.078
Dunkirk..........................	1,095,364	271,688
Oswego..........................	235,382	16,878,917
Ogdensburg..........................	576,394	1,828,974
Cape Vincent..........................	48,576	598,829
Total..........................	4,801,738	76,142,686

It is clear that this does not cover the total lake trade, not to mention that of the districts of the west south of its proper line, since the receipts at New York alone are larger than the total. The following statement of receipts at New York is from the Buffalo trade report for 1862:

	1860.	1861.	1862.
Flour .... barrels..	3,892,358	5,013,053	5,379,417
Wheat .... bushels..	18,039,384	28,749,909	28,897,110
Corn .... bushels..	12,999,659	23,169,469	18,409,465
Oats .... bushels..	4,358,824	4,031,395	4,832,330
Barley .... bushels..	1,168,065	1,742,895	1,627,790
Rye .... bushels..	143,927	659,368	923,016
Total grain	36,759,864	58,373,036	54,669,711

The flour and grain trade of Buffalo has been large for many years, and until about 1854 it constituted the sole statistical return of that class of trade on the lakes. The following statement of receipts at Buffalo of flour and the several kinds of grain shows the growth of the trade from 1836 to 1862, and that at no time has its increase been so rapid as from 1860 to 1862:*

Receipts of flour and grain at Buffalo from the west from 1836 to 1862.

Years.	Flour.	Wheat.	Corn.	Oats.	Barley.	Rye.
	Barrels.	*Bushels.*	*Bushels.*	*Bushels.*	*Bushels.*	*Bushels.*
1836........	139,178	304,090	204,455	28,640	4,870	1,580
1837........	126,805	450,350	94,490	2,553	....	3,227
1838........	277,620	933,117	34,145	6,577	....	909
1839........	294,125	1,117,262	....	....	....	....
1840........	597,142	1,004,561	71,327	....	....	....
1841........	730,040	1,635,000	201,031	14,144	....	2,150
1842........	734,308	1,555,420	454,530	....	4,710	1,268
1843........	917,517	1,827,241	223,993	2,480	....	1,352
1844........	915,030	2,177,500	137,978	18,017	1,617	456
1845........	746,750	1,770,740	51,200	23,100	....	....
1846........	1,374,529	4,744,184	1,455,258	218,300	47,550	28,250
1847........	1,857,000	6,489,100	2,862,300	446,000	....	70,787
1848........	1,249,000	4,520,117	2,298,000	560,000	0	17,889
1849........	1,207,435	4,913,978	3,321,651	362,384	....	....
1850........	1,103,039	3,681,347	2,593,378	357,580	3,000	....
1851........	1,258,224	4,167,121	5,988,775	1,140,340	142,773	10,652
1852........	1,299,513	5,549,778	5,136,746	2,596,231	497,913	112,251
1853........	975,557	5,420,043	8,065,793	1,580,655	401,098	107,152
1854........	739,756	3,510,792	10,108,983	4,401,739	313,885	177,069
1855........	936,761	8,022,126	9,711,430	2,093,222	62,304	209,591
1856........	1,120,048	8,465,671	9,633,277	1,738,342	46,387	245,810
1857........	845,953	8,334,179	5,713,611	1,214,760	37,844	48,538
1858........	1,536,109	10,671,550	6,621,668	2,278,241	308,371	125,214
1859........	1,420,333	9,214,652	3,113,653	2,394,502	361,500	124,693
1860........	1,122,335	18,502,649	11,386,217	1,209,584	262,158	80,823
1861........	2,150,591	27,105,219	21,024,657	1,797,905	313,757	337,764
1862........	2,846,029	30,435,831	24,288,627	2,024,958	423,184	991,564

* The following incidents connected with the origin of this vast trade are from the Board of Trade report of Buffalo for 1862:

"The history of the produce trade of Buffalo, which is now of such vast magnitude, dates back but a few years, and is in fact the history of the produce trade of the Great West. Previous to 1836 there was very little, if any, grain received at this port for sale. The grain received prior to this date was mostly purchased by millers from the interior of this State, who made their purchases in Ohio and shipped it to place of destination, but the quantities were insignificant as compared with our present grain trade.

"In the fall of 1836 the steamer Great Western brought to this port from Chicago thirty-nine bags of wheat consigned to a miller in Otsego county, which was the first grain shipment from Lake Michigan ports, and the only shipment made during that year.

The trade of Buffalo in pork, beef, bacon, and provisions generally, is as greatly extended in 1862 over former years as is that in flour and grain. The following table gives the total of receipts and the shipments by canal eastward for fourteen years. The shipments by railroads eastward are large, but they cannot be distinguished, being simply classed with other freight:*

Years.	Receipts of provisions by lake for fourteen years.				Canal exports of provisions for fourteen years.			
	Pork.	Beef.	Bacon.	Lard.	Pork.	Beef.	Bacon.	Lard oil and lard.
	Barrels.	Barrels.	Pounds.	Pounds.	Barrels.	Barrels.	Pounds.	Pounds.
1849	[illegible]	[illegible]	[illegible]	5,311,007	41,178	54,978	1,322,164	4,421,614
1850	[illegible]	81,719	[illegible]	[illegible]	27,517	[illegible]	1,791,416	5,604,167
1851	[illegible]	73,074	[illegible]	[illegible]	23,640	61,773	6,146,140	4,376,000
1852	[illegible]	[illegible]	[illegible]	[illegible]	[illegible]	55,015	[illegible]	10,060,237
1853	[illegible]	62,779	21,075,645	[illegible]	[illegible]	49,746	15,474,377	8,730,454
1854	[illegible]	50,897	20,455,400	[illegible]	[illegible]	86,730	16,702,288	14,613,348
1855	[illegible]	[illegible]	[illegible]	10,357,130	[illegible]	34,925	6,784,919	5,169,138
1856	60,477	30,350	[illegible]	5,337,502	[illegible]	8,443	3,948,377	3,905,708
1857	[illegible]	50,911	3,612,519	613,006	9,135	5,236	[illegible]	718,435
1858	[illegible]	122,915	[illegible]	1,916,540	[illegible]	[illegible]	[illegible]	3,884,019
1859	76,619	81,815	[illegible]	[illegible]	[illegible]	30,338	1,518,147	3,130,508
1860	[illegible]	37,522	[illegible]	1,618,300	5,416	6,440	4,478	108,064
1861	[illegible]	[illegible]	[illegible]	[illegible]	4,980	17,301	772,416	691,778
1862	171,522	123,301	25,687,657	22,471,204	153,421	53,686	4,442,480	8,349,454

The receipts by lake and the exports by canal of whiskey at Buffalo for thirteen years are as follows:

Years.		Imported by lake.	Exported by canal.
1850	barrels..	30,169	19,644
1851	barrels..	76,524	60,300
1852	barrels..	79,306	73,398
1853	barrels..	60,707	45,693
1854	barrels..	50,287	24,757
1855	barrels..	27,067	18,989
1856	barrels..	36,009	5,501

"In October, 1839, the brig Osceola brought from Chicago, for Durfee & Kingman, then millers at Black Rock, 1,678 bushels of wheat, which was the first grain shipment in bulk from Lake Michigan ports. In 1840 a small schooner called the General Harrison, of about 100 tons burden, was laden at Chicago with 3,000 bushels of wheat, for Buffalo, which is said to be the first full cargo of grain exported from Lake Michigan. During the same year the schooner Ouselle brought from Chicago 3,000 bushels of wheat, the brig Erie 2,000 bushels of wheat, and the schooners Major Oliver and Illinois each a small cargo. Such was the beginning of the grain trade of the upper lakes which has now grown to such vast magnitude. From this period to the opening of the Illinois canal, 1848, the trade was slowly progressive. In the year 1844 Charles Walker, of Chicago, was said to have had at one time five vessels afloat, loaded with wheat, destined for Buffalo, and this was then considered to be of great magnitude, while, during the season just passed, it has been no unusual event to have two to two and one-half million bushels of grain afloat on the lakes, destined for this port, mostly from Lake Michigan. Previous to 1843 the only grain coming from Lake Michigan was wheat, and it was not until 1848 that any corn worthy of notice was received from Illinois, and what little there was brought to Buffalo came from Ohio."

* Note appended to this table in the Buffalo Trade report:

"It will be seen from the foregoing table of canal exports from 1849 to 1855, that there was a gradual augmentation of the movement by canal.

"After the consolidation of the roads composing the New York Central, and the opening of the New York and Erie railway, these roads divided the business with the canals, taking the lion's share, but the subsequent action of the canal board in adjusting the rates of toll has gained to the canals a larger share than under the higher rates of toll. If the revenues of the State are to be augmented, a lower rate of toll than the present would secure to the canals a larger tonnage from pork, beef, lard, and bacon than is now carried by the several railway lines."

1857	barrels..	42,140	20,900
1858	barrels..	59,446	51,160
1859	barrels..	16,211	15,930
1860	barrels..	49,204	15,282
1861	barrels..	111,372	45,759
1862	barrels..	113,253	38,007

Staves and lumber from the lakes are principally received at Buffalo, so far as they are designed for the market there and eastward. Chicago is a great market for supply of the interior of Illinois, but no port of Lake Michigan exports staves or lumber eastward. The Buffalo Board of Trade report speaks of this trade as follows:

"The lumber and stave trade constitutes a very large portion of the freight carried on the lakes and canals, and is only second to grain. The larger portion of the eastward movement usually take place in mid-summer, when low rates of transportation rule. The principal sources of supply are the States of Ohio, Indiana, Michigan, Canada West, and Pennsylvania, of which more than fifty per cent. is from Michigan alone. In the northern peninsula of that State, in and around Saginaw, at Port Huron, on St. Clair river, are the largest and finest lumber districts in the west and northwest.

"The supply of staves is derived from Ohio, Indiana, Michigan, Wisconsin, and Canada West, of which more than eighty per cent. of the receipts at this port come from these States first named."

The table of comparison of receipts by lake at Buffalo and of exports by canal is for fourteen years.

LAKE IMPORTS.

Years.	Staves, No.	Lumber, feet.
1846	10,762,500	34,536,000
1847	8,800,000	18,313,000
1848	8,091,000	21,425,000
1849	14,183,902	33,935,768
1850	18,052,890	53,076,000
1851	10,696,006	08,006,000
1852	12,998,814	72,337,225
1853	9,215,240	69,294,000
1854	15,464,554	67,407,003
1855	16,421,568	72,028,651
1856	18,556,039	60,584,812
1857	23,024,213	66,283,319
1858	15,119,019	67,059,173
1859	23,277,028	111,072,476
1860	22,307,839	111,094,496
1861	25,228,978	58,082,713
1862	30,410,252	125,289,071

CANAL EXPORTS.

Years.	Staves, tons.	Lumber, feet.
1849	62,127	40,694,095
1850	79,740	45,791,525
1851	37,964	55,881,000
1852	41,565	63,424,388
1853	38,033	61,885,663
1854	60,157	59,109,520
1855	74,606	48,989,289
1856	72,932	38,617,501
1857	92,961	43,727,523

1858	77,621	31,991,067
1859	111,469	94,364,597
1860	132,420	91,612,607
1861	117,380	33,343,470
1862	148,679	88,327,976

The receipts at Buffalo given in the above tables as from the west are altogether by lake, and do not include the carriage by two important railroads—the Lake Shore road, from the southwest, and the Buffalo and Niagara Falls road. Nor do they include the large amount of flour taken over the Niagara river at Suspension Bridge.

The receipts at Buffalo by lake of many other articles are important. Live stock, transported both by lake and railroad, at that point are stated as follows in the trade report from which we quote:

The following will show the receipt of live stock by lake from 1850 to 1862, inclusive:

	Cattle.	Hogs.	Sheep.
1851 ... number..	8,211	89,120	.....
1852 ... number..	15,926	171,223	16,590
1853 ... number..	20,460	114,952	20,466
1854 ... number..	19,047	74,276	19,441
1855 ... number..	14,049	64,954	26,508
1856 ... number..	25,283	72,713	41,467
1857 ... number..	39,799	75,174	44,972
1858 ... number..	32,522	136,849	41,364
1859 ... number..	17,606	42,476	23,695
1860 ... number..	18,266	33,350	34,685
1861 ... number..	32,275	43,243	39,630
1862 ... number..	18,938	35,024	29,033

The sources of supply are Ohio, Indiana, Michigan, Wisconsin, Illinois, and Canada West.

This does not show the extent of the trade in live stock, as a large number are daily coming here by the different railways converging at this point.

The following exhibit of the totals of receipts at the different yards for several years will more nearly approximate to the true state of the trade in live stock. The receipts by lake include the imports by the Buffalo and Lake Huron railway, both of which being deducted from the total receipts at the several yards in each year, will show more nearly the receipts of live stock by the Lake Shore railway for the several years indicated:

	Cattle.	Hogs.	Sheep.
1857 ... number..	108,203	307,549	117,408
1858 ... number..	136,043	345,731	92,194
1859 ... number..	103,337	189,579	73,619
1860 ... number..	150,972	145,354	85,770
1861 ... number..	141,629	238,952	101,679
1862 ... number..	129,433	524,916	105,671

	Cattle.	Hogs.	Sheep.
1862. Receipts ... number..	129,433	524,976	105,671
Less by lake ... number..	18,938	35,024	29,033
By State Line railroad ... number..	110,495	489,952	76,638
1861. By State Line railroad ... number..	109,354	195,709	64,049
Increase ... number..	1,141	294,243	12,589

It will be seen by the foregoing statement that of the totals of receipts at the different yards 110,495 cattle, 459,952 hogs, and 78,638 sheep were received by the Buffalo and State Line and Niagara Falls railways, nearly all of which came by the former road.

The magnitude of the trade in live stock when expressed by the valuation in money will be about the following estimate, viz:

129,433 cattle, at $50	$6,471,650
524,976 hogs, at $7	3,674,832
105,671 sheep, at $3	317,013
Total valuation	10,463,495

The valuation of this report is in excess of those before assumed as regards cattle, but otherwise somewhat less. It cannot be far from correct.

Hides were imported by lake as follows:

	No.		No.
1852	95,452	1858	148,950
1853	98,008	1859	148,046
1854	67,427	1860	78,837
1855	90,964	1861	50,993
1856	111,856	1862	268,695
1857	139,051		

The imports and exports of hides by the Erie canal were as follows:

		Received.	Shipped.
1856	pounds..	442,525	469,465
1857	pounds..	130,500	780,855
1858	pounds..	573,904	569,312
1859	pounds..	386,789	342,029
1860	pounds..	137,345	79,431
1861	pounds..	173,441	169,258
1862	pounds..	193,503	466,003

The following will show the receipts by lake and canal from 1855 to 1862, inclusive:

	Receipts by lake. Bulls, No.	Receipts by canal. pounds.
1855	2,265	1,886,236
1856	2,326	1,603,057
1857	2,513	714,135
1858	4,291	800,863
1859	5,342	1,172,260
1860	1,608	1,172,417
1861	3,778	(*)
1862	3,159	1,108,883

The following will show the lake imports and canal exports of wool from 1856 to 1862, inclusive:

	Lake imports. Wool, bales.	Canal exports. Wool, lbs.
1856	41,592	2,009,497
1857	35,613	1,326,289
1858	31,485	1,736,883

* No report of receipts by canal in 1861.

1859	-32,480	1,747,556
1860	32,108	1,079,942
1861	32,480	1,288,394
1862	42,619	1,371,098

There is a very considerable amount of wool received here by rail, of which we are unable to obtain any accurate account, which will augment the receipts as given above.

Since the opening of the five great through lines of railway the transportation of this commodity has been divided between these railway lines and the New York canals, the former taking nearly the whole amount moved to eastern markets.

The following table shows the miscellaneous receipts at Buffalo by a comparatively new line—the Buffalo and Lake Huron railroad—connecting with Port Sarnia, at the outlet of Lake Huron:

Statement showing the receipts at Buffalo by the Buffalo and Lake Huron railway for the year ending December 31, 1862.

Articles.		Quantity.	Articles.		Quantity.
Apples, dried	barrels	367	Ginseng	casks	10
Ashes	casks	142	Glassware	package	1
Alcohol	barrels	250	Horses	number	313
Buckwheat	bushels	10	Hogs, live	number	22,687
Beef	barrels	5,181	Hides	number	4,700
Bacon	pounds	7,508,660	Hoop-poles	number	2,969,300
Barley	bushels	112,122	Hogs, dressed	number	4,383
Butter	pounds	224,237	Hemp	bales	109
Boat knees	number	664	Hops	bales	2
Beans	bushels	5,346	Iron	pounds	663,302
Bladders	barrels	10	Lumber	feet	3,985,300
Broom-corn	bales	138	Lard	pounds	4,920,740
Barrels, empty	number	900	Lath	pieces	437,200
Buffalo robes	bales	82	Leather	rolls	7
Beeswax	pounds	100	Lead	pounds	19,600
Copper	barrels	2,096	Mill feed	pounds	161,400
Cheese	pounds	16,650	Molasses	barrels	2
Copper plates	number	570	Nails	kegs	16
Corn meal	barrels	1,926	Nuts	barrels	59
Cloverseed	bushels	2,845	Oatmeal	barrels	90
Cattle	number	16,215	Oats	bushels	4,852
Copper	tons	544	Oil	barrels	42
Corn	bushels	100,209	Onions	bushels	3
Cotton	bales	521	Pork	barrels	11,069
Candles	boxes	361	Peas	bushels	12,387
Cranberries	barrels	28	Potatoes	bushels	71
Cedar posts	number	100	Piles	number	2,340
Deer, dressed	number	32	Pelts	bundles	161
Eggs	barrels	1,046	Rags	sacks	1,314
Flour	barrels	187,402	Railroad ties	number	2,600
Fish	barrels	129	Rye	bushels	2,314
Flax	pounds	7,925	Staves	number	274,800
Flaxseed	bushels	56	Stave bolts	cords	94
Furs	packages	64	Sheep	number	23,140
Feathers	sacks	43	Skins	bundles	973
Grease	pounds	264,400	Sundries	pounds	458,000

Shingles........number..	165,500	Timber.............feet..	9,250
Sheep, dressed...number..	127	Turnips.........bushels..	2
Sheep-pelts.....bundles..	165	Tobacco......hogsheads..	31
Stone............boxes..	80	Tobacco..........boxes..	162
Tallow..........pounds..	249,720	Whiskey........barrels..	2,993
Tow.............bales..	43	Wool.............bales..	1,415
Timothy seed....bushels..	3,677	Wheat.........bushels..	600,719
Tobacco.........barrels..	5	Wood............cords..	144
Tails.............bales..	19		

The preponderance of through freights is large, apparently, though it is impossible to distinguish that originating in Canada from that shipped by lake to Port Sarnia, and thence taking the railroad to Buffalo.

The following is a table of general receipts at Buffalo from the lake in 1862, including the Lake Huron railroad, and it embraces the greatest attainable quantities of miscellaneous western freight sent eastward from the lakes exclusively:

Articles.	Quantity.	Articles.	Quantity.
Ashes, casks.........	3,046	Cider, barrel	1
Alcohol, barrels......	15,580	Cranberries, barrels...	138
Apples, dried, barrels..	846	Copper, packages.....	44
Ale, barrels..........	16	Deer, dressed, No.....	32
Buckwheat, bushels...	10	Eggs, barrels.........	14,173
Bones, sacks.........	5,073	Flour, barrels........	2,846,022
Bones, hogsheads.....	134	Fish, barrels.........	9,647
Bones, tons..........	225	Feathers, sacks.......	247
Boat knees, No.......	901	Flax, pounds.........	7,925
Beeswax, packages....	114	Furs, boxes..........	66
Bread, boxes and barrels	70,361	Flax seed, bushels....	36,812
Beans, bushels......	21,048	Glassware, packages..	6,441
Barrels, empty, No...	5,345	Glass, tons..........	35
Barley, bushels.......	423,124	Grease, pounds.......	1,421,594
Beef, barrels.........	123,301	Glue, packages.......	1,090
Bacon, pounds.......	25,687,657	Grindstones, No......	1,631
Butter, pounds.......	4,119,173	Gunstocks, tons......	3,106
Broomcorn, bales.....	8,839	Gunstocks, barrels....	972
Brick, No...........	5,000	Gunstocks, No.......	35,399
Buffalo robes, No.....	82	Gunstocks, boxes.....	59
Bladders, barrels......	19	Ginseng, packages....	136
Barytes, barrels.....	86	Horses, No..........	445
Broom-handles, No....	5,750	Hogs, live, No........	36,024
Copper, barrels.......	9,077	Hogs, dressed, No....	7,606
Copper, tons.........	2,373	Hoop-poles, No.......	5,867,290
Cedar posts, No......	991	Hoops, No..........	7,977,137
Candles, boxes.......	9,995	Hides, No...........	268,685
Corn, bushels........	24,288,627	Hemp, bales.........	2,301
Corn meal, barrels....	31,268	Hair, bales.........	835
Coal, tons...........	84,523	Horns, sacks.........	5,545
Cattle, No.........	18,938	Hay, bales.........	28
Cheese, pounds.......	1,313,030	Hops, bales..........	316
Cotton, bales.........	7,282	Iron, pounds.........	8,329,811
Clover seed, bushels...	5,047	Iron, pig, tons........	3,163
Copper bars, No......	458	Iron ore, tons........	10,027
Copper, plates........	1,179	Junk, pounds........	28,750
Clay, barrels.........	492	Lead, pounds........	8,535,992

Articles.	Quantity.	Articles.	Quantity.
Lard, pounds........	22,471,204	Rafts, No............	1
Lumber, feet.........	125,289,071	Staves, No	30,410,252
Leather, rolls	3,159	Sundries, pounds	6,869,009
Lath, packs........ ..	959,750	Shingles, No..........	21,782,680
Molasses, barrels......	2	Shooks, bundles......	61,875
Moss, bales..........	50	Skins, bundles.......	1,822
Malt, bushels........	6,730	Stone, tons..........	336
Mill feed, pounds	247,300	Ship-knees, No.......	1,662
Nails, kegs..........	16,490	Ship-knees, tons......	693
Nuts, barrels	184	Sheep, No...........	29,033
Oats, bushels	2,624,932	Steel, pounds	160,220
Oatmeal, barrels & bags	133	Sand, tons	540
Onions, bushels	221	Starch, packages	9,842
Oil-cake, sacks	46,798	Soap, boxes..........	972
Oil-cake, tons........	1,446	Stave-bolts, cords.....	411
Oil-cake, barrels......	459	Saw logs, No	290
Oars, No	298	Salt, barrels	118
Oars, feet............	114,820	Sheep, dressed, No....	127
Oil, barrels	9,862	Stearine, barrels......	72
Oil-cake, pounds......	1,075,650	Stone, boxes.........	80
Potatoes, bushels	18,409	Stone pipe, pieces.....	299
Peas, bushels........	78,266	Tallow, pounds.......	4,363,684
Peaches, bags........	31	Tobacco, hogsheads...	5,269
Provisions, bbls. & t'c's	6,809	Tobacco, barrels......	1,026
Pork, barrels	171,552	Tobacco, boxes	7,261
Paint, barrels........	154	Tobacco, casks.......	1,498
Pickets, No..........	5,490	Tobacco, bats........	785
Plaster, tons	275	Tails, bales..........	19
Pelts, bundles........	824	Timber, cubic feet....	83,000
Piles, No............	24,036	Timothy seed, bushels.	61,278
Paper, bundles	4,167	Tow, bales..........	401
Pike-poles, No.......	70	Wool, bales.	42,619
Paraffine, boxes......	165	Wheat, bushels	30,435,831
Rye, bushels.........	791,564	Wood, cords..... ...	11,978
Rags, sacks..........	8,965	Whiskey, barrels.....	97,673
Railroad ties, No.....	33,615	Wine, packages......	25
Rack-sticks, No......	186,000		

THE EXCHANGE OF GENERAL MERCHANDISE EASTWARD AND WESTWARD AT BUFFALO.

The exchanges at Buffalo, conducted at the terminus of the Erie canal, can only be stated from the form of records kept on the canals, indefinitely classified as "products of the forest," "products of animals," &c. The following is the general statement in this form:

Statement showing the eastward movement of freight from Buffalo, by the Erie canal, for nine years.

Years.	Products of the forest.	Products of animals.	Vegetable food.	Other agricultural products.	Manufactures.	Merchandise.	Other articles.	Total.	Total value.
	Tons.	*Tons.*	*Tons.*	*Tons.*	*Tons.*	*Tons.*	*Tons.*	*Tons.*	
1854..........	134,416	42,750	457,153	5,674	8,505	1,[illegible]	[illegible]	691,816	[illegible]
1855..........	151,994	25,[illegible]	681,044	2,419	7,149	4,457	19,254	[illegible],107	29,[illegible]
1856..........	177,651	10,611	492,138	[illegible]	1,[illegible]	1,040	16,650	664,219	31,870,119
1857..........	146,700	4,[illegible]	387,529	[illegible]	5,804	301	24,191	571,529	16,956,740
1858..........	185,397	23,[illegible]	[illegible],649	2,093	19,184	3,[illegible]	82,497	776,[illegible]	24,[illegible]7,171
1859..........	201,684	14,[illegible]	[illegible],447	1,378	9,553	2,[illegible]	52,363	639,540	24,[illegible],101
1860..........	283,044	3,109	735,849	296	6,018	3,[illegible]	51,769	1,113,754	24,412,[illegible]
1861..........	176,325	4,708	1,323,638	491	18,118	2,438	53,[illegible]	1,579,745	32,300,[illegible]
1862..........	201,919	35,[illegible]	1,575,469	1,189	16,130	3,224	46,523	1,860,9[illegible]	52,424,[illegible]

Statement showing the receipts of westward moving freight at Buffalo, by the Erie canal, for nine years.

Years.	Products of the forest.	Products of animals.	Vegetable food.	Other agricultural products.	Manufactures.	Merchandise.	Other articles.	Total.	Merchandise going to western States and Canada.
	Tons.	*Tons.*	*Tons.*	*Tons.*	*Tons.*	*Tons.*	*Tons.*	*Tons.*	*Tons.*
1854..................	64,105	519	2,219	109	59,118	190,450	80,[illegible]	342,772	167,530
1855..................	54,536	367	8,[illegible]	109	87,749	171,176	77,991	404,[illegible]	115,[illegible]
1856..................	67,794	310	10,347	810	61,473	149,769	85,314	375,[illegible]	114,[illegible]
1857..................	76,046	95	5,473	311	51,088	85,728	100,[illegible]	318,949	74,730
1858..................	46,849	997	4,872	516	55,610	66,301	64,670	218,965	47,350
1859..................	26,[illegible]	291	7,749	340	67,318	85,678	80,[illegible]	249,971	72,707
1860..................	25,[illegible]	93	4,[illegible]	208	60,199	61,152	89,730	246,1[illegible]	74,[illegible]
1861..................	16,013	103	4,779	93	90,088	42,096	86,739	237,[illegible]	55,976
1862..................	23,004	100	6,839	124	121,705	63,218	141,389	353,4[illegible]	....

The shipments of flour and grain by canal, it will be seen, cover the greater share of the receipts before stated, confirming the position assumed, that the receipts and shipments of western produce may be considered as substantially identical.

The following comparative statement shows the shipments of flour and grain by canal from Buffalo for four seasons:

	1862.	1861.	1860.	1856.
Flour......barrels..	451,814	306,236	180,853	220,466
Wheat.....bushels..	27,751,786	23,713,713	13,951,458	6,108,068
Corn ......bushels..	22,487,185	19,112,125	10,306,048	2,159,538
Oats.......bushels..	2,164,776	1,705,395	1,282,646	953,169
Barley .....bushels..	201,744	134,341	130,189	308,626
Rye.......bushels..	653,480	337,764	80,822	124,093
Totals.......	53,258,973	45,003,338	25,751,103	9,713,994

The commercial statements prepared at Buffalo supply the deficiency only for a limited period.

The following is a statement of the quantities of produce of all distinguishable articles sent eastward by the Erie canal from Buffalo:

General exports from Buffalo eastward by canal.

Articles.	1860.	1861.	1862.
Ashes ....casks....	1,376	1,156	1,059
Lumber ....feet....	91,602,567	33,343,470	68,327,978
Timber ....hundred cubic feet....	47,802	19,401	14,570
Staves ....pounds....	264,538,920	234,760,706	207,357,627
Pork ....barrels....	5,406	4,290	128,421
Beef ....do....	6,400	17,341	55,826
Bacon ....pounds....	4,452	212,416	4,242,493
Cheese ....do....	754,289	58,955	60,228
Butter ....do....	160,418	80,671	103,907
Lard ....do....	100,660	682,778	6,549,454
Wool ....do....	1,079,942	1,228,394	1,371,068
Hides ....do....	79,431	173,141	426,063
Flour ....do....	180,853	390,236	451,814
Wheat ....bushels....	13,951,458	23,713,713	27,751,768
Rye ....do....	50,804	282,724	653,490
Corn ....do....	13,306,048	10,112,125	22,447,185
Barley ....do....	130,199	134,341	201,744
Oats ....do....	1,292,646	1,705,325	2,164,778
Bran, &c. ....pounds....	3,921,731	5,106,140	8,209,674
Peas and beans ....bushels....	62,215	69,874	58,692
Dried fruit ....pounds....	3,534	602,968	11,770
Cotton ....do....	....	....	2,380
Potatoes ....bushels....	117	19,601	1,250
Tobacco ....pounds....	21,153	781,663	680,550
Hemp ....do....	90,412	10,325	....
Seed ....do....	158,839	122,455	473,981
Flax seed ....do....	235,328	80,900	1,170,819
Hops ....do....	6,384	2,219	337
Domestic spirits ....gallons....	631,180	1,631,600	1,520,280
Leather ....pounds....	30,172	44,227	14,489
Furniture ....do....	332,175	800,456	238,474
Lead ....do....	6,159,048	10,329,630	....
Pig iron ....do....	4,000	708,000	9,551,668
Bloom and bar iron ....do....	....	....	2,700,921
Castings, &c. ....do....	70,234	128,961	358,907
Domestic salt ....do....	16,700	12,560	12,800
Iron and steel ....do....	2,403,845	2,377,118	6,147,357
Railroad iron ....do....	317,830	....	....
Crockery and glassware ....do....	808,075	180,277	141,304
All other merchandise ....do....	1,390,414	1,177,092	1,418,776
Stone, lime, clay ....do....	146,543	2,841,076	9,185,378
Coal ....do....	71,872,850	76,060,650	57,894,000
Copper ore ....do....	6,587,812	6,446,540	6,285,308
Sundries ....do....	18,840,172	22,580,534	19,075,081
Oil meal ....do....	....	10,196,705	7,814,119
Molasses ....do....	....	156,500	1,843
Nails, spikes, &c. ....do....	....	1,070,101	2,731,628

The following approximate calculation of values for this eastward freight sustains the estimate of total values made in the report of the State auditor of New York. That report gives the sum of $72,131,136 as the value of property "from other States" going eastward on the canal in 1862. It is here shown that nearly the sum of $60,000,000 in value left Buffalo, and it is clear that the other points of receipts of canal freight—Tonawanda, Black Rock, and Oswego—would add $12,000,000 to $15,000,000 in addition.

Calculation of values of eastward freight by canal from Buffalo in 1862.

Ashes, casks, 1,059, at $10 per cask	$10,590
Lumber, feet, 88,327,978, at $15 per M	1,324,920
Timber, cubic feet, 1,475,000, at $20 per M	29,500
Staves, tons, 148,678, at $30 per ton	4,460,340
Pork, barrels, 126,421, at $15 per barrel	1,896,315
Beef, barrels, 53,826, at $10 per barrel	538,260
Bacon, pounds, 4,242,493, at 10 cents per pound	424,246
Cheese, pounds, 80,238, at 10 cents per pound	8,023
Butter, pounds, 103,807, at 15 cents per pound	15,571
Lard, pounds, 6,549,454, at 10 cents per pound	654,945
Wool, pounds, 1,371,098, at 60 cents per pound	822,659
Hides, pounds, 486,003, at 10 cents per pound	48,600
Flour, barrels, 451,814, at $6 per barrel	2,710,884
Wheat, bushels, 27,751,786, at $1 10 per bushel	30,526,964
Rye, bushels, 653,480, at 70 cents per bushel	477,436
Corn, bushels, 22,487,185, at 50 cents per bushel	11,243,592
Barley, bushels, 201,744, at $1 per bushel	201,744
Oats, bushels, 2,164,778, at 45 cents per bushel	974,150
Bran, bushels, 5,299,674, at 20 cents per bushel	1,059,935
Peas and beans, bushels, 58,682, at $1 per bushel	58,682
Dried fruit, pounds, 11,770, at 10 cents per pound	1,177
Cotton, pounds, 2,320, at 60 cents per pound	1,392
Potatoes, bushels, 1,250, at 50 cents per bushel	625
Tobacco, pounds, 680,550, at 25 cents per pound	170,140
Seeds, pounds, 473,891, at $3 per bushel	23,694
Flax seed, pounds, 1,170,819, at 4 cents per pound	46,233
Hops, pounds, 357, at 25 cents per pound	90
Spirits, gallons, 1,520,280, at 33⅓ cents per gallon	506,760
Leather, pounds, 14,429, at 25 cents per pound	3,607
Furniture, pounds, 238,474	10,000
Pig iron, pounds, 9,551,666, at $50 per ton	238,791
Bloom and bar iron, pounds, 2,700,921, at $70 per ton	94,538
Castings, pounds, 368,907, at 5 cents per pound	18,445
Salt, pounds, 12,600	200
Iron and steel, pounds, 6,147,357, at 10 cents per pound	614,735
Crockery, pounds, 141,304, at 10 cents per pound	14,130
Merchandise, pounds, 1,418,776, at 20 cents per pound	283,755
Stone, lime, and clay, tons, 4,593, at $10 per ton	45,930
Coal, tons, 28,947, at $7 per ton	192,629
Copper ore, pounds, 6,283,308, at 5 cents per pound	314,165
Sundries, pounds, 19,675,081, at 10 cents per pound	1,967,508
Oil-cake, tons, 3,607, at $50 per ton	180,350
Molasses, pounds, 1,843, at 10 cents per pound	184
Nails and spikes, pounds, 2,731,636, at 10 cents per pound	273,164
Total value	62,489,643

The following statement gives the detail of articles brought westward to Buffalo by the Erie canal for three years:

Imports into Buffalo by the Erie canal, 1860 to 1862.

Articles.	1860.	1861.	1862.
Lumber.... ....feet....	277,055	391,381	119,797
Timber........ ......hundred cubic feet....	20,988	11,470	145,891
Staves..............................pounds....	691,000	1,101,000	....
Wood......... ....cords....	9,075	5,214	5,743
Cheese..............................pounds....	4,600	650	916
Hides................ ....do......	137,843	189,258	193,503
Flour ....barrels....	3,867	2,788	521
Wheat...............................bushels....	24,108	40,049	3,103
Rye.................................do......	24,116	6,416	....
Corn ....do......	64,623	60,700	403
Barley ....do......	24,208	3,900	....
Oats ....do......	9,734	9,739	....
Bran, &c............................pounds....	111,500	370,000	228,586
Beans and peas.................bushels....	448	....	....
Potatoes............................do......	10,237	3,368	7,374
Dried fruit....... ....pounds....	261,354	2,607	250,311
Hops........ ....do......	385,864	108,740	84,440
Domestic spirits...... ....gallons....	102,800	161,547	11,858
Leather.............................pounds....	19,414	18,630	1,108,883
Furniture...........................do......	1,295,857	1,307,473	1,894,764
Pig iron............................do......	13,708,369	9,272,612	13,976,076
Castings, &c........................do......	11,425,929	9,500,758	12,251,949
Domestic cottons....................do......	5,065	....	660,235
Domestic salt.......................do......	92,949,229	159,191,278	177,680,435
Foreign salt........................do......	112,563	46,015	32,901,873
Sugar...............................do......	31,179,408	11,518,608	27,581,579
Molasses............................do......	16,159,122	5,059,570	8,438,769
Coffee..............................do......	2,848,048	2,029,795	1,979,114
Nails, spikes, &c...................do......	2,772,372	1,217,763	2,015,039
Iron and steel......................do......	13,621,529	6,204,029	4,982,421
Railroad iron.......................do......	3,803,857	1,584,353	6,747,043
Crockery and glassware..............do......	4,295,601	3,053,289	4,824,801
All other merchandise...............do......	93,652,751	49,488,651	69,359,473
Stone, lime, &c.....................do......	42,838,446	25,655,619	96,659,568
Gypsum..............................do......	573,550	392,700	....
Coal................................do......	68,259,212	134,788,740	193,544,618
Sundries............................do......	27,785,110	19,710,181	18,248,179
Iron ore............................do......	....	....	46,188,633

The following is an addendum comparing the grain receipts at Buffalo for 1863 with 1862:

Deficiency in wheat, as compared with..........	1862	9,195,483	bushels.
" " corn, " "	1862	4,201,675	"
" " rye, " "	1862	369,275	"
Increase in 1863 in flour, " "	1862	132,067	barrels.
" " " " "	1861	618,498	"
Deficiency in totals of grain, as compared with	1862	8,190,498	bushels.
" " " "	1861	3,206,433	"

LAKE TRADE AT TORONTO, CANADA.

The relation held by towns and ports of Canada to the general lake trade, and particularly to the movement of flour, grain and produce eastward, is one of the most interesting and important branches of inquiry into its character. The statistics of many of these points are, however, difficult, if not impossible of collection. The trade is irregular as well as large, and it is often through points of mere transit, along new lines of railroad, or of propeller shipment on the lakes. The principal feature apparent at the outset is the general tendency to return to the United States markets all along the frontier, and even from Montreal.

The following table gives the quantities and destination of the leading exports from Toronto for a series of years:

Exports of flour and wheat from Toronto, and destination.

Destination.	1857.		1858.		1859.	
	Flour.	Wheat.	Flour.	Wheat.	Flour.	Wheat.
	Barrels.	*Bushels.*	*Barrels.*	*Bushels.*	*Barrels.*	*Bushels.*
Oswego	27, 703	163, 584	15, 150	257, 088	16, 617	290, 300
Ogdensburg	35, 721	130, 550	8, 746	100, 156	12, 357	109, 353
Cape Vincent	17, 169	102, 261	853	100, 294	1, 148	145, 249
Rochester	8, 235	30, 641	1, 922	31, 664	......	67, 180
Montreal	34, 371	84, 502	70, 815	67, 557	20, 310	13, 770
Quebec	11, 400	6, 825	9, 250	11, 010	1, 955	8, 774
Other ports	23, 621	44, 229	15, 980	14, 817	4, 633	25, 021
Total	182, 478	533, 622	114, 385	579, 833	72, 523	570, 514

Exports of flour and wheat from Toronto, and destination—Continued.

Destination.	1860.		1861.		1862.	
	Flour.	Wheat.	Flour.	Wheat.	Flour.	Wheat.
	Barrels.	*Bushels.*	*Barrels.*	*Bushels.*	*Barrels.*	*Bushels.*
Oswego	21, 812	514, 108	30, 529	395, 412	10, 627	271, 380
Ogdensburg	20, 540	60, 146	26, 473	68, 015	8, 745	7, 586
Cape Vincent	4, 788	141, 961	3, 657	70, 220	2, 524	106, 234
Rochester	......	67, 806	179	8, 368	421	8, 925
Montreal	40, 341	234, 171	89, 320	547, 470	70, 959	451, 917
Quebec	7, 300	5, 654	6, 844	93, 274	645	17, 740
Other ports	72, 429	169, 129	6, 021	119, 176	12, 404	36, 389
Total	178, 310	1, 192, 417	163, 727	1, 098, 639	108, 174	933, 973

The following is a more detailed statement for 1862.

It is apparent that the larger amounts, up to the close of 1860, were sent to United States ports, from Rochester to Cape Vincent, since which year Montrea was the leading destination. As an average, the division is nearly equal between the United States and Canada, outward.

The origin of these quantities is not clearly stated, but it is probable that a share was western State produce, previously entering Canada at Sarnia, the Welland canal or elsewhere, since Toronto appears as a point of destination in many of the statements for western shipping cities.

MONTREAL.

The produce and grain trade of Montreal also exhibits return shipments to the United States at Portland and Boston, though probably all for further export across the Atlantic. The imports to Montreal of flour and grain in 1862; and the exports to all points, are given in the following statement by the trade and commerce report of that city:

Imports of flour by Grand Trunk railroad	405,553	barrels
" " Montreal and Champlain	196	"
" " Lachine canal	735,529	"
Total	1,141,278	"
Milled in the city	220,981	"
Total receipts for the year	1,362,259	"

Shipments of flour direct from Montreal	626,070	barrels.
" " via Portland and Boston	66,123	"
Exports down the river	226,177	"
Total exports	918,370	"

The exports of wheat show a still larger proportionate diversion to Portland and Boston, undoubtedly for foreign export.

Imports of wheat by Grand Trunk railroad	673,779	bushels.
" " " Lachine canal	7,952,782	"
Total	8,626,561	"

Exports of wheat via St. Lawrence	6,538,053	bushels
" " " Portland and Boston	478,595	"
" " to river ports	199,482	"
Total exports	7,216,030	"

[The Montreal Herald's annual review of the trade and commerce of Montreal for 1863.]

Exports of flour, grain, and produce from Montreal.

Articles.	SHIPMENTS IN 1861.			SHIPMENTS IN 1862.		
	By river St. Lawrence.	By Lachine canal.	Total.	By river St. Lawrence.	By Lachine canal.	Total.
Flour ...... barrels.	605,492	10,341	616,[illegible]	597,477	28,593	626,070
Wheat .... bushels.	5,584,727	17,044	5,601,771	6,500,796	37,257	6,538,053
Peas .... do...	1,529,136	2,029	1,531,165	711,191	1,628	712,819
Barley ...... do...	2,472	105	2,577	373	84	457
Oats .... do...	276,375	2,800	279,175	8,072	16,716	24,788
Oatmeal .... barrels.	25,158	....	25,158	4,040	963	5,003
Corn ...... bushels.	1,477,114	....	1,477,114	1,774,546	....	1,774,546
Ashes ...... barrels.	22,147	244	22,391	23,135	700	23,835
Butter .... kegs.	49,540	170	49,522	59,801	....	59,801
Pork .... barrels.	626	2,677	3,303	3,225	4,581	7,806
Lard .... do...	178	....	178	455	17	472
Beef.. tcs. and bbls.	1,618	....	1,618	222	....	222
Tallow ..... barrels.	112	28	140	154	35	189

Flour and grain trade of Montreal compared for three years, 1861 to 1863.

Articles.	1861.		1862.		1863.	
	Receipts.	Shipments.	Receipts.	Shipments.	Receipts.	Shipments.
Wheat ...... bushels.	7,829,684	5,010,100	8,589,029	6,045,815	5,606,324	3,806,306
Corn .... do...	1,565,477	1,477,114	1,661,011	1,774,347	855,328	655,387
Oats .... do...	192,390	287,877	96,792	8,072	373,063	3,001,766
Peas .... do...	1,400,850	1,409,859	634,679	727,277	....	....
Barley .... do...	132,749	2,457	236,930	373	204,324	640,390
Rye .... do...	24,812	....	92,665	200	32,278	170
Flour .... barrels.	1,081,160	654,906	168,174	632,052	1,173,096	692,868
Meal, oat and corn. do.	21,221	32,015	2,436	4,039	1,760	9,353

RECEIPTS AT OSWEGO.

The receipts of flour and grain at Oswego have been very large for many years, but no great quantity of provisions or miscellaneous western produce arrives there from the lakes. The following are the receipts of grain, in totals, by each of the leading routes bringing freight to that port, for 1862 and 1863:

Total receipts of grain at Oswego in 1862 and 1863.

	1862.	1863.
	Bushels.	*Bushels.*
Welland canal..................................	11,367,609	9,043,613
Welland railway................................	2,071,914	1,717,371
Buffalo and Lake Huron railway.................	1,296,601	292,635
Collingwood....................................	237,273	130,957
Lake Ontario...................................	1,885,517	2,634,385

The following is the detail of different grains received by different routes in 1863:

Routes.	Wheat.	Corn.	Oats.	Barley.	Rye.
	Bushels.	*Bushels.*	*Bushels.*	*Bushels.*	*Bushels.*
By Welland canal...........	7,037,253	1,810,800	48,515	93,837	52,192
Welland railway...........	900,053	720,460	58,600	29,259	....
Lake Huron and Buffalo railway...............	161,984	123,533	....	....	7,118
Collingwood............	107,548	21,449	....	....	....
Canadian lines..........	8,215,778	2,676,242	107,151	123,096	59,310
Lake Ontario...........	569,647	125	325,996	1,701,572	57,045
Total receipts.........	8,785,425	2,676,367	433,147	1,824,667	116,355

SUMMARY OF THE GENERAL MOVEMENT EASTWARD OF FLOUR AND GRAIN.

The summary of movement eastward in flour and grain having been made up with care in the Buffalo Board of Trade Report for 1862, for years preceding as well as including that particularly examined in this report, that statement will first be considered. It includes several points at which no regular reports have been made in any published or accessible form, and there is reason to accept them in most cases as sufficiently close approximations.

Statement showing the quantities of flour and grain sent eastward from the lake regions, comprising Ohio, Indiana, Michigan, Illinois, Wisconsin, Iowa, Minnesota, and Canada West, 1856 to 1862.

Received at—	1856.				1857.				1858.				1859.	
	Flour.	Wheat.	Corn.	Other grain.	Flour.	Wheat.	Corn.	Other grain.	Flour.	Wheat.	Corn.	Other grain.	Flour.	Wheat.
	Barrels.	Bushels.	Bushels.	Bushels.	Barrels.	Bushels.	Bushels.	Bushels.	Barrels.	Bushels.	Bushels.	Bushels.	Barrels.	Bushels.
West terminus of—														
Baltimore and Ohio railroad	469,797	....	....	417,100	428,403	....	....	338,163	682,314	....	....	330,878	485,482	17,080
Pennsylvania Central railroad	213,088	....	....	403,878	384,011	....	....	216,793	430,088	....	....	820,083	340,080	....
Dunkirk	350,088	....	....	....	334,073	83,423	114,638	....	351,007	168,449	94,870	94,983	438,080	867,083
Buffalo	1,011,189	8,465,471	9,632,177	2,025,319	923,411	8,392,815	5,730,413	1,381,466	1,614,330	10,735,300	5,431,098	2,788,076	1,502,198	9,559,928
Suspension Bridge	304,329	....	....	800,643	160,104	148,138	....	....	180,410	892,484	....	....	41,376	57,688
Oswego	802,930	8,392,378	3,590,211	810,992	101,363	5,332,038	2,003,893	379,949	83,730	6,579,438	2,913,610	1,888,494	84,943	4,873,088
Ogdensburg	334,864	610,837	377,975	37,478	381,670	319,360	317,070	14,740	381,054	790,178	730,878	44,108	594,683	308,010
Cape Vincent	63,033	403,893	43,087	50,045	80,478	477,373	60,537	40,419	72,833	410,191	40,080	138,401	9,308	688,738
Montreal	712,630	1,046,330	637,989	67,328	637,038	1,718,963	353,163	38,365	654,173	1,389,480	165,087	138,537	597,863	838,900
Rochester	....	....	....	....	....	....	....	....	7,110	278,618	....	9,863	1,784	416,088
Totals eastward	3,885,448	19,335,330	14,289,632	4,388,685	3,387,604	16,783,683	8,779,638	2,256,844	4,489,613	21,643,838	10,485,334	8,035,087	2,789,574	16,085,709

Statement showing the quantities of flour and grain sent eastward from the lake regions, &c.—Continued.

Received at—	1859.		1860.				1861.				1862.			
	Corn.	Other grain.	Flour.	Wheat.	Corn.	Other grain.	Flour.	Wheat.	Corn.	Other grain.	Flour.	Wheat.	Corn.	Other grain.
	Bushels.	Bushels.	Barrels.	Bushels.	Bushels.	Bushels.	Barrels.	Bushels.	Bushels.	Bushels.	Barrels.	Bushels.	Bushels.	Bushels.
West terminus of—														
Baltimore and Ohio railroad	....	156,486	358,413	....	....	128,380	970,089	....	....	80,000	*880,000	....	....	*550,000
Pennsylvania Central railroad	....	130,000	459,080	....	....	664,160	1,045,038	....	....	1,948,256	891,038	....	....	1,088,088
Dunkirk	77,916	14,400	542,765	800,898	644,081	8,843	718,329	604,381	870,408	7,178	1,085,388	112,688	149,654	16,178
Buffalo	3,151,387	1,683,140	1,138,335	18,808,048	11,386,837	1,631,980	2,138,891	27,108,379	21,024,637	8,532,770	2,848,082	30,435,833	24,838,687	3,843,088
Suspension Bridge	....	73,348	630,000	....	....	1,073,080	754,915	....	....	2,073,948	*873,081	....	....	*3,730,089
Oswego	804,645	1,342,010	131,185	9,449,461	4,988,928	8,043,535	117,087	8,809,475	8,502,799	1,785,813	825,347	10,978,138	4,888,985	1,457,013
Ogdensburg	688,518	64,705	88,940	873,678	23,380	188,507	441,898	677,380	1,119,304	85,088	576,374	689,928	1,120,176	18,988
Cape Vincent	80,105	316,435	949,800	863,058	657,016	44,311	63,487	878,810	194,411	104,398	48,578	816,483	192,384	48,047
Montreal	71,430	834,638	818,309	2,808,738	138,814	913,648	837,388	7,330,555	1,316,767	1,504,807	†1,191,433	†18,018,773	†12,848,128	†1,319,930
Rochester	....	8,800	5,250	415,785	....	10,730	*2,300	*580,618	....	*30,798	*2,082	*130,000	....	*6,088
Totals eastward	4,423,088	4,264,031	4,108,057	32,334,301	18,683,778	9,712,082	4,533,880	46,364,144	39,304,828	19,048,113	4,388,890	50,480,130	31,085,985	10,044,130

* Estimated. † To December 4 only, as per report of Montreal Gazette. The *Witness* says the total receipts of breadstuffs, in bushels, were 28,887,791 in 1862, and the exports were 16,762,685 bushels.

The percentage of the total carried by each of the several lines is given by the same authority, as follows:

Table showing the per cent. of receipts at the principal receiving points for six years from 1857 to 1862, inclusive of the foregoing eastward movement.

Locality.	1857.	1858.	1859.	1860.	1861.	1862.
Buffalo	44.8	47.1	50.0	47.9	51.6	53.4
Oswego	16.3	19.2	17.1	21.7	15.5	13.3
Montreal	11.8	9.9	8.7	9.2	12.6	12.3
W. Ter. R. & O. R. R.	5.3	6.5	5.7	2.4	3.0	2.9
Ogdensburg	6.9	6.0	5.8	3.5	3.4	3.4
West Ter. Pa. C. R. R	4.3	4.3	4.2	3.9	4.1	4.4
Dunkirk	4.4	3.4	5.6	4.9	3.8	4.3
Suspension Bridge	2.3	2.0	0.7	6.5	5.4	5.3
Cape Vincent	1.9	1.8	1.3	0.8	0.6	0.7
Rochester	....	0.5	0.9	0.6	0.1	0.0
	100.0	100.0	100.0	100.0	100.0	100.0

The following is a comparison of total quantities of flour and grain moved eastward for seven years, to 1862:

Table showing the variations in the movement eastward from 1856 to 1862.

	Flour.	Wheat.	Corn.	Other grain.
1856	3,665,449	19,506,358	14,292,039	4,593,589
1857	3,397,954	16,763,195	6,779,832	2,256,914
1858	4,499,013	21,843,650	10,495,654	5,085,097
1859	3,760,274	16,865,709	4,403,030	5,264,051
1860	4,106,157	33,334,391	18,075,778	7,719,038
1861	6,531,069	46,384,144	29,624,028	10,656,116
1862	6,339,910	50,699,130	32,965,925	10,844,939

Reducing the flour to bushels of wheat, the following table will show the total eastward movement, in bushels, and the receipts at Buffalo for the years indicated;

	Total eastward movement.	Receipt at Buffalo.	Buffalo per cent. of total movement.
1856	57,707,769	26,270,791	45.5
1857	44,789,851	20,072,040	44.8
1858	60,672,546	28,219,855	47.1
1859	44,354,225	22,215,485	50.0
1860	78,652,443	37,130,461	47.9
1861	119,264,233	61,460,601	51.5
1862	136,329,549	72,704,169	53.4

GENERAL TABLES OF THE TONNAGE AND TRANSPORTATION OF THE ERIE CANAL.

Capacity, passages, and aggregate carriage of Erie canal boats eastward.

Years.	Average cargo of boat.	Days' time between Buffalo and Albany.	Toll & freight on a barrel of flour.	Tons delivered at tide-water from the Erie canal.
1841	41	9	$0 71	532,520
1844	49	7½	60	799,816
1847	67	10½	77	1,431,252
1848	71	9	58	1,184,337
1849	68	8½	50	1,266,724
1850	76	9	68	1,554,675
1851	78	8½	49	1,508,677
1852	80	9	53	1,644,699
1853	84	9	66	1,851,438
1854	94	8½	59	1,702,693
1855	92	8½	52	1,420,715
1856	100	8½	60	1,587,130
1857	100	8½	46	1,117,199
1858	126	8½	34	1,406,087
1859*	143	8½	31	1,451,333
1860	140	8½	42	2,270,061
1861	157	8½	40	2,449,609
1862	167	8½	48	2,917,094

Quantities of flour, distinguishing western and New York reaching tide-water through the Erie canal.

Years.	Barrels from west'n States.	Barrels from New York.	Barrels arriving at tide-water.	Price.
1837	284,909	747,676	1,032,578	$9 50
1838	552,283	637,036	1,189,319	8 60
1839	683,509	425,544	1,109,053	6 60
1840	1,068,616	1,080,044	2,148,659	4 84
1841	1,239,587	690,057	1,929,644	6 00
1842	1,146,292	543,064	1,776,061	5 18
1843	1,569,045	670,532	2,239,177	4 86
1844	1,727,714	746,939	2,474,653	4 50
1845	1,653,740	1,288,416	2,942,156	5 57
1846	2,723,474	929,330	3,652,804	5 05
1847	3,059,232	701,106	4,760,338	6 84
1848	2,981,028	770,114	3,753,808	5 68
1849	2,849,821	888,938	3,738,759	5 00
1850	3,084,958	905,277	3,990,235	5 00
1851	3,496,734	496,407	3,991,901	4 00
1852	3,937,356	677,731	4,615,087	4 63
1853	3,092,289	957,984	4,050,273	5 77
1854	1,646,901	367,858	1,954,213	9 25
1855	2,096,780	*	2,375,415	9 76
1856	3,240,741	976,034	3,465,775	7 60
1857	2,247,092	*	1,985,288	6 53
1858	3,778,009	*	3,563,901	5 50
1859	2,210,030	*	1,925,408	5 70
1860	4,344,387	737,321	5,081,708	5 75
1861	6,712,233	745,023	7,457,256	5 50
1862	7,616,387	743,693	8,360,080	6 00

* The arrival at tide-water in three years, being less than the quantity from western States, is proof of one of two things—either that none of the surplus product of this State came by the canal in those years, or that, if it did, its place was supplied from the west.

Tonnage of wheat and flour eastward to the Hudson river on the Erie canal, with the points of shipment, and the total value.

Years.	From Buffalo.	From Black Rock and Tonawanda.	From Oswego.	From way stations.	Total tonnage.	Total value.
	Tons.	*Tons.*	*Tons.*	*Tons.*		
1837..........	27,206	....	7,429	81,856	116,491	$9,640,156
1838..........	57,977	....	10,010	65,053	133,040	9,893,698
1839..........	60,082	7,627	15,108	41,796	124,063	7,217,841
1840..........	86,573	12,825	15,075	121,389	244,862	10,302,688
1841..........	106,271	24,843	16,677	53,509	201,300	10,165,354
1842..........	107,628	13,035	14,338	63,336	198,231	9,124,778
1843..........	140,180	12,882	25,858	63,914	248,760	10,223,454
1844..........	145,510	15,069	42,293	74,391	277,863	11,211,677
1845..........	118,614	17,066	44,560	140,223	320,463	16,068,859
1846..........	247,880	16,504	63,905	91,037	419,306	18,838,412
1847..........	380,053	18,480	87,329	65,334	551,205	32,890,928
1848..........	253,325	10,376	90,411	68,529	431,641	21,148,491
1849..........	229,083	22,106	119,201	63,064	434,444	19,308,698
1850..........	206,457	38,071	131,473	81,780	401,781	20,218,188
1851..........	229,668	48,773	146,204	33,121	457,624	16,487,852
1852..........	240,362	65,208	182,434	82,778	570,772	22,664,858
1853..........	219,868	68,401	247,631	87,058	613,858	30,034,871
1854..........	116,468	18,457	72,975	33,755	240,655	18,498,377
1855..........	219,111	15,109	124,004	....	302,125	23,163,691
1856..........	233,900	4,573	222,542	15,070	475,385	29,008,973
1857..........	200,727	4,007	104,322	....	263,141	14,043,681
1858..........	322,174	8,051	174,674	....	454,801	19,632,087
1859..........	208,854	8,970	93,345	....	250,872	9,970,409
1860..........	438,070	29,915	249,829	....	710,178	29,087,687
1861..........	744,484	10,571	277,679	21,561	1,064,295	42,800,199
1862..........	881,330	2,174	276,287	17,538	1,177,329	50,160,617

Statement of the tonnage and value of merchandise going to other States by way of Buffalo and Oswego, in each year, from 1836 to 1862, both inclusive.

Years.	Value.	Buffalo.	Oswego.	Total.	Value.
	Per lb.	*Tons.*	*Tons.*	*Tons.*	
1836	$0 12½	30,874	8,019	38,893	$8,723,850
1837	12½	22,270	3,061	25,331	6,329,750
1838	12½	32,047	2,642	34,689	8,657,250
1839	15	29,699	4,438	34,137	10,259,100
1840	16	18,863	3,193	22,056	7,057,920
1841	18	25,551	5,489	31,040	11,174,400
1842	15	20,625	3,638	24,063	7,218,900
1843	17½	32,798	4,537	37,335	13,067,250
1844	17½	32,767	9,648	42,415	14,845,250
1845	17½	37,713	11,905	49,618	17,366,300
1846	17½	44,487	16,540	58,380	20,415,506
1847	18	57,290	18,843	76,850	27,298,800
1848	18	64,428	20,444	84,872	30,553,920
1849	18	68,020	20,287	88,316	31,793,400
1850	18	79,405	35,091	144,496	41,218,560
1851	18	99,918	74,981	174,899	62,963,640
1852	18	143,787	76,012	219,709	79,127,640
1853	18	163,198	98,560	261,758	94,230,720
1854	18	107,550	64,329	231,879	83,476,440
1855	18	145,530	74,878	220,408	79,367,760
1856	18	114,696	68,817	183,513	66,064,680
1857	18	74,733	43,393	118,126	42,525,360
1858	18	47,350	29,540	76,890	27,680,400
1859	18	72,767	26,109	98,876	35,595,360
1860	18	72,930	47,652	119,682	43,085,520
1861	18	35,278	17,184	52,462	18,886,320
1862	18	52,945	18,094	71,039	25,574,040

Statement of the estimated value of property coming from, and merchandise going to, other States than New York, by way of Buffalo, Black Rock, Tonawanda, and Oswego, from 1836 to 1862, both inclusive.

Years.	Products coming from.	Merchandise going to.	Total.
1836	$5,493,816	$9,723,250	$15,217,066
1837	4,813,626	6,322,750	11,136,376
1838	6,380,045	8,657,250	15,036,895
1839	7,164,908	10,359,100	17,516,008
1840	7,877,359	7,057,600	14,934,958
1841	11,880,273	11,174,400	23,054,673
1842	9,215,808	7,218,900	16,434,708
1843	11,937,943	13,067,250	25,005,193
1844	16,875,558	14,844,250	27,720,808
1845	14,182,129	17,366,300	31,520,529
1846	20,471,940	20,415,500	40,887,439
1847	32,608,324	27,298,800	59,905,124
1848	23,245,353	30,553,920	53,799,273
1849	28,713,798	31,793,400	60,507,198
1850, Tonawanda included	25,339,605	41,272,491	66,612,096
1851	27,007,149	63,660,440	90,668,589
1852	37,041,390	79,127,640	116,169,030
1853	42,357,564	94,230,720	136,588,284
1854	39,346,283	83,476,440	122,822,723
1855	43,565,243	79,870,680	123,435,923
1856	38,043,813	66,061,680	104,105,493
1857	20,466,121	48,525,360	68,991,481
1858	35,182,406	24,891,063	60,073,469
1859	24,484,412	35,590,360	60,074,779
1860	42,915,046	45,154,114	88,069,160
1861	49,405,375	18,886,320	68,291,695
1862	72,131,136	25,674,040	97,706,176

COMMERCE OF THE PACIFIC COAST.

Since the era of gold discovery in the mountain ranges which girdle the whole Pacific coast, the United States, England, and Russia have made nearly equal advances in colonization in that quarter of the world. England is firmly planted in the Australian colonies and British Columbia; Russia has annexed Manchooria and the island of Saghalien, which, with her possessions in America, almost constitute a dominion of the North Pacific ocean; California and Oregon, with the settlements converging to the harbors of San Francisco and Puget's sound, have become an important section of the United States; and France probably finds a motive for Mexican intervention in the circumstance that her power in the New Pacific World is limited to the Society Islands and the recent successful crusade in Cochin China.

A review of these results of Pacific colonization will be the best illustration of existing and prospective commerce.

THE AUSTRALIAN COLONIES OF ENGLAND.

The statistics of the Australian colony of Victoria and of the State of California present many analogies.

At the commencement of the golden era in Victoria, 1851, the wool-created colony of Victoria contained 77,345 people who owned 6,032,783 sheep, 378,806 head of cattle, and 21,219 horses, and the wool-created city of Melbourne had a population of 25,000 souls. In eleven years the population of Victoria, under the gold impulse, has increased to 550,000; the average exports and imports are, respectively, £12,000,000, and the population of the city and suburbs of Melbourne has increased to 136,000.

In 1849 California had a population not exceeding 75,000; its industry and production were pastoral, the chief export being the hides of cattle; and San Francisco was an insignificant seaport. In 1864 the population of California and its colony, the Territory of Nevada, cannot be less than 500,000, and the average exports and imports are, respectively, $55,000,000 per annum.

The average annual exports of treasure from Victoria and California since 1854 have closely approximated, being nearly $40,000,000 annually. In both countries the aggregates have decreased with the diversion of labor to agriculture and manufactures. In Victoria, the culminating point was in 1856, when the export of gold was 2,985,696 ounces, of the value of £12,000,000; and the least export has been during 1863, viz., 1,634,377 ounces, of the value of £6,537,508. In California, the greatest annual export was, in 1853, $57,331,034, while, for the last two years, California alone has not exported more than $35,000,000 per annum.

The entire gold product of Australia and New Zealand stood, in 1862, as follows:

Victoria	1,711,508 ounces.
New South Wales	584,519 ounces.
New Zealand	445,902 ounces.
	2,741,929 ounces.

Or nearly as much as Victoria alone produced in 1856. So with California. When credited with the production of Nevada, Oregon and British Columbia, which the course of trade brings to California for exportation to different parts of the world, the aggregate retains and even exceeds the amount recorded in 1853; but California, like Victoria, has found more productive industries than gold mining.

Both countries now produce an immense number of consumable articles which they used formerly to import and pay for with gold. A summary of these new sources of value in Victoria is compiled from the London Statistical Journal, for December, 1863. In 1856, the year of the greatest production of gold, the colony had only 115,135 acres in cultivation; in 1862, 540,000 acres. The crop of wheat has increased from 1,148,011 bushels in 1856, to 4,152,000 bushels in 1862, with a saving of 60 per cent. in price. Oats increased from 614,679 to 2,033,692 bushels, with a gain in reduction of price of £400,000. The same comparison extends to all agricultural productions—the local supply now effecting a saving of gold export in lesser articles of £5,000,000.

Great changes may be anticipated from the success of the vine and tobacco cultivation. In 1843 four acres were planted by a Swiss vigneron, near Geelong. In 1862 there were 1,464 acres planted with 3,818,355 vines, (one-half only in bearing condition,) from which 16,972 cwt. of grapes were sold, and 47,568 gallons of wine manufactured. In 1862, 920 acres were planted to tobacco, yielding 2,552 cwt.

The successful manufactures of Victoria are machinery for mines, carriages, refined sugar, spirits, woollens, ale, furniture, soap, candles, biscuits, brick and tiles, cement and lime, leather, hats and caps, iron rolling mills, jewelry, paper bags and pasteboard boxes for tradesmen.

The bank circulation for 1862 was £1,605,253.

In railroad construction Victoria is in advance of California. At the close of 1863 the colony had 351 miles of railroad in operation, constructed by the government, and yielding a revenue of £433,615, against £297,949 in 1862, when the total mileage in operation was only 220 miles. Mr. H. S. Chapman, of Melbourne, one year ago, (in January, 1863,) wrote as follows on this interesting subject (see London Statistical Journal for 1863, p. 439:) "In the early part of 1862, the railway from Geelong to Ballarat was opened, but the double line not being completed, the department was not in a condition to carry goods to any extent. In October the Melbourne and Murray River line was opened to Sandhurst. The distance of the two is, in round numbers, 200 miles. There are also short railways having their termini at, and radiating from, Melbourne, constructed by four distinct companies. These connect the surrounding suburbs with the city, and are of great convenience to the inhabitants; but it is only one of these (that which connects Hudson's Bay with the metropolis) which is of great importance. The total extent of railways in operation is 221 miles, [351 in January, 1864.] The government has in its hands the means of completing the northern line to Echuca, on the banks of the Murray, where the Campaspe empties itself into that river. The embouchure of the Goulbourne is only a little to the eastward. This line measures a trifle over fifty miles. These government lines have been constructed with borrowed money, as everybody knows, £7,000,000 raised in England, £1,000,000 raised in Victoria. There was a premium of £385,000, and they would have been constructed for some hundreds of thousands less than the original estimates had not the government obtained the sanction of the legislature to purchase the Geelong line of a private company, which, with the repairs to that line, will require about £300,000, or perhaps £400,000 in addition. This the government have authority to raise in the colony. Upon these loans the annual charge is half a million. It is not easy as yet to ascertain what the net revenue from the government lines will be. They are scarcely yet in a condition to do all the work they will ultimately be capable of, and undoubtedly the revenue will be greatly increased when the line is open to Echuca. The revenue at present is £45,000 per month, and is increasing. This will give £540,000 for the year. The working expenses are roughly estimated at one-half, but I am informed they will not exceed, and will probably be kept below, £260.000. In round numbers we may call the net revenue £300,000 for the year 1863, [it was £433,615.] to go towards the payment of the interest which is charged on the consolidated revenue. This net revenue is 3½ per cent. on the capital. I do not think there can be any reasonable doubt that in two or three years the net revenue will be worked up to the interest, or 6 per cent. I am not, however, upon conjecture or speculation, but upon the facts as I find them: and the fact with which I am now to deal is a deficiency of £200,000, which the people of the colony now have to meet by taxation. Not that we should care to be taxed less if that were not the case, but we should have £200,000 more to expend on other improvements. Is that £200,000 a loss to the community? I answer it is not. It is in the nature of a guarantee premium, to secure the great economical gain to the country from the cheapness of transport generated by these railways. There is no country in the world which has illustrated, and still illustrates, this so perfectly as Victoria. Our existence has been of such short duration, and our progress so rapid, that everything may be said to have passed before the eyes of everybody. We can all recollect our roads in the condition in which General Wade is said to have found them in the north of England. In 1852–'53 we saw these roads "before they were made"—1854–'58 was the era of macadamization—1859–'62 that of railways. The revolution from the second to the third period was not so marked as from the first to the second. More than £100 per ton has been paid for the carriage of goods to Bendigo; £40 and £50 was not uncommon. As MacAdam moved, Melbourne cartage got down to £18, then to £12, and latterly to £5 and £6 per ton. We now think that enormous. The government charge is 50*s*. to Sandhurst, and 42*s*. to Ballarat, and in proportion for shorter distances, and the public are actually agitating for reduced rates. At present I have not data to make an exact calculation of the gain, but I can make one which will certainly be on the safe side. At present, as I have said, the goods traffic is in its infancy; but if we take the twelve months at no more than the first two months, the number of tons conveyed will be, on the Sandhurst line, 128,073; on the Ballarat line, 72,840; on both, 200,913. Deducting one-third for short distances, it is equal to 134,000 tons carried the whole way. In 1860 the winter rate of cartage to Bendigo was £6 10*s*., the summer rate £5 10*s*.; mean rate £6 per ton, and even then the carriers had the benefit of twenty miles of railway. In 1861 the winter rate was £5, the summer rate £4 5*s*.; mean, £4 12*s*. 6*d*. This makes an average saving of £2 6*s*. 6*d*. per ton, or a total of £311,550 gain, against the revenue deficiency of £200,000. In this calculation nothing is allowed for the superior condition of the goods when delivered, nothing for time, nothing for the absence of depredation, which used to be considerable; nothing for passengers and their convenience; and nothing for the revenue of the Echuca line, when completed, for the £200,000 is charged on the whole. Taking all these into account, I do not doubt that the economical advantage distributed over the whole country is at least *half a million*, secured at a guarantee or insurance charge of £200,000; and as the charge is not subject to increase, but may be reduced as the traffic extends, the advantage must be deemed progressive. The Echuca line will add a fourth to the length of the lines, and ought, consequently, to add one-fourth to the net revenue; that will reduce the deficiency to £125,000; but it will also add one-fourth to the sum of economical advantages. Englishmen, who only know the change from our four-horse coaches, so splendidly appointed and worked, to the railway, can form no conception of the revolution which we have experienced. It is a change from misery to comfort—a sudden jump from the eighteenth to the middle of the nineteenth century."

This extract is given without paraphrase, on account of its suggestiveness in regard to the indispensable internal improvements of mining districts. California has recently opened fifty miles of railroad eastward of San Francisco.

The leading statistics of the Australian group of English colonies are as follows:

Colonies, &c.	Area, square miles.	Population according to latest returns.	Revenue raised in the colony in 1862.	Commerce in 1862.	
				Value of imports.	Value of exports.
New South Wales	323,437	365,635	£1,300,000	£7,510,000	£5,072,000
Victoria............	86,831	548,944	3,039,000	16,094,000	12,063,000
Queensland..........	678,000	56,000	179,400	742,000	710,000
South Australia	383,328	126,830	439,000	1,649,000	1,784,000
Western Australia	978,000	16,691	61,000	160,000	89,000
Tasmania............	26,215	90,211	268,000	1,006,000	1,025,000
New Zealand.........	106,259	155,070	465,000	1,548,000	589,000
	2,582,070	1,358,381	5,760,000	27,718,000	22,282,000

The revenue of Victoria since 1860 has been nearly £3,000,000. In 1863 it was reduced to £2,722,299, but will reach the former point in 1864. The sources of the revenue for the year ending with December, 1863, are thus presented by the Melbourne Argus of January 25, 1864:

I.—Customs:	Rate of impost.	Revenue for 1863.
Spirits....................................	10*s*. per gallon.	£494,045
Wine.......................................	3*s*. per gallon.	44,073
Beer.......................................	6*d*. per gallon.	53,537
Tobacco, manufactured......................	2*s*. per pound.	120,320
Tobacco, unmanufactured....................	1*s*. per pound.	
Cigars.....................................	5*s*. per pound.	10,118
Tea..	6*d*. per pound.	92,780
Sugar......................................	6*s*. per cwt.	118,736
Coffee.....................................	2*d*. per pound.	11,918
Opium......................................	10*s*. per pound.	23,644
Rice.......................................	2*s*. per cwt.	15,560
Dried fruits...............................	10*s*. per cwt.	16,633
Hops.......................................	2*d*. per pound.	5,825
Malt.......................................	6*d*. per bushel.	8,445
Sheepwash tobacco..........................	3*d*. per pound.	5,218
Registration fees, ("unit of entry").......	2*d*. per package.	28,026
Total from customs.........................		1,048,586
II.—Excise:		
Spirits distilled in Victoria..............		£6,181
Publicans' licenses........................		54,625
Spirit merchants' licenses.................		14,123
Auctioneers' licenses......................		4,350
Brewers....................................		976
All other licenses.........................		9,144
Total from excise..........................		89,408
III.—Income from public works:		
Railways...................................		£433,615
Electric telegraph.........................		24,222
Total from public works....................		457,837

IV.—Territorial:	
Sales and leases of lands, miners' rights, &c.	£750,603
Export duty on gold, 1s. 6d. per oz.	121,508
Total territorial	872,111
V.—Post office	£117,664
VI.—Ports and harbors:	
Tonnage, pilotage, &c.	£20,453
VII.—Miscellaneous:	
Fees, fines, and forfeitures, &c.	£116,240
Grand total	£2,722,299

The expenditure of Victoria covers the whole field of what in the United States is divided into national and state expenditure. Taxation of the entire population of the United States in equal measure would produce a revenue of $800,000,000.

Hittell, in his Resources of California, (1862,) estimates that the inhabitants of Nevada, Oregon, Washington, the western part of New Mexico, (now organized as Arizona,) the northwestern part of Mexico, British Columbia, Vancouver's island, and the Hawaiian islands, are an aggregate population of 1,700,000, and destined to an identity of commercial interests.

San Francisco and California hold the same relation to this Pacific population which Melbourne and Victoria bear to the 1,400,000 inhabitants of the Australian group of English colonies. Omitting further comparative statements, it is now proposed to exhibit the present nature and relations of the Pacific trade which concentrates at the city of San Francisco. This will be done chiefly by compilations from the San Francisco Mercantile Gazette, showing the transactions and situation of 1863.

THE TRADE OF SAN FRANCISCO.

The following table shows the destination and value of exports from San Francisco, exclusive of the precious metals, during the past three years:

To—	1861.	1862.	1863.
New York	$1,605,034	$2,245,633	$2,738,435
Boston	98,345	1,192,469	1,506,620
Great Britain	2,838,004	1,355,217	1,697,829
Australia	1,056,401	352,315	487,085
British Columbia	1,177,159	2,195,903	1,740,801
Mexico	1,094,930	1,014,629	1,819,659
Peru	163,264	271,251	216,206
China	711,841	722,229	1,240,254
Hawaiian islands	288,877	293,370	357,389
Japan	15,677	21,528	43,901
Other countries	838,647	940,630	930,564
	9,888,072	10,565,294	12,877,399

This table includes the productions of Oregon, British Columbia, and northern Mexico, as well as of California.

The Gazette adds the following comparative statement of the value of different articles of California produce exported during the past three years:

Articles.	1861.	1862.	1863.
Barley	$361,458	$131,882	$65,044
Beans	10,214	40,599	11,608
Bones	1,044	6,400	171
Bran	1,131	3,061	1,871
Bread	64,809	69,865	65,290
Copper ore	135,240	370,800	719,300
Fish	21,828	21,868	11,285
Flour	868,426	689,234	707,870
Glue	7,320	1,240	930
Hay	4,863	10,898	11,914
Hides	444,896	947,263	924,667
Horns	2,350	2,484	1,807
Leather	3,605	11,040	3,773
Lime	357	989	2,403
Lumber	69,931	149,500	123,084
Mustard seed	1,867	2,417	11,230
Oats	156,879	78,045	130,082
Potatoes	21,016	12,018	91,929
Quicksilver	1,079,850	1,134,981	1,073,078
Skins	30,652	25,011	68,338
Silver ores	211,345	34,740	118,109
Tallow	35,659	37,740	80,170
Wheat	2,709,434	1,379,679	1,754,116
Wine	8,000	25,838	60,141
Wool	519,677	1,009,104	1,119,098
Sundries of manufacture	27,145	23,843	45,565
Sundries of agriculture	4,938	2,498	7,637
	6,795,758	6,811,788	7,208,289

The destinations of these California products were classified as follows:

To—	1861.	1862.	1863.
New York and Boston	$1,293,391	$2,465,811	$2,870,897
Great Britain	2,744,637	1,290,889	1,080,812
Australia	1,078,118	827,075	398,018
China	660,860	689,907	1,010,931
Mexico	457,953	829,927	600,312
Peru	158,774	210,270	102,094
Hawaiian Islands	42,627	47,135	68,930
British Columbia	71,315	373,611	860,746
Other islands	390,283	394,237	240,449
Total	6,795,758	6,811,788	7,208,289

Including exports of treasure, the entire exports of California productions during three years, may be classified as follows:

	1861.	1862.	1863.
Products of the mine	$42,103,193	$44,106,662	$47,049,398
Products of agriculture	3,265,471	1,645,350	2,013,075
Products of the herd	1,041,917	2,027,024	2,164,165
Products of the forest	69,831	149,500	124,695
Products of the sea	21,828	21,848	11,965
Products of manufacture	902,878	798,101	873,654
Products of the vine	8,000	25,800	81,456
Total	47,472,217	48,773,549	53,290,809

The following table shows the value and destination of treasure shipments from San Francisco during the years 1854 to 1863:

Years.	To eastern ports.	To England.	To China.	To Panama.	To other countries.	Total.
1854	$46,533,166	$3,781,080	$935,887	$804,592	$500,908	$52,045,633
1855	38,730,564	5,182,158	889,675	230,207	128,129	45,161,731
1856	39,895,294	8,666,289	1,308,852	258,208	573,722	50,697,434
1857	35,531,778	9,347,743	2,993,264	410,929	692,978	48,976,697
1858	35,891,236	9,265,739	1,916,007	299,266	176,779	47,548,025
1859	40,146,437	3,910,930	3,100,756	270,949	208,300	47,640,462
1860	35,719,298	2,672,506	3,374,680	300,819	258,165	42,325,916
1861	32,689,011	4,061,779	3,541,279	349,709	95,920	40,676,758
1862	26,194,035	12,950,140	2,660,754	434,508	322,324	42,561,761
1863	10,329,330	28,407,258	4,206,370	2,503,298	605,607	46,071,920
Total	341,659,147	88,308,054	24,957,624	5,857,809	3,510,010	463,708,338

The imports, answering to these exports, are, in some measure, indicated by the following statement of the tonnage which arrived at San Francisco during the year 1863:

From—	No. of vessels.	Tons.
Domestic Atlantic ports	102	114,962
Domestic Pacific ports	1,414	153,017
Great Britain	30	28,927
Panama, New Granada	39	64,671
France	13	5,698
Hamburg	11	4,115
Australia	95	13,968
China	44	31,444
Japan	2	693
Manilla	7	5,758
Calcutta	3	1,336
Java	2	981
Malaga	1	295
Rio Janeiro	4	1,034
Chili	4	1,751
Peru	11	2,977
Mexican ports	65	20,648

STATEMENT—Continued.

From—	No. of vessels.	Tons.
West Indies	2	600
British Columbia	44	46,605
Hawaiian Islands	18	6,580
Society Islands	13	2,176
Central America	13	2,771
Russian Possessions, northwest coast	9	3,148
Russian Possessions, Asia	4	737
Whaling voyages	13	4,604
Total arrivals	1,899	641,383

Recapitulation for the year 1863.

	No. of vessels.	Tons.
American vessels arrived from domestic ports	1,510	307,980
American vessels arrived from foreign ports	228	214,655
American vessels arrived from whaling voyages	13	4,304
Foreign vessels arrived from whaling voyages	1	300
Foreign vessels arrived from foreign ports	138	64,164
Total	1,889	641,390

By a return from the Register's office of the Treasury Department, the total value of foreign imports at San Francisco for the year ending June 30, 1863, was as follows: In American vessels, $7,348,969; in foreign vessels, $3,333,173; total, $10.682.142. To which add for the third quarter of 1863, in American vessels, $1.037.441; in foreign vessels, $750.956; making an aggregate for the period of fifteen months ending September 30, 1863, of $13,370,539. During the same period of fifteen months the value of foreign imports to Oregon are stated on the same authority at $79,764. There is no return from Puget's Sound district, though estimated to import at least $100.000 yearly. These custom-house returns indicate an annual importation on the Pacific coast of $10,826,957.

The present tendencies of the Pacific trade in regard to different countries are worthy of observation.

To New York and Boston the leading articles of export are hides, wool, and even copper:

Articles.	1860.	1861.	1862.	1863.
Copper ore ... sks.	....	11,155	72,038	100,470
Hides ... No.	200,116	177,998	315,751	30[illegible],1[illegible]9
Wool ... bales.	11,767	14,791	21,011	[illegible],078

The exportation of wheat, which in 1860 was 203,528 bags, fell to 19,288 in 1861, and is not reported for the last two years.

To Great Britain the exports from California chiefly consist of wheat and flour, as follows:

Articles.	1860.	1861.	1862.	1863.
Flour.........................barrels.	36,375	70,945	8,682	19,900
Wheat.........................bags.	458,496	1,028,664	590,465	644,029

To the Sandwich Islands and Mexico, lumber is the leading export, amounting in 1863 to 772,794 feet for the Sandwich Islands, and 1,162,360 feet for Mexico.

The export of lumber to Peru reached 1,936,166 feet in 1862, and 890,009 feet in 1863.

China is also a considerable market for the lumber of the Pacific coast, receiving 2,659,190 feet in 1862, and 2,709,733 feet in 1863. The San Francisco Mercantile Gazette of January 12 remarks: "The shipments of California products to China during the year just ended have been very much greater than ever before. Flour, wheat, lumber, bacon, butter, cheese, lard, wine, vegetables, &c., have all been sent forward in quantities that indicate a rapidly expanding market. The people of that country who have lived among us these many years, much to the disgust of certain political classes, and in spite of the most determined efforts to drive them away, have done us a great service in teaching their countrymen at home the use and value of our products, and in overcoming their ancient prejudices against 'barbarian' diet. The trade requires judicious management, and is in good hands. We regard its present aspect as perhaps the most important feature in our outward commerce which the past year has developed. Its progress may be comparatively slow for some time to come, and may yet undergo many vicissitudes; but once fairly inaugurated, as indeed it now seems to be, the wants of a population almost illimitable give assurance of a market for any surplus we may have to spare at prices reasonably remunerative."

To Australia and New Zealand the leading export is lumber; the former demand for breadstuffs being much below the exportation of 1861.

The East Indies send to California coffee, sugar, rice, hemp, spices, &c., but take little in return except gold and silver.

The exports of California produce to British Columbia, New Granada, Chili, Society Islands, Manilla, Japan, France, Cape of Good Hope, Central America, and Russian possessions, are reported by the San Francisco Gazette as follows:

Articles.	1860.	1861.	1862.	1863.
Barley.........................bags	99,243	92,814	39,034	27,303
Beans.........................bags.	291	4,683	8,940	3,074
Bran.........................tons.	....	25	....	....
Bran.........................bags.	5,806	1,098	5,762	3,709
Buckwheat.........................bags.	....	36	75	....
Bread.........................bbls.	245	68	28	60
Bread.........................cwt.	1,753	1,513	1,044	2,327
Bread.........................packages.	....	....	249	96
Brooms.........................dozen.	....	302	518	....
Flour.........................bbls.	33,677	21,480	50,170	67,634
Furs.........................packages.	....	....	....	....
Hay.........................bales.	7,318	3,002	5,524	6,103
Hide cuttings.........................packages.	....	10	....	....
Horns.........................No.	....	5,400	....	....
Leather.........................packages.	61	68	77	67
Lumber—boards.........................feet.	1,740,576	1,631,506	2,607,752	940,699
boards .....bundles and packages.	1,428	3,549	704	306
shingles.........................No.	490,000	218,000	450,000	....

STATEMENT—Continued.

Articles.	1860.	1861.	1862.	1863.
Lumber—shingles......bundles.	411	....	400	....
pickets......No.	2,000	5,000	....	....
pickets......bundles.	....	400	....	....
laths......No.	....	....	1,000	....
Lime......bbls.	290	....	30	310
Oats......bags.	3,199	2,504	7,788	6,453
Potatoes......bags.	6,351	4,055	4,514	6,223
Quicksilver......flasks.	1,497	2,382	2,210	703
Salmon......bbls.	230	73	215	37
Salmon......cwts.	....	17	8	60
Tallow......packages.	1,484	327	423	251
Wheat......bags.	37,357	4,184	5,118	27,257
Wool......bales.	....	3	546	....

The table of treasure shipments indicates a great change of destination since 1861. Then the shipments to our Atlantic cities reached $32,628,011, while during 1863 they amounted to only $10,389,330. The treasure shipments to England increased from $4,061,779 in 1861 to $23,467,256 in 1863.

The attention to wool-growing on the Pacific coast during the last five or six years has resulted in a very rapid increase of the crop in California. In 1857 the whole product of the State was only 1,000,000 pounds; now it is estimated at 7,600,000 pounds. The shipments of wool from San Francisco have been as follows for the last four years:

	1860.	1861.	1862.	1863.
	Bales.	*Bales.*	*Bales.*	*Bales.*
To New York......	11,767	13,244	13,127	9,869
To Boston......	....	1,547	8,734	6,216
To England......	315	1,193	78	319
To other countries......	....	3	626	....
Total......	12,082	15,987	22,616	16,398

The export of the important article of quicksilver for the past six years is shown by the following table:

To—	1858.	1859.	1860.	1861.	1862.	1863.
New York and Boston......	3,559	250	400	600	9,965	95
Great Britain......	....	....	....	9,500	1,600	1,062
Mexico......	12,901	103	3,840	12,061	11,778	11,520
China......	4,132	1,069	2,715	13,788	8,725	8,849
Peru......	2,000	571	750	2,804	3,439	3,376
Chili......	1,364	930	1,040	2,069	1,746	600
Central America......	....	....	....	110	40	40
Japan......	....	....	....	50	25	....
Australia......	....	325	100	1,060	800	300
Panama......	....	130	135	67	424	120
Victoria, V. I......	186	10	347	110	5	43
Total flasks......	24,142	3,399	9,348	35,995	33,749	28,014

The manufactures of California are unexpectedly prosperous, and materially reduce importations. Cordage, cement, blankets, white and colored flannels, cloths and cassimeres, gunpowder, leather, malt liquors, tar, rosin, turpentine, paper, soap, wine, are now manufactured with a degree of success which will probably control the home market.

The California supply of coal, chiefly from the Mount Diablo mines, is on the increase, reaching 37,000 tons in 1863; but the demand is so great as to warrant shipments from Vancouver island, Bellingham Bay, and Chili, and even from England and Australia. The monthly consumption from the Diablo mines during the last three months of 1863 was fully 6,000 tons per month.

The product of gold and silver on the Pacific coast is estimated at $55,000,000 for 1863, of which fully $7,000,000 was received from British Columbia. The total coinage at the San Francisco mint during the year 1863 was $20,251,417 97.

It is contended by the commercial journals of San Francisco that the currency of California, which is mostly coin, is more abundant in proportion to population and wealth than that of the Atlantic States. The Mercantile Gazette of February 12, 1864, represents the amount in circulation on the Pacific coast as $25,000,000; that the population of California with adjoining State (of Oregon) and Territories is 600,000, which gives forty-one dollars and sixty-six cents *per capita*. The total value of real and personal property on the Pacific coast is estimated by the Gazette to be $340,000,000, of which $25,000,000 is about seven per cent. The currency of the loyal States east of the mountains, notwithstanding its expansion to meet the exigencies of the nation, is below those ratios to population and property. The population of the loyal States and of the insurrectionary districts which are held by the army (in June, 1864) is 24,000,000. If the currency was at the California standard—$41 *per capita*—its aggregate would be $984,000,000, and a proportion of 7 per cent. upon the total valuation of property would give an equal aggregate.

VANCOUVER'S ISLAND AND BRITISH COLUMBIA.

Except Australia, British Columbia, and the islands adjacent to its coast, would be the only important colonial occupation of the Pacific coast by Great Britain—Mauritius, Hong Kong, and Labuan having their chief significance in the convenience of the mercantile marine. The station of England on the northwest coast of North America will prove of great value in the future struggle for commercial, if not political, ascendancy in the Orient.

The island of Vancouver, with its excellent harborage in Puget's sound, is in the latitude, and is not unlike the climate, of Ireland. The coldest weather of the year is in December; but little snow falls, disappearing usually in a few days. The frosts which precede and follow penetrate the soil but a few inches, and the lakes are covered with ice sufficiently strong to bear the skater only during a few weeks. The climate is mild and equable, but warmer in summer than in England. Cattle, horses, sheep, and hogs are seldom housed. Probably not more than half the surface of the island is adapted to agriculture, but the soil is of excellent quality, and all other conditions favorable. Wheat, oats, barley, hay, and vegetables are produced, and the almost evergreen turf is well suited to grazing. The section of country now in course of agricultural settlement is within sixty miles of Victoria, the leading town of the island, and is known as the district of Cowichan. The conditions on which land may be taken there, as elsewhere in Vancouver's island, are easy. A single man may pre-empt one hundred and fifty acres; a married man, with his wife in the colony, two hundred acres; and for each child under ten years of age, ten acres additional. The government price for the land is one dollar an acre. If unsurveyed land be pre-empted, the settler has to pay for it when surveyed. If surveyed, he has three years in which to pay the purchase money. Another condition makes it incumbent on the pre-emptor to occupy and improve his claim. When two dollars an acre is expended in improvements the government will make a title; but not so unless the settler has resided on his claim two years.

Vancouver's island is the naval station of England in the North Pacific. The harbor of Esquimalt, three miles from Victoria, and near the Straits of San Juan, is a magnificent haven, fit to shelter a whole navy in safety. The forests of the island are an inexhaustible resource for ship-building, while the coal mines at Nanaimo, sixty miles from Victoria, on the sheltered navigation of the Gulf of Georgia, are of the best possible quality—bituminous and extensive. The seams now worked at Nanaimo are, respectively, three feet ten inches, five feet, and two feet five inches, and have been traced to the northwest extremity of the island, where Johnson's straits furnish excellent land-locked harbors. Up to 1858 the Hudson Bay Company had, in nine years, taken 63,000 tons; but, during 1863, 22,000 tons have been exported to San Francisco alone, where it found a remunerative sale, though the price at the pit-mouth is six dollars per ton. Behind Nanaimo a remarkable natural cleft known as Albeoni canal leads into Barclay sound, where a London firm have established saw-mills, which, during nine months of 1863, cut and exported 15,000,000 superficial feet of the finest planking from the Douglas and other pines. These details of the coal and lumber trade indicate the great advantages of Vancouver for the construction, repair, and coaling of vessels.

Northward of Puget's sound the coast of British Columbia is so broken with fiords or inlets, and sheltered by islands, as to present the greatest possible advantages for fisheries and a coasting trade. The salmon, herring, and other fisheries of this region will equal those of Norway.

British Columbia, in respect to capacity for agriculture, may be compared with Scotland, while its mineral resources are destined to a development fully equal to the gold product of the colony of Victoria.

The progress of the colony of British Columbia, during the first four years of its organization, will be illustrated by a statement of revenue which is raised almost entirely by customs duties levied at New Westminster, or the mouth of Frazer river, and by a mining license of twenty shillings per year for each man. During the first year of the existence of British Columbia as a colony—that is, to the 31st of December, 1859—the customs duties amounted to £16,464, the receipts from other sources being quite trifling. In the succeeding year, 1860, the customs receipts reached £30,416, and those from other sources, such as land sales, port and harbor duties, licenses, &c., nearly £23,000 more. In 1861 the receipts from customs were £41,177; from other sources, £38,192. In 1862 the customs receipts were estimated by Governor Douglas at £58,980; other sources, £47,050. One-third of the gross revenue is devoted to the construction of roads and bridges, which are objects of first necessity in a rugged mining country. By the improvement of the roads from the mouth of the Frazer river to stations three hundred miles distant, the cost of transport has been reduced to about twenty shillings a ton, which is 300 per cent. less than in 1860.

The land system of British Columbia is identical with that of Vancouver's island, the price of land being 4*s.* 2*d.* per acre on easy terms of payment.

The mineral wealth of British Columbia, especially the interior district called Cariboo, which parts the waters of the Columbia, Frazer, Saskatchewan, Athabasca, and Peace rivers to every point of the compass, has lately been attested by papers read at the London Geographical Society, and is confirmed by the returns of treasure exports at New Westminster and Victoria.

Allen Francis, esq., United States consul at Victoria, Vancouver's island, states that the export of gold from that port during the year 1863, as obtained from reliable sources, amounted to $2,935,170 16, and he computes that an equal amount has been taken away in private hands, or about $6,000,000 as the total export.

Mr. Francis communicates the following statistical tables:

Table of imports to Victoria, Vancouver's Island, for the years 1861, 1862, *and* 1863.

	1861.	1862.	1863.
From San Francisco	$1,2[illegible],350	$2,345,066	$1,890,117
From Washington Territory and Puget's sound	228,350	224,703	242,781
From Oregon	216,603	75,370	108,003
Total	1,753,919	2,645,[illegible]	2,230,501
From England	516,041	604,279	1,472,021
From Sandwich Islands	54,382	112,109	113,498
From British Columbia	31,454	32,424	65,870
From China	....	22,258	45,434
From Melbourne	....	32,170	....
From Valparaiso	....	17,000	....
Total	601,877	910,243	1,657,311

Statement of exports from the port of Victoria, Vancouver's Island, during the six months ending December 31, 1863.

To what place.	July.	Aug.	Sept.	Oct.	Nov.	Dec.	Total.
San Francisco	$20,673	$25,015	$16,650	$28,112	$23,217	$25,450	$139,123
Port Angeles	5,970	6,804	6,187	8,863	3,944	10,412	42,084
Astoria	945	1,727	637	4,208	2,580	301	10,464
New York	....	349	....	....	....	....	349
Total	27,688	33,896	23,474	40,983	29,701	36,229	191,960

Statement of the export of gold from Victoria, Vancouver's Island, from 1858 *to* 1863, *inclusive.*

1858. Wells, Fargo & Co	$337,765 17
1859. Wells, Fargo & Co	823,488 41
1860. Wells, Fargo & Co	1,298,466 00
1861. Wells, Fargo & Co	1,340,395 72
1862. Wells, Fargo & Co	1,573,096 16
1863. Wells, Fargo & Co	1,373,443 39
McDonald & Co. from 1858 to 31st December, 1861	1,207,656 00
1862. Not included in Wells, Fargo & Co.'s statement	335,379 00
1863. Bank of British North America	585,617 85
1863. Bank of British Columbia	824,876 92
Hudson Bay Company and others from 1858 to 1863, inclusive, approximate	500,000 00
	10,200,184 64

Shipment of gold by express and on freight during the year 1863	$2,936,170 16
Same for the year 1862	$2,167,183 18

Statement of the tonnage of shipping entered and cleared at Victoria, Vancouver's Island, from 1st July to 31st December, 1863.

Nationality.	Tonnage entered.	No. crew.	Tonnage cleared.	No. crew.
American	47,075	2,412	46,067	2,344
Foreign	43,800	1,616	47,048	1,711

RUSSIA IN ASIA.

In 1858, before the English and French fleet had reached the Pei Ho, the Russians appropriated the best results of the campaign. In May of that year General Mouravieff concluded a convention at Algoor with the Chinese authorities, which enlarged Siberia almost to the absorption of Manchooria—securing to Russia a region abounding with the elements of commerce. Along the Amoor river, fed by numerous navigable tributaries and capacious enough to admit steam vessels two thousand miles from its mouth, the Russo-Chinese treaty fixed the dividing line of the two empires, only varying from its channel by a line running to the tide-waters of the Pacific at a point which gives to Russia the best harbors on the sea of Japan. The territory thus acquired can hardly be estimated under three hundred thousand square miles, rich in the products of the forest and in mineral wealth. In securing Manchooria, or the best half of the native land of the tribes, whose dynasty is dominant in China, Russia has virtually pushed her frontier to the wall of China.

In the wilderness of Central Asia, west and northwest of China proper, Russia is constantly making territorial acquisitions. Even Khiva, Kokand and Khorassan are dependencies of the Czar. Indeed, the desert of Gobi on the east, and the Himalayan range and the frontiers of Afghanistan and Persia on the south, are natural boundaries within which Russian influence is paramount. Mongolia, Thibet, Turkestan, are at this moment less members of the Chinese than of the Russian Empire. This portion of Asia, known historically as the birthplace and scene of empire of Genghis Khan, has a considerable capacity for commerce. Stretching from the Suliman range to Siberia, from the Caspian to the sea of Okhotsk, it certainly contains a considerable population, possibly a large one, which wants clothes, weapons, iron instruments—most of the appliances and some of the luxuries of civilization—and can give in exchange hides, horns, goats' wool, camels' hair, tallow, silk, borax, gems, metals, drugs, and all that wealth which is sure to be discovered in very wide tracts of earth. "Englishmen think of the provinces of Central and Northern Asia," observes the London Economist, "as if they were covered with desert, but they comprise every kind of climate, and contain every variety of mineral, while over half their extent fat grapes grow in the open air, and every traveller records the luxurious quality of their fruits."

Upon the question of practical communications with Central Asia, the same authority reaches conclusions which demonstrate the value of the Amoor river and its tributaries. "The true route towards these countries," continues the writer in the Economist, "is through Russia and China, for it is the only one on which we have much help from water communication. By following the

Yangtseo and Hoongho to the utmost limit of navigation, we bring ourselves to points from whence the Chinese merchants have traded with the people east of the Himalayas—points from which traffic in wheeled carriages may begin. In northern Asia, the true access is by the Amoor, a river which, if travellers may be trusted, is navigable for more than two thousand miles, and cleaves into the very heart of that secluded region. The western division, which we call Central Asia, as if Thibet were not more central, is cloven by the Jihon, which flows from Bokhara to the Caspian, and the navigation of which has never been fairly tried. * * * The notion of opening the Amoor has been repeatedly entertained at St. Petersburgh, and if all sovereign rights were fully reserved, and the advantages of such a course to the revenue made quite clear, the government might be disposed to go gradually much further. To enfranchise the great eastern Asiatic rivers by agreement with St. Petersburgh and Pekin should be the line to which our efforts ought to be directed."

Proceeding upon such a commercial policy in 1859, Lord Elgin, who was fully conscious of the advantages gained in the Russian treaty of May, obtained from the Chinese government concessions of free travel through the empire and of a port of Shingking, at a point easily attainable from Shanghae and open to the importation of foreign manufactures. These concessions have been extended to American traders.

Russia has followed the initiative of 1858 with extraordinary vigor. The telegraph already connects St. Petersburgh with Irkoutsk, a distance of 5,000 miles, and will be extended to the Pacific coast during 1865. The colonization of the valley of the Amoor has been undertaken, and already eighty steam vessels are employed in the trade with the Russian possessions of the North Pacific, while the government of St. Petersburgh extends all possible encouragement to the enterprise projected by English and American capitalists to unite the telegraph lines of the United States and British America with the Russo-Siberian line now advancing to a junction across the Behring straits and through Russian America.

COMMERCE OF THE SANDWICH ISLANDS.

The Hawaiian islands should not be omitted from the consideration of the great commercial changes which the contact of European and Asiatic civilization is destined to produce. In 1863 the external commerce of the islands had reached an aggregate of $2,201,345, and its progress is indicated by the following table:

Years.	Domestic produce exported.	For'n merchandise exported.	Total exports.	Total imports.
1846	$301,625	$62,325	$363,750	$598,363
1850	460,278	214,540	670,824	1,150,483
1860	480,526	326,932	807,459	1,223,749
1861	470,872	162,902	639,774	701,109
1862	586,542	251,842	838,424	998,239
1863	744,413	281,439	1,025,852	1,175,493

The official returns of 1863 are classified as follows by the Honolulu Commercial Advertiser:

		Paying duty.	Bonded.
Imports from United States, Pacific side		$304,502	$36,617
" " " " Atlantic side		122,770	40,827
" " Bremen		194,429	62,651
" " Great Britain		63,400	9,227
" " Vancouver's island		32,210	2,277
" " Sea		6,291	179,454
" " Islands of Pacific		6,457	5,468
" " Sitka, (Russian America)			4,586
		730,061	341,303

Of articles exported, 3,512 pounds of cotton were sent to the United States, and the exports of sugar increased from 3,000,000 pounds in 1862 to 5,292,000 pounds in 1863.

THE GOLD PRODUCT OF THE PACIFIC COAST.

The extension of English and American settlement since 1850, expressed by the foregoing statistics of Australia, California, and British Columbia, is the result of gold discovery. The London Economist estimates the production of gold from the islands and coast of the Pacific during the fifteen years 1849–'63 at £350,000,000 sterling, or equal to 58 per cent. upon the total computed stock of £600,000,000 sterling of gold existing in various forms in Europe and America in 1848, and conjectures that the following numerical distribution of these £350,000,000 has taken place:

Employed and absorbed in Great Britain	£60,000,000	
" " France	110,000,000	
" " United States	50,000,000	
		£220,000,000
" " Australia	30,000,000	
" " California	20,000,000	
" " Turkey and East	40,000,000	
" " Brazil, Egypt, Spain, Portugal, &c.	40,000,000	
		130,000,000
		350,000,000

The cheapening of the price of quicksilver, and the large discoveries of silver in Nevada and Arizona, have increased the annual supplies of that metal, but only to a small extent compared with gold.

Upon the question, now elaborately discussed, of the effect of this gold production upon its exchangeable value, the London Economist of February 20, 1864, calls attention to the evidence afforded by comparing the average annual rates from 1841 to 1863 of the foreign exchange between England, using a gold standard, and Paris, Hamburg, and Amsterdam, using a silver standard, and according to this statement the fall in the value of gold as compared with silver (the best available test at present) in no case exceeds 2½ per cent.

The result of this comparison adds, if possible, to the force and significance of the following language by an eminent English writer:*

* Tooke, History of Prices, vi, 235, published in 1857.

"Set at work and sustained by the production year by year of large quantities of new gold, there is at work a vast and increasing number of causes all conducing to augment the real wealth and resources of the world—all conducing to stimulate and foster trade, enterprise, discovery, and production—and therefore all conducing with greater and greater force to neutralize, by extensions of the surface to be covered, and by multiplying indefinitely the number and magnitude of the dealings to be carried on, the *a priori* tendency of an increase of metallic money to raise prices by mere force of enlarged volume. Already the boundaries within which capital and enterprise can be applied, with the assurance and knowledge alone compatible with durable success, have been extended over limits which ten or even five years ago would have been regarded as unattainable. There have come into play influences by which it seems to be the special purpose to contribute, by the aid of the gold discoveries and by the aid of the concurrent advance of knowledge, to the removal or mitigation of many chronic evils against which past generations have striven almost in vain."

It has been estimated that the populations of China and India, when the benefit of a strong and stable government is assured, will develop a commerce fully equal to the proportions now witnessed in France. The beginning of such a state of things, attested by the movement thither of the precious metals, is a fruitful topic of discussion, and will be briefly considered.

THE DRAIN OF SILVER TO THE EAST.

The absorption of silver in Asia has never been so great as since the gold discoveries of California and Australia. With the increase of bullion Europe ceased to regard with apprehension the oriental demand for silver in exchange for silks, teas, indigo, and other staples of eastern production. When it was known that the Pacific gold stream was yearly increasing in volume, and could readily fill any vacuum which the shipment of silver to India and China might produce, a great expansion of trade to Asia followed. The precious metals came to be regarded as merchandise, and it was deemed wholly unessential whether payment was made for eastern products in the coin or the manufactures of Europe.

The following table of the imports of Indian products into England in a series of years indicates the nature of this increase of trade:*

Imports from British India—value.

Articles.	1855.	1856.	1857.	1858.
Cotton	£2,241,970	£3,530,410	£6,416,683	£2,898,779
Hemp, jute, and other articles	504,264	638,300	610,913	685,048
Indigo	1,518,097	2,190,131	1,791,044	1,907,511
Seeds	1,968,501	2,645,372	1,328,336	1,774,568
Silk	659,319	605,405	188,097	600,601
Sugar	1,043,480	1,871,279	1,028,008	1,059,291
Tea	25,661	82,903	147,040	91,158
Wool	490,977	576,044	673,400	490,521
	8,354,268	12,000,544	19,063,961	9,507,321

* See an article in Hunt's Merchants' Magazine, August, 1863, on "Silver: its Production, Coinage, and Value."

Imports from British India—value—Continued.

Articles.	1859.	1860.	1861.	1862.
Cotton	£3,901,109	£3,339,076	£9,334,115	£21,223,774
Hemp, jute, and other articles	637,167	671,176	729,172	906,834
Indigo	1,619,604	2,220,119	2,005,634	1,784,334
Seeds	2,344,898	2,075,274	1,071,449	1,751,003
Silk	296,263	60,893	136,505	438,572
Sugar	1,101,716	939,026	821,458	368,493
Tea	132,255	230,064	165,904	101,768
Wool	402,100	690,601	614,099	749,607
	10,695,108	10,235,491	16,379,226	29,087,605

The steady rise in value to an aggregate of $60,000,000 in 1857, producing a drain of silver, was one of the causes of the revulsion in that year. Since then the purchases of Indian produce, mostly cotton, have risen to $90,000,000 in 1862, while in 1863 England imported cotton from India to the enormous value of $200,000,000.

The quantity of silver annually exported from England and the Mediterranean to Asia has been as follows, per English official reports:

Year.	England.	Mediterranean.	Total.
1851	$8,362,500	....	$8,362,500
1852	12,116,210	....	12,116,210
1853	23,550,000	$4,240,000	27,790,000
1854	15,555,000	7,255,000	22,821,000
1855	32,075,000	7,620,000	39,695,000
1856	60,590,000	9,950,000	70,540,000
1857	86,477,170	10,180,291	96,657,461
1858	25,441,250	16,150,000	31,594,250
1859	33,298,120	7,340,280	40,638,400
1860	40,620,182	8,120,204	48,740,386
1861	36,389,175	7,980,000	44,379,175
1862	52,551,045	9,150,000	61,701,045
1863, six months	21,258,514	11,737,271	32,995,781
	430,306,102	88,723,040	539,029,203

France, although the richest country of the world in the precious metals, has since 1848 parted with $165,947,253 of silver, and taken in exchange gold. This is the case with England, Russia, and the United States, who no longer hesitate to encourage and extend their trade with the non-importing population of Asia, although at the hazard of a drain of silver coin. The trade of California with China is more reciprocal, owing, it is supposed, to the new demands for American provisions and manufactures, which the Chinese immigrants, attracted by the mines to our Pacific coast, carry back with them to China. But in India, notwithstanding a century of British occupation, the apathy of the natives—their aversion to any exchange except for silver—seems unbroken. To this condition of the market there has been added, during the last ten years, an investment of £50,000,000 of English capital in the railroads of Hindostan, which has greatly contributed to the influx of silver.*

* See the Bankers' Magazine, Journal of the Money Market, and Commercial Digest, January, 1864, London, p. 18.

From the time of imperial Rome bullion has flowed from west to east, and Pliny complained that India was the "sink" of the precious metals. Gibbon has also observed that this continuous drain was "a complaint worthy of the gravity of the senate;" and Humboldt, estimating the produce of the South American mines in the beginning of this century at $43,000,000, states that $25,000,000 were sent to Asia. The tendency to hoard the precious metals partakes of the proverbial immobility of the Asiatic character. Silver is less used in India for purposes of luxury and ornament than in Europe; and it is probable that silver, and perhaps gold, will continue to be the leading article of import until the whole Asiatic world, with its population of six hundred millions of souls, shall be in possession of the same money supply relatively which is found in European or American states. This proportion between population and its industry on the one hand, and the medium of commerce recognized by the world, once established, then, and perhaps not before, will the oriental torpidity be succeeded by new and more advanced modes of traffic. The population of Great Britain is computed at 30,000,000, with an amount of gold and silver in circulation assumed to be £80,000,000; and this amount is found essential, notwithstanding the great extension of paper substitutes for coin. The circulating medium of India in 1857 was about £80,000,000, but the population of India is 180,000,000, or sixfold that of Great Britain. India can, therefore, absorb £400,000,000 in addition to the amount she is now supposed to hold before she will exceed the monetary level of Great Britain.

France affords a more impressive illustration of the inevitable absorption of the precious metals by Asia before the monetary equilibrium will be adjusted between the Orient and the Occident. The population of France is, in round numbers, 36,000,000; its specie supply 6,600,000,000 francs, or about £264,000,000. The population of India will therefore require £1,320,000,000 to reach a circulation of coin proportionate to that of France.

But this is not all. It is estimated that there are 600,000,000 Asiatics, fully equal as to industrial capacity to the people of India; many of them—the Japanese and Chinese especially—superior to the Hindostanese. Before the orientals reach the monetary level of England, they must be in possession of £1,600,000,000, while to attain an equality with France no less than an aggregate of £4,400,000,000 must be permanently absorbed by the 600,000,000 Asiatics, who are soon to be brought into close commercial relation with christendom.

The capital and industry of Europe and America were never so active as now. How immeasurable, under the impulse of machinery, is the energy and the amount of production. Fully proportionate is the exigency of distribution and the development of commerce; and as money is the grand instrument both of production and distribution, it must be permitted to diffuse itself proportionately. Until every land is saturated to the full standard of Europe and the United States, there will be no excess of supply from the mines of all the continents. The golden age is here, but we stand only on its threshold.

OVERLAND TRADE AND COMMUNICATIONS

BETWEEN THE

PACIFIC COAST AND THE MISSISSIPPI STATES.

Having considered the external commerce of the United States, mostly concentrated on the Atlantic seaboard, and the volume of internal trade between the Mississippi States and the cities and communities east of the Alleghanies, the grand result of nearly three centuries of American civilization, and having also anticipated, from less than twenty years of similar colonization on the Pacific coast, a still more remarkable phenomenon of social and material progress, it remains to consider the situation and prospects of those interior American States which are destined to connect the two great oceans by a railway across the American continent, itself the precursor of other communications of the kind.

The California division of the Union Pacific railroad consists of three sections, under the control of three companies: First, the San Francisco and San José Railroad Company, which has a section of fifty miles between these two places; secondly, the Western Pacific Railroad Company, which has a section of one hundred and fifteen miles from San José to Sacramento; thirdly, the Central Pacific Railroad Company, which has the section from Sacramento to the eastern boundary, in Truckee valley, a distance of one hundred miles. The first section, from San Francisco to San José, is completed and in operation. The further distance to Sacramento is rapidly advancing to completion. With the aid of the California legislature there is a probability that the railway will be pushed to the eastern boundary of the State sooner than the lines west of the Missouri river will be constructed for an equal mileage.

When recently the people of Nevada Territory were represented in a convention to frame a State constitution, there was no dissent from the proposition that the credit of the State to the amount of $3,000,000 might be applied to aid the construction of a Pacific railway, all other loans of credit for internal improvements being prohibited. This provision will doubtless be inserted in the constitution soon to be presented. Utah, Colorado, and Kansas will also co-operate with efficiency.

But the surest guarantee will be the resources, present and prospective, of the organizations named, which will now be considered in geographical sequence.

NEVADA.

The population of Nevada Territory by the census of 1860 was 6,857. At the close of 1863 it had reached 60,000, of which nearly 20,000 was concentrated at Virginia City, the centre of the most productive silver district. Within four years $5,000,000 have been expended in erecting quartz mills and reduction works; another $5,000,000 have been laid out in opening the mines, and three times as much in various kinds of improvement. In wagon roads alone, leading into and through the Territory, $500,000 have been spent, an investment that has paid from forty to eighty per cent. per annum. The tolls collected on these roads during the year 1863 reached at least the sum of $200,000. The money paid on freights coming into the Territory from the Pacific coast amounted to fully $3,000,000. About 3,000 teams of various kinds are employed in this business, besides numerous pack trains.

The argentiferous lodes of Nevada, first known as the Washoe silver mines, are not confined to the neighborhood of the first discoveries, although none have elsewhere been met with carrying so large a body of rich ores as the original Comstock, at Virginia City. Some claiming to be equally rich, but comparatively small, have been found at other points. The localities of the other principal mines of Nevada, naming them in the order of their discovery, are the Esmeralda mines, a little over one hundred miles south-southeast of Virginia City; the Humboldt, one hundred and sixty miles northeast; the Silver Mountain, sixty miles south; the Peavine District, thirty miles north; and the Reese River Country, one hundred and seventy miles east-northeast, embracing, like the other sections named, many districts, and flanked by two of more than ordinary promise—the Cortez, seventy miles north, and the San Antonio, one hundred miles south of Austin, now the principal town in the Reese River region. Besides these, there are many isolated districts in various parts of the country, all advancing claims to great mineral wealth.

Extensive districts of California, along the course of the Sierra Nevada, are argentiferous. On both the California and Arizona sides of the Colorado river silver lodes of manifest value are met with. In Utah Territory silver-bearing ledges, not unlike those found in the vicinity of Reese river, are numerous, and similar discoveries in the Boise country and other portions of Idaho have been made; but Nevada as yet sustains her pre-eminence as the silver-bearing region of the United States.

There are now more than a hundred quartz mills in operation in the Territory of Nevada. These carry from five to forty stamps each, and have been erected at a cost ranging from $10,000 to $100,000, three or four at least having exceeded the latter sum. The Gould and Curry mill, with its surrounding improvements, has already involved an expenditure of $1,200,000. About three-fourths of these mills are driven by steam, and the balance by water. Of the entire number in the Territory, seven-eighths are in the vicinity of Virginia City, the most remote being not over fifteen miles distant.

It is calculated that every stamper will crush a ton of rock in 24 hours. Supposing 100 mills to be in constant operation, carrying an average of 10 stamps each, 1,000 tons of ore are crushed daily. This ore will yield at the rate of $50 per ton, giving a daily product of $50,000 for the Territory, or a total, allowing 300 working days for the year, of $15,000,000 per annum. With proper allowance for the increased production of 1864, the estimate of $20,000,000 for the current year will not seem an exaggeration.

The colony of Victoria, in Australia, had a population in 1861 of 540,322, about equal to that of California and Nevada. The total number of persons residing within the mining districts of Victoria is given as 233,501, of which 90,364 are returned as directly employed "in the extraction by washing, crushing or other mode, of gold." Upon this basis the colony of Victoria has undertaken and constructed 351 miles of railway at a cost of £35,000 per mile; while society in the gold-fields, under the necessity of co-operation imposed by quartz mining, has been transformed from the violence of the first epoch of gold discovery to a remarkable condition of order and sobriety. Heavy and expensive machinery employed on works which extend over a period of several years have obliged the miner to adopt a settled mode of life. Attractive homesteads are everywhere seen, and flourishing cities are founded almost in a day. The same results are soon to be observed in Nevada—perhaps are already visible. Virginia City (in the language of the Edinburgh Review, describing the populous towns of Victoria) "contains as many as 20,000 or 30,000 inhabitants, with streets well metalled and paved, lighted with gas, and supplied with water, with churches, three daily newspapers, and other public institutions." The construction of 300 miles of railway will soon be added to the analogy of comparative progress.

UTAH.

The settlements of Great Salt Lake City, and elsewhere in Utah Territory, have directed their industry exclusively to agriculture and domestic manufactures. Their ecclesiastical rulers, by giving such a direction to the labor of the people, have shown great sagacity, for not only is society organized on surer foundations than in mining districts, but the demand for all the products of Utah has been so constant and remunerative as to furnish an advantageous home market. Simultaneously with the first settlement at Salt Lake the overland emigration to California commenced, and has increased from year to year until in 1863 it meets a return column of adventurers who are pushing eastward and northward to the gold-fields of Colorado, Idaho, and Montana. The consumption by the crowds in transit, both east and west, sustains the prices of provisions and manufactures at rates which encourage population and accumulate wealth.

By the census of 1860 the population of Utah was 40,273, an increase of 253.89 per cent. since 1850. The total valuation of property was $986,083 in 1850, and $5,596,118 in 1860, or an increase of 467.50 per cent. If these proportions continue during the present decade, the population of Utah will be 142,525, and the valuation of property $31,757,966 in 1870.

Most of Utah is barren; perhaps one-fiftieth of the surface, with the aid of irrigation, is available for agriculture; but over other and more extensive districts grazing and wool-growing will reward industry. The native grasses, especially the bunch grass, are heavily seeded, fattening cattle like grain, and giving great consistence and richness to the milk of cows. This concentration of nutriment is a result of the arid climate, and to the same cause may be attributed the health of sheep, and the fine quality of their fleeces.*

Iron and copper mines, which have been discovered in the Wahsatch mountains of Utah, have received more attention from the Mormons than the indications of gold and silver, but the time is at hand when the precious metals will be mined as successfully as in Nevada.

The present population of Utah is variously stated—by Peter A. Dey, esq., engineer of the Union Pacific Railroad Company, at 75,000; by Fitzhugh Ludlow, esq., in the Atlantic Monthly Magazine, at 80,000; and by Hon. J. F. Kinney, delegate from Utah to Congress, at 100,000. They are producing, besides fruits and cereals, wool, cotton, silk, paper, leather, iron, lead, copper and salt, having introduced machinery for manufactures.

---

* The following paragraph from the San Francisco *Bulletin* relates to the subject:

THE PASTURES OF THE GREAT BASIN.—These are generally found abundant on the elevations and rounded hills from 500 to 5,000 feet above the foot plains and level deserts coming west from the Salt Lake ranges. Hay is made from wild rye and barley, with many other grasses unknown heretofore to our hay-makers, and mostly undescribed in science. In several parts a species of wheat has been met with, and also several varieties of clover have long been used by passing emigrants, since 1846. Brush and shrub pines, and oaks not over one or two yards high, and covered with acorns and nuts, are common in many districts, and make excellent food for stock animals, being also necessary articles of the Papato cuisine; the dwarf oak acorns being particularly nutritious. An American gambusino, who had tramped up and down Arizona and Nevada in 1862-'63, lately stated to a correspondent of the *Bulletin* that the grasses of the eastern slope, or the other pastures with which they are mixed, have the property, when a little advanced in the season, of making the milk of domestic cows much thicker and more like the consistence of warm cream, and very rich in making cheese. It is many times more sustentative than that of the coast, and much more sweet and toothsome, though less in quantity, these being its usual peculiarities at all seasons. A variety of stiff, short grass is found in these places, not over a foot high, which is full of fine seeds and is greedily eaten by cattle and horses, and keeps them in excellent condition.

The late F. W. Lander, in a communication to the Secretary of the Interior, dated February 13, 1858, speaks of the inhabitants of Utah in the following terms: "Having been much exposed in the passes of the central mountains during two protracted explorations, with very small parties of men, and especially the last season, when the Mormons were expecting attacks from the government military forces, I wish, in this connexion, to place on record my own opinion and that of my party in favor of the masses of the Utah population. Often reduced to great straits for provisions and supplies, I was uniformly relieved, and in several instances most kindly and hospitably entertained by that distant class of our fellow-citizens. It cannot be denied that among this peculiar people exists as much thorough push, practical energy and determined movement, as are found in the republic. Both in founding the colonies of Salt Lake and throwing open that arid, desolate section to settlement, they have overcome some of the most remarkable obstacles of nature. In fact, the initiative steps taken by this singular people first gave great impetus to our own overland emigration, by imparting knowledge of the resources of travel, and by furnishing supplies." Again, in a subsequent communication, Colonel Lander remarks: "The existence of this Mormon population, and the supplies they are enabled to furnish, is a most important matter in making estimates for any public work to be carried on in that section of country. They are very excellent laborers, many of them Cornish miners, who understand all sorts of ledge work, masonry, &c. The majority of the lower classes are trained in the use of implements of excavation, from the amount of picking and digging which is required in the building of the great irrigating ditches, and in the erection of the earth and rock fences by which the farms of the country are separated. They will prove of remarkable service should the proposed line of the Pacific railroad pass anywhere in the vicinity of their settlements. Ex-Governor Young told me that he would engage to find laborers and mechanics to build that portion of a Pacific railroad which should extend across the Territory of Utah."

COLORADO.

Colorado Territory, with a white population of 34,231 in 1860, and an estimated area of 100,000 square miles, or 66,880,000 acres, has nearly doubled in population during the first three years of the current decade. The population in January, 1864, may be fairly stated at 60,000. The production of gold in 1862 was $10,000,000, which will probably reach $15,000,000 during 1864.

A message of honorable John Evans, governor of Colorado, to the Territorial legislature, delivered February 3, 1864, indicates quite distinctly the future situation of the State in regard to agriculture, grazing, and mining. He estimates that not over one-half of the supplies of provisions for the Territory are yet produced from the soil, and anticipates that this relation between supply and demand will be maintained for years to come. He admits that "the arable lands of Colorado, except for purposes of grazing, are limited exactly by the quantity of water that may be found applicable to purposes of irrigation," while claiming that lands are very productive when irrigated. The governor presents the following comparison between the returns of agriculture in Colorado and Illinois:

Colorado.—1 man's labor—10 acres corn, 15 acres wheat.

10 acres corn, 40 bushels per acre—400 bushels, at $3..........	$1,200 00
15 acres wheat, 30 bushels per acre—450 bushels, at $3	1,350 00
Corn fodder from 10 acres, at $10 per acre....................	100 00
Wheat straw from 15 acres—20 tons, at $10....................	200 00
Total..	2,850 00

Illinois.—1 man's labor—30 acres corn, 15 acres wheat.

30 acres corn, 60 bushels per acre—1,800 bushels, at 30 cents..	$360 00
15 acres wheat, 15 bushels per acre—225 bushels, at 75 cents..	168 75
Straw and fodder, estimated..........................	100 00
Total..	628 75
Profits in Colorado over those in Illinois on the annual labor of one man..	$2,221 25

Even more significant than these extraordinary prices of corn and wheat in Colorado is the suggestion by Governor Evans, that one claim of each quartz lode discovered hereafter shall be reserved, by act of Congress, for the purpose of creating a school fund, "as the usual grant of school-lands by the general government *will be comparatively valueless for such a purpose in Colorado.*"

Governor Evans alludes to the progress of quartz mining in the following terms:

"The improvement in the modes of saving gold from the ores of our mines that have been made during the past year have given a new impulse to mining operations. By these new processes, ores that paid $25 per ton by the old process are readily made to yield $100 per ton, while many varieties produce much more largely, and this without greatly increasing the expenses."

The improvements here alluded to are chemical as well as mechanical, and are thus described by a writer in the New York Commercial Advertiser:

"The gold in the quartz is associated with iron pyrites; it is held very tenaciously, as if combined itself with the sulphur always present. The old plan, after drawing off the sulphur, was to pulverize very fine and then apply quicksilver, which united with all the gold free, forming a part, which, exposed to heat, lost the quicksilver in vapor, leaving the gold pure. By this process much gold was lost because it adhered to the pyrites and passed off in the tailings. A new process of roasting at a certain heat drives off the sulphur without adding to the cohesion of the pyrites or causing the gold to volatilize. This process increases the product threefold. In other cases, where the ores are finely pulverized, the gold becomes so fine as to float in the air, thus escaping the quicksilver. This difficulty has been met by heating the quicksilver into vapor enclosed in a cylinder, into which the dust penetrates. The vapor thus fixes the floating particles of gold, and the yield has been raised in the proportion of two to five."

On the western slope of the Snowy mountains, in Colorado, extensive silver mines have been discovered. Iron, lead, quicksilver, and coal have also been found in the Territory, and have already attracted capital. With the ratio of increase since 1860, the population of Colorado will be 200,000 in 1870.

The discoveries and development of the Gregory district is the sole basis, hitherto, for the settlement of Colorado. This district extends from Gold Hill to Empire City, about thirty miles along the base of the Snowy range, and is, on the average, about ten miles in width—an area of three hundred square miles of gold-producing mountains, in which a hundred quartz mills are now in operation.

Governor Evans, in his message of July 17, 1862, thus describes the mines and the manner of mining in the Gregory district:

"The veins of quartz are found within an average distance of one hundred feet of each other. They are by the mining laws divided into claims of one hundred feet in extent, making surface enough on quartz lodes in this region alone for over eight hundred thousand claims. These veins are from six inches to nine feet in thickness, and vary even more in their quality—from those that will not pay at all, to those that produce the richest ore that has been found in any part of the world."

He estimates that ore yielding $12 per ton pays all expenses, and that the average result of quartz mining in Colorado is $36 per ton.

Intelligent observers express the conviction that the range of the gold-bearing quartz is not limited to the Gregory district, but is as extensive as the Snowy range itself; and that recent discoveries in the vicinity of the South Park, and along Clear and Boulder creeks and their branches, are but the precursors of developments in the mountain chain that separates the three parks that will, in a very few years, yield a greater amount of treasure than is now furnished by California, building up important points north as well as south of the present centre.

Professor James T. Hodge, geologist of the Union Pacific railroad, reports the existence of iron and coal near Fort Laramie and the Cheyenne Pass—localities north of Colorado. The Black Hills and Medicine Bow mountains contain these minerals, while the Laramie plains, in the vicinity, will be available for agricultural settlement. In the vicinity of Denver City, Colorado, Professor Hodge visited coal-beds which present a thickness of five feet ten inches pure coal, with no mixture of slate, and thus describes its appearance and quality:

"The coal is of a brilliant jet black, and is easily mined in large lumps, which appear to be firm and sound, but are said to crumble after exposure for a few weeks to the air. It contains but little bitumen, burning with little smoke, no unpleasant odor, and a yellow flame. It does not melt or coke, and, however high the draught, produces no clinker. The ashes of most of the beds are usually white and bulky. A welding heat in a forge is obtained with difficulty. Sulphur is observed in it, in small quantity, in the form of exceedingly thin disks of iron pyrites disseminated through the seams. Particles of mineral rosin are much more abundant, scattered through the coal of the size of pin-heads."

Another coal-bed, worked for the supply of the Denver market, is in the hills along South Boulder creek, only two and a half miles from the base of the Rocky mountains. This locality also affords an abundance of iron ores, and has been selected for the establishment of the first blast furnace erected in the Territory, which went into operation in March, 1864. "The principal coal-bed is opened a few rods southeast from the furnace, and has been worked one hundred feet down a slope of about ten degrees from the horizontal toward the east. The bed is twelve feet thick, almost uniform in quality, with no intermixture of slate, and presents a beautiful appearance in the brilliant lustre of the coal. A little sulphur (pyrites) may here be detected in the seams." Two other beds are described, one of them affording coal of a firmer quality than the others.

These specimens of coal were submitted to Professor John Torrey, who, after analysis, describes them as belonging to the class of lignites—not technically a bituminous coal, neither cannel nor an anthracite. "Still, in common parlance, it will be regarded as coal. In calorific power the Rocky mountain coal may be placed between dry wood and bituminous coal, and therefore it is a most valuable fuel. It may be used for the smelting of iron and other ores. For locomotives it could be employed to advantage, with some modification of the fireplace. The ash is so small in quantity, and so light, that most of it would be carried off by the blast of the furnace. The coal burns freely in a small stove, making a hot and clear fire, and leaving no clinkers. The specimens, that were examined had a tendency to break up and crumble after being soaked with water and allowed to dry; hence the necessity of protection from moisture."

The iron ore found at the eastern base of the mountains, near Denver City, is characterized by Professor Torrey as "lemonite, a compact variety derived from carbonate of iron, and commonly known by the name of brown hematite or brown iron ore." "It is found," continues Professor Hodge, "in irregular deposits, scattered over the summits, ends, and slopes of many of the ridges which border South Boulder creek and Rock creek. These deposits extend to a depth of only one to three feet, and, as they evidently do not form a part of the strata in the hills, it is impossible to make any estimate of the quantity of ore they will afford. One can judge, only from seeing numbers of acres thus covered, that supplies may be obtained for one or more blast furnaces for several years; but extended observations would be necessary before positively asserting that large works could be supported from this source. The ore is found in pieces of all sizes up to masses of half a ton weight, and large quantities of it are so fine that it would have to be collected for the furnace by screening. There is scarcely any intermixture of foreign stony materials in these deposits. The quality of the ore is generally pretty good, though the larger masses are not so fine-grained and pure as the smaller ore. I should judge that an average of three tons would be required to make a ton of iron. The ore is in excellent condition for the blast furnace, its long exposure at the surface having prepared it for smelting almost as thoroughly as if it had been roasted. Its unusual mode of occurrence, unconnected with the strata in the hills, was for some time a source of perplexity; and it seemed necessary to explain it correctly in order to judge better of the probability of the ore being found in large quantities in other places on the range of these formations. On examining the country up to the base of the mountains I discovered what I believe is the true explanation. At the distance of two and a half miles from the mines the marginal ridge, already noticed, rises suddenly with a very steep face and dip of its strata. The surface at its foot is covered with large rounded boulders from the granite rocks of the mountains. Some, also, are of the red sandstones and conglomerates of the outer ridge. They decrease in size and numbers towards the east, indicating the movement in that direction of vast bodies of water or ice. These, together with the evidences of denudation I had observed further north, evidently not referable to the diluvial or drift formation, appeared to me as more strongly marked evidences of glacial action than I had ever before seen. The extension of this over the hills near the furnace must have excavated the soft beds, of which they are in great part composed; and the light clayey materials of the strata containing the iron ores being swept away by currents of water, these, by their weight, were left behind, and are now found spread over the surface of the hills. By long exposure they have been oxidized and converted from the clay iron stone, or 'blue case iron' as it is here called, into the shelly hematite. Such a derivation of the ore, if correct, must itself make the quantity in any locality always uncertain. Found as it is, it is collected and delivered at the furnace at a cost of $3 per ton, making about $9 to the ton of iron."

"The furnace, owned by Messrs. Langford, Lee, and Marshall, is a very small stack, of daily capacity of only four or five tons of pig iron. It is twenty feet square at base, twenty-two feet high, and seven feet diameter at the boshes The hearth is five feet high and eighteen inches diameter. It is intended to work the furnace with cold-blast, and the consumption of charcoal will probably be from two hundred and fifty to three hundred bushels to the ton of iron. The cost of charcoal at the furnace is ten cents per bushel, making the cost of fuel from $25 to $30 per ton, while that of ore, as above stated, may be rated at $9. The cost of the limestone for flux will probably not exceed fifty cents, and the remaining items of labor, repairs, &c., may be estimated at about $7. The total cost will probably be about $45 per ton of pig metal. In large establishments the expenses should be less, especially if the raw mineral coal could be substituted, wholly or in part, for the charcoal. The quantity of fuel, too, would be diminished by the use of the hot-blast."

The prospects of agriculture are thus considered by Professor Hodge: "The agricultural resources of the prairies are somewhat limited by the extreme dryness of the climate. Rain seldom falls, and were it not for the never-failing supplies of water in the numerous streams running from the snowy central range of the Rocky mountains, the country would be an uninhabitable desert. Yet the soil is in great part fertile, warm, and mellow, and abounds in gypsum and salts of soda, which appear upon the surface in the form of an incrustation resembling frost. This is particularly abundant about the edges of dried-up ponds. The alkaline salts affect the waters of many of the wells, rendering them nauseous to the taste and unwholesome, and mixed with the dust of the roads, this is said to be, in the summer season, very injurious to the eyes of travellers. It is remarkable that, notwithstanding the want of rain, no great trouble is experienced over the plains for the want of water at the ranches and stations along the roads. I crossed the Platte river at Fort Kearney in October, over its dry, sandy bed, and yet the wells along the valley contained abundant water, and, in general, they were not twenty feet deep, their bottoms not reaching to the level of the stream. It is difficult to explain from whence these supplies are derived. The dryness of the soil renders irrigation necessary for its successful cultivation, and this is already practiced to a considerable extent in Colorado, after the system of the Mexicans, which consists in the excavation of *acequias* or ditches, often several miles in length, by which the water of the streams, taken out at an upper level, is carried at this elevation past the farming lands, over which it is let out, as occasion requires, by tapping the *acequias* at any desired points. The cultivation is thus limited to lands lying below the level of the *acequias*, and such lands are met with of considerable extent along most of the streams, spreading out to great width, even before these have fairly emerged from the mountains. Very productive and extensive farms thus situated are seen running up among the basaltic hills, on Clear creek, and similar improvements extend all along this stream to its mouth, below Denver. The streams north of it, so far as and including the *Cache à Poudre*, afford the same advantage for cultivation of the soil, and along most of them the lands are occupied in continuous lines of farms. In the newness of the country, which has been occupied only two or three years, the crops are limited to a few of the most necessary articles. Flour being supplied to the Territory from the States and New Mexico, the cultivation of wheat is not so important as of the more bulky articles, which will not pay for transportation from such distances. Some wheat, however, is raised, and the crop is a successful one. But attention is chiefly directed to procuring the large supplies of hay, corn, oats, and vegetables, required by the numerous gold-mining population in the mountains. The hay being made from the wild prairie grass, its supply is limited only by the amount of labor employed in cutting and stacking it; still, owing to an overstock of it the previous year, the quantity put up in 1863 has proved too small for the demands of the country, increased as they are by the extraordinary accumulations of snow, which, covering the plains, cut off the herds of cattle and horses, with which the country is abundantly stocked, from their accustomed support by grazing during the winter. This, together with the obstructed condition of the roads, caused the price of hay in December last to rise to $105 per ton at the gold mines. Corn, which is a good crop, and may be raised to any extent along the streams, was worth at the same time nine or ten cents per pound. Potatoes are produced in abundance, as also onions, cabbages, and many other vegetables; but in this unpropitious season the prices of all these range high. Onions are raised with scarcely any of the labor attending their cultivation in the States, yet they were from ten to twelve cents a pound. They grow so luxuriantly that a single one often weighs more than a pound. Such prices cannot be sustained in a favorable season, and particularly when the country is supplied with a more numerous agricultural population.

"It is an important question whether the cultivation of these prairies is always to be limited to those portions capable of being irrigated only by the system now in use. The mountains, it appears, are abundantly provided with water, derived chiefly from the melting of the snows in the great central range. A large part of this, without doubt, penetrates under the stratified rocks, which on both sides dip away from the mountains. These waters probably flow in underground channels far from the mountains, and if tapped by artesian wells sunk down to them, they might reasonably be expected to rise to the surface in never-failing springs. The stratification of the country is certainly remarkably encouraging to such an enterprise; and another inducement to its prosecution would be the discovery of the mineral beds, whatever they may be, beneath the surface. This would be a certain and most economical method of determining the existence or non-existence of beds of coal in localities where it might be especially desirable to obtain this fuel. Artesian wells must at some time be exceedingly useful at Laramie plains, which are not so well watered as the country east of the mountains. These plains, hitherto entirely uncultivated, afford, in places, good pasturage, and a considerable amount of prairie-grass hay, for the use of the overland stage line and of emigrants."

The Laramie plains and the mountain valleys of the Black hills and the Medicine Bow chain are mentioned by Professor Hodge as repositories of iron and coal, and having the constituents of agriculture with the aid of irrigation. These statements were anticipated by Lieutenant (now General) G. K. Warren in his report, as topographical engineer, upon Nebraska Territory, published in 1858–59, (Executive Documents, volume 2, part 2, p. 643,) from which an extract is given:

"In the mountain formations which border the great plains on the west are to be found beautiful flowing streams and small, rich valleys, covered over with fine grass for hay, and susceptible of cultivation by means of irrigation. Fine timber for fuel and lumber, limestone and good stone for building purposes, are here abundant. Gold has been found in places in valuable quantities, and, without doubt, the more common and useful minerals will be discovered when more minute examinations are made. I think it exceedingly desirable that something should be done to encourage settlements in the neighborhood of Fort Laramie. The wealth of that country is not properly valued, and the Indian title not being extinguished, there is no opportunity to settle it. Those who live there now support themselves by trade with the Indians, which being already overdone, it is to their interest to keep others away. If the Indian title were extinguished and the protection of a territorial government extended there so as to be effectual, there would soon spring up a settlement that would rival that of Great Salt lake. The Laramie river is a beautiful stream, with a fine, fertile valley, and there are such everywhere along the base of the mountains. Pine timber of the finest quality in abundance grows there, easy of access, from which the finest lumber can be made. Building-stone of good quality abound. The establishment of the military post and the constant passing of emigrants have driven away the game, so that the Indians do not set a high value on the land, and it could be easily procured from them.

"The people now on the extreme frontiers of Nebraska and Kansas are near the western limit of the fertile portions of the prairie lands, and a desert space separates them from the fertile and desirable region in the western mountains. They are, as it were, on the shore of a sea, up to which population and agriculture may advance, and no further. But this gives them much of the value of places along the Atlantic frontier in view of the future settlements to be formed in the mountains, between which and the present frontier a most valuable trade would exist. The western frontier has always been looking to the east for a market, but as soon as the wave of emigration has passed over the desert portion of the plains to which the discoverers of gold have already given an impetus that will propel it to the fertile valleys of the Rocky mountains, then will the present frontier of Kansas and Nebraska become the starting point for all the products of the Mississippi valley which the population of the mountains will require. We see the effects of it in the benefits which the western frontier of Missouri has received from the Santa Fe trade, and still more plainly in the impetus given to Leavenworth by the operations of the army of Utah in the interior region. This flow of products has, in the last instance, been only in one direction, but when those mountains become settled, as they eventually must, then there will be a reciprocal trade materially beneficial to both.

"These settlements in the mountains cannot be agricultural to the same extent as those in the Mississippi valley, but must depend greatly upon the raising of stock. The remarkable freedom here from sickness is one of the attractive features of the region, and will, in this respect, go far to reconcile the settler from the Mississippi valley for his loss in the smaller amount of products that can be taken from the soil."

The late General F. W. Lander, while employed in the exploration of the Rocky mountains, (1858,) thus indicated the prospects of grazing in the northern valleys of the mountains, (Executive Documents, 1st session 35th Congress, volume 9, No. 70:) "From the arable grounds of the Salt Lake valley, through the numerous valleys and timbered regions of the Wahsatch mountains toward the head of Wind river, to the Beaver Head and to the St. Mary's valley of the north, occur available and peculiarly favorable locations for settlements. There are the numerous herding grounds of the Indians and mountaineers, and here are recruited and fattened, in the open air and during winter, the worn-down cattle, mules, and horses bought up by traders from the later overland emigration. The half-breed horses raised by the mountaineers from a cross between the larger animals of the settlements and the Indian pony, reared in the open air and without forage, are some of the finest animals I have ever seen. Durham short-horned cattle, a delicate breed, and not usually thought adapted to exposure, are raised here and wintered without shelter upon the natural grass of the mountains. Hay is never cut by the mountaineers, yet this celebrated stock, fattened upon the bunch-grass, grows larger than any I have seen in the States. John Grant, a well-known trader, who has raised a large stock of Durham milch cows and steers and American horses, winters yearly in the great valleys of the mountains with no shelter but the common Indian lodge of dressed elk or buffalo skin."

KANSAS AND NEBRASKA.

The census of 1860 returned the population of the interior districts, which are connected with the overland trade west of the Missouri river, as follows:

New Mexico	83,009
Colorado	34,277
Utah	40,273
	157,559

In 1860 a special correspondent of the New York Herald furnished the following statement:

Table showing the amount of freight forwarded across the plains from the various ports on the Missouri river during the year 1860, with the required outfit.

Where from.	Pounds.	Men.	Horses.	Mules.	Oxen.	Wagons.
Kansas City	10,439,134	7,084	464	6,140	27,920	3,033
Leavenworth	5,656,082	1,216	....	206	10,925	1,003
Atchison	6,097,943	1,591	....	472	13,640	1,280
St. Joseph	1,672,000	490	....	520	3,980	418
Nebraska City	5,496,000	896	....	113	11,118	916
Omaha City	713,000	324	377	114	340	272
Grand total	36,074,150	11,601	841	7,574	67,060	6,922

In 1863 a population of 60,000 in Nevada employs for the transportation of machinery, merchandise, provisions, &c., from the Pacific coast, a number of men, animals, and wagons fully half as great as the foregoing exhibit of overland transportation west of Kansas and Nebraska. That this table is inadequate to express the traffic of 1864 may also be inferred from the consideration of the present population of the mountain Territories, viz:

New Mexico, (no increase)	83,009
Colorado	60,000
Utah	80,000
Montana	12,000
	235,009

It is not an excessive estimate that the present transportation is 50,000,000 pounds, employing 10,000 trains, and at a cost of $5,000,000 annually. In consequence of the war and other causes, a considerable diversion of the traffic across the plains has taken place in favor of the northern points of departure from the Missouri river; Kansas city by no means leading in the degree indicated in 1860. Whether the traffic will resume its former proportions, depends altogether upon the railway construction of the next twelve months.

Kansas and Nebraska, for an average distance of one hundred and fifty miles west of the Missouri river, are as well adapted to agriculture as the States of Missouri and Iowa, but beyond that limit agriculture is dependent upon irrigation. Hence, as shown by Lieutenant Warren, a steady and remunerative market for breadstuffs and other agricultural products is at the door of the farmer in Kansas and Nebraska, which will divert all his surplus from the Atlantic coast. The foregoing review of the Territories east of the Sierra Nevada of California suggests a permanent deficiency of agricultural production, while their mineral resources will concentrate a large population. Grazing and wool-growing are future interests, which, with domestic manufactures, will diversify industry and occupy labor at no distant stage of progress; but for the next decade of years, manufactures, and even meats, will be largely imported across the Sierra Nevada from the west, and across the plains from the Missouri river.

The spring of 1864 witnesses an exodus of population from the western borders of Missouri and Iowa to the mining districts of Colorado and Montana, which far exceeds that of 1860. Peter A. Dey, esq., engineer of the Union Pacific railroad, writing from Omaha, under date of May 17, 1864, says: "Four thousand wagons and six thousand tons of freight have crossed the Missouri river at Omaha since April first. There is now a daily movement of two hundred teams, three hundred tons freight, and one thousand persons. The teams are equally divided into those drawn by four horses, and those drawn by five yoke of cattle. No emigration has ever been known to bear any comparison to this. The line of teams waiting ferriage reaches nearly to Council Bluffs, or three miles in length. This rush will undoubtedly continue to the middle of June. The ferry-boat runs night and day. This does not include government transportation."

The statistics of the spring emigration of 1864, on the basis of this statement, are 75,000 men, 22,500 tons of freight, 30,000 horses and mules, and 75,000 cattle. It is probable that similar aggregates represent the emigration from other points on the Missouri river, and in that case 150,000 will be added to the population of the mountains from the Mississippi States during 1864.

UNION PACIFIC RAILROAD.

That the overland trade on the average latitude of 40 degrees north has already reached proportions which assure the prosperity of the Central Pacific railway from the way business alone, as soon as constructed, is a probability which can be made to appear from the general railroad statistics of the country.

Take the proportion of mileage to population. In 1860 the population of the States, not including the Territories, was 31,148,047, and the number of miles of railroads in operation was 30,598. The population on the 1st of January, 1861, is estimated at 31,615,267; while on that date official reports show that there were 31,168 miles of railroad constructed in the United States, at an aggregate cost of $1,777,993,818, or $37,794 97 per mile. Thus, the proportion of one mile of railroad to every thousand of population seems to be established as a practical law of railroad progress by the American people. This ratio is exceeded in many of the States. For instances: Ohio, in 1860, had a population of 2,339,511, and 2,900 miles of railroad in operation; Illinois, 1,711,951 of population to 2,867 miles of railroad; Massachusetts, 1,231,066 population to 1,272 miles of railroad; while the most advanced southern States were, Virginia, 1,596,318 of population to 1,771 miles of railroad; Tennessee, 1,109,801 to 1,197; Georgia, 1,057,286 to 1,404.

If the Union Pacific railroad, assured by the extent of overland traffic, and aided by the land grant and credit of the general government, should organize measures for the completion of a central trunk line through California, Nevada, Utah, Colorado, and Kansas, by the year 1870, the census of that year would doubtless return populations exceeding the ratio of one thousand per mile. During the decennial period of 1850–'60, the population of those Territories increased five-fold. Connect by railroad the agricultural districts of the Pacific coast and the Mississippi valley with the varied consumption and commerce of the interior mining regions, and the ensuing six years, or the period occupied in effecting that connexion, would probably witness an advance of population three-fold the aggregates which appear in 1864, viz:

	1850.	1860.	1864.	1870.
California	92,597	365,439	500,000	1,500,000
Nevada	......	6,857	60,000	180,000
Utah	11,380	40,273	80,000	240,000
Colorado	......	34,271	60,000	180,000
Kansas	......	107,206	120,000	360,000
	103,957	554,052	820,000	2,460,000

A comparison of the statistics of the English colony of Victoria and the State of California has already been presented, and is instructive. Victoria, in April, 1861, had a total population of 540,322, almost equally divided between the mining districts and the remainder of the colony. Including the Washoe district, now Nevada, California had a population in 1861, nearly equal to Victoria, and which was divided in the same proportion. San Francisco and Melbourne are cities of equal commercial importance. The California revenue for State purposes is $1,462,690; for national treasury, $7,128,399; total $8,591,089, or about $17 per capita. The provincial revenue of Victoria was, in 1862, $15,123,465; in 1863, $13,968,510, or an average per capita of $29. California has only 75 miles of railroad in operation, while Victoria has 351 miles, constructed at an expense of £35,000 per mile, from which the Victoria government received an income in 1863 of £433,015.* The first section of the California Central railroad, which was opened in January from San Francisco to San José, a distance of $49\frac{3}{10}$ miles, was constructed at a cost of $40,000 per mile. If we suppose the next 600 miles across the Sierra Nevada, and the State of Nevada, to cost $80,000 per mile, the expenditure will not exceed the cost of the Victoria railroads, which connect the city of Melbourne with the Ballarat and Bendigo gold fields, and with the wool-growing districts of the river Murray.

There is abundant evidence that the mountain valleys are favorable to stock-raising, and that animals and their products will largely contribute to the return business of the Pacific railroad, in addition to the movements of Asiatic merchandise, and of the precious metals. As far north as the sources of the Columbia, the Missouri, and the Saskatchewan rivers, cattle and horses require no winter shelter, but are found in the spring in the best health and condition. For many years the emigrant trains will take to the mountains a multitude of domestic animals. The climate and natural grasses are favorable to their increase, and if the cattle of Texas have been profitably transported to the New York market, it is possible that the Mississippi and Atlantic States may yet receive a considerable portion of their consumption of meats from the Rocky mountains. Wool and dry hides are a considerable export from New Mexico and Colorado; and the San Francisco Mercantile Gazette of March 2, 1864, reports the departure of 1,500 head of beef cattle to the gold mines of Montana, or the sources of the Missouri, which cost but $6 per head in California. "They can be produced in every Rocky mountain district at as low a figure.

The construction of a continental telegraph from the Missouri river to San Francisco, three years since, was regarded as premature; but its successful operation has justified the enterprise. So will it be with the Union Pacific railroad. California alone is better able to carry its construction to the Missouri river than New York was competent, by the resources and credit of the State in 1824, to undertake the Erie canal. As its sections advance westward and eastward, a population will attend fully able to sustain the investment by dividends; nor is it improbable that the perforation of the Rocky mountains and the Sierra Nevada by tunnels will prove the most successful and gigantic traverse of gold and silver lodes ever yet developed in the annals of quartz mining.

A SOUTHERN PACIFIC RAILROAD ROUTE.

A route from the Lower Mississippi States to the Gulf of California and San Diego on the Pacific coast, which should be a trunk for communications with Memphis, Vicksburg and New Orleans, is a measure which only awaits the re-

* The returns for the first quarter of 1864, as reported in the London Times, make it certain that the net profits of the Australian railways will henceforth discharge an interest of six per cent. on the entire cost of construction.

storation of the federal authority in all the gulf States, to be favorably considered by the country.

There are two events which will direct attention to the latitude of 35° as a scene of rapid settlement and overland communication. The first is the agricultural advantages of the Neosho district, or the country due west of Arkansas, which was conceded by treaties to the Cherokee, Choctaw, Creek, Chickasaw and Seminole Indians; and in the second place, the new discoveries of mineral wealth in the central and northern districts of Arizona Territory. Neosho, on the east, will soon equal Kansas; while the San Francisco mountains of Arizona, situated geographically south of Nevada, will doubtless be the scene of similar excitement and development as have attended the settlement of the Washoe silver district. It is proposed to compile the latest intelligence of the agricultural region of the east, and the mineral district of the west, under the average latitude of 35°.

It was observed in a report presented by the territorial committee of the United States Senate, in 1854, that the country occupied by the Cherokee Indians is as rich and beautiful, as well watered and healthy, as the finest portions of Iowa and Wisconsin, and as lovely in its prairie scenery, as the choicest parts of Texas. It consists of 13,000,000 acres, mostly lying within latitudes 36° and 37°. One Indian agent represents the staple productions of the people to be corn, wheat and oats; that the country is well adapted to apples, peaches, plums, and similar fruits; that stone-coal, iron, and salt-springs are abundant and profitable; and that the country is admirably adapted for grazing cattle, of which the Indians have extensive stocks. In consequence of the climate, only a portion of the country, resembling the northern part of Alabama, is suited for the cultivation of cotton; tobacco and hemp flourish as in Kentucky.

The Creeks occupy 13,140,000 acres, except a small tract assigned to the Seminoles, on the deep fork of the Arkansas, in latitude 97°. The Creek country lies immediately west of Fort Gibson, extending from the Canadian river to the 36th parallel of latitude. It is noticed by James Logan, who was an Indian agent in 1847, as "a country of abundant extent, well timbered and watered, of fertile soil, and of comparative healthfulness, offering every facility for the raising of stock." The scene of Washington Irving's "Tour of the Prairies" is comprised in the Creek district.

The Choctaw country, of which the western half has been assigned to the Chickasaws and some smaller bands of Indians, extends from the Red river to the Canadian, and from the western boundary of Arkansas to the 100th meridian of longitude. Between longitude 94 and 97 degrees, or the Choctaw territory, as reduced in 1854, cotton has been grown near Red river, but corn and wheat are the prominent crops. An Indian agent wrote in 1851: "The soil produces the finest of wheat, weighing sixty-five to seventy pounds to the bushel; as a grazing community it is likewise unsurpassed, the extensive prairies, clothed with luxuriant grass, being capable of sustaining innumerable flocks and herds throughout the year." In 1854, Mr. A. J. Smith, Chickasaw agent, described some medicinal or "oil" springs on the Washita river, as very efficacious. Coal, copper and salt are found in ample quantities.

In the "Exploration of the Red River of Louisiana in 1852," by Captain (now Brigadier General) R. B. Marcy, the Chickasaw district, between longitude 97° and 100°, is described as about one hundred and eighty miles in length, and fifty in width, containing 9,000 square miles of valuable and productive lands, or 1,000 square miles more than the State of Massachusetts. Various portions of this country are more specifically described. Captain Marcy speaks of "charming landscapes; of soil remarkable for fertility; vegetation in old Indian cornfields twelve feet high; of beautiful springs and streams; of natural meadows covered with luxuriant grasses; broad and level bottom lands, covered with dense crops of wild rice, and of excellent timber, large and abundant." He adds: "Indeed, I have never visited any country that, in my opinion, possessed greater natural local advantages for agriculture than this."

There is no reason for doubt that the valleys of the Red River of the South, the Arkansas and the Canadian, for a distance of four hundred miles west of the State of Arkansas, are fertile, well watered and timbered, and supplied with coal and iron—comparing favorably with Kentucky and Tennessee in these respects. The colonization of this district will no longer be postponed, but will follow the termination of the war, and a reasonable adjustment of the interests of its Indian occupants.

Ten degrees of longitude west of the Neosho district, in the northern portions of the Territory of Arizona, recent discoveries of gold have occurred, which are attracting population and capital from San Francisco and southern California. This gold district is near the line of the 34th parallel of latitude, and west of the 110th degree of longitude, and is approached from the Gulf of California by steamboat navigation on the Colorado. The San Francisco mountains on the route of Captain A. W. Whipple's Pacific railroad survey are its central landmark. The Colorado river is navigable for a distance of 500 miles to latitude 36° 06', or to the mouth of the Rio Virgen, by a class of stern-wheel steamers, described as follows by Lieut. J. C. Ives, topographical engineer: "100 feet long, 22 feet beam, built full, and with a perfectly flat bottom, having a large boiler and powerful high-pressure engine, and drawing, when light, but twelve inches." The miners of Northern Arizona will be supplied from the Pacific coast by this navigation.*

The silver mines of southern Arizona, in the valley of the Gila, have been well known for several years. They are not less rich, and will be as productive as those of Nevada.

With peace restored, Indian hostility suppressed, and individual title to mineral lands assured, Neosho, (as the country west of Arkansas has been called,) western Texas, New Mexico, and Arizona, may be expected to follow the central cordon of States in the increase of population and wealth; and if so, and whenever so, a great central highway of commercial communication will be opened. When that period of development shall arrive, the Union Pacific railroad, like the Union Pacific telegraph, will have vindicated all the intervention by the national government in its behalf, and a great impulse will be given to the construction of a more southern line.

When, in 1853, the initiative of Pacific railroad exploration was presented to the United States Senate, resulting in a congressional appropriation of $150,000 for the purpose, attention was directed to three routes—the northern, the central, and the southern. Legislation has followed in behalf of one—the central—not so much from any demonstration of greater feasibility, but because the mineral discoveries of the interior, followed by population, suggested the selection. The same causes are now active on the two other routes. Discoveries, not only of gold and silver, but of coal, iron, lead, and salt, diversify the map of the Rocky mountain region everywhere within our boundaries; and an emigration from the Pacific coast meets the Atlantic column even upon the great plains, which are drained by the Missouri, the Platte, and the Rio Grande.

The necessity of more than one route between the Mississippi States and the Pacific coast will appear from an enumeration of the railroad lines which are indispensable to the commerce between the Atlantic and interior States. These

* A San Francisco paper says, under date of March 2, 1864: "The discovery of valuable lodges of gold and silver ore is now reported in such numbers, of such richness, and so well authenticated, that if any doubt has existed in regard to the vast mineral wealth of Arizona, it must soon be dissipated. One of the great drawbacks to the prospects of that region for mining enterprises has been the scarcity of fuel; but late advices announce the discovery of coal near La Paz, on the Colorado."

are seven well-defined thoroughfares: (1) From Portland, by the Grand Trunk, to Detroit, and thence, with a traverse of the State and Lake of Michigan, to Milwaukie and La Crosse; (2) by the New York Central, the Great Western, of Canada, and the Chicago and Northwestern railroad, to Prairie du Chien; (3) by the New York and Erie, the lines of Ohio and Indiana south of the great lakes, and the Illinois Central, to Galena; (4) the Pennsylvania Central, and its western connexions, to Rock Island; (5) the Baltimore and Ohio, by way of Cincinnati, to St. Louis; (6) from Richmond, through the Cumberland valley, to Memphis; and (7) from Charleston and Savannah, traversing the States of Georgia, Alabama, and Mississippi, to Vicksburg and New Orleans. All these highways are thronged and prosperous, and, with the wonderful impulse to colonization and commerce induced by mining investments, a period of twenty-five years will probably witness the completion of four great continental communications within the limits of the north temperate zone, and upon the following lines:

1. Through the southern tier of States, on or near the parallel of 35°, which is central to the region of cotton, the sugar cane, and the vine, and which will be supported by the populations of Louisiana, Arkansas, Neosho, (or the Territory occupied by the Cherokee and Choctaw Indians,) Texas, New Mexico, Arizona, Sonora, and southern California. This may be called the Gulf route, from its relation to the Gulfs of Mexico and California.

2. The central, which is now in course of construction, on the average latitude of 40°. With its present prestige and aid from the federal government, soon to be increased by the intervention of State governments in its behalf, the speedy construction of this road may be anticipated. If in operation at the present moment, the road would be financially successful. All the resources of Kansas, Nebraska, Colorado, Utah, Nevada, and, in a great degree, of Missouri and California, are pledged to such a result.

3. The lake route, hitherto designated in congressional debates as the Northern Pacific route, connecting the western coast of the great lakes, and the navigable channel of the Columbia river, by the most direct and feasible communication with which the Territories and future States of Dakota, Montana, Idaho, and Washington, as well as the States of Minnesota and Oregon, are identified.

4. The international route, or an extension of the Canadian railway system across the Peninsula of Michigan, and through Wisconsin and Minnesota, to the English colony of Selkirk in latitude 50°, and thence, through the valleys of the Saskatchewan and upper Frazer rivers, to the Pacific coast in latitude 54°.

The prediction is hazarded that the year 1890 will witness the consummation of the 8,000 miles of interior railroad above indicated. A more accurate statement would be, that whenever, along either of these routes, a population shall be assembled of two millions of souls, then will follow, by an irresistible social law, the construction and support of two thousand miles of railroad. The probability of that aggregate of population by the year 1870 has been considered on the central line. The situation of the more southern communication has been also referred to, and some space will now be given to the probabilities that, by the year 1890, the great lakes will be connected by railroad with the Columbia river and Puget's sound, while 1880 is likely to witness the completion of the international railroad upon the average latitude of 52° north.

THE NORTHERN OR LAKE ROUTE.

The latitude of 45° north, extended west of Minnesota, is not only central to the lake coast and the railroads of northern Illinois and Iowa, Wisconsin and Minnesota, but in its traverse of the Great Plains and the Rocky mountains it is most accessible from the mining districts now developed, or soon to be occupied, in the Territories of Dakota, Montana and Idaho. Other conditions being favorable, the future emigrant route will follow the parallel of 45° or 46°, and when population warrants. that will be the general direction of the northern or lake railroad route.

Explorations by officers of the general government, and publications of their reports, have made the general features of this route quite familiar. Fully nine-tenths of the area between the 100th meridian of longitude and the Cascade range of Oregon will never be available for agriculture, although districts far more extensive will support herds and flocks. The climate, owing to the reduced altitude, is not more severe than in the corresponding districts of Colorado and Utah. The Great Plains are characterized geologically by a development of the cretaceous formation, which is observed over large Asiatic areas, and concurring with aridity, constitutes the American desert. Population would have been slowly attracted to those localities, except for the discovery of gold. The "northern mines," as they are termed, upon the sources of the Columbia and Missouri, were discovered not more than two years since, and now have a population of 30,000, of which 12,000 are east of the mountains. In addition to the Salmon river mines of Idaho, and the Missouri and Yellowstone mines of Montana, under the average longitude of 108°, it is now well ascertained that the Black hills of Dakota Territory, situated on the 44th parallel of latitude, and between the 103d and 105th meridians of longitude, are rich in gold and silver, as well as coal, iron, copper, and pine forests. With the pacification of the Sioux nation, and the establishment of emigrant roads, Dakota will be the scene of great mining excitement, as the gold field of the Black hills is within two hundred miles of the steamboat navigation of the Missouri river, at the intersection of its channel with the forty-fifth parallel of latitude. Admitting the general sterility of the Great Plains, and the physical difficulties of the mountains, yet the great productiveness of the northern mines warrants the opinion that the Territories of Idaho, Montana and Dakota will advance in population in a ratio fully equal to that observed in Nevada and Colorado since their first settlement. The discoveries at Washoe and Pike's Peak date from 1859. Five years is the whole period of the settlement and progress of Nevada and Colorado, and within that period each Territory has reached a permanent population of 60,000. Both have been subject to the mutations of a mining population, but each has increased at the rate of twelve thousand souls per annum. So with the Salmon river district, twenty months of productive gold-mining having assembled 20,000 people, while east Idaho, or Montana, at the expiration of twelve months from the first discovery of gold on the Jefferson fork of the Missouri, had a population of 12,000. If such a rate of accretion is accepted, the result in the year 1890 will be indicated as follows:

	1863.	1870.	1880.	1890.
Idaho	20,000	104,000	224,000	344,000
Montana	12,000	96,000	216,000	336,000
Dakota	10,000	94,000	214,000	334,000
	42,000	294,000	654,000	1,009,000

An estimate of the increase of population in Oregon and Washington is annexed. Oregon in 1850 had a population of 13,294, which was increased in 1860 to 52,465, or a ratio of increase of 294.65. Assuming a ratio of increase from 1860 to 1870 of 200 per cent.; for the decade closing with 1880, of 100 per cent., and of 50 per cent. from 1880 to 1890, the population of Oregon during and at the expiration of twenty-seven years will be as follows:

1860	52,465
1870	157,396
1880	314,490
1890	472,185

The population of Washington is estimated on the hypothesis that the ratio of increase during the first decade will be 300 per cent., (or about the same as that of Oregon from 1850 to 1860;) then 200 per cent. for ten years closing with 1880, and 100 per cent. for the decade of 1890, as follows:

1860 (by census)	11,168
1870 (assumed)	44,672
1880 "	134,016
1890	268,032

The ratio of increase registered as to Michigan and Wisconsin, from 1830 to 1860, far exceeds these estimates.

	1830.	1840.	1850.	1860.
Michigan	31,639	211,560	397,654	749,113
Wisconsin	......	30,945*	305,391	775,881

An American railroad from the west border of Minnesota to the Columbia river may be anticipated by the year 1890, on the following basis of population, ascertained as above:

Dakota	334,000
Montana	336,000
Idaho	344,000
Oregon	472,185
Washington	268,032
	1,754,217

THE INTERNATIONAL ROUTE.

Public sentiment in Canada and England has long demanded measures for the colonization of Central British America, as that fertile belt of territory is now called, which extends from Canada and Lake Superior to the Rocky mountains. It includes the valleys of the Red River of the North and the Saskatchewan river, which belong to the hydrographical system of Hudson's bay, and are covered by the charter of the Hudson Bay Company.

Selkirk settlement, on the Red River of the North, was founded in 1812, and has a population of 10,000—an industrious, moral, and well-ordered community. Fort Garry, in this settlement, is the North American headquarters of the Hudson Bay Company. The posts of this company, more than fifty in number, occupy very commanding situations over the immense area, bounded by Hudson's bay and Lake Superior on the east, the Rocky mountains on the west, and the Arctic ocean on the north. The fur trade of this immense territory concentrates its annual product on the Red River of the North, at Fort Garry, from which point, by the annual voyages of brigades of batteaux, merchandise and supplies are distributed to the most distant post. Prior to 1858, the imports and exports of the Hudson Bay Company were principally transported by the difficult and dangerous route of Hudson's bay and Nelson's river, or over the numerous obstacles intervening from Lake Superior to Red river, on the British side of the international line. In 1858, however, materials were transported from the navigable waters of the Mississippi river to construct a steamer on the Red river, and in 1862 two such vessels navigated that stream. The trade previously existing between St. Paul and Selkirk has been greatly increased in consequence. The imports of Central British America for the use of the Hudson Bay Company and the Selkirk settlers amount to $500,000 annually, while the average annual exports, almost exclusively furs, amount to $1,000,000.

It is now well known that, northwest of Minnesota, the country reaching from the Selkirk settlement to the Rocky mountains, and from latitude 49° to 53° on the longitude of 94°, and to latitude 55° on the Pacific coast, is as favorable to grain and animal production as any of the northern States; that the mean temperature for spring, summer and autumn observed on the 42d and 43d parallels, in New York, Michigan and Wisconsin, has been accurately traced through Fort Snelling and the valley of the Saskatchewan to latitude 55° on the Pacific coast, and that from the northwest boundary of Minnesota this whole district of British America is threaded in all directions by the navigable water-lines which converge to Lake Winnipeg.

These facts, however favorable to agricultural settlement, would have failed to revolutionize the policy of the Hudson Bay Company, except for the violent excitement of gold discovery. The year 1858 directed a column of adventurers to the channel and sources of Frazer river: the organization of British Columbia followed, and it was soon ascertained that the richest and most extensive gold fields of northwest British America—the Cariboo mines—are so far within the Rocky mountains, so far up to the utmost sources of Frazer river, as to be practicably more accessible from Selkirk than from the coast of Puget's sound. At length, in 1862, the tributaries of the Saskatchewan and Peace rivers, on the eastern flank of the Rocky mountains, were discovered to be auriferous; while eastward stretched, towards Canada and Lake Superior, not less than 100,000,000 acres of fertile lands destined to cereal cultivation, whenever reached by emigration. English and Canadian exploration also established, in favor of this district, that its average elevation above the sea was far less than in American territory; that the Rocky mountains were diminished in width, while the passes were not difficult; that the supply of rain was more abundant, and the carboniferous and silurian formations were of greater extent than further south; and, owing to the greater influence of the Pacific winds through the mountain gorges and the reduced altitude, that the climate was no material obstacle to civilized occupation.

The Hudson Bay Company, in 1863, was reorganized to meet the exigencies of imperial and provincial policy in Central British America, "in accordance (to quote the circular of the new directory) with the industrial spirit of the age, and the rapid advancement which colonization has made in the countries adjacent to the Hudson's Bay territories."

While the present most effective organization of the fur trade will be continued and even extended, the company now proposes to avail itself of all possible agencies for the rapid colonization of the Saskatchewan basin and the gold districts at the sources of the Columbia, Frazer, Saskatchewan and Peace rivers. A telegraph line from St. Paul to Pembina, and thence through Selkirk and the Rocky mountains to the Pacific coast, is first announced as the special enterprise of 1864. Then a connexion of the Selkirk settlement by railroad with St. Paul, and by a direct emigrant road with Fort William, on the British coast of Lake Superior, will receive effective aid, concurrently with the prosecution of American and Canadian enterprises. Steamboat navigation is to be extended upon Lake Winnipeg and the Saskatchewan river. The systems of land survey and gratuitous allotments of land to colonists which prevail in the United States are proposed, the company reserving alternate blocks or sections to support future railroad construction, since, at the earliest practicable moment, a railroad will be undertaken traversing the colonies of Central British America and British Columbia. It is in the power of the modernized Hudson Bay Company, and it is its well-defined purpose, to connect Lake Superior and the Pacific coast by a cordon of settlements, and to carry forward the construction of two thousand miles of railroad simultaneously with the advent of population, and as the sure means to encourage the settlement of Northwest British America, or the interval which separates the lake coast of Canada from the coast of the North Pacific ocean.

This international railroad (as it may properly be called, until the development of British America warrants a direct communication with Canada) will be the favorite object of English capitalists on this continent, as the Union Pacific railroad will combine in its behalf the energies of the government and citizens of the United States. These two enterprises will therefore precede the construction of railroads on the gulf and lake routes, but only by a decade of years. All four routes will be demanded by the wants of 8,000,000 of people, which the next twenty-five years will witness permanently seated on the average latitudes of 35°, 40°, 45° and 50°, between longitude 95° and the Pacific ocean.

STATISTICAL MAP.

To illustrate the communications, present and future, between the Atlantic, Mississippi, Interior and Pacific States, a map is annexed, which has been prepared for publication in this connexion, and which also indicates the boundaries of the Territories at the close of the congressional session of 1863-'4. The statements of population are from the census of 1860, except the estimates for later dates. The map has been extended beyond the northern frontier of the United States, that the arable districts of British America, as shown by their respective northern boundary lines, may be studied with reference to the railway and commercial movements on the continent.

THE MINERAL WEALTH OF LAKE SUPERIOR.

The whole basin of Lake Superior indicates the presence of iron and copper The mountains which divide the waters of Lake Michigan to the southeast, of the Mississippi river and its tributaries to the southwest and west, of the Rainy Lake river to the northwest, and of Hudson's bay to the north and northeast—the outer rim of the Superior basin—are found, wherever explored, to contain iron ore. The mines at Marquette, Michigan, have been successfully worked, in consequence of the construction of a railroad from the harbor of Marquette to the Iron mountain, eighteen miles distant; but iron deposits in the same mineral range are situated at no greater distance south of Bayfield and Superior, in Wisconsin, and thence have been traced around the north shore of the lake, in Minnesota and in Canada.

Nearer the lake coast, and apparently a lower formation, are the copper districts. The only locality on the southern shore which has attracted attention is a district extending from Keweenaw Point to the Montreal river, 100 miles in length by four to twenty miles in width. On the north shore of the lake, in Minnesota, near the western extremity of the lake, and in Canada for a distance of 200 miles northwest from the Sault St. Marie, are well-defined copper regions which are now attracting the attention of capitalists, and will probably prove as productive as the Keweenaw, Portage Lake, Ontonagon, and Carp Lake districts, as the subdivisions of the Michigan copper-bearing territory are termed.

During the year 1863 discoveries were made in the vicinity of Marquette, which suggest that Michigan is destined to become, at an early day, a great silver-yielding State.* The newly-discovered district is known as the granite range, lying between the schistose or iron range and Lake Superior, and is from ten to twenty miles in breadth and about fifty miles in length. Lodes of argentiferous galena have been found in this region, yielding from ten to thirty pounds of silver to the ton of metal. Assays made on some of the ores have discovered gold in them to the value of $60 to $240. If these statements are confirmed, the silver district of Lake Superior will exceed in value either of the ranges now yielding copper and iron.

Under the impulse of the present demand for iron and copper, the Minnesota district, extending from Fond-du-Lac to the Grand Portage at the mouth of Pigeon river, has been thoroughly explored with satisfactory results; while Canada has taken effective measures for the encouragement of mining enterprises on the remainder of the northern shore. Title to mineral lands on Lake Superior can now be acquired from Canada at one dollar per acre, subject to a tax of one dollar per ton of ore. This order will have the effect to transfer English capital to the Nepigon, Pic and Michipicoton districts of Lake Superior, as it is now admitted that the copper mines of Great Britain have lately failed of their former productiveness. A correspondent of the London Mining Journal states that "the very rich mines of Cornwall and Devon are limited in the present day, and that some thirty or forty of the greatest and richest mines in those countries are exhausted, at least for copper." There were, in March, 1864, more than fifty bills before the Canadian Parliament to incorporate companies for mining gold, silver, lead, antimony, iron, and copper.

Similar and greater activity prevails in all the American districts of Lake Superior. The total amount of capital invested in the fee-simple and development of the copper mines now worked in Michigan, not including the value of the metal produced, is estimated at $6,000,000, while their stocks are worth over, $15,000,000. The aggregate amount of copper produced in 1863 was not less than 9,000 tons of stamp work, barrel and mass, or about 7,500 tons of ingot, worth at its present value over $6,000,000; but as the largest portion was probably sold at an average of 35 cents per pound, the aggregate receipts of sales will not be much over $5,000,000. The products of the Marquette iron mines for 1863 are reported as 185,000 gross tons of ore, and 13,732 gross tons of pig iron. In 1855 the product of the same mines was only 1,447 tons of iron ore, with no production of pig iron; in 1858, 31,035 tons of iron ore and 1,627 tons of pig iron.

The exports, of all values, for 1863, from Lake Superior, will amount to $10,000,000, imports $12,000,000, consisting, in addition to provisions and merchandise for the mining villages, of shipments of machinery and other materials for permanent improvements.

---

* In the same vicinity, the Huron mountains are reported to be gold-bearing, and at the latest date (June 13, 1864) there is a probability that the discoveries and production of gold in this district of the Lake Superior basin will fully equal the facts in regard to silver.

www.ingramcontent.com/pod-product-compliance
Lightning Source LLC
Chambersburg PA
CBHW030317270326
41926CB00010B/1403

9783741144905